The Role of Agriculture in Economic Development

Søren Kjeldsen-Kragh

The Role of Agriculture in Economic Development

The Lessons of History

Copenhagen Business School Press
2007

The Role of Agriculture in
Economic Development
The Lessons of History

© Copenhagen Business School Press, 2007
Printed in Denmark by Narayana Press, Gylling
Cover design by Morten Højmark
1. edition 2007

ISBN 10: 87-630-0194-2
ISBN 13: 978-87-630-0194-6

Distribution:

Scandinavia
DJOEF/DBK, Mimersvej 4
DK-4600 Køge, Denmark
Tel +45 3269 7788
Fax +45 3269 7789

North America
International Specialized Book Services
920 NE 58th Ave., Suite 300
Portland, OR 97213, USA
Tel +1 800 944 6190
Fax +1 503 280 8832
Email: orders@isbs.com

Rest of the World
Marston Book Services, P.O. Box 269
Abingdon, Oxfordshire, OX14 4YN, UK
Tel +44 (0) 1235 465500, fax +44 (0) 1235 4656555
E-mail Direct Customers: direct.order@marston.co.uk
E-mail Booksellers: trade.order@marston.co.uk

All rights reserved.
No part of this publication may be reproduced or used in any form or by any means – graphic, electronic or mechanical including photocopying, recording, taping or information storage or retrieval systems – without permission in writing from Copenhagen Business School Press at www.cbspress.dk

"The ideas of economists and political philosophers, both when they are right and when they are wrong, are more powerful than is commonly understood."

J. M. Keynes, The General Theory of Employment, Interest and Money, 1936

Table of Contents

Preface 11

I   General economic trends 15

1.   Economic development in the modern era... 17
1.1   The modern era started around 1750 17
1.2   The data available for comparison.. 18
1.3   Population growth from 1500 to 2000 19
1.4   Economic development from 1500 to 1820.................................... 21
1.5   Economic development from 1820 to 2000.................................... 23
1.6   Industrialisation.. 24
1.7   Different economic conditions in Western Europe and the USA in different periods 28
1.8   The business cycle 33
1.9   Factors influencing economic development 34
1.10   Summary 43

2.   Integration and trade 47
2.1   New ideas in a world with little integration 1750-1815 48
2.2   The increase in international trade 1815-2000............................... 50
2.3   Increasing integration and liberalisation 1815-1875...................... 51
2.4   Increasing integration and tariff protection 1875-1914.................. 55
2.5   A turbulent period of disintegration 1914-1945 61
2.6   The revival of integration 1945-2000 66
2.7   Summary 67

II   Agricultural development.. 71

3.   Employment, productivity and prices in agriculture............................. 73
3.1   The relative decline of agriculture 73
3.2   Production resources in agriculture 76
3.3   Productivity in agriculture 79
3.4   Productivity differs between countries 82
3.5   Demand for agricultural products 84
3.6   Agricultural prices in the short term 85
3.7   Agricultural prices in the medium term 87
3.8   Agricultural prices in the long term 88

Table of Contents

3.9	Real agricultural prices	92
3.10	Summary	95

4.	Technological and institutional changes in agriculture 1750-1914	99
4.1	What are technological and institutional changes?	99
4.2	An overview of industrial and agricultural changes	100
4.3	The farming system in Europe before the agricultural revolution	102
4.4	The first technological changes	103
4.5	Institutional changes in the form of agricultural reforms	104
4.6	Technological changes continued	108
4.7	Institutional change in the form of economic integration	112
4.8	The importance of markets	115
4.9	Summary	118

5.	Agricultural reforms in Europe 1750-1914	123
5.1	The feudal system was not the same everywhere	124
5.2	Britain	127
5.3	France	133
5.4	Germany	137
5.5	Denmark	140
5.6	Mediterranean countries	143
5.7	Austria-Hungary and the Balkans	144
5.8	Russia	145
5.9	Summary	148

6.	Trade policy and agricultural performance in different countries 1815-1914	151
6.1	Britain	152
6.2	France	155
6.3	Germany	161
6.4	Denmark	166
6.5	The USA	169
6.6	Summary	175

7.	Agricultural markets and public intervention 1914 – 1945	181
7.1	The First World War and the restoration of peace 1914-1929	181
7.2	The introduction of agricultural support policies in Europe 1929-1939	183
7.3	The Great Depression and agricultural policy in the USA 1929-1939	191
7.4	Lack of international co-operation	196
7.5	How did agriculture perform?	197
7.6	Agriculture in the Soviet Union 1917-1939	200
7.7	The debate about development strategy in the Soviet Union	204
7.8	Summary	208

Table of Contents

8.	Adjustment and agricultural policies 1945-2000	213
8.1	The immediate post war period 1945-1950	213
8.2	GATT and agriculture	214
8.3	Agricultural policies 1950-1960	216
8.4	The foundation of the European Economic Community and the Common Agricultural Policy	218
8.5	Agricultural policy problems 1968-1973	224
8.6	The agricultural trend of falling real prices	225
8.7	The Common Agricultural Policy 1973-1990	228
8.8	Why was the CAP allowed to be developed?	231
8.9	US agricultural policy 1960-1990	232
8.10	Agriculture more dependent on world markets and macroeconomic policies	236
8.11	Agricultural reforms since 1990	238
8.12	Summary	240
III	*Lessons from the past*	243
9.	The determinants of agricultural development	245
9.1	A development model	245
9.2	Common characteristics of feudal societies	252
9.3	The different stages of agricultural development	255
9.4	The first stage of agricultural development	257
9.5	The second stage of agricultural development	259
9.6	The third stage of agricultural development	265
9.7	The fourth stage of development	267
9.8	What will happen in the fifth stage?	270
9.9	Summary	273
10.	Agriculture in the early stage of economic development	277
10.1	Agriculture or industry as the engine of growth	277
10.2	Agricultural demand stimulated industrialisation	280
10.3	Agriculture supplied resources	281
10.4	Interrelationship between agriculture and industry	284
10.5	Agricultural development and population growth	286
10.6	Agricultural reforms and farm size structure	288
10.7	Summary	291
11.	Markets and institutions for further development	295
11.1	The market mechanism and development	295
11.2	The implementation of the market economy	297
11.3	Markets are of special importance to agriculture	301
11.4	Agriculture is a biological production	302
11.5	The institutional framework and agriculture	304
11.6	The experience of the Soviet planned economy	308
11.7	Summary	314

Table of Contents

12.	Economic policy intervention	319
12.1	Trade policy	320
12.2	Agricultural policy	325
12.3	Problems caused by agricultural policy	330
12.4	Macroeconomic policy and agriculture	336
12.5	Summary	343
13.	Agriculture in the developing countries after 1950	347
13.1	The long-term trends in the Third World	347
13.2	Why did the developing countries choose industrialisation?	350
13.3	Was it wise to focus on industrialisation?	354
13.4	Production structures and patterns	359
13.5	The importance of prices	361
13.6	Macroeconomic policies in the developing countries	365
13.7	Summary	368
14.	The lessons of history	371
14.1	Different methods of analysis	371
14.2	General economic trends	373
14.3	Agricultural development	373
14.4	A development model	381
14.5	Productivity increases and agricultural reforms	383
14.6	Economic integration, markets and economic environment	386
14.7	Economic and agricultural policy intervention	389
14.8	Post-war experiences of the developing countries	392

Literature 397

Index 405

Preface

The purpose of this book is to analyse the role of agriculture in the process of economic development. It is a study of economic history based on the role of agriculture in the economic development of Europe and the USA in the period 1750 – 2000.

Such a study is interesting for several reasons. Firstly, it is interesting to know how the different countries in Europe and the USA have developed differently. The agricultural developments varied from country to country, and these differences had an impact on overall economic development. It is valuable in itself to know how societies which started with overwhelmingly dominant agricultural sectors gradually developed into the modern societies we know today.

Secondly, it is important to understand and to explain why the rural sector developed differently in different countries. It is important to explain how rural development contributed to the development of the urban sector and vice versa. What were the driving forces behind the development of agriculture as a major sector in the western world? An analysis of the historical development contributes to a better understanding of the processes of economic and social development.

Thirdly, a better understanding of the processes which led to the development of today's industrialised countries can contribute to improving the economic performances of contemporary developing countries. The lessons from the past should be taken into account when developing countries choose their development strategies. The purpose of investigations into economics is to acquire an understanding of economic relationships and processes. Such knowledge makes it possible to intervene so as to achieve certain goals.

This book is divided into three parts. In the first part, containing Chapters 1 and 2, there is a description of the general economic trends in the western world from 1750 to 2000. The two chapters focus on population, economic growth and international trade. The data used draws heavily on the comprehensive studies of Angus Maddison who has made estimates of populations and gross domestic products over several centuries for most countries in the world.

The second part of the book analyses agricultural development in the western world. Agricultural development started in the north-western part of Europe, so the focus is on that area. From the second half of the eighteenth century there was a radical change in farming that started a development which has totally changed European society. What were the causes, what were the initiatives, and what were the consequences? The essential elements of agricultural history in the period 1700 - 2000 are discussed in the Chapters 3 - 8.

The third part of the book deals with the lessons that can be learnt from studying the agricultural and economic development of the past. The framework of a development theory is set-out in Chapter 9. Economic development depends on the amount and quality of the resources, technological innovations, institutional changes and attitudes. Chapter 10 covering the period 1750 – 1850 shows how the agricultural sector of the time became the engine of growth, once technological changes and agricultural reforms had taken place. Chapter 11 covers the period 1850 – 1914, when economic integration between the rural and the urban sectors and between countries accelerated. Economic integration was achieved through the establishment of markets and the necessary economic environment. Up to 1914 agriculture played a major role in the development process, but this crucial role was not maintained after the First World War. Chapter 12 shows how the agricultural sector became heavily dependent on public policy interventions in the period 1914 - 2000.

When decolonisation started after the Second World War, the developing countries had to choose development strategies. They did not follow the development pattern of the western world. Why did they choose the strategies they did, and why were their choices of development strategy not successful? These questions are considered in Chapter 13.

In Chapter 14 the lessons of history are summarised. To get a more detailed summary of the main topics and arguments of this book, the reader is recommended to start by devoting some time to the last chapter.

The writing of a book takes time, and during the process several persons are involved. I have discussed parts of the book with many of my students and with colleagues, and I would like to thank them for their inspiration and for suggestions. In particular, the Director General of the Institute of Food and Resource Economics at KVL (The Royal Danish Agricultural University) in Copenhagen, Søren E. Frandsen, has followed the work with great interest. The original manuscript was written in English, but I am grateful to Steven Harris who revised the text so that it corresponds to one written by a native English speaking person. Finally, but not least, I would like to thank Lisbeth Balle, who has with great

Preface

patience transcribed my hand written notes and prepared the figures and tables in this final edition, and all the previous drafts, which preceded it.

Søren Kjeldsen-Kragh
Copenhagen,
August 2006

I General economic trends

1. Economic development in the modern era

1.1 The modern era started around 1750

The start of the modern era is often dated to around 1750. Around that time several important changes occurred. Firstly, the population started to increase at a higher rate than previously. Secondly, the average gross domestic product per capita also seems to have increased somewhat more rapidly than previously. Thirdly, at that time some important structural changes started to have an impact on society.

It is true that some parts of the world did experience development and progress before 1750. In Europe, for example, there was development before 1750, but the rate of change was slower. Around 1750 there was a significant increase in the rate of population growth, and there was some increase in the rate of growth of the gross domestic product per capita. Most importantly, the period around 1750 saw the start of changes in social and economic structures, especially in Europe.

The period around 1750 saw the start of a process which both continued and accelerated. It was a time of important technological and institutional change. It was also the Age of Enlightenment, when new ideas had an important impact on the development of modern societies. Since 1750 societies have gradually been transformed, first from agrarian societies to industrial societies, and then from industrial to service societies.

The structural changes at the start of the modern era began in Britain, which was the first country to industrialise. At the same time, there were also important changes in agriculture. Again Britain was the country where new technological and institutional changes in agriculture took root at an early stage.

The agricultural changes and the start of industrialisation in the eighteenth century are often called the agricultural revolution and the industrial revolution, respectively. It is true that industrial and agricultural changes led to a radical change to the previous way of life, but it is problematic to speak about an agricultural revolution and an industrial revolution.

The term 'revolution' usually refers to a sudden and unexpected event with rapid, dramatic and far-reaching consequences. As will be seen in the following, there was some economic development prior to 1750, but it took a long time to realise the industrialisation and transformation of the agricultural sector.

The initiation of the modern era was dependent on technological and institutional changes, and these took place over a long period. Historical research shows that "the technological changes around 1750 were the completion of tendencies, which had been significantly evident since Leonardo da Vinci" (Usher, 1970). The institutional changes were to a large extent influenced by a new prevailing ideology of liberalism. Also here it took some time before the new ideals were put into practice.

It is the purpose of this chapter to give a short overview of economic developments in Europe, the USA and other parts of the world since 1500, with a special focus on developments since the start of the modern era. At the end of the chapter it is shown how a series of interrelated factors influenced this development.

Clearly, the analysis of economic history is more difficult if the necessary data are not available. The further back one goes, the more difficult it is to get reliable statistics. Fortunately, statistical data collection has improved significantly in recent decades, thanks to the work of Angus Maddison. He has collected and estimated data for the population and the gross domestic product of different countries and different parts of the world. He has estimated data for the selected years 1500, 1600, 1700, 1820, and has provided annual data for the period 1820-2001 (Maddison, 2003).

Gross domestic product per capita may be useful for comparative purposes, but there are some problems which should be considered before the data are applied.

1.2 The data available for comparison

Economic activity in a society is measured by the gross domestic product (GDP) in fixed prices, and the GDP per capita is often used as a measure of the average living standard. There is a series of difficulties in constructing GDP data which are used for cross-section analyses, such as comparisons of GDP in different countries at a given moment, and time series analyses which compare the GDP at different times in a given country.

Comparative analyses between countries can only be made when the GDP is calculated in the same currency. The exchange rate used for conversion to the same currency should be an equilibrium exchange rate, which is not necessarily the same as the present exchange rate because a currency may be overvalued or undervalued. Even where such an equilibrium exchange rate has been found, there is the problem of different price structures. The purchasing power of an equal amount of income in two countries is not able to buy the same amount of goods, regardless of how the money is spent on different goods and services. In some countries, food is relatively expensive, in other countries industrial products are expensive, and in a third group of countries services such as housing, are expensive. When a country is moving from a low income level to a higher income level, productivity increases will often be highest in the agricultural sector, followed by lower productivity increases in manufacturing, and the lowest productivity increases in the service sector. With this pattern, at a given moment services will be relatively cheap in lower income countries with low wages and relatively expensive in high income countries. Therefore, GDP estimates should be based on the concept of purchasing power parity (PPP), which means that the same GDP in two countries should be able to buy the same basket of goods and services in each of the two countries.

There are also problems related to inter-temporal comparisons of data within a given country. It is well-known that inflation rates vary over time, and may replaced by periods of deflation. Comparisons can only be made when the GDP is calculated in fixed prices. A more serious problem relates to the fact that the assortment of products available also changes through time. Many of the products produced today did not exist in the past, and even if they did exist, they would typically be of a lower quality. If the price of a product has increased, this need not necessarily be due only to inflation; it could partly be a result of the extra costs associated with the production of goods of higher quality.

Maddison has tried to eliminate these problems in his calculations, as far as possible. Of course, the reliability of the estimated data can be disputed, especially the older data and data relating to countries outside Europe and North America, where it may be more difficult to find sources. However, Maddison's work provides us with the most comprehensive and most reliable data set.

1.3 Population growth from 1500 to 2000

Table 1.1 shows the population growth in the different parts of the world from 1500 onwards. The total population of the world grew during the period 1500-1700. In the sixteenth century, the increase was approximately 25 per cent, whereas the increase in the seventeenth century was only about 10 per cent. In the following 120 years, from

1700-1820, the population increased by about 75 per cent. This pattern is found in most regions and certainly in the two regions with the largest populations, namely Asia and Western Europe.

Table 1.1: The population of the world 1500-1820

	1500	1600	1700	1820	1913	2001
Western Europe[1]	48.2	62.6	68.8	114.6	228.0	325.1
Southern Europe[2]	8.8	10.8	12.3	18.5	33.0	67.0
Eastern Europe	13.5	17.0	18.8	36.5	79.5	120.9
Former USSR	17.0	20.7	26.6	54.8	156.2	290.3
USA	2.0	1.5	1.0	10.0	97.6	285.0
Latin America	17.5	8.6	12.1	21.7	80.9	531.2
Asia	283.8	378.5	401.8	679.4	977.4	3653.5
Africa	46.6	55.3	61.1	74.2	124.7	821.1
World	438.4	556.1	603.5	1041.8	1791.1	6149.0

[1] The EU(15) except Spain, Portugal, Greece and Luxembourg plus Norway and Switzerland
[2] Spain, Portugal and Greece
Source: Maddison (2003)

The conclusion is that the population grew before 1700, but that the rate of increase accelerated significantly after 1700. This sharp increase in population growth seems to have been world-wide. From 1700 to 1820, the total world population increased by 438 million. This was followed by an increase of 750 millions in the period 1820-1913, and an increase of 5.3 billion from 1913 to the present.

From 1820 to 1913, the rate of population growth increased in all regions of the world, except Asia, compared to the period 1700-1820. From 1820 to 1913, the population of Europe doubled, while the population increased three times in the former USSR, ten times in the USA and four times in Latin America. The population increase in Asia was much lower, less than 50 percent.

This pattern changed dramatically during the last period, 1913-2001. In the European countries, the former USSR and the USA, the population increased from 0.6 to 1.1 billions, whereas the population in Latin America, Asia and Africa increased from 1.2 to 5.0 billions. In the twentieth century, high economic growth in the developed countries was combined with a decrease in the rate of population growth. In the developing world, low economic growth was combined with an increase in rate of population growth.

1.4 Economic development from 1500 to 1820

Table 1.2 displays the gross domestic product (GDP) per capita in the world for the period 1500-1820. The estimates show no growth per capita in Asia and Africa during these three centuries. In 1500, Western Europe had a GDP per capita which was around 40 per cent higher than in China, India and the other countries in Asia. This disparity increased during the period 1500-1820 because the GDP per capita in Europe increased gradually during the period, while it was stagnant in Asia. GDP per capita in Western Europe grew 30 per cent during the period 1500-1700, and a further 20 per cent during the period 1700-1820, corresponding to a growth of 32 per cent over two centuries.

The comparison between Western Europe and Asia during the period 1500-1820 is interesting. In both parts of the world, the population increase followed the same pattern, see Table 1.1. During the sixteenth century, the population increase was higher than in the seventeenth century, and then there was a significant increase in the growth rate in the period 1700-1820.

Table 1.2: The gross domestic product per capita in the world 1500-1820. Measured in 1990 US$[1]

	1500	1600	1700	1820
Western Europe[2]	798	908	1033	1245
Spain	661	853	853	1008
Eastern Europe	496	548	606	683
Former USSR	499	552	610	688
USA	400	400	527	1257
Latin America	416	438	527	692
Asia except Japan	572	575	571	577
Africa	414	422	421	420
World	566	595	615	667

[1] 1990 international Geary-Khamis dollars. This indicator is based on fixed 1990 prices and exchange rates which are calculated according to purchase power parity.
[2] Including the same countries as in Table 1.1
Source: See Table 1.1

This pattern of population increase was not matched by a similar increase in GDP. In Asia, GDP increased at the same rate as the population so that GDP per capita was stagnant. In Western Europe the growth of GDP was much stronger than the population growth, and GDP per capita increased approximately 50 per cent from 1500 to 1820.

However, this growth was small compared to the growth during the succeeding period 1820-1913, when GDP per capita increased by 200 per cent.

Around 85 per cent of the population of Western Europe lived in the areas which today constitute the United Kingdom, France, Germany and Italy. Developments in these four large countries were very different, as can be seen from Table 1.3. The rate of population increase was much higher in the United Kingdom than in the other countries.

Table 1.3: The population and the GDP per capita in the UK, France, Germany and Italy 1500-1820

	Population in millions			GDP per capita, 1990 $		
	1500	1700	1820	1500	1700	1820
United Kingdom	3.9	8.6	21.2	717	1250	1706
France	15.0	21.5	31.2	727	910	1135
Germany	12.0	15.0	24.9	688	910	1047
Italy	10.5	13.3	20.2	1100	1100	1117

Source: See Table 1.1

Together with the high rate of population increase in the United Kingdom there was also a large increase in GDP per capita. In 1500, GDP per capita was at the same level in the UK, France and Germany, but, by 1820, GDP per capita was around two-thirds higher in the UK. In 1500, GDP per capita was significantly higher in Italy, but over the next three centuries, GDP per capita in Italy stagnated.

The figures for the UK, France and Germany confirm that there was significant economic development before 1700. The economic dynamics were located in Britain, and had their roots far back, earlier than the eighteenth century. It is interesting to note that there was a significant increase in GDP per capita in Britain before industrialisation started around 1750. There was also an increase in France and Germany, though this was much smaller. The British development can be explained by Britain becoming an important trader. Trade meant urbanisation, and this may have been an important stimulus for increased agricultural production.

It is tempting to explain the different developments in Britain, on the one hand, and France, German and Italy, on the other hand, as resulting from industrialisation. There is no question that industrialisation is part of the explanation. According to the estimates, in 1830 industrial production in Britain was seven times the level of 1750, while industrial production had not even doubled in France and Germany during the same period (Bairoch, 1982). In all three cases, it was an increase from a very low level of industrial production in 1750. There are reasons to believe that the increased GDP per capita was to a large extent due to agricultural developments, also in the case of Britain.

1.5 Economic development from 1820 to 2000

Together with the large population increase illustrated in Table 1.1, there was unprecedented economic growth measured as GDP per capita. Table 1.4 shows that the growth rate per capita was very different in different parts of the world, and that the growth rate varied from period to period.

In 1820, GDP per capita in Western Europe, the USA, and other countries settled by European immigrants, was around double the world average. By 2001, Western Europe, North America and Japan were far ahead, and others, especially Africa and to a lesser extent Asia, were lagging behind. The disparities between the different regions had become much wider.

Table 1.4: The GDP per capita in 1820 and 2001 and the growth rates in different periods

	GDP per capita 1990-dollars[1]		Annual compound growth rate Percent				
	1820	2001	1820-1870	1870-1913	1913-1950	1950-1973	1973-2001
Western Europe[2]	1204	19265	0.98	1.33	0.76	4.05	1.88
Eastern Europe	683	6027	0.63	1.39	0.60	3.81	0.68
Former USSR	688	4626	0.63	1.06	1.76	3.35	-0.96
USA and others[3]	1202	26943	1.41	1.81	1.56	2.45	1.84
Latin America	692	5811	-0.03	1.82	1.43	2.58	0.91
Japan	669	20683	0.19	1.48	0.88	8.06	2.14
China	600	3583	-0.25	0.10	-0.62	2.86	5.32
India	533	1957	0.00	0.54	-0.22	1.40	3.01
Other Asia	584	3998	0.19	0.74	0.13	3.51	2.42
Africa	420	1489	0.35	0.57	0.92	2.00	0.19
World	667	6049	0.54	1.30	0.88	2.92	1.41

[1] See Table 1.2
[2] Including all European countries, apart from the Eastern European countries
[3] USA, Canada, Australia and New Zealand
Source: See Table 1.1

The last columns in Table 1.4 show the economic performance in different periods during the last two centuries.

The next almost centennial period, 1913-2001, is split into three sub-periods, 1913-1950, 1950-1973 and 1973-2001. In the period 1913-1950, there was an average annual increase in GDP per capita of nearly 0.9 per cent, which is below the growth rate of 1.3 in the pre-war period, 1870-1913. The years 1950-1973 can be described as a golden period when the highest annual growth rate per capita was achieved at 2.9 per cent. Around 1973, there were exogenous shocks which caused unemployment and inflation. These were the oil price shock in 1973, the breakdown of the Bretton Woods exchange rate system and a decrease in the rate of productivity increase. In the years 1973-2001, the rate of annual increase in GDP per capita fell to 1.4 per cent.

When comparing the different regions of the world there are interesting differences for the different periods. In the first phase, 1820-1870, growth was concentrated in Western Europe and the USA. Growth was less in Eastern Europe and Russia, and non-existent in Latin America and Asia. In the second phase, 1870-1913, there was an increase in the growth rate in all regions apart from China which had a stagnant economy. Western Europe and the USA achieved high growth rates, but they were now accompanied by the rest of Europe, Latin America and Japan. Asia and Africa were still lagging behind.

During the third phase, 1913-1950, the western hemisphere and the USSR performed significantly better than the rest of the world, where especially Asia performed poorly. Africa performed at the rate of the world average. Around 1950, when decolonisation started in Asia and later in Africa, GDP per capita was on average 40 per cent higher in Africa than in Asia, excluding Japan.

During the golden age, 1950-1973, there was a significant increase in GDP per capita everywhere, but Europe and Japan performed markedly better than the global average, whereas America and Africa had performances below average. In the subsequent period, 1973-2001, Asia performed better than any other region. The regions with problems were the former USSR with an annual decline of 1.0 per cent and Africa where the population increase neutralised the growth of GDP.

1.6 Industrialisation

Industrialisation is the process by which labour-intensive small-scale manufacturing is gradually replaced by more capital-intensive manufacturing production on a larger scale. Industrial production is made possible by technological and institutional changes. Industrialisation was an extremely slow phenomenon, especially at the beginning. It is reasonable to speak about two industrial revolutions.

The first industrial revolution took place in Britain during the period 1750-1830. It was only around 1830 that the first industrial revolution gathered momentum in Belgium and Northern France and later, around 1850, in Germany and the USA.

The first industrial revolution, 1750-1830, was started in Britain. It was based on a series of important innovations. Steam was a new power source captured by steam engines. Industrialisation was dependent on coal for producing energy and on iron ore for the production of iron, which was necessary for the production of machinery. There were also significant innovations in the textile sector, such as mechanised spinning and weaving. The first industrialisation was largely concentrated on light consumer goods such as textiles. Industrialisation depends on the existence of a sufficiently developed infrastructure so that the raw materials can be brought to the factories and the finished goods can be distributed to consumers. Such conditions existed in Britain in the form of sea, river and canal transport, although the improvements to transport facilities made by the building of railways and steam ships only started in around 1830.

The period 1870-1914 can be considered as the second industrial revolution when further innovations were introduced. These innovations were the use of electricity, improved iron and steel production, production of chemicals and synthetic materials and engineering and construction in the form of new machinery, better engines, better ships and the construction of cars.

The first industrial revolution was very much concentrated around Britain. According to estimates made by Bairoch, the disparity between the level of industrialisation between European countries, measured as the coefficient of variation, increased from 1800 to 1880, when it reached its maximum. Since 1880, the disparities have been reduced. Although Britain was a small country, with less than 10 per cent of the population of Europe, including Russia, in the period 1860-1880, Britain was responsible for one third of the total industrial production of Europe (Bairoch, 1982).

In global terms, industrialisation was a phenomenon very much associated with Europe and the USA. The present developing countries did have some industrial production in 1750, and there was a slight increase of around 20 per cent up to 1830. The period 1830-1900 was one of de-industrialisation. Their industrial production declined from 1830 to

1900 by 50 percent. Around 1900, the developing countries were responsible for only little more than 10 per cent of total industrial production (Bairoch, 1982). It was only from this very low level that industrial production in the developing countries started to increase.

Industrialisation in Europe was very much concentrated around the countries in the north and to the west. In Europe around 1900 the most industrialised areas were Britain, Belgium, Northern France, Germany and Switzerland.

Table 1.5 gives an idea of the degree of industrialisation in different European countries in around 1900. For each country, the industrial production, as a share of the total economic activity, has been calculated as an average for the years 1898-1902. The percentage share of industrial production is an indicator of the degree of industrialisation in each country. Then a similar calculation has been made for all European countries together, which indicates the average degree of industrialisation in Europe. When the national indicators for the degree of industrialisation are divided by the European average, it is possible to rank the European countries, indexing the European average at 100.

According to the figures in Table 1.5, in around 1900 Europe can be divided into three groups of countries. The first group is industrialised countries with an indicator above 110. These are the United Kingdom, Belgium, Germany, Switzerland and France, especially the northern part of France. The second group consists of countries with an indicator between 70 and 110, and this group includes the Scandinavian countries (Denmark, Norway and Sweden), the Netherlands, Austria-Hungary (especially Austria and the later Czech Republic) and Italy (especially the northern part of Italy). In these countries there was a certain industrial base, but the countries could not yet be considered as industrialised, as the primary sectors still played a major role. In the third group of countries, with an indicator below 70, there was no firm industrial base yet, and the countries should be considered as agrarian societies. This group consists of the Mediterranean countries (Portugal, Spain, the southern part of France, southern part of Italy and Greece), the Balkan countries (Serbia, Romania and Bulgaria) and Russia, including Poland and Finland, which were parts of Russia at that time.

There seems to be a clear positive correlation between the GDP per capita and the industrialisation level in 1900. This is illustrated in Figure 1.1, where the horizontal axis shows the industrialisation index from Table 1.5, and the vertical axis marks the GDP per capita in 1900. GDP per capita in the industrialised countries is significantly higher than the GDP per capita in Southern and Eastern Europe. There is also a positive correlation between the increase in GDP per capita in the period 1820-1913 and the industrialisation index in 1900. Those countries which industrialised first had the highest growth rate per capita during the first stage of industrialisation.

Table 1.5: *Industrialisation index in 1900 for different European countries[1]*

United Kingdom	254	Spain	52
Belgium	230	Greece	48
Germany	177	Portugal	46
Switzerland	150	Serbia	39
France	140	Russia	34
Sweden	104	Bulgaria	33
Netherlands	97	Finland	32
Norway	93	Romania	13
Denmark	85	Europe	100
Austria-Hungary	82	Continental Europe	83
Italy	71	Continental Europe without Russia	109

[1] The degree of industrialisation in the country for the period 1898-1902, when the average European industrialisation level is indexed at 100
Source: Bairoch (1976)

Figure 1.1: *The relationship between the GDP per capita and industrialisation in 1900*

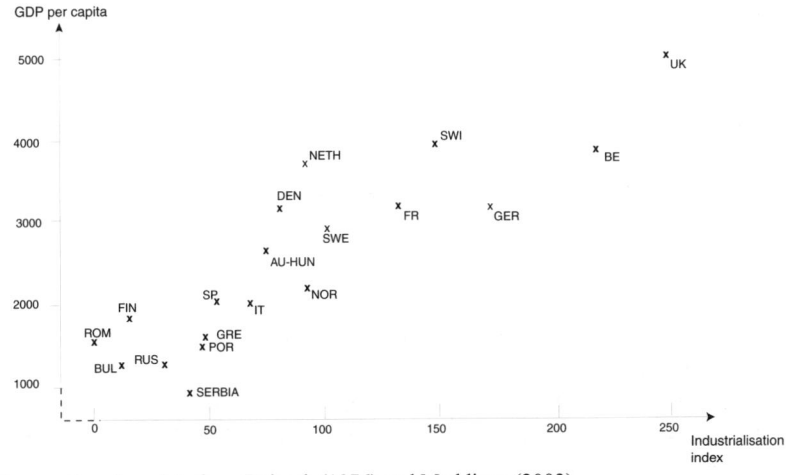

Source: Based on data from Bairoch (1976) and Maddison (2003)

High average income per capita is correlated with a high degree of industrialisation. However, there are some important exceptions. Switzerland had a higher GDP per capita than Belgium, even though its industrialisation index is much lower. The Netherlands and Denmark were among the less industrialised countries, but they had a GDP per capita equivalent to some other countries that were more industrialised. The reason for this is that these two countries specialised in agriculture and trade, and greatly benefited from their proximity to the industrial centres of Western Europe. In the Mediterranean area, Portugal, Spain and Greece reached the same level of industrialisation, but the income level in Spain was significantly higher than in the two other countries.

The less industrialised and rural societies of Western Europe in 1900 all developed into industrialised and later into post-industrialised societies during the 20th century. The relative income disparities between Western European countries in 1900 were greatly narrowed, especially during the second half of the 20th century.

Economic development is often associated with industrialisation, but a one-sided theory of development which only focuses on industrialisation is dangerous. Important improvements in living standards can also be obtained through agricultural development. Industrialisation can be considered as a demand element, pulling the economy, while agricultural improvements can be considered as a supply element, pushing the economic development. To focus either on the demand side or the supply side is dangerous because there are important links between the two in the economy.

A high correlation between industrialisation and GDP per capita does not indicate anything about the development process in which both industry and agriculture have an important role to play. This important issue will be discussed in more detail later.

1.7 Different economic conditions in Western Europe and the USA in different periods

The last two centuries can be characterised as a period of unprecedented growth. Development has been uneven, in the sense that periods of higher growth have alternated with periods of lower growth as it has already been shown in Table 1.4.

It is reasonable to divide the first centennial period, 1820-1914, into four sub-periods and the second centennial period 1914-2000 into five sub-periods.

Different economic conditions in Western Europe and the USA

The choice of periods is to a large extent based on the growth rates and the price trends in the three important economies in Western Europe (United Kingdom, Germany and France) and the USA. The three big western European countries have been chosen as representatives of Western Europe. Table 1.7 shows the increase in the real gross domestic product per capita in the United Kingdom, Germany, France and the USA.

Table 1.6: Economic performance during the period 1820-2000

First centennial period 1820-1914

1820-1850	Moderate growth with falling prices
1850-1875	High growth with rising prices
1875-1895	Moderate growth with falling prices
1895-1914	High growth with rising prices

Second centennial period 1914 - 2000

1914-1929	War and recovery
1929-1939	Great depression and recovery
1939-1950	War and recovery
1950-1973	Extremely high growth
1973-2000	High growth

Table 1.7: Increase in the real GDP per capita in the United Kingdom, Germany, France and the USA. Average annual increase[1]

	UK	Germany	France	USA
1820-1850	1.2	1.1	1.2	1.4
1850-1875	2.1	2.0	1.4	1.7
1875-1895	1.0	1.4	0.8	2.0
1895-1913	1.1	2.0	2.0	2.7
1913-1929	0.3	0.8	1.2	1.9
1929-1939	1.4	2.8	1.5	-0.5
1939-1950	1.4	-2.2	1.0	4.0
1950-1973	3.1	9.0	6.4	3.0
1973-2001	2.4	2.0	2.2	2.4

[1] The percentage increase in real GDP per capita, measured in 1990 dollars, from the first year of the period is divided by the number of years in the period.
Source: Calculations based on data from Maddison (2003)

Economic development in the modern era

The development of prices is the other important indicator characterising these periods. Table 1.8 shows the rise in price levels in the different periods for the three most important economies of Western Europe and the USA.

Table 1.8: Changes in wholesale price levels in the United Kingdom, Germany, France and the USA. Average annual increase[1]

	UK	Germany	France	USA
1820-1850	-1.2	-0.7	-0.9	-0.4
1850-1875	1.3	1.6	0.7	1.5
1875-1895	-1.7	-1.4	-1.7	-1.1
1895-1913	1.6	2.2	2.0	2.2
1929-1933	-6.2	-8.0	-9.5	-7.7
1933-1939	3.3	2.5	12.3	2.7
1950-1970	3.9	1.6	6.3	-0.4

[1] The percentage increase from the first year to the last year of the period is divided by the number of years in the period
Source: Calculations based on data from Mitchell (1981) and Historical Statistics of the United States (1949)

It is clear that price shifts have great economic implications, because wages and profits, in both nominal and real terms, are influenced by prices. Price changes also have an impact on the real burden of debt. If prices fall, debtors will loose and creditors will gain. The opposite is the case, when prices rise.

The period 1820 -1914

It seems that the first centennial period, 1820-1914, can be divided into two sub-periods, 1820-1875 and 1875-1914. Each sub-period is divided into two halves where the first half is characterised by moderate growth and falling prices, whereas the growth rate per capita was markedly higher in the second half, and the price level rose.

The first period, 1820-1850, was one of moderate growth in Western Europe. This pattern can be explained by productivity increases in agriculture and industrialisation in Britain which was slowly spreading to other Western European countries. At the same time price levels were falling, especially during the 1820s. During the 1830s, prices were stable, and during the 1840s they fell again.

The period 1850-1875 was a prosperous one with higher growth rates than previously, accompanied by rising price. There was an increase in

Different economic conditions in Western Europe and the USA

the investment ratio. It was the period of construction of extensive rail networks. Improved transport was a major step towards integrating the agricultural sector into the national economies. Industrialisation gathered pace and the agricultural sector benefited from rising agricultural prices. Higher farm incomes created a demand for industrial inputs and consumer goods, so the farming sector contributed to the ongoing industrialisation.

During the period 1875-1895, the rate of economic growth slowed and price levels fell. During the first half of the period, real GDP per capita was nearly stagnant and it then increased during the last half. Prices fell during the first half and then levelled out. During the whole period, agricultural production continued to grow, but farmers suffered from falling prices. The growing urban population benefited from the falling food prices, and this contributed to the increase in real incomes of non-agricultural workers.

The economic trend shifted again in the period 1895-1914, when the economy grew at a higher rate than in the preceding period, and prices also rose. There were improvements in productivity, which seems to have been an important factor in explaining the higher growth rate. The investment ratio was still high, but there was a shift in the composition of investments away from investments in infrastructure, such as railways, towards investments in the production of other capital and consumer goods. Investments in infrastructure are a prerequisite for growth in the longer term, but the capital output ratio is very high for these investments. Investments in infrastructure were now largely replaced by investments in manufacturing industries, where the capital output ratio is significantly lower. The period was also a prosperous one for agriculture in Europe and the USA with rising prices. Agriculture was still an important sector, so there was an interdependence between improved business conditions in agriculture and manufacturing industries.

Table 1.7 shows the economic performance of the three largest economies in Western Europe and the USA. The growth rate in the period 1820-1875 was approximately the same in Western Europe and the USA. However, initially in 1820 Britain had a higher real GDP per capita than Germany, France and the USA, which were all at the same level. The real GDP per capita in Britain has been estimated as having been around 40 per cent higher than in the other countries. In 1875, Britain was still 40 per cent ahead of the USA and even further ahead of France than it had been in 1820.

In the following period, 1875-1914, the growth rate in the USA was significantly higher than in Europe, where Germany had the highest growth rate. The United Kingdom grew more slowly and in 1914 the USA had caught up, having the same real GDP per capita.

The Period 1914 - 2000

When comparing the economic performances of Britain, Germany, France and the USA during the second centennial, 1914-2000, there seem to have been wider divergences between the individual sub-periods than in the previous centennial period. This is not surprising, since the two World Wars and the Great Depression affected these countries differently. During the First World War, the US economy performed much better than the Western European economies. The USA did not suffer the destruction of war, and the 1920s were boom years in the USA. By contrast, the British economy was stagnant during the 1920s. Britain wanted to go back to the gold standard at the pre-war parity, but its cost levels were much too high for such a foreign exchange policy, so Britain lost competitiveness. The USA and Germany suffered most from the Great Depression. Before the outbreak of the Second World War, the GDP per capita in the USA had not reached the 1929-level. In Germany, the economy was marked by the takeover of power by the national socialists in 1933, and rearmament stimulated the economy so much that real GDP per capita was significantly higher in 1939 than in 1929.

Not surprisingly, during the war and the years immediately following it, the US economy continued to expand at a rapid pace, whereas the European economies suffered from the devastations of war, especially Germany.

Since 1950, there has been a rapid increase in GDP per capita in nearly all Western European countries. Europe was to some extent catching up with the USA, except the UK which had a growth rate corresponding to the US rate. After 1973 there was a general slowing down of economic growth. Unemployment levels rose, but the rate of increase in productivity also slowed down.

The political and economic turbulence of the period 1914-1950 also manifested itself in relation to prices. During all wars and the years immediately following them, prices soar and in some cases inflation takes off into hyperinflation. This was the case with the First and the Second World Wars. After high inflation during the First World War, prices fell sharply in all Western European countries in 1921, apart from in Germany where inflation developed into hyperinflation. During the rest of the 1920s, prices either rose, as in France, or fell as in the United Kingdom, according to the choice of monetary policy. During the worst years of the Great Depression, 1929-1933, prices fell between 25 and 40 per cent in Western Europe and the United States. Later in the 1930s, price levels rose again, but in most Western European countries they did not reach the 1929 level. High inflation during the Second World War continued in most countries after the war until 1949-1950, and in Germany the monetary system broke down.

From 1950 to 1980, there was a relatively high inflation rate, except in Germany, which was very successful in establishing price stability. The inflation rate rose from a lower level in the 1950s to a higher level in the 1960s and it became markedly higher during the 1970s, when two oil-price shocks contributed to the high inflation rates which only began to level off from the beginning of the 1980s. During the 1990s inflation was further reduced.

1.8 The business cycle

In the previous section it has been shown how the economic conditions in the period 1820-1914 seemed to change every 20-25 years. There seem to be some longer-term cycles where a period of slow growth and falling prices is followed by a period of higher growth and rising prices.

Besides these long-term cycles, there seemed to be some shorter cycles during the period 1820-1914. These shorter cycles are called the business cycle. Early researchers into business fluctuations found impressive regularity in the intervals separating the peaks of the booms, being of roughly equal length, 9-10 years. The same regularity is found in the intervals between the troughs of the years of slumps. The booms were especially strong when they occurred during a longer-term growth trend and the slumps were more serious in the periods with a longer-term trend of lower growth (Heaton, 1968 and Scheiber et al. 1976).

During the second centennial period, 1914-2000, there was not a similar pattern of regular long-term cycles. The period can be split into two stages, namely 1914-1950 and 1950-2000. The first stage was a turbulent period with two world wars, separated by the Great Depression. The second stage, 1950-2000, was characterised by extraordinary growth in 1950-1973, followed by lower growth in 1973-2000.

It is not possible to identify regular business cycles in the period 1914-2000. It may be understandable that regular business cycles cannot be found in the period 1914-1950, but it could have expected that regular business cycles would have returned when more normal economic conditions were re-established after 1950. However, it is not possible to identify shorter business cycles after 1950, corresponding to those in the period 1820-1914.

It seems that regular business cycles have disappeared in the second half of the twentieth century. Why has the more or less regular business cycle disappeared? The expansion of the public sector could be a part of the explanation. The decline in the importance of the agricultural sector could be another part of the explanation.

There are some automatic economic stabilisers connected with the public sector. During periods of low economic activity, tax revenues fall more than activity, and public expenditures, such as unemployment payments, are automatically increased. Lower taxes and increased social transfers both stabilise disposable incomes in the economy. When the public sector is larger, the automatic stabilisers become more powerful.

Economic conditions for the agricultural sector change more than in other sectors. Agricultural income depends on the product prices, the volumes produced and the costs. The volume produced is subject to external events such as the weather influencing the harvest, and plant and animal diseases influencing the harvest and animal production. Agricultural prices also fluctuate a great deal. The level of agricultural income has a major impact on the macro economy when agriculture is a dominant sector. These erratic events have important impacts on the non-farm sector, although it is not evident why erratic events should be transformed into regular business cycles. Nevertheless, the declining role of agriculture has eliminated the impact of such external events, which were so important in the past.

1.9 Factors influencing economic development

Growth is closely linked to increases in labour productivity

The amount of goods and services available for the citizens of a country depends on the volume produced and the capacity to import. The available volume of goods and services (Y) is the sum of the volume of domestically produced goods and services for private consumption (C), for private investment (I), for public consumption and investment (G) in the country and the volume of imported goods and services (M). The following equation can be written:

$$Y = C + I + G + M$$

When a country wants to have balance of payments equilibrium, the import capacity M is equal to the export revenue, namely the export price level multiplied by the export volume X, divided by the import price level P_M, so the following applies:

$$M = \frac{P_X}{P_M} X$$

The average amount of goods and services available per person can be found by dividing by the population D:

$$\frac{Y}{D} = \frac{C}{D} + \frac{I}{D} + \frac{G}{D} + \frac{P_X \, X}{P_M \, D}$$

Economic growth is defined as the increase in the GDP per capita, which is equal to Y/D. The labour force (L) is smaller than the population, but it is assumed that the proportion of the population belonging to the labour force (L/D) is constant. When labour productivity is defined as (C + I + G + X)/L, it can be concluded that the growth in GDP per capita (Y/D) depends on the average increase in the productivity of the labour force and the change in the terms of trade (P_X/P_M).

When a country obtains improved terms of trade, the growth rate in the country will increase. A trading partner suffering from a deterioration of its terms of trade will get a corresponding decrease in its growth rate. If the international aspects of economic growth are set aside, the size of the GDP per capita growth rate is determined by changes in labour productivity. There are many factors influencing the productivity of the labour force. One of them is the employment rate. Only the employed produce, so an increase in the employment rate will increase labour productivity because the production level (Y) will increase while the labour force (L) is constant.

Therefore, the realised economic growth, which depends on the increased productivity of the labour force, is a result of supply and demand factors. The stock of capital, the size of the labour force and the level of knowledge and technology are factors which determine the potential output from the supply side. The size and quality of the capital stock and the labour force determine the production potential, but whether it will be realised depends on the demand side. If there is a lack of demand, there may be unemployment and spare capacity. In such cases there will be less willingness to invest, and the growth rate will be lower than in a situation with full employment and full capacity utilisation. If demand fluctuates, the growth rate will also fluctuate, even if the potential growth rate determined by the supply factors is constant.

Economic development in the modern era

Technology, institutions and capital accumulation

If we disregard international trade, and if the labour force is a constant proportion of the population, then the growth rate in GDP per capita is determined by the increase in the productivity of the labour force. In the following it will be shown how labour productivity depends on technology, institutions and capital accumulation.

The neo-classical macroeconomic production function illustrates the relationship between the gross domestic product (Y), the labour force (L), the capital stock (K) and a parameter (A) which depends on infrastructure, institutions and technology. The Cobb-Douglas function is one such neo-classical function:

$$Y = AK^\alpha L^{1-\alpha}$$ or

$$Y/L = A(K/L)^\alpha$$

It shows how the GDP per capita depends on the capital-labour (K/L) ratio and the level of A. This production function is depicted in Figure 1.2.

Curve 1 shows the production frontier. The infrastructure and institutional set-up in the country is the best attainable, and the applied technology is the best available. GDP per capita depends on the capital-labour ratio. Capital can either be increased by investing in a larger stock of physical capital, such as buildings and machinery, or by investing in human capital through education and vocational training. If the time preference is equal to the slope of the tangent at point A, the corresponding capital-labour ratio is optimal, because the value of the marginal capital return is equal to the time preference. The most advanced countries are on curve 1.

The countries which lag behind may either be on curve 2 or curve 3. The countries on curve 2 have infrastructure and institutions which are as good as those in the countries on curve 1. They are on a lower production function because they are using a lower level of technology than that used in the frontier countries.

The countries on curve 3 are also using a lower level of technology, just like the countries on curve 2. However, the production level at a given capital-labour ratio is lower than on curve 2 because the infrastructure and the institutions are inadequate. A country with the production function 3 will strive for a capital stock corresponding to B if the time preference in the society is equal to the slope of the tangent in B.

Factors influencing economic development

Figure 1.2: Growth depends on technology, infrastructure, institutions, and capital accumulation

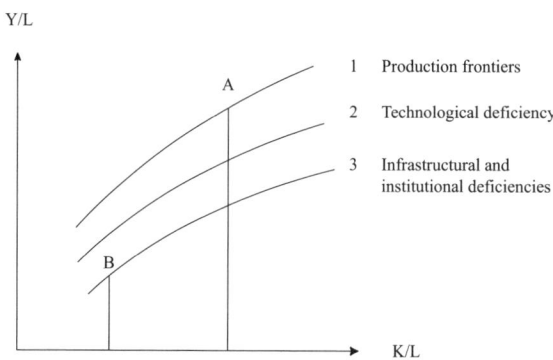

When a country producing at B lags behind a country producing at the frontier at A, it can only reach the position of A by taking a number of steps. The country must improve its infrastructure and institutions; it must apply a higher level of technology; and it must enlarge its stock of physical and human capital. The country at B, which is lagging behind, can catch up by moving gradually from B to A.

The country producing at A, at the frontier, cannot grow unless the production frontier moves upwards through improved technology or better institutions. The model in Figure 1.2 shows the different factors influencing the growth rate, but it does not say anything about the relationships between the different factors. The model is presented in such a way as to suggest that the different factors can be separated. They are, in effect, interlinked and the total effect on growth of several factors combined may have a greater impact than the sum of the partial effects of each.

The separability of the impacts of the different factors is known from the neo-classical production function of the Cobb-Douglas type. Using this function one gets:

$$\frac{\dot{Y}}{Y} = \frac{\dot{A}}{A} + \alpha \frac{\dot{K}}{K} + (1-\alpha) \frac{\dot{L}}{L} \rightarrow \frac{\dot{Y}}{Y} - \frac{\dot{L}}{L} = \frac{\dot{A}}{A} + \alpha \left(\frac{\dot{K}}{K} - \frac{\dot{L}}{L} \right)$$

where a dot signifies an increase and where, for example, $\dot{Y}/Y$ is the percentage increase in the GDP. The growth rate of GDP per capita is broken down into two terms, one term related to the change of the capital-labour ratio (K/L) and another term being equal to the percentage change of A, which is associated with technological and institutional changes. So the impacts of capital investments, technological changes and institutional changes are considered to be independent of each other.

The different factors which influence the growth rate are: investments in machinery and equipment, investment in structures such as infrastructure, investments in human capital, new technology and institutional changes. It is not possible to separate the growth impacts of the different factors. This will be illustrated in the following.

Different kinds of capital accumulation

There are different kinds of capital accumulation, and they have different impacts on GDP per capita. Investments which increase capital stock can be capital widening, capital deepening or associated with technological progress.

Capital widening means increasing the capital stock by using the same technology as the present capital stock. The capital stock is increased in the same proportion as the increase in the labour force, so the capital intensity is unchanged. This is illustrated in Figure 1.3 where the capital stock is increased from K_A to K_B and the labour force is increased from L_A to L_B. If the production function is homogenous, and if there is constant return to scale, the percentage increase of the capital stock, the labour force and production is the same. In this case, the new investments are replicating the applied technology of the initial capital stock, so there will be no increase in GDP per capita.

In the case of capital deepening, the production point is moved from A to C in Figure 1.3. This is the case where capital is substituted for labour when the production level is constant. The production technology has changed because the production has become more capital-intensive, which is often described as application of a higher production technology.

In practice, it is nearly always impossible to distinguish between capital widening and capital deepening, because most investments involve both. This is the case when investments move the capital stock from K_A to K_D, which involves a larger and more capital intensive production.

Three different cases are illustrated: the pure capital widening case, the pure capital deepening case, and the mixed case of capital widening and deepening. All three cases are characterised by capital accumulation in a given technology. The fact that technological progress occurs continuously is disregarded.

Figure 1.3: Capital widening and deepening *Figure 1.4: Investment and technological progress*

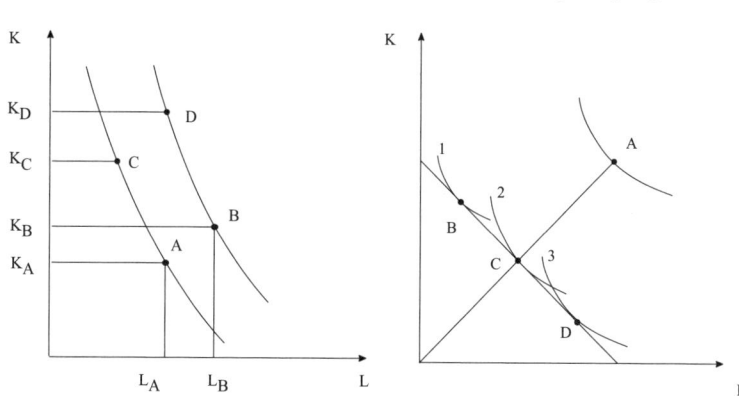

When technological progress occurs, the isoquant of a given production level moves closer to its point of origin, as illustrated in Figure 1.4. The same production level can be obtained by a reduced use of production factors. There are different kinds of technological progress which can influence the way in which the isoquant moves. If the isoquant moves to curve 1, the technological progress is capital intensive, if it moves to curve 2, the technological progress is neutral, and if the new isoquant is curve 3, the technological progress is labour intensive.

In industrialised countries most technological progress is inevitably labour saving because of market forces. When there are labour shortages, and when wage levels are steadily rising, there is an incentive to develop labour saving technology.

Technological progress takes place continuously, and investments in machinery and equipment are normally made in the newest technology. In such a case, the vintage, meaning the year when the machinery or equipment was made, influences the productivity of the capital investment. Older capital investments of a given size are less productive than newer capital investments of the same size.

Different parts of the capital stock have different vintages. When looking at the stock of machinery, the oldest machines may be, for example, 15 years old and will soon be scrapped. Others may be quite new, and it may take 15 years before they are scrapped. The capital stock is gradually renewed and enlarged by gross investments. New technology is embodied in the new machinery, but the total stock of machinery is not immediately replaced by the newest machinery. This only takes place gradually as the older machinery become outworn and obsolete. A higher rate of replacement of old machinery by new will lead to a higher growth rate due to higher labour productivity.

Where there has been technological progress in the past, but there is no future technological progress, a country can still increase its capital productivity. This will occur gradually as the old machinery is replaced by new machinery using newer technology. Capital productivity increases until the oldest machinery with the oldest technology has been replaced by new machinery embodying the newest technology.

The leading countries with high technology will be closer to the technological frontier than countries with lower technology. This gives an advantage to non-leading countries, as they have the possibility of catching up with the leading countries through gross investments in known higher technology. By renewing its capital stock, a country can increase its GDP per capita.

A leading country which is already producing at the production frontier with an optimal capital stock can only increase its GDP per capita through technological progress. If the future rate of technological progress is lower than in the past, a country at the production frontier may have a lower rate of increase of its GDP per capita than countries that are further from the production frontier. On the other hand, richer countries are better able to finance research programmes which can increase the rate of innovation.

Other factors influencing the growth rate

There are factors other than technology, institutions and capital accumulation which can have an impact on the growth rate. Economies of scale, changes in production structure, the discovery of natural resources and increased international trade can each contribute to additional growth.

Until now it has been assumed that there are constant returns to scale in production. The Cobb-Douglas function on page 36 assumes constant returns to scale, because the sum of the exponents of K and L is equal to one. However, in many productions there are economies of scale. Often, average unit costs decline up to a certain level when the firm size is increased, and beyond that level a further increase in size may increase the unit costs. These are the internal economies of scale. But there are also some external economies of scale. There are linkages between different sectors so that investments in some firms may induce other firms to invest, and when there is an agglomeration of firms, the existing infrastructure and institutions will be more fully utilised, or new infrastructure and new institutions which need a certain population base may be established. Up to a certain size, urbanisation will be beneficial.

If the inputs of capital and labour are both increased by 10 per cent, and output increases by 20 per cent, there are economies of scale which will lead to an increase in GDP per capita.

Reallocation of resources is an important cause of economic growth. When the labour force in one sector, for example agriculture, earns less than the labour force in industry, there will be a migration of labour from agriculture to industry. The lower income can relate to a lower increase in the total factor productivity and/or a deterioration of the terms of trade for agriculture.

The total factor productivity in agriculture is Q_A, and when the agricultural price is P_A and the general price level P, the real price of agricultural products is P_A/P. The term $Q_A \cdot (P_A/P)$ is an indicator of the real value of the agricultural output per resource unit. For the non-agricultural sector, the corresponding term is $Q_{NA} \cdot (P_{NA}/P)$. When the real value output per resource unit is higher in industry than in agriculture, the real GDP per capita will increase by moving the resources from agriculture to industry.

Unused natural resources are a potential source of economic growth. The growth is realised when the natural resources are used in production. Potential arable land can promote economic activity and economic growth as was the case after the agrarian reforms in Europe and the settlement of new land in the USA in the nineteenth century.

It is also clear that natural resources, such as coal mines and iron-ore deposits, were important when industrialisation started. Most industries had to be located near to the sources of coal or iron. Modern industries can be more flexible; they are no longer so dependent on proximity to natural resources, thanks to improvements in transport technology.

An increase in international trade will cause an increase in the growth rate. When the level of international trade between two countries increases, because international trade barriers are lowered, the GDP per capita will increase in both countries. The reason for this is that in both countries expensive domestic goods will be replaced by cheaper imported goods. The same labour and capital resources are now applied more efficiently. When the share of export and import volumes of the total production volume increases the GDP per capita will increase. It is assumed that either existing labour or capital resources can be reallocated or additional resources are allocated to industries which are successful in competing with foreign producers.

International trade increases the GDP per capita growth rate in various ways. Firstly, each country does not have the same relative productivity in different industries; each country does not have the same relative factor endowment. Each country can specialise in production where it has a comparative advantage. Secondly, trade makes it possible to exploit the advantages of economies of scale and product specialisation, where the product assortment is reduced. Thirdly, the opening up of international trade creates stronger competition on the domestic market. Fourthly, trade may speed up technological progress, not only through a higher degree of specialisation, but also through better transmission of information about foreign technology. International trade is of special importance for smaller countries which have less diversified factor endowment and fewer opportunities for exploiting gains from economies of scale and specialisation in a closed economy

Technology alone is not sufficient

Technological progress involves the production of new goods, both consumer goods and capital goods, and it involves the application of new production processes. Technological progress is embodied in physical capital through better and more advanced machinery, and in the labour force through new skills. New IT-technology can illustrate the complex relationship between technological progress, and physical and human investments. The IT revolution is based on new knowledge about electronic circuits and chips. This new basic knowledge, which is an invention, is then applied in the construction of a computer, called an innovation. An innovation, as such, does not have a real impact on the growth rate. This technological progress will only have an effect on the growth rate and labour productivity when computers are widely used in a society. This will only occur when there has been a large investment in the capital stock of computers, and when the human capital invested in the labour force has increased. The labour force can only use the computers efficiently when they have been taught how to do so. The conclusion is that innovations will only have an overall impact on the growth rate per capita when they are combined with investments in physical and human capital.

New technology alone is not the engine of growth. Capital formation is a complementary element, as illustrated above. A further complementary element is institutional changes. These are important, especially at the stage when a society is moving from being a traditional static society to a society transformed by technological and social changes. In the period 1750-1914, there were important institutional changes. A new liberal economic philosophy penetrated the industrialising countries. In any society there will always be resistance to change. As the new opportunities are realised, the resistance will weaken, especially when the majority of the people benefit from increasing earnings. Agrarian reforms were undertaken, capital markets were created, research and development were supported by governments, education and training took place at all levels, and the dissemination of know-how became much easier.

Trade unions were formed to look after the interests of the workers. Later, public benefit schemes to compensate for loss of income due to unemployment and other social events were started and gradually extended.

1.10 Summary

The purpose of this chapter is to give an overview of economic developments since the start of the modern era, which is traditionally dated to around 1750, and to look at some of the important factors behind economic development.

Compared with previously, the data show a significant and universal increase in the rate of population growth after 1700. During the eighteenth century there was also an increase in GDP per capita in Western Europe, especially in Britain, and in the USA which had a very small population.

However, it is interesting to note that the GDP per capita increase was not a new phenomenon. There was some economic growth in Western Europe from 1500 to 1700, again especially in Britain. The economic growth in the eighteenth century can be considered a continuation of the previous growth but at a higher level. It was only after 1820 that Western Europe witnessed a significant increase in the growth rate per capita. During the nineteenth century the highest growth rates were found in Western Europe and the USA, while the growth per capita was especially low in Asia and Africa. The income disparities, which already existed in 1820, between Western Europe and the USA on the one hand and the rest of the world on the other hand, increased in the period 1820-1913.

Economic development accelerated from the period 1820-1913 to the period 1913-2000. Globally, the population increase was significantly higher in the twentieth century than in the nineteenth. The growth rate of GDP per capita was also much higher in the twentieth century than in the previous century, in spite of two world wars and a severe depression during the 1930s. The income disparities between the industrialised countries (Western Europe, North America and Japan) on the one hand, and the rest of the world on the other hand, became much wider during the twentieth century.

When looking at the period 1700-2000, it can be concluded that the overall economic development of the world has accelerated from century to century. This is the pattern for the population, for GDP per capita, and for the income disparities between the richest and the poorest parts of the world.

However, the acceleration of development has not been at a constantly increasing rate. The last two centuries can be split into a series of periods in which a higher growth rate has been followed by a lower growth rate, followed in turn by a higher growth rate.

For different countries and different regions, growth rates have varied markedly from period to period. In some periods one region has grown more than another region, and in other periods it has been the reverse. In some periods some countries have taken the lead, and in other periods other countries have caught up.

Western Europe and the USA were at the same level in 1820, but up to 1950 growth was much more rapid in the USA than in Western Europe; since then Western Europe has narrowed the gap. Japan was at a lower level than Western Europe in 1950 but it has since caught up. During the nineteenth century, the disparities between the countries of Europe seemed to increase, but since 1950 there has been a clear trend towards greater equality between western European countries.

During the last two centuries, Latin America has performed better than Asia which has in turn increased its GDP per capita more than Africa. Development has been uneven, because Asia has to a large extent caught up with Latin America since 1973, whereas Africa has fallen behind not only Asia but also Latin America over the last 30 years.

These figures raise a lot of questions. Why do some countries develop quickly? Why do other countries fall behind? And why do some countries more or less stagnate? Industrialisation has often been considered as a cause. When looking at Europe in around 1900, there is a clear positive correlation between the degree of industrialisation and the income level per capita, although there are some exceptions such as Denmark and the Netherlands

After the Second World War, when de-colonisation started, nearly all the newly independent countries chose to follow industrialisation and

Summary

import substitution strategies. Experience shows that it is difficult to argue that these strategies have been universally successful.

A positive correlation between industrialisation and GDP per capita in Europe does not reveal anything about causality. So a series of questions remains unanswered. Which factors start the development process? Why do they occur in some countries and not in others? How is development continued once it has been started?

Why does development continue in some countries but not in others? What is the role of agriculture and the role of different industries in the development process? When it is accepted that certain industries matter, it should be asked why such industries started, since at one time all countries were agricultural societies.

In the traditional economic growth theory the emphasis has been on investment and technological progress. It has been implicitly assumed that markets are more or less perfect, and that the "necessary" institutions exist. When the development process over the last 250 years is analysed, it appears that these assumptions are not reliable.

Development is concerned with building institutions so that existing potential can be realised. At the end of the chapter some fragments of a development theory are set out. Economic performance during development depends on institutions, technology and investments. Each element is a necessary but not sufficient condition for development. There are some important interrelationships between these different elements.

2. Integration and trade

Economic development is associated with economic integration, which in turn depends on the development of markets. Economic integration is concerned with movements of goods and of production factors. The more easily goods and production factors can move, the more integrated markets are.

There are various barriers to trade and to production factor movements. There are both natural barriers and political barriers. The natural barriers concern the difficulties of overcoming physical distances. Technology determines how easily goods can be transported from one place to another, and the same applies to the mobility of production factors. Also, the technical possibilities of communication are very important for trade and factor movements. If there is no information about supply and demand in different areas, there will be no incentives for trade and factor movements.

The political barriers to trade include customs duties, import quotas, differing technical standards and exclusive rights, which all hamper free competition in goods. There may also be political barriers in the labour market and the capital market. Some of the trade barriers are inherited from the past. Others are introduced due to current ideological influences on economic policy in relation to international trade.

Economic integration has both a national and an international dimension. National integration concerns breaking down economic barriers between different regions and between the different sectors within a country, such as the rural sector with agriculture on the one hand and the urban sector, dominated by manufacturing, trade and services, on the other hand. International integration concerns breaking down economic barriers between countries.

In the following, the focus will be mainly on international economic integration, because it is easier to get data illustrating international integration. The trend towards national integration is similar to the trend towards international integration, because, to a large extent, they both depend on the same factors, namely the development of transport and communications technology.

Integration and trade

2.1 New ideas in a world with little integration 1750-1815

Little integration

In the second half of the eighteenth century, the European economy was still characterised by a great fragmentation of markets just as it had been before. The feudal system, which was still the predominant system, made most regions more or less self-sufficient. Urbanisation had started, giving rise to some trade, but this was mostly between towns and their hinterlands. Trade over long distances was mostly limited to luxury goods. The low integration of commodity markets was the result of the existing transport technology, the inheritance of a system of trade barriers and the predominant ideology influencing economic policy.

The existing means of transport were primitive, especially land transport. Land transport was slow and expensive, involving wagons or pack animals. Transport by sea and by river was easier, so countries and regions with access to water transport traded more than land-locked regions, although the tonnage of the fleet of river barges and sea-going vessels was limited.

Many of the trade barriers were internal, and national frontiers did not have the economic significance they acquired later. Tolls were levied at town gates, on roads, at bridges, at sea-crossings, etc., rather than at national frontiers. The purpose of the tolls was not to protect local traders, but to raise revenues for national or local government. Different systems of weights and measures and different coinage, even within the same country, made trade difficult. There were staple rights, navigation rights and trading monopolies under royal charter.

Until about 1750, the dominant ideology of economic policy was mercantilism. The idea was that a country should strengthen its economic and military position vis-à-vis other countries by supporting its own industries through levying import duties and through export embargoes on strategic goods.

The movement of production factors was also limited. Labour mobility was low. East of the Elbe, serfdom, which bound the peasants to the land of their landlords, still existed. The possibility of getting an alternative occupation was very low, even where peasants were allowed to move. There was no freedom of trade because of the guild system, which regulated the number of craftsmen and merchants in a given district.

New ideas in a world with little integration 1750-1815

In principle the movement of capital was free, but in practice capital movements were hindered by the defective monetary system and the limited means for conveying money from one place to another.

The *physiocrats* in France were in favour of agricultural reforms. However, their ideas did not have an important impact on European agriculture. In the second half of the eighteenth century, significant agricultural reforms were only undertaken in Britain and Denmark. Agricultural development in Britain was in accordance with the philosophy of the physiocrats. There is some debate about how much influence the physiocrats had in Britain, because the agricultural transformation had already started. In Denmark, agriculture developed differently than in Britain, and was more influenced by German than by French ideas.

Much more important was the book, *The Wealth of Nations*, by Adam Smith, published in 1776. It was Smith who launched the idea of the importance of markets and specialisation. In time, this idea gained many supporters because it fitted so well with the industrial revolution which was under way. Adam Smith argued that all market barriers, internal as well as external, should be removed. Specialisation was an important element in raising the living standard, and larger markets were needed if specialisation was to be successful.

Even in the short run, the idea of liberalising international trade had some impact. In 1786, France and Britain signed a trade treaty by which Britain admitted French wines and spirits to Britain at much lower tariff rates, in return for lower French tariffs on British cottons, pottery and iron. The French Revolution and the Napoleonic Wars prevented the treaty from having any practical impact. During the period 1789-1815, trade was regarded as a weapon to be used by each side against the other. In 1806, Napoleon launched the Continental System, which aimed at prohibiting British cargoes from entering harbours on the continent controlled by Napoleon and his allies, and similarly prohibiting the sale of goods to Britain.

The French Revolution was also important from an economic point of view. A series of measures was taken in France to integrate the local and regional economies into a national economy. All internal tolls and rules impeding the free traffic of goods were removed. A uniform system of weights and measures was adopted to facilitate internal trade. Customs duties were shifted to the external frontiers and a system of external tariffs and quotas was introduced to protect domestic production. The construction of new and better roads was important. The legal rights of the landlords vis-à-vis the peasants were abolished and the peasants were given their personal freedom. The privileges of companies and guilds were abolished.

The idea was to create an internal market with free movement of goods, labour and capital. Internal liberalisation was combined with external protection. This philosophy was adopted by Napoleon and extended to the European countries conquered by France during the Napoleonic Wars. The Continental System was intended to make the continent independent of Britain.

2.2 The increase in international trade 1815-2000

The increase in GDP from 1815 to 2000 was associated with an even greater increase in international trade. Table 2.1 shows the increase in the volume of world exports and the exports of Western Europe and the USA as a share of GDP in fixed prices. From 1820 to 1913, there was an annual increase in the world exports of around 4 per cent. In the following period 1913-1950, there was a sharp decline in the growth rate.

Table 2.1: *Increase in export volume and exports as a share of GDP 1820-1992.*

	Increase in export volume[1]	Exports as a share of GDP in percentage[2]		
	World	World	Western Europe	USA
1820	4.2	1.0	n.a.	2.0
1870	3.4	5.0	10.0	2.5
1913	1.3	8.7	16.3	3.6
1950	7.0	7.0	9.4	3.0
1973	3.7	11.2	20.9	5.0
1992		13.5	29.7	8.2

[1] Annual average compound growth in export volume
[2] Exports and GDP in 1990 prices
Source: Maddison (1995)

In the golden period of economic growth, 1950-1973, international trade increased 7 per cent per year, and in the subsequent period, the growth rate declined to 3.7 per cent. The level of trade in 1820 was low. It has been estimated that only 1 per cent of the world GDP was internationally traded. In the period 1820-1913, the increase in trade was much greater than the increase in GDP so that international trade increased its share of global GDP to 5 per cent in 1870 and 8.7 in 1913. The increase in the export-GDP ratio was much greater for Western Europe and less for the USA, compared to the world average. In the period 1913-1950, trade increased less than GDP, and the export-GDP ratio fell, especially in Western Europe, but also in the USA. In the period 1950-1973, there was a significant decline in the level of protection for industrial products, due to the GATT co-operation and the establishment of the EC. The export-GDP ratio more than doubled in Western Europe, and it increased by two thirds in the USA. Between 1973 and 1992, international trade continued to expand at a higher rate than the growth of GDP. In Western Europe the export-GDP ratio increased 8.8 percentage points, and in the USA 3.2 percentage points.

The conclusion is clear. Between 1820 and 1913 there was a marked trend towards increased international economic integration, which was manifested by the significant increase in trade. In addition, international integration was strengthened through international capital movements and labour migration, especially to North America, but also to South America and Australia. It was especially in the period 1870-1913 that international factor movements increased. The period 1913-1950 was one of international disintegration. The increase in protectionism in the 1930s caused a decline in international trade. In the period 1870-1913, international capital movements were dominated by British savings being invested abroad, but from the time of the First World War, capital flows changed direction as Britain repatriated a substantial part of its foreign assets. In particular, the USA became the new international creditor nation. A new era of strong international integration developed from 1950 to the present. International trade, especially between the industrialised countries, increased strongly, and since the beginning of the 1970s, international capital movements have gradually been liberalised. The international movement of labour has been modest, compared with the period 1870-1913, though there has been an increase in the movement of labour over the last 20 years.

2.3 Increasing integration and liberalisation 1815-1875

When considering trade policy in Europe during the period 1815-1875, it is reasonable to speak about three stages. In the first stage 1815-1846, Britain gradually took steps to liberalise its imports, while the rest of Europe maintained or even increased its protection levels. In the second stage 1846-1860, free trade ideas did gain ground in several continental European countries. During the third stage 1860-1875, trade liberalisation had taken place in most European countries, and tariff protection levels reached their lowest point in most European countries.

Trade policy 1815-1846

After the Napoleonic Wars there were large adjustment problems. Severe inflationary problems, high customs duties and excise taxes had distorted national economies. Now the economies had to adjust to more normal conditions, without war demand. The war itself had constituted a protection measure, and production patterns had been adjusted to the needs of self-sufficiency. Many of these productions had difficulty in competing when trade was opened up again. There was a great demand for protection, in order to facilitate the adjustment process. In agriculture, prices were falling, and to maintain farm prices, Britain passed a Corn Law in 1815, which banned imports of wheat if the domestic prices of grain fell below a certain level. In 1828 the Corn Law was changed. The import ban was removed and replaced by a sliding scale mechanism with a variable import levy, equal to the difference between a fixed domestic price and the world market price. In other European countries there were even stricter protectionist moves. In France, the tariffs on textiles and other industrial products were raised on several occasions, and there were similar trends in Prussia, Austria and Russia. Also in the United States, industries established under the shelter of the war were protected by higher customs duties.

When economic conditions improved in around 1830, discussions began on the reduction of the levels of protection, first in Britain, and later in other European countries. British manufacturers in particular argued for free imports of agricultural products, especially cereals, to keep down food prices. Lower food prices meant lower wages, which would increase the competitiveness of British industries. Landowners were against this, and they prophesied the ruin of British agriculture if the Corn Laws were repealed. However, landowners were losing political power as agriculture was less important than before, and in 1846 the Corn Laws were repealed. Grain could be imported freely, apart form a very small duty which was later removed. Bad harvests in England in the preceding years and the potato blight in Ireland contributed to the decision which was made following much debate. In fact, there was no negative impact on British agriculture, because the grain market was booming with prices increasing until 1875 when the British market was flooded with US grain.

The repeal of the Corn Laws in 1846 can be considered the ultimate victory for the free trade ideology in Britain. The free traders got intellectual support, not only from the work of Adam Smith but also the work of David Ricardo. His theory of comparative advantage showed that two trading nations would both gain from free trade between them. Ricardo also predicted that the real prices of agricultural products would rise. To avoid price rises on food products, free imports of cereals were considered appropriate. Another important event was the repeal of the Navigation Act of 1691. According to the Act, all imports from Continental Europe had to be transported either in British ships or ships belonging to the exporting country. Imports from other continents could only be carried in British ships. These requirements were first relaxed and then finally abandoned in 1849.

There had also been barriers to factor movements, such as labour migration and exports of capital goods. In 1825, Britain abolished all legal barriers to the emigration of skilled workers, and in 1842, the export ban on capital goods was removed.

Following the Napoleonic wars, the German area consisted of more than 38 states, of which Prussia was the largest. Prussia passed a protective tariff law after the wars. Gradually other German states agreed to enter into a customs union with Prussia, so that internal trade could take place freely and the Prussian tariff rates became those of the outer tariff wall. In 1834, seventeen states agreed to form a *Zollverein* (customs union), which played an important role in forming the unified German state. Internal German trade was liberalised, but this did not apply to external trade before 1850, when the outer tariff level was gradually reduced.

Trade policy 1846-1875

The period 1815-1846, especially up to 1830, was a less prosperous period. It was a period in which economic difficulties led to demands for strong tariff protection. The following period, 1846-1875, was a prosperous one with high growth rates, and it was from 1850 that trade liberalisation gained momentum. Figure 2.1 shows the level of trade protection for Great Britain, France and Germany from 1850 to 1938. After the repeal of the Corn Laws in 1846, there was a significant reduction in the level of protection in Great Britain. The same was true for France where Napoleon III was in favour of trade liberalisation. The signing of the Cobden Treaty between Britain and France in 1860 was a significant event. Under this treaty, France removed its bans and reduced its tariff rates on British imports, and similarly Britain gave access to its markets for French products, especially wine and silk. It was also important, as each country promised the other most-favoured-nation treatment. If France subsequently signed tariff treaties with other countries giving them lower rates, these should also be enjoyed by Britain. So, French or British tariff reductions for other countries would also apply in their mutual trade.

As already mentioned, the German *Zollverein* reduced its common tariff protection from 1850. There was a similar pattern nearly everywhere, in the Netherlands, Belgium, the Scandinavian countries, Russia, as well as in Italy, where numerous formerly independent states were united, as in the case of Germany.

Figure 2.1: The average tariff rates for protection in the United Kingdom, France and Germany 1850-1938

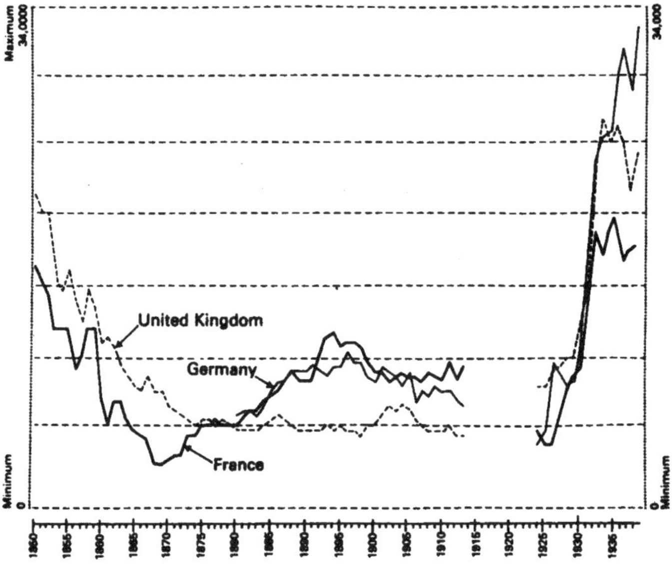

Source: Messerlin and Becuwe (1986)

Technology and integration

Industrialisation, founded on technological innovation, stimulated economic integration in Europe. Industrialisation was associated with increased internal and external trade, mostly of an intersectoral kind. The most industrialised country, Britain, exported industrial goods and imported raw materials and agricultural products. Different industrialised countries specialised in different industrial goods belonging to different industrial sectors. Britain, for example, had a highly developed textile sector, while Germany soon acquired a comparative advantage in the chemical sector. Industrialisation also led to the geographical concentration and specialisation of production. As a result, it was necessary to have a larger geographical market for the sale of products.

Technological development and industrialisation in general contributed to economic integration. Technological innovations and investments in the transport and communication sectors were especially significant. The period 1850-1914 witnessed a tremendous accumulation of capital in the construction of railways. The European railway system expanded from 24,000 km in 1850 to 351,000 km in 1910 (Bairoch, 1976).

Technological innovations gave rise to better infrastructure and industrialisation which in turn led to further economic integration. Better economic integration gave rise to expanded markets and increased capital accumulation, and this in its turn had a positive impact on industrialisation and technological innovation.

At the end of the period, around 1875, international trade, migration and capital movements were practically free all over Europe. This situation had been achieved through negotiations, leading to bilateral agreements. Bilateral agreements, such as the Cobden Treaty 1860 including the most-favoured-nation clause, triggered considerable Europe-wide tariff reduction.

Bilateral agreements were reached through the usual diplomatic channels. There were no international organisations at the time, apart from two dealing with postal services and telegraphs. The International Telegraph Union was founded in 1865, and the Universal Postal Union in 1874. Their objectives were to harmonise all national regulations with respect to international rates, procedures, cables, etc.

2.4   *Increasing integration and tariff protection 1875-1914*

During the period 1875-1895, Britain continued its free trade policy, but in other European countries, such as Germany, France, Italy, Austria-Hungary, Russia, and Spain, the liberalisation of trade was reversed, and protection was increased. In the following years, 1895-1914, there was a revival of calls for protection in Britain, which now felt the competition from Germany and the USA. Nevertheless, Britain continued its free trade policy, but there were discussions about whether the free trade policy towards other countries should be conditional on some level of reciprocity. Protectionism was maintained in most other European countries.

Trade policy 1875-1895

The less prosperous period of 1875-1895 started with the collapse of an almost world-wide boom in 1873 and was followed by a sharp increase in American and Russian grain exports. In most countries, there were widespread demands, both in agriculture and in industry, for higher tariff protection to relieve the crisis. Figure 2.1 shows that in France and Germany the protection level was raised, whereas it was unchanged in Great Britain. Both industrial and agricultural protection increased in France and Germany. In Germany the land-owning class (*junkers*) of Prussia, growing cereals, had great political power and they formed a coalition with the industrialists to increase overall protection. In France, too, domestic cereal production was protected. Both in Germany and in France, agricultural protection was raised more and more as market prices fell. Tariff schedules were frequently changed as tariffs became a bargaining weapon. In Germany and France there were two schedules of tariff rates, a set of maximum rates and a set of minimum rates. The maximum rates were the normal rates, but if a trading partner gave concessions on German or French products, the two countries would only charge the minimum rate on imports from such country. In Austria, Russia and Italy there were similar increases in protection levels, as in Germany and France.

As shown in Figure 2.1, the level of protection was unchanged in Great Britain where the free trade idea was not abandoned, even in agriculture which was suffering from the decline in cereal prices. A couple of a smaller countries, Denmark and the Netherlands, shifted towards animal production, benefiting from the low cereal prices which reduced the fodder costs, and from the smaller decline in prices of animal products compared to arable products.

In the United States, the high protection level dated from the Civil War. After the Napoleonic wars, the US tariff protection was increased, but the level was not exorbitant, and from the mid 1830s to the Civil War in 1861, tariff protection declined. The American economy was prosperous when a new protective Tariff Act was passed for political reasons in 1861, just before the outbreak of the war.

The North, which was industrialised, was interested in protection, whereas the South, having substantial exports especially of cotton, was interested in free trade. The passing of more protectionist laws contributed to the outbreak of the Civil War. To finance the Civil War, internal excise duties were levied, and to compensate manufacturers, added protection from foreign goods was granted. The USA came out of the Civil War with extortionately high protection levels and an average duty of not much less than 50 per cent (Scheiber et al., 1976). From the end of the Civil War in 1865 until 1890, there were several tariff laws which slightly lowered the tariff rates. The McKinley Bill in 1890 restored the average tariff level at 50 per cent. The finer grades of industrial products were charged especially high customs duties and tariffs were imposed on agricultural products. In 1897, the adoption of a new tariff raised the average tariff level to a new high, 57 per cent.

Did the increase in protection raise the trade barriers?

It is evident that, all things being equal, tariff increases raise barriers to trade. But in the period 1875-1895 there was a significant fall in transport costs.

Table 2.2 shows that the cost of transport for wheat from Chicago to Liverpool fell from 179 pence per quarter in 1870-1874 to 70 pence per quarter in 1895-1899. This meant that the transport costs at the end of the nineteenth century were only 40 per cent of what they had been twenty-five years before. The table also shows that the price of US wheat in Britain fell by more than the reduction in freight rates. However, 40 per cent of the price fall for US wheat in Britain can be explained by reduced transport costs. Before 1875, high transport costs were a natural barrier to

Table 2.2: Transport costs and the price of wheat

	1870-74	1875-79	1880-84	1885-89	1889-94	1895-99
	pence per quarter					
Freight Chicago-New York by rail	113	72	63	61	53	47
Freight New York - Liverpool by steamer	66	60	35	25	20	23
Price of US wheat, c.i.f. Liverpool	625	568	531	402	379	356

Source: Tracy (1982)

Integration and trade

international trade. This barrier was removed over the next 20-25 years. In response, many countries raised their tariffs, but if the tariffs were not raised more than the reduction of transport costs, it can be argued that the increased tariffs did not cause a higher protection level, taking into account both natural and political barriers.

The tariff increases were typically less than the reduction of the transport costs, so there was effectively trade liberalisation, which can also be demonstrated by the increase in wheat exports by the USA, Russia and other countries, see Table 2.3.

Table 2.3: Exports of wheat from main suppliers, 1850 – 1900

	USA	Canada	Russia	India	Australia
			million bushels[1]		
1851-60	5	-	41	-	-
1861-70	22	-	75	-	-
1870-74	59	1	55	1	-
1875-79	107	3	71	6	-
1880-84	136	4	65	29	-
1885-89	110	3	95	36	-
1890-94	170	9	104	30	8
895-99	184	16	107	15	3

[1] Three bushels equals approximately 100 kg
Source: Tracy (1982)

The period 1875-1895 was thus one of trade liberalisation despite the raising of customs duties. Raising tariff barriers could be considered as reflecting a desire to moderate the free trade which followed from declining transport costs.

Trade policy 1895-1914

In around 1895, there was a reversal of the long-term economic trend. The period 1895-1914 was characterised by a high average growth rate. Tariff protection declined somewhat in Germany and in France, as illustrated in Figure 2.1. In Germany the alliance between manufacturers and farmers broke down. Higher protection of agricultural products meant higher living costs for industrial wage-earners, so manufacturers asked for lower protection of farm products. The farmers responded by attacking the protection of manufactured products.

In Britain, the tariff protection level was more or less constant. At the end of the century, British industry was expanding more slowly than previously, and it felt the stronger competition from Germany and the USA. This new situation caused a change in British attitude towards tariffs. Previously, British industry had been in favour of unconditional free trade, but now the concepts of 'fair' trade and trade retaliation made their appearance. It was now argued that Britain should only lower its tariff rates if its trading partners did the same. As a result, in 1903 the Conservatives started a campaign for tariff reform involving more protection against countries with low paid workers, combined with a system of imperial preferences. Against this it was argued that, as a net exporter of industrial products and a net importer of food products, Britain would not gain from such a policy. Both the Liberal Party and the Labour Party were opposed, so the tariff policy remained unchanged.

In the USA, the highly protectionist Tariff Act of 1897 remained in force in spite of the prosperity sweeping the country. Some people attributed the prosperity to the protection level, but others were dissatisfied with the increased cost of living, and there was also a revival of antitrust sentiment. During the period 1895-1914, agricultural prices rose more than general price levels. In 1913 there was a revision of the tariff level. Certain agricultural products were put on the free list, but industrial protection remained high. Imports of steel, iron, and raw wool became free of duty, and although the tariffs on manufactured cotton and woollen goods were reduced, their effective protection was still high, and the rates on chemicals and other products were in fact increased.

Increasing economic integration

1875-1914 was the period of the second industrial revolution. New technology was quickly put to use due to a high investment ratio. There were important institutional changes. Research and development were supported by governments, and education and training took place at all levels so the dissemination of know-how was much easier than previously. New employment possibilities arose and resistance to new technologies was weakened.

International economic integration within Europe and between Europe and some overseas countries, such as the USA, increased significantly. Large free trade areas without internal trade barriers had existed since Germany and Italy had been unified and Austria-Hungary and Russia already formed large areas with free internal trade.

Economically, there was healthy competition between European countries even though there was also some unhealthy political competition. There was no co-operation to restrain protectionism, or to restrain colonialism or the arms race between the larger countries of Europe.

In 1914, Europe was part of a global economy, but more importantly, Europe was to a large extent economically integrated. In 1913 the share of exports of total GNP was 16 per cent. This share had increased from 1870, when it was 10 per cent, despite the increased tariff protection.

1875-1914 was also a period in which emigration from Europe, especially to the USA, increased significantly, and when international capital movements became an important element of the world economy.

Labour emigrated from Europe especially to the USA. The population of the USA increased from 5.3 million in 1800 to 31.4 million in 1860, and to 105.7 million in 1920 (Scheiber et al., 1976). From 1860 to 1920, around 30 million people, corresponding to the population of the USA in 1860, emigrated to the USA. Europeans also emigrated to Canada, South America and Australia, but in much smaller numbers, even though the economic impact of this immigration was significant.

International migration within Europe was less important and mainly related to seasonal workers. Several thousands of Italians were employed in France, Germany and Austria. Some hundreds of thousands of Poles went to Germany, as did a large number of other East Europeans (Heaton, 1968). The immigrants worked mainly in manufacturing, mining, construction and agriculture. In agriculture they filled the jobs left open by rural people moving to urban areas.

International capital movements were practically free. Europe became the banker to the world. Its total stock of foreign capital rose significantly and by 1913 it exceeded GDP. The annual flows amounted to 4-5 per cent of GDP. One quarter of the outgoing capital went to other European countries, another quarter went to the USA, and half to the rest of the world (Molle, 1990). Integration was stimulated by the monetary system of the period. Most European countries and the USA were on the gold standard, and accordingly an integrated monetary system was established. The automatic rules of the gold standard meant that exchange rates were fixed, and each country had to abstain from conducting an independent monetary policy.

Economic integration in 1875-1914 was very much based on the rules of the free market. There was a feeling of confidence; people could travel without passports until 1914. There was also a feeling of general trust, because of the general rules on law enforcement in different countries.

Only in a few areas was the need felt for international organisation and international policy co-ordination. In the case of telegraphs and postal services, international organisations to harmonise regulations were set up in 1865 and 1874 respectively. International committees were also established in the transport sector, with the aim of agreeing common technical standards for railway equipment and the co-ordination of other elements, such as the exchange of rolling stock, the treatment of goods, scheduling, etc.

In other areas, even where there was not a need for technical co-operation, there were some attempts of co-ordination. Agriculture was a sector which had economic difficulties in the period 1875-1895. There were some attempts to establish a European tariff for foodstuffs to counter competition on the European markets. These general attempts failed, but there was some success in co-ordinating sugar policy in Europe. Sugar-beet production had been stimulated by export subsidies. In 1902, a sugar agreement was reached between European countries according to which these countries agreed to refrain from subsidising sugar beet.

There was also some concern about differences in social policies. There was a fear that the improvement of social security and work conditions in one country would put that country at a competitive disadvantage. However, it was only after the First World War that the problem was discussed at various conferences, and this led to the creation of the International Labour Organization (ILO).

At that time, countries did not implement macroeconomic policies. Foreign exchange rates were fixed, so a country could not have an independent monetary policy. Active fiscal policy, for the purpose of regulating purchasing power and economic activity, did not exist. It was only during the Great Depression in the 1930s this kind of policy was introduced.

2.5 *A turbulent period of disintegration 1914-1945*

1815-1914 was a period of calm and stability, without major wars. Such wars as there were, were either short or local. The following period was both politically and economically turbulent, with the greatest depression ever experienced sandwiched between two world wars. The two wars lasted for several years and involved more countries than ever before.

The period 1914-1945 was one of disintegration, lack of co-operation and macroeconomic problems.

The result of the First World War and the peace treaties

Firstly, material war damage was relatively limited geographically to Northern France, East Prussia and some Russian areas. In France, the physical war damage was quite quickly repaired. In Russia, the damage of war was followed by the turmoil of the Bolshevik revolution in 1917, and the civil war with foreign intervention in 1917-1920.

Secondly, the allies, France, Britain and the USA, agreed that Germany should pay war reparations, which caused problems for the German economy. Inflation in Germany in the years 1918-1920 took off into a hyper-inflation in the years 1921-1923. This was the worst inflation ever experienced and the German monetary system collapsed in 1923.

Germany tried to meet its war debt obligations by taking foreign loans. Other countries like France also borrowed internationally to overcome the adjustment problems which showed up as balance of payments problems. France and other European countries borrowed in Britain which, in turn, borrowed in the USA, because Britain also had balance of payments problems. Britain, which had previously been a net creditor nation, became a country with foreign debt. The USA which had been a debtor nation before the war now became a creditor nation. Many of the international loans were short-term loans, and this caused major problems when trust in international capital markets evaporated with the Great Depression.

Thirdly, as a result of the peace treaties, new international boundaries were drawn and new countries appeared such as Finland and the Baltic countries, which were formerly parts of Russia. The Austrian-Hungarian Empire was split up into a series of smaller nations such as Austria, Hungary, Czechoslovakia, Romania and Yugoslavia. Poland also became independent getting most of its territory from Russia. This dislocation created major economic problems, which can easily be illustrated by the case of Austria-Hungary. Before the war it was a large free trade area with a high degree of specialisation and internal trade between its different parts. After the war, each state had to establish its own institutions and its own government with their own centres, replacing Vienna in particular, but also Budapest, which had previously been the centres. There was widespread distrust between the nations, hampering co-operation as they tried to solve their post-war difficulties with high tariff protection.

A turbulent period of disintegration 1914-1945

Lack of trust and lack of co-operation

Firstly, general distrust between countries was a main cause of lack of co-operation up to 1925, when the international climate improved, and there were also some efforts of co-operation between France and Germany. When the economic crisis started in 1929, these fragile efforts were replaced by unilateralism, where each country strived to protect itself. This lack of co-operation was especially prominent in the area of foreign exchange. Britain returned to the gold standard in 1925 at pre-war parity, which caused sterling to be greatly overvalued. Germany returned to the gold standard in 1924 after a new currency was introduced. France returned to the gold standard in 1928 at a value less than a quarter of the pre-war parity, which meant the franc was undervalued. The result was the misalignment of the different currencies.

This economic disequilibrium between countries caused by the currency misalignment was reinforced by the fact that the pre-war rules of the gold standard no longer applied. Countries with balance of payments surpluses, such as France and the USA, were supposed to expand their credit in order to facilitate the adjustment of the balance of payments disequilibrium. But the surplus countries did not expand their credits, which made the problems of the deficit countries even worse.

Secondly, pre-war international economic co-operation had been concentrated around Britain, as the leading industrial and commercial economy with London as its financial centre. This status was lost after the war, when Britain had its own economic problems. There was chronic unemployment during the 1920s and 1930s. The British economy was to a large extent based on the coal, iron, textile and shipbuilding industries, which were all stagnating. The over-valuation of the pound made it difficult for Britain to compete in the new expanding industries, and Britain had balance of payments problems.

The USA became the new strong industrial power with a booming economy based on innovations. There were new products to be produced. The motor car industry gave a lead to many auxiliary industries, such as the petrol, rubber, steel and tin industries, as well as the road construction and road-transport industries. The use of electricity became common and gave rise to a whole range of new industrial and domestic electrical appliances. Apart from new products, there were also innovations applied to old products, which led to a considerable increase in the use of capital and electricity. In manufacturing, labour productivity increased by around one third during the 1920s. In spite of its economic leadership, the USA followed a policy of political isolation and was not willing to take on any international responsibilities.

Thirdly, there was a rise of totalitarianism. Totalitarian regimes were established in Russia, Italy, Germany and Spain. The socialist regime in the USSR was based on a planned economy, and the fascist regimes were based on corporatist ideas and strong state intervention. Economically, they were very much inward-looking and they contributed to the general distrust and lack of international co-operation. In addition, in Central and Eastern Europe there was a series of smaller states, which had recently become independent; these had to build up their own institutions, and wanted to protect their own fragile economies.

Adjustment problems 1918-1929 and the Great Depression

During the First World War prices soared, as they always do in wartime. Overseas exports to Europe, especially of agricultural products, increased. After the war there were adjustment problems. Production had to be adjusted from a war economy to peace time economy. The devastation in the war zones had to be repaired, and production capacity which had not been maintained had to be restored.

1918-1925 can be considered as the recovery period after the war. However, Britain had longer-term problems, mostly of structural nature. Since 1875, the growth rate in Britain had declined compared to the period 1815-1875 when Britain was the dominant industrial country. From 1875, Britain lost market share as Germany and the United States forged ahead. In addition to this structural problem, Britain was conducting an inadequate economic policy, especially its foreign exchange policy. British price levels fell significantly from 1920 to 1925 when Britain returned to the gold standard. In spite of the fall in prices, the pound was overvalued and this hampered British competitiveness.

Germany had huge adjustment problems because a severe inflation in 1918-1920 and hyperinflation in 1921-1923. However, its recovery from the effects of the war was rapid. The manufacturing sector expanded quickly, and production volume in 1929 was more than double of the 1921 level. Agriculture did not adjust so easily. By 1929 agricultural production was still below its pre-war level.

The worst economic crisis ever, the Great Depression, started in 1929. There was a dramatic fall in industrial production between 1929 and 1932. The USA and Germany were the two countries that experienced the sharpest decline in industrial production. There was mass unemployment and deflation. The depression spread because of lack of international co-operation.

A turbulent period of disintegration 1914-1945

Table 2.4: *Industrial production index in 1932. 1929 = 100*

USSR	183	Belgium	69
Japan	98	Italy	67
UK	84	Poland	63
Romania	82	Canada	58
Hungary	82	Germany	53
France	72	USA	53

Source: Lewis (1953)

The USA was not hit by the war like the countries in Europe. Its manufacturing sector continued to expand during the 1920s. However, the agricultural sector was influenced both by the war and its aftermath. During the war, farmers in both European and overseas countries benefited from high prices which persisted for a time after the war because of food shortages. The reduction of soil fertility and loss of livestock and of capital in the countries where there had been war damage were gradually made good. Overseas production had expanded greatly during the war and continued to rise afterwards. In 1921, there was a sharp fall in food prices. In the following years, prices remained low and farmers found themselves in difficulties. Although there was a revival in prices in 1924, they fell again in 1926, and the low price levels continued until 1929 when the Great Depression hit.

Tariff policy and the decline of international trade 1914 - 1945

As illustrated in Figure 2.1, the pre-war tariff levels were restored during the 1920s in France and Germany. In Britain the protection levels were higher than before the war. In the USA the tariff levels during the 1920s were similar to those before the war. Also, during the 1920s, agricultural products in the USA were protected to a high degree, although this protection was hardly needed and did not perceptibly affect the decline in prices. When the Great Depression developed from 1929, protection levels increased dramatically, first in the USA with the passing of the Smoot-Hawley Act in 1930.

As also illustrated in Figure 2.1, there was a dramatic increase in tariffs in the UK, Germany and France after 1930. Similar tariff increases took place in other European countries. Tariff increases were supplemented by the use on non-tariff measures such as restrictions and subsidies.

There were also devaluations of the main currencies. The gold standard was abandoned, and each country devalued to increase competitiveness against foreign suppliers. This ended with a currency agreement in 1936 by which approximately the same exchange rates were established between the main currencies as had existed before 1931 when the competitive devaluations had started.

The rise of protectionism started with the Smoot-Hawley Act. Other countries retaliated by increasing their tariff protection, so there was a fall in international trade. Exports, as a share of GNP, were 16 per cent in Europe in 1913, 9 per cent in 1920, 9 per cent in 1930, and 6 per cent in 1938 (Molle, 1990). These figures illustrate that, between the two world wars, international trade in Europe was never restored to the pre-war level.

The decline in international trade was not only due to protectionist trade policies, but also to the new totalitarian regimes. The USSR withdrew from international trade because it chose a self-sufficiency development strategy. A similar strategy was followed by the various fascist governments which came to power in Europe. The autarky philosophy in Germany after 1933 was part of the national socialist preparations for war. The autarky philosophy of the dictatorships together with the beggar-my-neighbour policies of the democracies were the background to the decline in European trade in the 1930s.

2.6 *The revival of integration 1945-2000*

After the Second World War, one of the main objectives was to establish international co-operation, which had failed so badly especially during the 1930s.

The General Agreement on Tariffs and Trade (GATT) was signed in 1947, and under the auspices of the GATT there was a significant decrease in the tariff protection levels of the industrialised countries in the years 1947-1973. During 1973-1995, there was a trend towards an increased use of protective measures, such as voluntary export agreements, voluntary import increase agreements, subsidies, anti-dumping measures, and countervailing duties. More discipline was introduced in international trade matters by the conclusion of the Uruguay Round of GATT in 1993, which established the World Trade Organization (WTO). The establishment of the WTO was also a significant event in the sense that developing countries were integrated in the international trade system to a much greater extent.

In addition, exchange rate stability was introduced by the establishment of the IMF at the Bretton Woods conference in 1944. This system broke down in 1973, when a floating exchange rate system was introduced between the main currencies, such as the dollar, yen, sterling and D-mark.

ized and this
later developed into the European Monetary Union.

2.7 Summary

The story of the economic development of Western Europe and the USA is the story of the gradual increase in economic integration, internally between the different regions of each country, and internationally between different countries.

In the countries of Western Europe, markets did not play an important role before these developments started in around 1750. Each country consisted of a series of smaller regions, each with a town and its surrounding area, each being largely self-sufficient. The rural sector was characterised by the feudal system, while in the urban sector, mercantilist ideas prevailed.

There was a change of ideology during the second half of the eighteenth century. The Age of Enlightenment focused on rationality and there was an interest in improving living standards through improved production methods. Adam Smith, who published *The Wealth of Nations* in 1776, became the most influential economist and he stressed the importance of the market.

There cannot be economic development without economic integration, and economic integration requires the establishment of markets. The improved transport systems and the institutional changes, which will be discussed in Chapter 4, were crucial for the development of markets and the removal of trade barriers. Together with internal integration, there was also international integration between countries. This can be illustrated by the sharp increase in the ratio between exports and the gross domestic product.

The trend towards economic integration due to technological improvements and institutional changes has been supported or slowed down in varying degrees by trade policies.

The period 1815-1845 was, generally speaking, one of lower economic growth and falling prices. Most countries reacted to these conditions by reintroducing protection after the Napoleonic wars, and by maintaining their protection levels despite the free trade policies pursued by Britain, including the repeal of the Corn Laws in 1846.

Economic trends were more positive in the period 1845-1875, when the economic growth rate was higher and the prices rose. After a period of adjustment in 1845-1860 when tariffs were lowered in the European countries, by 1860 a situation had been reached which can be characterised as being very close to free international trade in Europe. This situation lasted until 1875.

In the period 1875-1895, growth slowed and prices fell. Protection was reintroduced to some extent in many but not all European countries. In spite of the increased tariffs, trade barriers did not increase. Trade barriers consist not only of political barriers but also of natural barriers such as transport and communication costs. Due to railway construction and improved sea transport there was a sharp fall in transport costs, especially those that affected the European cereal markets by increased supply from overseas. The result was a further increase in the ratio between exports and gross domestic product. This ratio increased in Western Europe from 10 per cent in 1870, to 16.3 per cent in 1913.

The last decades before the First World War, 1895-1913, were a period of higher growth and rising prices. The tariff level which had been reached at the end of the previous period was maintained.

Altogether, the period 1815-1914 was one of ever-increasing economic integration. Even during 1875-1914, when protection increased in some European countries and in the USA, economic integration continued because the tariff increases were more than offset by the fall in transport costs.

During the second industrial revolution, 1875-1914, Europe became part of a global economy, but more importantly, Europe itself became largely an integrated economy. Large free trade areas without internal trade barriers existed after the unification of Germany and of Italy; Austria-Hungary and Russia already formed large areas with free internal trade. Besides the increased integration of markets for goods, there was also increased integration of factor markets. Capital markets were created and international capital movements in the form of portfolio investments became an important element in the world economy. Labour mobility increased, and 1875-1914 was a period of high emigration from Europe to overseas countries, especially the USA. This economic integration took place without the establishment of international institutions.

Altogether, the period 1914-2000 can be divided into the two sub-periods: 1914-1945 and 1945-2000. 1914-1945 was a turbulent period with economic disintegration due to two world wars and the deep economic crisis of the 1930s. There was distrust between nations, which made co-operation difficult, and there were no international institutions which could or should assist in creating a rule-based international economy. Some countries withdrew from the international economic scene for political reasons; others tried to solve their adjustment problems

Summary

by raising trade barriers. When the Great Depression started in 1929, there was no co-ordination between countries, and individual countries tried to solve their macroeconomic problems by introducing successively higher trade protection. The results were disastrous.

After the Second World War, the main goal was to create a system of international co-operation to avoid the economic and political disasters of 1914-1945. A set of international institutions was created under the auspices of United Nations. The objective was to agree upon a set of rules to be followed by the member countries, and to avoid unilateral policy initiatives which harmed other countries. The GATT was an agreement which contained a set of trade policy rules and which initiated a series of trade negotiations, called 'rounds', which removed trade barriers. The spectacular trade liberalisation of the period 1947-1973 promoted economic integration and an extraordinarily high rate of growth.

Growth slowed down in the period 1973-2000, but economic integration continued. Besides increases in trade, international capital markets were established, and it became easier for labour to move internationally. In addition to global co-operation, formal arrangements for regional co-operation, such as the EC/EU were also established.

II Agricultural development

3. Employment, productivity and prices in agriculture

Over the last two centuries there has been a dramatic shift in employment and productivity in agriculture in Europe and the USA. The amount of resources available in agriculture, together with productivity, determines the supply of agricultural produce. Supply and demand determine agricultural prices which fluctuate in the short term, but follow a more stable pattern in the long term. This chapter deals with the long-term trends in employment, productivity and prices in agriculture.

3.1 The relative decline of agriculture

Economic development in the industrialised countries is associated with the transformation of society. It is the history of how countries have been transformed from agricultural societies into industrial societies and from industrial societies into service societies.

Economic activity is traditionally grouped into three categories: the primary sector, which includes agriculture, forestry, fisheries, and mining; the secondary sector, which includes manufacturing, construction and public utilities; and the tertiary sector, which includes transport, trade, financial activities and services (Clark, 1940; Kuznets, 1966). Table 3.1 shows the importance of the primary, secondary, and tertiary sectors in Europe (excluding the UK and Russia) in the period 1800-1920. The UK is excluded because in the nineteenth century its primary sector share was already much lower than the average, and Russia is excluded because its primary sector share was higher than the average. In 1800, three-quarters of the labour force worked in the primary sector. This share was reduced by nearly 25 percentage points up to 1920, and the share of the employment in both the secondary and tertiary sectors doubled from 1800-1920. However, in 1920, more than half the labour force still worked in the primary sector.

In 2000 only 4.5 per cent of the labour force in the EU (15) worked in agriculture, forestry and fisheries. Around 30 per cent worked in the secondary sector, and the remaining two-thirds of the labour force worked in the tertiary sector.

Employment, productivity and prices in agriculture

Table 3.1: *Percentage of the labour force in different sectors in Europe, excluding the UK and Russia, 1800-1920*

	Primary sector	Secondary sector	Tertiary sector
1800	76.0	13.0	10.0
1880	60.4	23.1	16.6
1900	56.4	26.0	17.6
1920	52.5	26.0	21.5

Source: Bairoch (1976)

When Central and Eastern Europe are included, the picture changes somewhat, because agriculture is still relatively more important there. In 2000, there were 6.9 million annual working units (AWU) employed in agriculture in EU (15), whereas there were 9.7 million AWU working in the CEEC (10), which includes the 8 new member states from Central and Eastern Europe plus Romania and Bulgaria. An annual working unit is a full time equivalent worker for 1 year. In the EU (25) only 8.5 per cent of the labour force was working in agriculture in 2000.

In comparing the two periods 1800-1920 and 1920-2000 it can be concluded that the relative decline of agriculture was less in the first period, when the share of agriculture only declined by around 25 percentage points. In the second period, the decline was around 45 percentage points. A simple calculation shows that the number of people working in agriculture increased during the first period, 1800-1920, and fell dramatically during the second period, 1920-2000. In Europe (excluding the UK and Russia) there was a population of 160 million in 1820, 290 million in 1920 and 450 million in 2000. If it is assumed that the ratio of the labour force to the total population has been constant, at 1:2, the agricultural labour force can be estimated to have been approximately 60 million in 1820, 75 million in 1920 and 20 million in 2000.

Table 3.2 illustrates the employment patterns in the USA, France, Germany, the UK and Russia over the last two centuries. At the beginning of the nineteenth century, around 70 per cent of the labour force was employed in agriculture in the USA. Figures are not available for France or Germany, but it is reasonable to assume that a similar proportion was employed in agriculture in these countries, see Table 3.1. Agricultural employment in the UK was much lower, as the share of agriculture of the total labour force was only half that of the USA and Continental Europe. In the UK, both the manufacturing and the service sectors were relatively much larger than in the other countries.

The relative decline of agriculture

There was a gradual reduction of the agricultural sector in all countries, but the rate of reduction varied from country to country. In the period 1820-1870, there were similar declines in the USA and the three main Western European countries. From 1870 to 1913, the USA experienced the largest decrease of 23 percentage points, Germany 15 percentage points, the UK 11 percentage points, and France only 9 percentage points. In Russia, 70 per cent of the labour force was still employed in agriculture in 1913.

Table 3.2: The proportion of employment by major sectors, 1820-1992

	USA	France	Germany	UK	Russia
Agriculture, forestry and fisheries					
1820	70.0	n.a.	n.a.	37.6	n.a
1870	50.0	49.2	49.5	22.7	n.a
1913	27.5	41.5	34.6	11.7	70.0
1950	12.9	28.3	22.2	5.1	46.0
1992	2.8	5.2	3.1	2.2	17,0
Manufacturing, mining, construction and utilities					
1820	15.0	n.a	n.a	32.9	n.a
1870	24.4	27.8	28.7	42.3	n.a
1913	29.7	32.3	41.1	44.1	n.a
1950	33.6	34.9	43.0	44.9	29.0
1992	23.3	28.1	37.8	26.2	36.0
Services					
1820	15.0	n.a	n.a	29.5	n.a
1870	25.6	23.0	21.8	35.0	n.a
1913	42.8	22.6	24.3	44.2	n.a
1950	53.5	36.8	34.8	50.0	25.0
1992	74.0	66.8	59.1	71.6	47.0

n.a. = non available
Source: Maddison (1995)

At the time of the First World War, the agricultural sector in Europe was relatively much larger than in the USA. The share of agricultural employment was reduced by roughly the same number of percentage points in the USA, France and Germany from 1913 to 1950, so that by 1950 the relative importance of agriculture in employment in France and

Germany was around twice its importance in the USA. It can be concluded that by 1950, there had been greater agricultural adjustment in the USA than in France, Germany and the rest of Western Europe, apart from the UK. During the second part of the twentieth century, there was a significant adjustment in Western Europe. Today, the relative importance of agriculture in employment is at around the same level, namely 2 to 5 per cent of the labour force in the USA and in most Western European countries.

The relative decline of agriculture corresponds to an increase in employment in manufacturing and services. Table 3.2 shows that already in 1913, the service sector in the USA employed more people than manufacturing, etc. In 1913, the two sectors were of equal size in the UK.

The share of employment in manufacturing, etc. continued to increase in the USA and Western Europe until 1950, since when it has declined. From 1950 to 2000 there was a sharp decline in the share of agricultural employment and a more modest decline in the share of manufacturing employment, so it is not surprising that the share of service employment increased more than previously from 1950 up to 2000.

It is evident that the growth rate in a society is linked to structural change. When the value added per labour unit is higher in the industrial sector than in agriculture, a shift in the composition of the labour force will create more growth.

The high growth rate in the USA in the period 1870-1913 was linked to the large influx of labour and capital into the secondary sector. The lower growth rate in the UK may have been influenced by capital exports and by a lower supply of available labour for secondary industries. The agricultural sector was already relatively small, so it may have been more difficult to grow the industrial sector by drawing surplus labour from agriculture.

After the Second World War, economic growth was higher in Europe than in the USA. This was partly to do with war damage, which was relatively quickly repaired, stimulated by US support through the Marshall Plan. High growth in Western Europe was made possible by the existence of the relatively large agricultural sector at the beginning of the period. The agricultural sector contained a reservoir of labour from which expanding industries could draw additional workers.

3.2 *Production resources in agriculture*

The supply of agricultural products depends on the amount of resources used by agriculture. The primary production factors are land, labour and capital, and the variable production factors are fertilisers, feedstuffs, chemicals, etc.

When the agrarian reforms took place in Europe, there was an increase in the quantity of available arable land because more common land was put into production. Arable acreage increased in Europe during the nineteenth century, and there was a dramatic increase in arable acreage in the USA. From 1900 to the end of the Second World War, the amount of the arable land was either stagnant or slowly increasing. Since the Second World War there has been a slight decrease.

There also seems to be a clear pattern for the agricultural labour force. The agricultural labour force increased during the nineteenth century, although the increase was significantly lower than the increase of the total labour force.

The agricultural labour force in the USA increased during the nineteenth century, due to immigration and the expansion of the agricultural frontier. Table 3.3 shows that the number of male workers in agriculture reached its maximum around the First World War, since when there has been a decline.

In Western Europe, the picture differs according to the level of industrialisation. In the UK, the agricultural labour force declined from 1880 to 1920 by approximately 10 per cent. In France, the agricultural labour force was stagnant from 1880 to 1910, and then slightly declined during the First World War and the following decades. In less industrialised countries like Denmark, agricultural employment reached its maximum in the period 1920-1930. Other data seem to indicate that the less industrialised a country was, the later agricultural employment reached its maximum, and the smaller was the following decline in the agricultural labour force.

Table 3.3 and other statistics indicate that it is reasonable to divide the period 1820-2000 into three sub-periods, 1820-1914, 1914-1945 and 1945-2000. In the first period, 1820-1914, the agricultural labour force seemed to increase except in Britain, which was the first country to industrialise. At the end of the period, the agricultural labour force may have been stagnating in some countries like France, and there was a decrease in the UK. During the following period 1914-1945, there was a decline in the agricultural labour force, but this was modest compared to the sharp decline in the last period 1945-2000.

The reduction in the labour force in the period 1914-1945 was due to there being fewer agricultural labourers, whereas the number of farms and farmers was nearly constant. It was only after the Second World War that the number of farms and farmers was reduced. Typically, this was when old farmers retired and their farms were absorbed by other farmers.

Table 3.3: *The labour force in agriculture in different countries, 1880-1980. Index 1960=100*

	Number of male workers			
	USA	UK	France	Denmark
1880	200	151	193	107
1890	230	145	178	108
1900	248	139	195	103
1910	260	143	190	114
1920	256	135	176	130
1930	236	134	157	131
1940	214	126	150	129
1950	160	115	128	113
1960	100	100	100	100
1970	54	64	79	57
1980	45	57	51	40

Source: Hayami and Ruttan (1985)

Mechanisation started already in the nineteenth century, especially in the USA, but its development was slow compared to the twentieth century. In the USA, the rate of mechanisation increased in the period 1900-1930, especially during the 1920s when tractors were replacing horses. The use of tractors increased the productive land available, as land which had hitherto been used for fodder for horses could now be released for growing commercial crops. The sharpest increase in the rate of mechanisation in the USA took place during the period 1940-1960 (Gardner, 1992). The high degree of mechanisation is associated with the sharp decrease in the US agricultural labour force, especially from 1940 to 1960.

Mechanisation came later to Europe. It was after 1950 that mechanisation really took place in Western Europe. In Europe, too, mechanisation was associated with a sharp decrease in the agricultural labour force.

Up to around 1840, agriculture relied on its own resources. From then on, farmers started to buy fertilisers, first guano and later chemical fertilisers. They bought inputs for land improvement, such as marl for marling and tiles for drainage. In the last part of the nineteenth century,

Productivity in agriculture

when animal production increased, farmers also began to supplement their own feedstuff production with feedstuffs produced outside agriculture.

Buying inputs from outside was known during the nineteenth century, especially in the latter half, but it was only in the twentieth century, and especially after the Second World War, that agriculture in Western Europe became heavily dependent on non-agricultural inputs, such as fertilisers, feedstuffs and chemicals. In the USA the use of commercial fertilisers started early in the twentieth century and it especially increased after the Second World War. Today, the use per hectare of fertilisers in the USA is only half that of Western Europe.

3.3 Productivity in agriculture

Supply can also be increased by productivity increases, when a given amount of factor inputs delivers an increased production. It is problematic to calculate productivity for a whole sector such as agriculture. Agriculture produces different crops and different animal products. The total output has to be calculated as the weighted sum of the output of the different commodities. The volume of intermediate inputs such as seed, fertilisers, feedstuffs, etc. has to be deducted from the gross output to find the value added.

Total factor productivity is equal to the total value added, divided by the weighted sum of all the primary production factors, such as land, labour and capital. Rather than total factor productivity, it is easier to calculate partial productivities, such as labour productivity and land productivity.

Table 3.4 shows the historical evolution of wheat yields in Europe and North America from 1800. The wheat yield is not the same as land productivity. Land productivity is equal to the total value added in agriculture, divided by the amount of arable land. Land productivity depends on the yields of all the crops per year and depends on the animal production level.

In Europe, not including Russia, the wheat yield increased by 10 per cent from 1800 to 1850. The next 10 per cent increase in yield was accomplished over a shorter time, from 1850 to 1880. Over the next 30 years, from 1880 to 1910, the yield increase was 20 per cent. So there was a gradual increase in the wheat yield in Europe from 1800 to 1910. During the turbulent period 1914-1950, there was a decline in the rate of increase. In the post-war period from 1950 to 1990 there was a high

Employment, productivity and prices in agriculture

increase in the yield. By 1990 the wheat yield was more than three times the yield of 1950.

In North America the wheat yield shows a different pattern. In 1800 the yield in North America was higher than in Europe. From 1850-1870 there was a decline in yield, and in 1910 the yield was the same as in

Table 3.4 : Historical evolution of wheat yields (100 kg per hectare)

	Europe (less Russia)		North America	
	Yield[1]	Annual change (per cent)	Yield[1]	Annual change (per cent)
1800	8.6		9.6	
1850	9.4	0.18	9.6	0.00
1860	9.8	0.36	9.1	-0.52
1870	10.1	0.37	8.4	-0.82
1880	10.3	0.17	8.6	0.26
1890	10.9	0.53	8.7	0.12
1900	11.9	0.91	8.8	0.09
1910	12.6	0.58	9.6	0.93
1936	14.2	0.46	8.2	-0.60
1950	14.4	0.30	11.6	2.51
1960	18.1	2.01	15.2	2.74
1970	26.9	4.04	19.9	2.73
1980	37.1	3.27	21.7	0.86
1990	47.8	2.54	22.5	0.36
1994	47.1	-0.37	24.2	2.51

[1] Five-year annual averages around the given year
Source: Bairoch (1999)

1800. There was a significant increase in yield in North America during the period 1936-1960, and since then there has been only a relatively modest increase in yield. In Europe the yield increase came later, around 1960, but since then the increase has been much higher than in the USA. Today, the wheat yield in the USA is around half the yield in Europe.

Table 3.5 shows the evolution of labour productivity in the western developed countries and in all developed countries, which includes Eastern Europe and the former USSR. The rate of increase is higher than the rate of increase in the wheat yield.

Labour productivity in the western developed countries increased by 50 per cent during the first half of the nineteenth century, and it doubled

Productivity in agriculture

during the last half of the century. During the first half of the twentieth century labour productivity increased 80 per cent. It was during the last half of the twentieth century that the spectacular rise in labour productivity took place. Labour productivity level in 1995 was eight times the level of 1950. The labour productivity in Eastern Europe and the former USSR has always been lower than in the western countries.

Table 3.5: Historical evolution of labour productivity

	Western developed countries[1]		All developed countries[1]	
	Production per male worker[2]	Annual change (per cent)	Production per male worker[2]	Annual change (per cent)
1800	7.1		6.4	
1830	8.6	0.66	7.3	0.45
1840	9.6	1.19	8.0	0.90
1850	10.9	1.27	8.8	1.00
1860	12.5	1.35	9.7	0.99
1870	13.6	0.86	10.3	0.60
1880	16.2	1.79	11.8	1.38
1890	18.0	1.02	12.8	0.75
1900	20.2	1.16	14.2	1.05
1910	23.4	1.48	15.7	1.10
1930	29.2	1.23	18.8	1.01
1950	36.2	0.98	26.0	1.48
1960	61.0	5.36	43.0	5.16
1970	109.4	6.02	71.6	5.23
1980	175.9	4.85	97.8	3.17
1990	247.0	3.45	118.0	1.89
1995	290.0	3.27	122.3	0.73

[1] All developed countries' encompasses Europe, including the former USSR, USA, Canada and Australia. Western developed countries include all developed countries except Eastern Europe and the former USSR. The border prior to 1989 determines the division between Western and Eastern Europe.
[2] Production of million net direct calories per male worker. Calories in crop production plus animal calories recalculated to the crop calories needed to produce them. Five year annual averages around the given year.
Source: Bairoch (1999)

This can be seen from Table 3.5, where the average level for all developed countries is lower than the average level for the western countries. It is interesting to note that this discrepancy seems to have increased significantly. In 1800 labour productivity for all countries was

90 per cent of the western level, in 1900 it was only 70 per cent and in 1995 it was a little more than 40 per cent.

3.4 Productivity differs between countries

There is no doubt that the technological innovations and agrarian reforms of the eighteenth century did have important impacts on productivity. The productivity level was low, so that the relative productivity increase was important, even though the absolute productivity increase was modest compared with later gains. There were modest productivity gains during the nineteenth century, which varied from country to country.

Table 3.6 shows that in 1880, labour productivity in the UK was the highest in Europe. It was twice the productivity level of France and 50 per cent higher than the level in Denmark. From 1880 to 1920 productivity increases were modest, compared to the gains obtained later. The productivity increase was larger in Denmark than in France, and was lowest in the UK which had initially performed the best.

Table 3.6: Labour and land productivity in agriculture in different countries, 1880-1980[1]

	USA	UK	France	Denmark	USA	UK	France	Denmark
	Labour productivity				Land productivity			
1880	13.0	15.7	7.4	10.5	0.5	1.1	1.1	1.2
1920	18.3	18.3	10.2	16.1	0.5	1.1	1.1	2.0
1950	46.5	31.2	15.6	31.9	0.6	1.6	1.5	3.4
1960	88.8	44.0	33.2	47.4	0.8	1.9	2.5	4.6
1970	192.6	88.9	55.6	100.0	0.9	2.5	3.4	5.5
1980	287.8	116.6	108.5	151.4	1.2	3.0	4.5	6.4

[1] The total output is measured in wheat units. The outputs of the different commodities are weighted by the prices of the commodities. Labour productivity is equal to the production measured by wheat units divided by the labour force. Land productivity is the production divided by the number of hectares
Source: See Table 3.3

During the period 1920-1950, productivity increases accelerated, in spite of two world wars and the Great Depression. Productivity increases in Denmark were significantly higher than in France. In 1950, labour productivity in Denmark and the UK was twice the level of France. However, productivity increases were even higher in the USA which was now in the lead.

From 1920-1950 to 1950-1980, there was a dramatic acceleration in productivity increases. In the USA, the labour productivity level of 1980 was more than 5 times higher than in 1950, in Denmark 5 times higher, and in France 7 times higher. During this period, French agriculture was catching up with agriculture in other countries. In 1980, the productivity level in France was equal to the level in the UK.

The increase in land productivity was much less than the increase in labour productivity, although the land productivity increases were significant. In 1880-1920, there was no increase in land productivity in the USA and the UK, and the increase in France and in Denmark was modest. The productivity increase was higher in the period 1920-1950 and again much higher for the last period 1950-1980. The higher increase in labour productivity than land productivity, especially during the period 1950-1980, was due to the substitution of capital for labour.

Care is needed when comparing absolute productivity levels between countries. The absolute productivity level depends on the product composition. US agriculture is more based on arable production, while, relatively speaking, European agriculture focuses more on animal production. Most animal production is more labour intensive than most arable production, so that the labour productivity level will be expected to be lower in countries with a high proportion of animal production. The opposite is true for land productivity. Intensive animal production does not depend on land to the same degree as arable production; so again, land productivity in countries with a high proportion of animal production will be expected to be higher.

There is a clear connection between labour productivity and land productivity, which can be illustrated by looking at the equation:

$$\frac{X}{L} = \frac{X}{A} \cdot \frac{A}{L}$$

where X/L, X/A and A/L are value added per labour unit, value added per area unit and area per labour unit, respectively.

The equation shows that labour productivity and land productivity do not necessarily move in the same direction. An increase in land productivity can be combined with a decrease in labour productivity when the area per labour unit declines. This could occur if the land is split into more but smaller farms because all the sons of the farmer inherit part of the land. On the other hand, labour productivity could be increased without an increase in land productivity if there is a large migration of farmers, increasing the land area per labour unit.

3.5 Demand for agricultural products

The demand for agricultural products increases at different rates from time to time. The following equation illustrates the relationship between the increase in food demand ($\dot{D}/D$) and its determinants, namely the changes in population ($\dot{N}/N$), the change in GDP per capita ($\dot{Y}/Y$) and the change in relative prices for food products and other products ($\dot{P}/P$):

$$\frac{\dot{D}}{D} = e_N \frac{\dot{N}}{N} + e_Y \frac{\dot{Y}}{Y} + e_P \frac{\dot{P}}{P}$$

where e_N, e_Y and e_P are the population elasticity, the income elasticity and real price elasticity for food products.

When it is assumed that food demand expands at the same rate as the population then e_N is equal to one. If the real price of food products is constant, the above equation illustrates that changes in food demand at a given real price level depend on the population increase, the growth rate of GDP per capita, and the income elasticity e_Y.

Table 3.7 shows how the population and GDP per capita have increased at different rates at different times. From 1500 to 1700 there was a very modest population increase and a small increase in GDP per capita. During the next period, 1700-1820, the population and GDP per capita increased at a higher rate, and these growth rates were further increased through the 1800s.

There is no doubt that the higher population increase and higher growth rate of GDP per capita in the period 1700-1914 greatly stimulated the demand for food products. During that period, the income elasticity for food products was very high, although it declined for staple products, such as cereal, as society became richer.

However, it should not be forgotten that the income elasticity differs for different agricultural products. As income levels rise there is a shift in the demand for food items. The demand for cereal for food stagnates or only increases moderately, whereas there is a greater increase in the consumption of animal products such as meat and dairy products. There is a derived demand for cereals for animal feed when the holdings of livestock increase due to the increased demand for animal products. During the period 1870-1914 the income elasticities for meat products and dairy products were high.

Table 3.7: Population increase and GDP growth per capita in Western Europe and USA, 1500-2001. Annual compound growth rate in per cent.

	Population		GDP per capita	
	Western Europe[1]	USA	Western Europe[1]	USA
1500 - 1700	0.15	-0.35	0.10	0.10
1700 - 1820	0.41	2.00	0.20	0.70
1820 - 1870	0.69	2.83	0.98	1.34
1870 - 1913	0.77	2.08	1.33	1.82
1913 - 1950	0.42	1.21	0.76	1.61
1950 - 1973	0.70	1.45	4.05	2.45
1973 - 2001	0.32	1.06	1.88	1.86

[1] Western Europe corresponds to EU (15) plus Norway and Switzerland
Source: Based on Maddison (2003)

Compared with the period 1700-1914, the years 1914-2000 are characterised by a lower rate of increase in food demand. The rate of population growth was lower than in the previous century. The opposite was the case for the GDP per capita, which rose at a significantly higher rate in the last two quarters of the 1900s, compared to the 1800s. This significant increase in GDP per capita did not cause a high increase in food demand because the income elasticity at this stage was low.

3.6 Agricultural prices in the short term

Agricultural prices depend on supply and demand. It is natural to distinguish between supply, demand and price changes in the short term, medium term and long term, because these changes differ according to the chosen time horizon. There can always be a debate about how short the 'short term' is, and how long the 'medium term' is. Here, the time horizon for the short term is taken to be 0-2 years; the horizon for the medium term is 0-10 years; and the horizon for the long term is more than 10 years.

Especially in the short term, agricultural prices fluctuate more than industrial prices. This is because of the differences between agricultural and industrial markets, and the characteristics of agricultural production.

Firstly, the markets for agricultural products are perfect competition markets, whereas industrial markets are characterised by monopolistic competition. Agricultural products, as delivered by farmers, are homogenous products and industrial products are differentiated. There are numerous farmers supplying agricultural products, but the number of industrial producers is often very limited. The farmer is a price taker, and he is able to sell as much as he wants at the market price. No single farmer has sufficient influence on supply to affect the market price. On industrial markets, the volume sold by an individual producer depends on the price he fixes.

Prices on perfect competition markets fluctuate more than on monopolistic competition markets.

Secondly, farmers are exposed to erratic disturbances which they cannot fully control. Agricultural production involves biological processes, so the harvest and the supply of animal products depend on weather conditions and the occurrence of diseases. Farmers can plan their production, but they can never be sure of the production level to the same extent as industrial producers.

The economic impact of a bad harvest depends on how much low supply influences agricultural prices and agricultural incomes. When limited supply, due to a small harvest, makes prices rise, agricultural incomes will not change so much. The volume sold is reduced, but this is compensated for by a higher price. This situation will occur if the agricultural market is in a community which is isolated from similar markets in other countries. This would be the case if it were not possible to buy the product internationally, either because of natural barriers such as lack of infrastructure, or because of political barriers such as trade restrictions.

If the market in a country is integrated into the world market, the impact of a bad harvest will be different. Limited supply in the producing country will not raise the domestic price as much because the country will start importing. The international price is presumed to be more stable, because bad harvests in some countries will be offset by more abundant harvests in other countries.

When a domestic market is isolated, agricultural incomes will fluctuate much less than when harvest yields fluctuate in an integrated market. This will have repercussions on the non-farm economy. When the agricultural market is isolated, farm incomes will be stable but the real incomes of the non-farm economy will fluctuate. A bad harvest will cause agricultural prices to rise and the real incomes of the wage earners to fall.

When an agricultural market is integrated internationally, farm incomes will fluctuate, but the real incomes of wage-earners will be stable because agricultural price levels will be stabilised through trade. However, the non-farm sector is not isolated from the impact of a bad harvest. When farmers earn less because of reduced sales volumes, they

Agricultural prices in the medium term

will buy fewer goods from the non-farm sector which will, of course, have a negative impact on employment and incomes in this sector.

Thirdly, it is more difficult for farmers to adjust to changing conditions than it is for industrial producers.

Most agricultural products are perishable and can either not be stored or can only stored for a short time. When a harvest is abundant, the increased volume will be sold and prices will fall. When demand fluctuates through the business cycle, it is much easier for industrial producers to adjust because they have inventories. In boom years they sell out of their inventories, and in slack years they accumulate inventories, stabilising market prices. It is not possible for farmers to make a similar adjustment.

3.7 *Agricultural prices in the medium term*

In the medium term, changes in general level of economic activity may influence the economic conditions of agriculture. The demand for food products will shift as income levels shift. The impact of income change depends on the income elasticity, which varies according to the average income level and the income distribution in a country. In low-income countries, income elasticity is high; in middle income countries it is lower; and in highly industrialised countries income elasticity for food products is close to zero. Income elasticity also depends on income distribution. If the income distribution is skewed, and if a large group of people on low incomes benefit from economic development, the overall income elasticity for agricultural products will be higher than if there is a more equal income distribution.

It is clear that income elasticity varies for different food items. Cereal products are less responsive to income change than animal products, so the relative prices of cereals and animal products may change during a business cycle.

The responsiveness of agricultural prices to changes in demand in a country during the business cycle depends on how internationally integrated the domestic market is, and how synchronised the business cycles of the countries trading with each other are. Where a domestic market is strongly integrated internationally and the business cycles of the countries are not synchronised, the price response to demand shifts will be small. When a domestic market is isolated or the business cycles are synchronised, the price response will be greater.

On the supply side, there are also changes in the medium term. When prices are high there is an incentive to increase production, and there is opposite incentive when prices are low. Such adjustments should stabilise prices, especially when a short time elapses between the decision and the production response. For many agricultural products it takes a long time before supply can be increased. Pig meat supply can only be increased when an increased number of sows deliver an increased number of piglets which then have to be fattened for slaughter. The supply of perennial crops can only be increased by planting new bushes or trees, and it takes time for bushes or trees to yield fruit. It takes several years from planting a new coffee tree to harvesting beans from it for the first time. The delay in supply response causes price fluctuations.

In agriculture it takes a long time to adjust production capacity, because the production factors are fixed. The fixed costs are high and the variable costs are low so the production level is relatively insensitive to output prices. In the medium term, when demand conditions change, it is easier for industrial producers to adjust production levels. This is done by adjusting inventories or adjusting the size of the labour force.

External shocks, in the form of wars, have an impact on economic conditions both in the short term and in the longer term, depending on the length of the war. Domestic supply in the belligerent countries will be reduced because of reduced production potential. The work force is reduced because of the demands of military service. The necessary inputs such as fertilisers are scarce, the supply of feedstuffs is reduced, and holdings of livestock have to be reduced. Because of the scarcity of civilian resources, the necessary reinvestments cannot be made. If a country was importing before, its supplies from abroad will be reduced due to the hostilities.

In wartime, general price levels rise. Periods of war are periods of inflation, when the price structure also changes. Agricultural prices typically rise more than the general price level.

3.8 *Agricultural prices in the long term*

In the long term, agricultural prices depend on the long-term trends in supply and demand for agricultural products. In the following, it will be shown how nominal prices have developed differently in different periods. There are statistical indices for wholesale prices in different countries in Europe (Mitchell, 1981). Data for Britain goes back to 1750, whereas data for France and Germany starts in around 1800.

It is not possible to get a price indices for agricultural commodities long way back, but it has been possible to collect prices for single agricultural products, such as wheat.

Agricultural prices in the long term

Price rises 1750-1815

The period 1750-1815 was characterised by rising prices. Wholesale prices in Britain rose by around 30 per cent from 1750 to 1790, and price levels nearly doubled from 1790 to 1815. There were similar spectacular price rises in France and Germany from 1790 up to the end of the Napoleonic wars. A large part of the commodities included in the wholesale price indices were agricultural products. Also, information about wheat prices seem to indicae a more or less parallel development in the prices in general, and in the agricultural prices.

There were several factors behind this rise in agricultural prices. Firstly the population increase was higher than previously, due to better health conditions and lower mortality rates. There were medical improvements from the middle of the eighteenth century. Secondly, economic growth was higher than before, especially in Britain where industrialisation started. Thirdly, the period was dominated by several wars up to 1789, and then by the Revolutionary and Napoleonic wars, up to 1815.

Price falls 1815-1850

In this period there were significant fall in prices in Britain, France and Germany, especially during the 1820s. Prices were more or less stagnant during the 1830s before they fell further during the 1840s

After the Napoleonic wars, there was a severe period of adjustment for agriculture. Agricultural supply increased when the labour force returned from war, when the production capacity of the land and the capital stock recovered after the necessary restoration and investments, and when the traditional trade channels were re-opened. During this period the population continued to grow, but the growth in the GDP per capita was modest.

Price rises 1850-1875

During this period, wholesale prices rose by around 30-35 per cent in Britain, France and Germany. It was a prosperous period with higher growth rates than previously, accompanied by price rises. There was an increase in the investment ratio. This was the period of extensive railway construction. The population increased, and the GDP per capita rose. The improved transport facilities were a major step in integrating the agricultural sector into the national economies. Industrialisation gathered pace and the agricultural sector benefited from rising agricultural prices. Higher farm incomes created a demand for industrial inputs and consumer goods, so the farming sector contributed to the ongoing industrialisation.

Price falls 1875-1895

There was a fall of around 30 per cent in wholesale prices during this period. There was a general fall in prices, but it seemed to be more marked for agricultural products than for other products. The agricultural terms of trade deteriorated by around 15 per cent in Britain and Germany (Koning, 1994).

The general rate of economic growth was lower than in the previous period. The agricultural sector suffered from falling agricultural prices, caused by the increased international integration of agricultural markets.

The cereal sector was especially influenced by a large increase in the volume of cereal imports from the USA. In the USA, virgin land was cultivated and the agricultural frontier moved westwards. The construction of railways was an important precondition for the expansion of arable land in the USA. The American railway system connected the Mid-West with the harbours on the east coast, bringing a significant decrease in freight rates, which fell by a little less than 50 per cent from the beginning of the 1870s to the beginning of the 1880s. There was a similar reduction in the steamer-freight rates from New York to Liverpool in the same period. This was due to technical developments. In the second half of the nineteenth century, ships began to be built, not of wood but of iron, and later of steel, and this made it possible to increase their size and carrying capacity substantially. Sail gave way to steam and the compound engine greatly reduced fuel costs.

In Russia, railways brought grain to the Baltic and Black Sea ports. In the Danube valley, railways were built from the plains of Hungary and Romania to the Danube, where, in 1856, navigation was made free to the ships of all nations.

There were excellent natural conditions for cereal growing in the USA, Russia and the Danube area, and these potentials could be exploited once the transport facilities were developed. The Crimean War, 1854-56, closed the Baltic and Black Seas for exports from Russia, and the Civil War in the USA, 1861-65, curbed American exports, but the effect of these technical developments was strongly felt from the mid-1870s.

In addition to the falling agricultural prices in the last quarter of the nineteenth century, the relative prices of cereals and livestock products changed in the same period. Table 3.8 shows price indices for cereal and livestock products in Britain. These figures show that the agricultural crisis was much more keenly felt in the cereal sector than in the livestock sector.

Table 3.8: Price indices of food products in the British market

	1867-77	1880-84	1895-99	1905-09
Cereal products	100	82	59	67
Livestock products	100	101	77	88

Source: M. Tracy (1982)

The prices of meat and dairy products only started to fall in the 1880s and fell relatively less than prices for cereals. The economic effect of falling livestock prices was compensated for by improved terms of trade, especially for pork, poultry and egg producers, because cereal is a major input in these productions. The later and more moderate fall in livestock prices can be explained by supply and demand factors. The import of ship-frozen meat from the USA and Australia only started in the mid-1870s when refrigeration began to be used on a commercial scale. In spite of the enormous increase in shipments, the additional supply of livestock products was relatively much less than the additional supply of cereals. The demand for livestock products increased rapidly, due to the higher living standard and the relatively high income elasticity for these products.

Price rises 1895-1914

The economic trend shifted again in this period, when economic activity increased at a higher rate than in the preceding period, and prices also rose. The investment ratio was still high, but there was a shift in the composition of investment away from investment in infrastructure, such as railways, toward investment in the production of other capital and consumer goods. Investment in infrastructure is a prerequisite for growth in the longer term, but the capital output ratio is very high for such investment. This investment was now largely replaced by investment in manufacturing industries, where the capital output ratio is significantly lower. The period was also a prosperous one for agriculture in Europe and the USA, with rising prices. Agriculture was still an important sector, so there was a link between the improved business conditions for agriculture and for manufacturing industry.

During this period, wholesale prices rose by 30-35 per cent and there was a significant improvement in the agricultural terms of trade, especially in the USA.

Prices 1914-1950

The political and economic turbulence of the period 1914-1950 was reflected in prices in general, and agricultural prices in particular. During all wars and the years immediately following them, prices soar and in some cases inflation develops into hyperinflation. This was the case during the First and the Second World Wars. After the high inflation of the First World War, prices fell sharply in all Western European countries in 1921, except Germany, where the inflation developed into hyperinflation. During the remainder of the 1920s, prices either increased, as in the case of France, or fell, as in the case of the United Kingdom, depending on the choice of monetary policy. During the worst years of the Great Depression, 1929-1933, prices fell by between 25 and 40 per cent. Later in the 1930s, price levels rose again, but in most Western European countries they did not reach the 1929 level. In most countries, the high inflation of the Second World War continued after the war up to 1949-1950, and in Germany the monetary system broke down.

Prices 1950-2000

For the general price level there are two sub-periods with different trends. During the first three decades, 1950-1980, the inflation rate increased from decade to decade. In the next two decades, 1980-2000, this trend was reversed. The inflation rate fell during the 1980s, and it fell further during the 1990s.

Agricultural prices were heavily influenced by agricultural support systems, which were different in EC/EU and the USA. In the EC/EU, the agricultural prices were more stable than in the USA where agricultural policy allowed greater price fluctuations.

3.9 *Real agricultural prices*

It is important to distinguish between the general price level and relative prices. The general price level depends on monetary policy. The quantity theory of money says that the price level is determined by the money supply, when activity is constant and the velocity of money is fixed. The

Real agricultural prices

quantity theory does not apply in the short term, because the assumptions about fixed employment and velocity are not fulfilled. However, it seems to apply in the long term. When the general price level rises or falls due to changes in monetary policy, agricultural prices will move correspondingly, unless there are changes in relative prices.

When goods are divided into two groups, agricultural and industrial products, their relative prices may change when the conditions of supply and demand develop differently for the two groups of goods. Rising nominal prices for agricultural products do not exclude the possibility of falling relative prices if the nominal prices for industrial products rise even more than agricultural prices. The real agricultural price level is defined as the nominal agricultural price, divided by an indicator for the general price level. The change in real agricultural prices is equal to the nominal price change for the agricultural goods, minus the change in the general price level.

The change in the real price of agricultural goods depends on changes in supply and demand for agricultural goods, compared to changes in supply and demand for non-agricultural goods. If the income elasticity of agricultural goods is below one, and if the industrial sector is the other sector in the economy, then the income elasticity for goods from this sector will be above one. This will not necessarily cause the agricultural terms of trade to deteriorate, because the supply increase must be known before such a conclusion can be drawn.

In Figure 3.1, agricultural demand is moving less to the right than the demand curve for industrial products. The agricultural supply curve moves from S_0 to S_1, due to increased labour productivity, as the agricultural labour force is assumed to be constant. The industrial supply curve moves more to the right than the agricultural curve, which is partly due to productivity increases and partly due to an increase in the size of the labour force. It is assumed that the total increase in the labour force is employed in industry. To simplify, in Figure 3.1, it is assumed that there are no changes in the prices of agricultural and industrial goods, so the terms of trade between the two sectors are unchanged. The result is clear. Agricultural production increases, but agricultural production as a share of the total production volume, and agricultural employment as a share of total employment, both decrease, even where the terms of trade between agricultural and industrial products are unchanged.

Employment, productivity and prices in agriculture

Figure 3.1: The markets for agricultural and industrial products

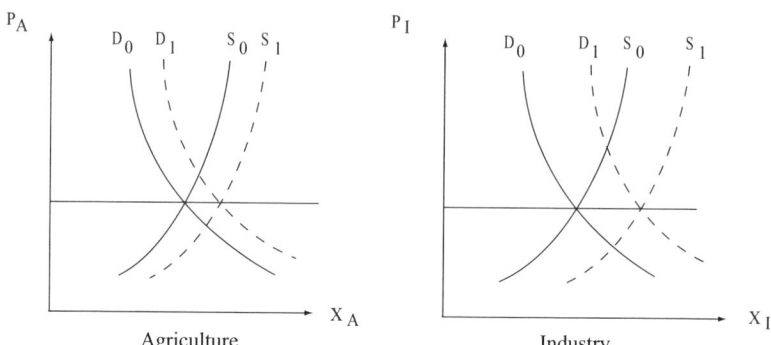

The relative price for agricultural products can rise if the demand increase is stronger than the supply increase. If the relative price rise is sufficiently strong, agricultural production value as a share of the total production value may increase. If the increase in agricultural productivity is more than in Figure 3.1, agricultural supply will move more to the right, and the agricultural terms of trade will deteriorate, so that the share of agricultural production value of the total production value could decline even further.

It can thus be concluded that a relative decline in employment in agriculture, as illustrated in Table 3.1, can be combined with rising, constant, or falling real prices for agricultural products. It is also clear that a nominal rise in agricultural prices can be combined with rising, constant or falling real agricultural prices.

How have real agricultural prices developed? The available data for different European countries does not indicate falling real prices for agricultural products for the period 1820-1850. Agricultural prices fluctuate more than other prices, but the longer trend does not show a general decline. During the period 1850-1875, the nominal price rises for agricultural products were so strong that real prices increased (Koning, 1994). In Britain and Germany there was a fall in the ratio between farm and non-farm prices of around 15 per cent from 1875 to 1895. It could be argued that this price ratio does not adequately describe the agricultural situation, because cereals are used as inputs in the production of animal products. Therefore, one could look at the ratio between the GDP deflator for agriculture and the GDP deflator for the whole economy. When animal product prices fall less than cereal prices, animal product producers will benefit. In Denmark, for example, the real prices of farm

Summary

products, measured as the ratio between the agricultural GDP deflator and the overall GDP deflator, did not change during the period 1875-1895.

Figure 3.2: Real farm prices for wheat and maize in the USA 1866-1981

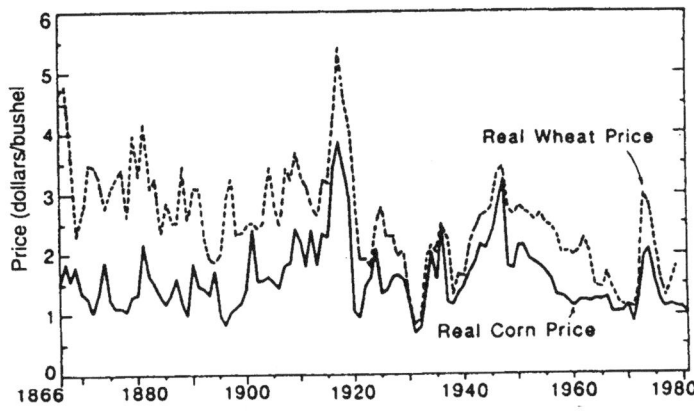

Source: Martin and Brock, 1983

Even when looking at the real prices for cereals in the USA 1875-1895, there is no clear trend for maize, though there might be a slight price fall for wheat. See Figure 3.2.

During the prosperous period 1895-1914, real agricultural prices rose in Europe and in the USA. During the 1920s, real agricultural prices fluctuated with a downward trend which accelerated sharply during the Great Depression 1929-1933.

Since the Second World War, the trend has been a fall in the real prices of agricultural products. This has been the case in Europe, in spite of heavy agricultural price support, and in the USA, as shown in Figure 3.2. This long-term trend was only interrupted in the short term in 1972-1974 by price hikes on the world market for cereals and vegetable oil products.

3.10 Summary

Economic development is associated with a dramatic shift in the relative importance of the primary, secondary and tertiary sectors. At the end of the eighteenth century, up to 80 per cent of the population was working in agriculture. Even in 1920, agriculture occupied around 50 per cent of the working population of Europe, but by 2000 the share of employment in agriculture in the EU and the USA in 2000 was less than 5 per cent.

Supply and demand determine agricultural prices. The trend of production increases over the trend of demand increases determines the trend of agricultural prices.

Production will increase if the amount of resources is augmented and/or if productivity increases. The amount of land and labour employed in agriculture increased from 1750 to 1920. Since then there has been a slight decrease in arable acreage and a large decrease in labour. Mechanisation started already in the nineteenth century, especially in the USA, but it was only after the Second World War that major mechanisation took place. The post-war period was also characterised by a large increase in the use of bought-in inputs such as fertilisers, feedstuffs and pesticides.

Agricultural productivity can be measured in different ways. Labour productivity has risen over the last two centuries. There seems to have been an accelerating rise in the productivity level. A slow rise in labour productivity in the first half of the nineteenth century was followed by a higher rate of increase in the second half and an even higher increase in the first half of the twentieth century. The greatest labour productivity increase took place in the second half of the twentieth century.

The demand for agricultural products is determined by the size of the population, income per capita, and income elasticity.

During the years 1750-1914, there was a relatively strong growth in the demand for agricultural products. There was a shift in the population growth rate in around 1750, and the high population growth continued through the 1800s. There was also an increase in the growth rate of GDP per capita, and at the same time, income elasticity was high. Supply also increased as more labour and land resources were used in agriculture, combined with productivity gains.

During the last century, 1914-2000, the rate of growth in demand slowed down. The population increased at a slower rate than before. During the last half of the twentieth century, GDP per capita increased more than in any previous period, but this only caused a slight increase in the demand for agricultural products because income elasticity fell to a very low level. Supply tended to increase more than demand in the period after the Second World War. The productivity increase outweighed the migration of labour.

Agricultural prices, which are determined by supply and demand, fluctuate in the short, medium and long term. Agricultural markets are different from industrial markets, and experience larger fluctuations in

Summary

the short and medium term. The degree of economic integration influences the extent of price fluctuations and the impact of exogenous shocks. The more agricultural products are processed, the less consumer prices will be influenced by fluctuations in farm-gate prices.

Monetary policy has an important impact on the general price trend, whereas relative prices are determined by supply and demand. The real prices of agricultural products do not seem to have deteriorated in the period 1750-1920. On the contrary, there seems to have been a rise in the real price level for agricultural products, apart from the period 1875-1895 when there was a slight fall. Real prices fell during the Great Depression, but it is only since the Second World War that there has been a long-term fall in real agricultural prices.

The long-term decline of agricultural employment as a share of total employment can be explained by a combination of three elements: income elasticity for agricultural products below 1, the high increase in agricultural productivity, and migration from agriculture.

4. Technological and institutional changes in agriculture 1750-1914

The economic transformation of societies in Europe and the USA during the period 1750-1914 was very much the result of agricultural change. But it was not only the result of agricultural development, because at the same time industrialisation started in Britain and later spread to the rest of Europe and the USA. Both in agriculture and industry, development was initiated and then carried forward by technological and institutional changes.

4.1 What are technological and institutional changes?

Technological change occurs when new product types are developed and new products are introduced. Product development and product innovation are normally combined with new production techniques. However, a new production process can be introduced even if the final product is unchanged. It is clear that technological change occurs both when there are product innovations and new production processes, and when these innovations are disseminated in society.

Technological change will also occur without product innovations when there are changes in the composition of outputs and changes in the production methods. It is clear that there will be technological changes when arable production is gradually supplemented by increased production of livestock products. It is also clear that production techniques will change when there is a shift in farm structures. Larger farms are typically more capital intensive than smaller farms which use relatively more labour.

What is meant by institutional change depends on the meaning of 'institution'. The term 'institution' is used to mean physical entities which deliver services. There are research institutions such as research centres and universities producing new knowledge. There are educational institutions such as schools and credit institutions such as banks and mortgage lending institutions. Development has much to do with establishing the entities which form the institutional framework of society.

The term institution is also used to refer to the rules of a society or of the organisations which influence the behaviour of people and co-operation between people. 'Institution' in this sense includes the rules or conventions which govern behaviour: (1) within economic units such as families, firms and public bodies, (2) between economic units such as firms and households acting in a market, and (3) between economic units and their environments, for example, the relationship between a firm and a regulatory agency. In the following, the term institution will be used in a broad sense, including both physical entities and the rules of a society and its organisations.

4.2 An overview of industrial and agricultural changes

The start of the modern era is traditionally associated with the start of industrialisation in Britain in around 1750. At that time, important technological and institutional changes started to take place in industry.

By around 1750, the first industrial revolution was under way. The first industrial revolution was based on a series of technological innovations and institutional changes. The technological changes included (1) the use of new kinds of power, in particular steam; (2) the use of coal as a fuel; (3) the ability to extract and use metals, especially iron, cheaply and in abundance; (4) the innovation of new machines and improved tools; (5) the accumulation of new knowledge based on practical improvements and on new scientific knowledge. With these technological innovations, production started to be based on power, coal, metals, machinery, and science. This first industrial revolution took place in those regions of Britain where coal and iron ore deposits were available.

Later, industrialisation spread to other regions where similar conditions existed. Industrialisation spread first to Belgium and Northern France and then to the Ruhr district and Silesia in Germany.

There were also institutional changes associated with industrialisation. The old crafts and trades were strictly regulated through the guild system. The guild system, with all its rules, could not survive industrialisation. Production was now organised by the establishment of the factory system, where many workers worked together. New classes arose and gained political power. A class of rich industrialists, organising industrial production, emerged. Industrial products had to be traded, so the class of

An overview of industrial and agricultural changes

merchants became more important. At the same time a broad class of middle-income earners and a large class of poorer workers evolved.

The first industrial revolution was concentrated around the development of the textile and iron industries and the production technology which lay behind them. The second industrial revolution took place during the period 1870-1914, and was also characterised by technological and institutional changes.

The second industrial revolution was based on new technologies such as the use of electricity and improved iron and steel production. Industrial production became more diversified. New production of chemicals and synthetic materials was started and developed, as was the use of new machinery in engineering and construction. Better engines and better ships were developed. Cars were introduced.

The institutional changes were very much associated with the development and improvements of markets. It was enlarged markets that enabled industrialisation to progress. Enlarged markets created economic integration, which was a prerequisite for economic specialisation.

When industrialisation started, up to 80 per cent of the population was engaged in agriculture. In such societies, there can only be pervasive economic improvements if agriculture is involved. There were important technological and institutional changes in agriculture during the period 1750-1914.

Agriculture went through two stages with different characteristics. The first stage started in around 1750 and continued into the nineteenth century. The second stage took place during the nineteenth century. It is difficult to put firm dates on these stages because to some extent they overlapped, and the stages occurred at different times in different places. In the first stage the agricultural sector progressed through technological and institutional changes. In the second stage agriculture continued to develop due to new technological and institutional changes.

During the first stage, the most important change was the introduction of new crops, which made it possible to cultivate the land more intensively. This technological change was combined with institutional changes in the form of agricultural reforms. These changes were based on internal agricultural resources.

Agriculture continued to develop during the second stage. The second round of changes was also a combination of technological and institutional changes. There were a series of technological changes in the form of land improvements, improved seed and livestock, new and improved tools, equipment and machinery. The technological changes were the results of innovations, the dissemination of know-how and the

Technological and institutional changes in agriculture 1750-1914

delivery of new inputs which depended on institutional changes. These institutional changes were connected with the development and improvement of markets and the enabling environment.

4.3 The farming system in Europe before the agricultural revolution

The farming system in any country depends on three elements: the methods of cultivation, the system of land ownership, and the social relations between the rural classes. Clearly, the farming system was not the same everywhere in Europe before the agricultural revolution, but the most typical characteristics are described briefly in the following.

In Europe, nearly all the land was owned by large estate owners, typically belonging to the aristocracy, the crown or the church. The land was cultivated in two different ways, either by the large estate system or by the open-field system of agriculture. The large estate system was based on large consolidated land areas cultivated by peasants and labourers. The conditions under which they worked differed from country to country. In the open-field system, the land was tilled by the peasants who typically worked as tenants. The arable land was divided into two or three open fields and these were cultivated according to a rotation system, where each of the fields lay fallow in turn in order to avoid the exhaustion of the soil. Each field was divided into a large number of plots, each of which was divided in turn into several strips, so each peasant had to till a great number of strips scattered around in different plots. In principle, each farmer had the right to cultivate what he wanted on his strips, but the crops had to be harvested at the same time, because the livestock were fed on the stubble after harvest. So that in practice, the peasants had to take collective decisions about the use of the land. The peasants lived close together in villages and the fields surrounded the villages. Around the fields there was common land, consisting of meadows, forests and waste land. The common land was used for grazing animals, and all the peasants and landless agricultural labourers were allowed to use the common land for grazing. There was also common grazing on the fallow field and on the other fields after the harvest.

The open-field system of farming had two main defects. Firstly, it made inefficient use of resources. The strip system wasted the land used for roads and footpaths. It wasted time in getting men, implements and draught animals from one strip to another or from the village to the more distant fields. The common grazing areas were often overstocked with animals and diseases spread easily when the animals were closely packed together. Secondly, the open-field system was a barrier to individual initiative and innovation. All the main decisions about cropping were taken collectively. It was difficult for an individual peasant to introduce new crops, and it was difficult to agree on turning the common land into arable land, even in times when there was an increasing demand for food.

In most of Europe, apart perhaps from Britain, productivity in the open-field system was either stagnant or increasing very slowly. Thus, the reform of the farming system was essential for increasing productivity. However, the reform of agriculture was a very complicated and slow process, not least because of the conflicting interests of estate owners, peasants and landless labourers. Agrarian reforms also implied radical changes to the way of life, and the consequences of reforms could be difficult for the uneducated and poor rural population to foresee. The landless labourers were afraid of losing their rights to graze animals on the common land. The peasants were mostly interested in reducing the rents they had to pay to the landlords who owned most of the village land. The peasants were also interested in reducing the work they were obliged to perform on the estate from which they rented their farms. The amount of work they had to perform varied substantially between countries. In the western part of Europe, west of the Elbe, it took the form of villeinage, where the legal status of the peasants was better than it was east of the Elbe, where the peasants were virtually subject to serfdom, with much lesser rights. The weak legal status of the peasants was a critical issue, and their dependent status meant that it was difficult for them to oppose the interests of the landlords.

4.4 The first technological changes

The farming system was more or less trapped in a vicious circle before some important technological changes were made. Cereals were cultivated on two out of three fields, while the third field lay fallow. It was necessary for a field to lie fallow in order to restore the fertility of the soil after its nutrients had been used by a grain crop. Soil fertility was dependent on the amount of manure available as fertiliser. The quantity of the livestock delivering the manure depended on the amount of fodder available, and most of the fodder came from meadows and pastures.

The productivity of this system, measured in grain yields per hectare, was determined by soil fertility. With a fixed cultivated area, an increase in the proportion of land sown with cereals would reduce the proportion of fallow and pasture, and so reduce fodder, soil fertility and yields. Any increase in grain output resulting from an increase in the area under cereals would be offset later by a fall in yields because of a reduction in soil fertility.

This vicious circle was broken when new crops were introduced. Turnips and clover were introduced on previously fallow areas. There were several important consequences of the introduction of the new fodder crops. Firstly, the new fodder crops increased the productivity of the arable land. It corresponded to an increase in the arable area with fixed productivity. However, it was less costly than expanding the actual arable area which would have involved high labour costs. A third of the arable land which had hitherto been more or less unproductive, because it lay fallow, was now used for production. Secondly, the increased fodder production made it possible to increase livestock production both by increasing the size of the herd and by increasing the productivity of the animals. The increased size of herd had a very important side effect, namely an increase in the amount of manure, which increased soil fertility. Thirdly, soil fertility could also be increased by growing clover. Clover has the valuable property of fixing atmospheric nitrogen in the soil. Cereals also need nitrogen, but cereal crops need to absorb nitrogen from the soil through their roots. Fourthly, the growing of turnips contributed to the cleaning of weeds from the fields. Fallow areas allow room for weeds to spread, but this was not the case with turnips, which had to be hoed. Turnips was also good for fodder, because it could be stored and used in winter.

The introduction of the new fodder crops was a crucial element in the new farming techniques associated with the agricultural revolution. These crops made it possible to increase agricultural productivity. This new farming technique relied solely on agricultural resources. No outside resources were needed.

The introduction of new crops, which proliferated in Britain during the eighteenth century and spread to other parts of Western Europe, was ground-breaking. Land productivity could be increased without depleting soil fertility.

4.5 Institutional changes in the form of agricultural reforms

In the second half of the eighteenth century, the population grew at an unprecedented rate. The population of Europe increased by around one third, due to a decline in the mortality rate (Heaton, 1968). This population growth could have been due both to medical and economic causes. With better hygienic standards, people's health improved and

Institutional changes in the form of agricultural reforms

doctors were better able to cure illness, so the mortality rate fell. The improved economic conditions, with an increased supply of food, improved nutritional levels.

The population growth stimulated the demand for food and prices rose. Technological improvements in agriculture increased productivity. Both these factors stimulated interest in agricultural production and in increased yields through agrarian reforms which could contribute to further productivity increases.

The trends were more or less the same everywhere in Europe, but the response differed from country to country. Three elements characterise the farming system of a country: the methods of production, the ownership of the land, and the social relations between rural classes.

A series of reforms

The agrarian transformation involved a long series of changes in the methods of production, land ownership and the working conditions and legal rights of peasants. The transformation depended on both technological changes and institutional changes. There were interrelationships between these two sets of changes. These institutional changes and agricultural reforms will be described below.

1. *Individual farming.* The open-field system was based on collective decision making. It was now replaced by individual farming, where each peasant took his own management decisions.
2. *Consolidation of land.* The numbers of small strips of land cultivated by each peasant were consolidated into coherent plots of farm land, and the fields were normally enclosed. The system of common land was abandoned and the land divided up into enclosed private plots.
3. *Relocation of farms.* The consolidation of the land could either take the form of a squared block pattern or a star-shaped pattern. In the first case, the individual farm consisted of a square block of land, where it was natural to place the farm in the middle. In this case, the farmer had to move his farm from the village out onto the farm land, and this required capital. In the case of a star-shaped pattern, the farm buildings and the dwellings could still be kept as a part of the village, and the dispersal of farms was not necessary.
4. *Size structure.* The land cultivated under the open-field system could be integrated into large estate holdings, so the number of farms was decreased. The common land could be taken over by the farm

estates. The alternative was to consolidate the land into a greater or lesser number of farms cultivated by the peasants. Should the strategy be to focus on larger commercialised farms or should agriculture be based on smallholdings?

5. *Ownership*. When the farms were consolidated, they could still be owned by landlords, who rented out the farms to the peasants. Alternatively, the landlords could sell the farms to the peasants. In the case of tenancies, it was important to establish laws to protect the interests of the tenants. In the case of transfer of the ownership of the freehold, there was a question of how to finance the transfer of ownership.

6. *Labour services*. Agricultural production on the large estates was based on the provision of labour services, either in the form of serfdom or villeinage. The working conditions changed. Serfdom was abolished and the amount of villeinage a peasant had to deliver could be fixed, reduced and finally removed. The labour service a peasant had to provide could be substituted by payments to the landlord. Personal freedom and reduced obligations of labour service were important for the development of the agricultural sector. A less suppressed peasantry opened the way for the establishment of an educated, self-organising peasant class that contributed to its own development. This was one way of creating social capital.

7. *Legal rights*. The peasants and landless labourers were in a weak position vis-à-vis the landlords, who exercised jurisdiction over their peasants, usually without a right of appeal. They had to pay rents. They had to pay charges for the use of estate facilities such as mills, ovens, wine presses, etc. They had to provide labour services. The peasants and landless labourers were often exploited because they were in a weak bargaining position without much protection from the law or from the way the law was enforced. The landlords both interpreted and enforced the law, and they often had the right to impose corporal punishment on peasants and labourers.

When one considers the range of elements associated with agrarian reform, it is not surprising that it took such a long time to decide on reforms and to implement all the different elements. The pattern of reform differed from country to country, as analysed in Chapter 5. The reforms differed in content, and they were not at all introduced and implemented simultaneously in the different countries.

Institutional changes in the form of agricultural reforms

The importance of attitudes and incentives

In the period 1750-1914, when many of the agrarian reforms took place in Europe, all the countries, apart from Britain, were governed by absolute monarchs, who ruled by decree. Some of the agrarian reforms were introduced by governments through legislation, such as the protection of legal rights or the abolition of adscription. Other laws, such as laws of succession, influenced the concentration of ownership and farm structure. Governments could stimulate agrarian reforms through public expenditure and tax legislation. Originally, the crown owned a large share of the land, and could introduce reforms on its own land. Many of the reforms, such as the abandonment of the open-field system, the consolidation of land holdings, and the removal of farms were highly dependent on the rulers, landlords and peasants.

Legislation depended on the absolute monarch and the political elite surrounding him. The prevailing philosophy or ideology influenced the content of the legislation. The economic and social interests of the king and the political elite also influenced the legislation. An important part of the political elite belonged to the landowning class.

The attitude of the landlords was important, not only in relation to the legislation, but also the implementation of reforms. The second half of the eighteenth century was the Age of Enlightenment, and the landlords could be more or less influenced by the new ideas. However, ideological attitudes were mixed with economic interests, which could be handled in two different ways. The landlords could react passively to the idea of agricultural reforms. When agricultural prices were rising they could choose the exploitation strategy, raising rents and extending villeinage and other rights over the peasants. Or the landlords could react more actively, by being interested in reforms, because they realised that such reforms could be beneficial to themselves. Some were only interested in technological changes; others were interested in both technological and institutional changes.

Whether or not agrarian reforms were initiated depended on the dominant attitudes of the rural classes and their economic incentives. The attitudes and class interests of the legislative powers also influenced the size structure which resulted from the changes.

The distribution of land ownership determined the size structure, which varied from country to country. The size structure had an important impact on the production methods, the agricultural produce and the developments in agriculture and in society.

The agricultural sector can be made up of two parts, one consisting of very large units and the other of small units. The dominant part, consisting of large farm estates, is managed by landlords or merchants, who hire the necessary labour from among the smallholders and landless labourers in the area. Large estates in temperate climate zones grow cereals or raise livestock. In developing countries, large farm units are often plantations owned by wealthy individuals, or national or multinational companies. The other sector of agriculture consists of a multitude of smallholders and landless labourers. The smallholders may be more of less quasi-subsistence farmers, who have to supplement their incomes from sources outside their own farms, either by working for the large estates or by working outside agriculture. This is a bimodal farm structure.

A unimodal farm structure is one where all the farms are of more or less the same size. The farmers themselves are both managers and workers, and they depend on hired labour to a lesser degree.

The performance of the agricultural sector also depends on the system of ownership. Are the farms state owned, collectively owned or privately owned? In the case of private ownership, the owner may be the day-to-day operator, but he may also let the farm to a tenant. When the farmers are tenants, the organisation of the tenancy system is crucial. Agreements between landlords and tenants should include incentives for both parties to make improvements which could benefit both parties.

When there are externalities connected with production, there are disadvantages associated with common ownership unless there are regulations which can be effectively enforced. When villagers have a right to graze their livestock on common land without charge and without limitation, the common land will typically be over grazed, and the value of the common grazing will decline.

4.6 *Technological changes continued*

Once the reform of agriculture had started, it continued. The continued development was due to new technological and institutional changes. The technological improvements depended on the institutional changes. New improved methods of production had to be introduced. Research institutions and universities had to be set up to deliver the basic and applied research which are the prerequisites for innovations. When there were innovations, information about them had to be disseminated to the farmers. The new production methods involved the use of new inputs, and these had to be made available. So the technological changes could only be made when innovations had been made, when information about

Technological changes continued

them had been disseminated, and when the necessary inputs were available.

In addition, the farmers would only be induced to change their production methods if the increased production could be sold. There had to be an organised market of a certain size, and this could only be established through infrastructural investments and the establishment of distribution channels. The new production methods required investments, and these would only be made if it was possible to finance them.

Improved inputs and new inputs

Land productivity and especially labour productivity continued to grow during the nineteenth century. This growth was based on improved inputs.

It was realised that crop yields could be raised by land improvements. Soil fertility was improved by marling and by different forms of drainage.

It was found that crop yields and livestock production could be increased by breeding programs based on the selection principle. When livestock grazed on the common fields and common land, it was impossible to manage a breeding programme. This became possible when the common fields and common land were enclosed in private plots.

The closed circuit system, where manure was used as fertiliser, was supplemented by a new system where additional fertilisers were bought in from outside. From around 1840, manure was supplemented by new sources of fertiliser. Firstly, guano from South America was imported to Europe, especially to Germany. Secondly, the supply of potassium, phosphorus and nitrogen was increased, especially in Germany. Potassium was found in Alsace. Phosphorus was known to be present in iron ore in Lorraine, and as the iron ore was extracted for steel production, a growing supply of phosphorus became available. Nitrogen was a by-product of coal and gas production. Thirdly, in 1913, just before the war, the first German factory produced chemical fertilisers on the basis of nitrogen "fixed" from the air. These new sources of fertiliser meant that arable production became less dependent on the size of a farmer's livestock.

New protein-rich oilseed cake was introduced as supplementary feed. This was a waste product from the industrial production of plant oil products. The plant oil industry started in the last quarter of the nineteenth century and the use of oilseed cake started at the same time.

New tools, new equipment and new machinery were introduced. For example, the introduction of the seed drill greatly reduced seed costs.

Less seed was lost when seed drills replaced the sowing of seed by hand broadcasting. The wheel plough, drawn by six horses, was replaced by the swing plough for which only two horses were needed, and this greatly increased the productivity of draught animals. Later, more and more advanced reaping and threshing machinery was introduced.

In the last quarter of the nineteenth century, innovation also played an important role in the development of the food processing industry, in the form of bigger slaughter houses and dairies. The introduction of the cream separator in 1878 was a big step forward in the development of the dairy industry, with much higher productivity than previously.

Technological progress through innovation is not a production factor as such, but technological progress has an important impact on productivity. Technology can either be embodied or disembodied. Embodied technological progress occurs when a farmer invests in a new herd of dairy cattle with higher yields obtained through improved breeding. The genetic technological progress is embodied in the cattle, and the farmer has to buy the better breed of cattle in order to benefit from the technological progress. Disembodied technological progress takes place, for example, when an improved fodder mix or an improved fodder item is produced. The new fodder will increase the milk yield as soon as it is used, and it is not necessary to scrap the old herd and buy a new one.

There were many different kinds of improved production methods. There were new livestock products, new seed and fertilisers, new machinery, breeding programmes, and new ways of combating plant and animal diseases. These technological changes could only be made because new institutions were established.

Innovations and institutions

To start with, the technological innovations and improvements were based on experiences at farm level. Often the innovations were made on estates owned by progressive landlords, and they were also active in applying new production methods. This was the case during the eighteenth century and the beginning of the nineteenth century.

Later, research became institutionalised in the sense that the innovations were the result of more planned and systematic efforts being made in institutions. Agricultural universities, colleges and experimental stations were established from around the mid-nineteenth century.

Soil and weather conditions varied from region to region, so it was important for the research to be based on the specific conditions of a region. The research topics chosen often reflected the most pressing needs of the region, and depended on the existing production bottlenecks.

Research institutions were only established when there was a collective initiative and collective financing. Farmers' organisations could invest in experimental stations, but this could also be done by public bodies. Investing in agricultural universities and colleges dealing with research and education is typically a task for the public sector. Public financing is reasonable when the research results contribute to increased supplies of agricultural products, which will benefit consumers by reducing prices.

Availability of inputs and institutions

The new production methods involved buying inputs such as fertilisers, new tools and new machinery. The new inputs had to be available, which meant not only that they had to be produced, but they also had to be available at farm level. The integration of urban and rural areas, through a well-functioning communication and transport system, was crucial. Such an infrastructure was also a prerequisite for farmers to move from subsistence or semi-subsistence farming to commercial farming.

The existence of distribution networks was also a prerequisite. There had to be a chain which linked farms to consumers. Inputs had to be produced domestically or imported before they were delivered to farmers through the distribution system.

When new technology involved investment and the buying of intermediate inputs, farmers had a need for finance. A rural credit system, where farmers in need of funds could borrow from others with surplus funds, greatly facilitated the introduction of new farming practices.

Information and institutions

Existing know-how and new knowledge about agricultural production only becomes useful when it is disseminated to farmers who are capable of turning the know-how to practical use. A veterinary service and an agricultural extension service were necessary links between the research institutes and the farmers. Information could only be disseminated once a series of conditions were fulfilled. Firstly, there had to be a sufficient number of veterinary surgeons and agronomists with the relevant education. Secondly, they should work in the countryside where they could assist the farmers. Veterinary surgeons treated the animals and delivered the necessary medicine, and participated in programmes to prevent the spread of infectious diseases. Agronomists were employed in extension services organised by farmers' unions, agricultural societies or public bodies. Here the farmers could get advice on all aspects of farming. Thirdly, farmers had to be sufficiently educated so as to understand the advice and take the necessary action. The elimination of illiteracy and general education were important because educated people can more easily absorb and apply new knowledge.

It is a great advantage for a country if information about new production methods can be disseminated quickly. This increases the chances of applying the new techniques quickly. The improved technology will lead to productivity gains and this will give the country an advantage over its competitors.

The dissemination of new technology depends on the economic integration of a country. The more integrated the economy is, the more easily the new technology will be spread. If a country is internationally integrated, it can also benefit from new technology from abroad.

Agricultural and farm associations were established in some countries in the latter half of the nineteenth century. They dealt with experimental research, the dissemination of know-how, and provided services to farmers. These associations were privately run, but their investments and their activities were often supported by the public sector.

4.7 Institutional change in the form of economic integration

Economic development in agriculture depends on the interrelationship between technological improvements and institutional changes. During the first stage of development, institutional changes were focused on agricultural reforms. During the second stage, the institutional changes were concerned with economic integration. Economic integration takes place through the establishment and improvement of markets. Increased labour productivity is based on specialisation and trade, combined with technical improvements. Specialisation is only possible when there are markets through which outputs can be sold and inputs can be bought. Economic development depends on economic integration, and economic integration cannot be realised without markets.

The creation and improvement of markets depend on infrastructure, distribution channels, institutions in the form of organisations, such as financial institutes, and institutions in the form of rules, such as property rights, the legal status of the different classes and the political power structure. In addition, the norms and the behaviour and attitudes of people influence the way markets work.

The importance of infrastructure

A market can be defined as the relationship between the actual and potential buyers and sellers of a given product. A market has a geographical extent, so transport and communication systems have an important impact on the way markets function. The network of roads, canals and railways determine the possibilities for moving goods and services from one place to another. Communication systems such as telegraphs, telephones and, today, modern information technology facilitate the gathering of information and make it easier to trade. The lower the transport and transaction costs, the better the market functions. Transport and transaction costs constitute trade barriers which limit the extent of the market and competition on the market. The physical infrastructure influences the way the market works.

Distribution channels

The market is the mechanism through which buyers and sellers co-operate. Farmers have to sell their produce for further processing; food processors then sell their products to wholesalers, who sell to retailers, who finally sell to consumers. There is a whole distribution chain, and farm-gate prices depend on consumer prices and the distribution and processing costs.

Farmers need inputs and it is important that the right inputs, such as seed and fertilisers, are available at the right time at a "reasonable" price. Storage capacity should be available, and it must be possible to transport the inputs to the farms.

The efficiency of the distribution system can be measured by the marketing margin between production prices and consumer prices. At a given wage level and a given distance level, a small margin indicates efficiency. Sometimes the public is involved in the purchase of farm products and the delivery of inputs through parastatals, which are semi-public agencies, or marketing boards. They are often quite inefficient. To leave the distribution system wholly to the private sector can also be problematic. Private buyers will often have monopsony power and the private sellers will have monopoly power. A common solution to this is the setting up of buying and selling co-operatives by farmers.

New markets such as credit markets

The existence of credit institutions is important for financing investments. Some farmers have savings which they want to lend. Others need to borrow funds for short-term or long-term investments. If there are no financial or credit institutions, it is difficult to allocate surplus funds to those who have a demand for funds. The result will be a lower savings ratio and a lower investment level. If there is no banking or mortgage system, farmers have to borrow on an unorganised market from private money lenders who usually charge high interest rates, partly due to the high risk of default. When the credit market is organised, the risks are reduced and the spread between the interest rate debtors have to pay and the interest rate creditors receive can be reduced.

The existence of an organised credit market is also important for the farmer's decision making. Farming is always risky because the harvest may fail, livestock may be hit by disease, and the prices for produce may fall. Therefore, it is risky, especially for poor farmers, to make investments if they have to be financed through an unorganised financial market with high interest rates for short term loans. When there are organised credit markets, it is easier for farmers to deal with the traditional farming risks of bad harvests and low prices, because the financing conditions are better. If a poorer farmer has invested, and if he has no possibility of borrowing if the harvest fails, he may be forced to sell his land or his farm. If the same farmer operates in a society with organised credit, he can survive by borrowing.

Rules, customs, initiatives and co-operation

A national market reflects the interrelationship between the citizens of a country. The more coherent the society is, the easier it is to establish co-operation within a country. The performance of international markets depends on international co-operation. How markets work depends on institutions in the form of the rules and norms of the society.

A legal system consisting of laws and legal institutions is necessary for the enforcement of agreements between persons and other entities in the economy. In a society it is important for people, organisations, and political parties to co-operate to create solutions which are beneficial for all or for most people. The ability of different individuals to act effectively together to pursue shared objectives depends on the norms of the society and trust between the participants. The ability to form societies and networks with common goals based on trust is a dynamic element in creating efficient markets and stimulating economic development. The ability to organise co-operatives which can sell their outputs and buy their necessary inputs can be of great importance to farmers. However, co-operatives can only be successful if there is trust, interest in civic participation and understanding of the need to co-operate.

The ability of a society to take initiatives and to co-operate to find solutions is often called its social capital. Social capital has been defined as the ability to facilitate "certain actions of work" (North, 1990). Social capital depends on norms, civic participation, trust, initiative and co-operation.

It has been recognised by sociologists and economists that culture influences norms and human behaviour. Max Weber (1905) emphasised the importance of religion in relation to economic activity. He thought that the Protestant religion was conducive to economic growth. Economists have emphasised the importance of competition in a society dominated by private ownership. J.M. Keynes spoke about "the animal spirit" as a driving force behind investment (Keynes, 1936). J. Schumpeter considered innovation to be an important driving force in the development process, and he described the effect of innovation as "creative destruction". "New" activities arise while "old" activities are out-competed (Schumpeter, 1943).

4.8 The importance of markets

The market and the enabling environment

Agricultural development depends on integration which takes place through markets. The establishment and improvement of markets depend on the five "in's": infrastructure, inputs, innovations, information and institutions (as described above in sections 4.6 and 4.7). Infrastructure is necessary to link different geographical areas. Distribution channels enable the delivery of inputs from other sectors, and they are also necessary for selling outputs outside the local market. Innovation and the dissemination of information are important for obtaining continuous productivity gains. The institutional framework, in the form of legal rights, legal rules and cultural norms has an important impact on the development pattern of the economy. Institutions in the form of physical institutions, such as research institutes, extension service centres and credit institutions deliver the necessary innovations, information and credit for investments at farm level. The five "in's" can be considered as the enabling environment. The farming sector can only perform adequately if the environment of its markets is satisfactory. It is a complex and resource-demanding task to create markets and the necessary environment. Therefore, there is a risk that the investments necessary for creating and improving markets and the environment may not be made.

Focus on agricultural development is important for two reasons. Firstly, the development of agriculture is of special importance because it is such a large sector. To a large extent, the development of society runs parallel to the development of agriculture. Secondly, agricultural development is also important because it contributes to the development of markets which are important for the whole of society. Agriculture needs infrastructure in the form of roads, railways etc., education in the form of a school system, and credit delivered by organised financial markets. If agriculture were not developed, there would not be the same pressure for infrastructure, education and credits, and this would hamper the development of the non-agricultural sectors. Agriculture contributes to developments elsewhere in the economy, because of the stimulation provided by the linkages between agriculture and other sectors. The backward linkages, forward linkages and income linkages mean that agriculture creates new possibilities for industrial producers. These linkages depend on the existence of markets and the enabling environment.

Who should take initiatives?

During the first stage of agricultural development, institutional changes in the form of agricultural reforms are important. This is the stage where peasants move from subsistence farming to a system where a greater part of their production is sold. This first step is a prerequisite for the second stage, where markets and the enabling environment are gradually developed.

During the first stage, the role of the monarch and the attitudes of the landlords are important. Agricultural reform without a revolution is only possible if the monarch and the land-owning class take the initiative.

During the second stage, private initiatives both inside agriculture and outside agriculture are needed, together with public initiatives. Some of the institutional structures, such as savings banks, mortgage institutions and other financial institutions can be initiated by private people either inside or outside agriculture. Distribution channels can likewise be established either as co-operatives formed by farmers or as traditional private firms, established by entrepreneurs.

The importance of markets

In other cases, governments must provide the necessary services, such as general education or agricultural research. Investments in roads and railways are also public undertakings. Public bodies may promote private initiatives when public finance is used to support the initiatives. Farmers' unions may introduce extension services, partly supported by public funds.

It is important to emphasise that the task is so great that it needs the joint efforts of the private and the public sectors. The capacity of the public sector to take initiatives and to make the necessary investments is often limited. That is why it is important to induce the private sector to participate. The initial stages will often need public support, but when a market is being developed, the way it functions will often indicate the initiatives and the investments needed. If the private return on investment is sufficiently large, private entrepreneurs will be induced to invest. If the social return is large, but the private return is low, the public sector will either have to invest in public initiatives or subsidise private initiatives.

What should be the guidelines behind the development strategy?

What should be the theoretical background steering interventions to support development? It is clear that a traditional neo-classical equilibrium model is not adequate. The neo-classical theory normally assumes the existence of fixed technology and a given institutional set-up. Markets are assumed to work perfectly, and when there are perfect markets, with all the necessary institutions, there is no need for institutional change. If technological and institutional changes are introduced, the changes are considered to be exogenous.

When dealing with economic development, it is important to treat the technology and the institutional set-up as variables, which interact with each other. The theoretical background for dealing with economic development should include a clear recognition of the complicated interrelationships between the following four cornerstones: factor endowment, technology, institutions and attitudes.

Development theory can be used as an overall framework for development policy, but it cannot be used as a method for choosing priorities during the development process. When changes take place, new bottlenecks will occur, hampering further development. It is important to identify bottlenecks and to take steps to eliminate them. Every change can be considered as a disturbance which creates both new opportunities and new problems. When these problems are confronted constructively so they are overcome, a dynamic process is started by the gradual removal of obstacles.

Economic development can be considered as a continuous process in which the realisation of new opportunities creates new bottlenecks. Technological and institutional changes create new opportunities. When the new opportunities are realised, new bottlenecks appear. There will be pressure for the removal of these bottlenecks, and when they are removed new opportunities will appear.

If markets work well, they play an important role in identifying the bottlenecks. They give information to research institutions about technical problems which have to be solved. They give information to entrepreneurs about whether new productions should be started or new markets should be opened. They give information to organisations and the political system about deficiencies which may need to be overcome by institutional changes.

When development occurs in this way, it is not possible to predict the different steps of the development process. It is not possible to make a master plan. Every step of the development process must be gradually evaluated to find out how the new bottlenecks and new problems can best be overcome.

4.9 Summary

From around 1750 there was a significant increase in population growth in nearly all parts of the world. In Western Europe and the USA this population increase was associated with a spectacular increase in GDP per capita.

Around 1750 there were feudal societies nearly everywhere in Europe, and these had been replaced by more or less industrialised societies in Western Europe by around 1914.

The transformation of these societies was linked to increased production resources, technological progress, institutional innovations and new social attitudes.

Feudal society was more or less stagnant, reproducing itself but without generating much development. Agriculture occupied around 80 per cent of the population. Production took place partly on large estates, managed by landlords, and partly in an open-field system, where peasants were in charge of production. There was slow technological progress and no fundamental changes to the institutions.

Economic development during the period 1750-1914 can be divided into two stages. In the first stage, the agricultural sector started to move.

Summary

In the second stage, economic integration between the rural and the urban sectors took off. The year 1850 has been chosen as the point of intersection between the two stages. It was around 1850 that extensive railway construction started to accelerate, promoting economic integration.

The first stage

During the first stage no economic development could have taken place without developments in agriculture, because agriculture encompassed nearly all the activities of society. Agriculture was caught in a productivity trap, with the three-field system in which one field was always laid fallow. If the fallow was taken into production, grain production could expand in the short run, but soil fertility would decrease in the longer run. The soil would be exhausted if there was either no time for recovery or no possibility of increasing the amount of manure for fertilisation. If the fallow system were abandoned, the supply of fodder for livestock would be reduced and so would the amount of manure. This vicious circle was broken when new crops, such as turnips and clover were introduced. Technological progress in the form of new crops made it possible to cultivate all three fields without making soil fertility poorer.

This technological change was combined with a series of agricultural reforms related to the methods of production, the ownership of the land and the relationships between peasants and landlords.

The open-field system was replaced by the consolidation of land holdings, which increased labour productivity by cutting out dead time. Farms were managed individually so farmers became accustomed to taking their own decisions. Private ownership made farmers more interested in working and investing in their farms. The legal protection of peasants made them more self-confident, and had a long-term effect on the establishment of a class of independent farmers.

The technological and institutional changes which started around 1750 were very much influenced by the ideas of the Age of Enlightenment. The period was influenced by ideas about rationality and human rights. The extent to which reforms were introduced depended on the attitudes of the monarch and of the land-owning class around him. In some cases, the landlords acted more as *rentiers* than as managers. They were mostly interested in receiving rents, and did not care about agricultural matters. When landlords were active managers, they were often split into two groups. One group was only interested in technological improvement and not interested in improving the position of the peasants. They were interested in introducing new technology on the estates managed by themselves, and were only interested in making improvements to the open-field system if it would lead to increased rents. The other group was interested both in technological improvements and in social improvements for the peasants. The position of the peasants attracted interest not only because of the ideas about human rights that were current, but also for purely economic reasons. This group of landowners believed that it was in their self-interest to improve conditions for the peasants. By doing so, they would become more productive and the landowners would obtain a benefit either from increased rents or by selling the land to the peasants on advantageous terms.

Some believed that technological change could be introduced without institutional change. Others believed that fundamental technological change could only be introduced in combination with institutional change. Experience shows that those countries that combined technological and institutional changes seemed to perform better, see Chapter 5.

During the first stage, industry played a minor role, apart from in Britain. Industrialisation was based on a series of technological innovations and some institutional changes. Production no longer took place in small craft units, but in factories with several workers under the same roof. The first round of industrialisation was based on the textile industry.

Technological and institutional changes in agriculture during the first stage, 1750-1850, got the agricultural sector moving. In feudal societies, agriculture was more or less stagnant, and it was only when technological and institutional changes started to occur that productivity increases accelerated. Technological and institutional changes made high demands on resources. The first changes were made using the internal resources of agriculture.

The second stage

Once the economic development of agriculture had started, it continued to develop. The reason for this was the introduction of further technological and institutional changes.

The increase in land productivity and labour productivity continued to accelerate through the nineteenth century up to 1914. This technological development was associated with improved inputs and new inputs.

The quality of the primary inputs, land, capital and labour was improved. The land was improved through investments in marling and

Summary

drainage. The capital stock was augmented. Livestock was improved by breeding programmes; arable production was improved by the introduction of new tools, new equipment and new machinery, such as seed drills, better ploughs, reaping and threshing machinery. The labour force became better educated.

New variable inputs were bought in from outside. Manure was supplemented by commercial fertilisers. Improved seed was developed through the selection principle. New protein-rich oilseed cake was introduced as supplementary feed.

The technological progress through improved inputs and new inputs also involved important institutional changes. Agricultural universities dealing with applied research and the education of agricultural specialists were founded, and so were experimental stations and agricultural schools. It is one thing to discover new and improved inputs, but it is another thing to disseminate know-how to farmers. Farmers' associations and extension services were needed for this task. Again, it is one thing to discover, a second thing to disseminate know-how, and a third thing to make inputs available. Farmers could only get the inputs if they were produced and available on the market.

Institutional changes, in the form of economic integration based on markets and the enabling environment, were a prerequisite. Infrastructural investments to facilitate transport and communication were necessary, as was the establishment of distribution channels. Farmers could only make the necessary investments if credit markets supplied funds.

The efficient functioning of markets not only depended on infrastructure, distribution channels and an enabling environment in the form of universities, experimental stations, agricultural schools, extension service systems, etc., it also depended on the rules and norms of society, and the initiatives and co-operation between farmers and between farmers and the rest of society. A well-educated class of peasants, who could take initiatives and who could co-operate, contributed to the development.

During the second stage, economic integration through markets was a fundamental part of the economic development. It required a high level of resources to set up markets and the enabling environment, and gradually improve the way in which markets operated.

This huge task could not be undertaken by the public sector alone. Close co-operation between the private and the public sectors was needed. The public sector had limited capacity, so success depended on contributions from the people in the private sector who were directly involved. A high degree of self-organisation among the peasants contributed to the solution of the task.

A great many steps had to be taken, and they could not all be taken at the same time. How should the different tasks be prioritised? It would make no sense to build a master plan following a fixed strategy. Such a strategy would need a development model, detailing how the development process occurs, but no such model exists.

A successful strategy uses the markets as a guide. When technological and institutional changes occur, new possibilities open up. When these possibilities are gradually realised, new obstacles or new bottlenecks to further development occur. These bottlenecks appear as no markets for inputs and services or as inefficiencies in existing markets. These non-existing or inefficient markets indicate where there is a need for further technological and institutional changes.

5. Agricultural reforms in Europe 1750-1914

Agricultural productivity depends on the farming system, and the farming system depends on three elements, namely: the methods of cultivation, the ownership of the land, and the social relations between the rural classes.

During the period 1750-1914 there were many important changes in the farming system in Europe due both to technological improvements and to institutional changes in the form of agricultural reforms. As shown in Section 4.5 there are a number of important elements to agricultural reforms. Some of them relate to the methods of cultivation, some relate to ownership, and others relate to the social position of the peasants.

The reforms occurred at different times in different parts of Europe. In terms of productivity, the most advanced agriculture in around 1750 was in Britain and the Low Countries. Agricultural reforms started in Britain with the enclosure movement in the eighteenth century. Agricultural reforms followed in other western European countries, such as Denmark, Germany and France. The Mediterranean countries were not immediately influenced by the new ideas which also came later to central and eastern Europe.

The extent of the reforms also varied between countries. The reforms were so fundamental that they changed societies and the lives of the different social classes, so it is natural that it often took a long time to make such far-reaching decisions and to implement the reforms.

The purpose of this chapter is to analyse the agricultural reforms in the different countries of Europe. When did they take place? Why did they take place in some countries and not in others? What were the ideological and political forces behind them? What was the content of the reforms? Agricultural reforms or the lack of them influenced agricultural performance. Other factors, such as the conditions of the markets and the enabling environment also had important impacts on agriculture, so the treatment of agricultural performance is postponed to Chapter 6, where all factors are taken into consideration.

5.1 The feudal system was not the same everywhere

The feudal system existed nearly everywhere in Europe up to about 1750. The feudal system was a preservative system and a constraint on development. While there were some common features in the feudal systems of the different European countries, the way the system worked differed as the peasantry was not equally oppressed in all countries. Social relationships between landlords and peasants differed in different parts of Europe.

The peasants could either work as villeins or serfs. The villeins were working at the estate, delivering villeinage, which was labour services, and they were personally free. The serfs were tied to their masters by hereditary personal bonds, forbidden to leave his service, unable, without permission, to marry a partner, who was not in his service, and unable to bequeath possessions to his children. The distinction had been blurred over time because serfs could be redeemed from all, or some of these servitudes and the freedom of ordinary villeins to leave the estates was often restricted. The landlord exercised jurisdiction over his peasants, usually without repeal.

This was the position of the peasants in medieval times nearly everywhere in Europe. Serfdom did exist in Britain when the Black Death broke out. In Denmark and the other Scandinavian countries serfdom in its strict sense was not known. Serfdom was never very common in France, but the distinction between serfs, who could hold land and have other possessions, and villeins, who were subject to restrictions on their personal freedom, became obscure.

It is difficult to come up with a general description of the peasants' conditions because they were not only different in different countries; they could also change from region to region and from time to time.

Europe was ravaged by the Black Death, which hit Europe for the first time in 1347. There were frequent renewed outbreaks of the plague over the next three centuries, but the worst period was from 1350 till about 1450, when the population of Europe fell between a quarter and half. Under the original system of feudalism, the lords competed with each other to attract peasants to fill empty plots or to open new land. The position of the landlords was weakened because it became more difficult to attract peasants after the fall in population. There was unavoidable competition between landlords to attract the peasants who provided their livelihood. Landlords were often in conflict about their rights over peasant communities, and the peasants could exploit this discord to obtain charters confirming their rights. As a result of the population crisis 1350-1450, the landlords had to restructure the system by which they took surpluses from their peasants. This was done in different ways in different parts of Europe (Brenner, 1997).

France

France, and the areas adjacent to it including parts of western Germany, was the original home of feudalism. The long-term result of the medieval crisis was the construction of the absolute state. Suffering from reduced revenues, the landlords were too weak to stand up to the monarch who expanded his power. The landlords were only too happy to co-operate with the monarch who granted them offices in a new centralised administration which was financed out of central tax revenues. In many cases the expanding absolutist state supported the peasants against local landlords as seigniorial rents competed with state taxes. The exploitation of the peasants continued as they became subject to the increasing taxation on which the officeholders of the state came to depend. There was a change in the feudal system, but the fundamental features of regeneration without renewal were preserved.

The Baltic area

In north-eastern Europe, east of the Elbe, and in eastern Germany and Poland, the feudal system developed later than in France and western Germany. The area east of the Elbe was colonised in the thirteenth century and the landlords, moving eastwards to open up vast estates, depended upon peasants to settle them. When the population in western Europe first stagnated and then declined, migration to the east stopped. The highly decentralised feudal structure, under which individual landlords tried to attract the necessary number of peasants, could not survive. In the long run, the problem was solved by constructing a new form of state in which competition between landlords was limited and peasant mobility restricted. The landlords organised themselves and formed local and national assemblies which defined the peasantry as being unfree and the property of their owners. Because of these rules, landlords east of the Elbe were able to extend considerably the size of their estates at the expense of the peasants' subsistence holdings. The peasants had to provide a far higher level of labour services than in western Europe.

England

In England, before the Black Death, the landlords were organised through the monarchic state, and they were able to achieve a high level of co-operation with each other in operating the decentralised system of exploitation by coercion. Feudal domination of the peasants was stronger in Britain than in France in this period. In the wake of the Black Death, the landlords tried to solve their problems by raising rents and tightening controls over peasant mobility. The peasants resisted, and by the first quarter of the fifteenth century they succeeded in winning personal freedom and securing low rents. This was a threat to the existence of the feudal structure.

After the Black Death, the landlords were unable to restore feudal domination, and they were not able to solve the problem in the same way as in France and western Germany by establishing an absolutist state.

In England, the landlords focused on their unconditional ownership of the land, and the concern of the landlords was to prevent a system where the peasants' rigthts prevented the landlords from getting the rents they wanted. The landlords wanted a system where their land was let to tenants who competed for leases

Different productivity in different parts of Europe

A series of data on yield ratios has been collected in a study of the agrarian history of western Europe (van Bath, 1963). The yield ratios show how much grain was harvested in relation to the grain sown. The conclusion of this study was that yield ratios in the countries bordering the North Sea (England, the Netherlands and Belgium) gradually increased from 4.5-5 in the 14th century to about 10 in around 1800. In the rest of Europe, progress had either been much slower (France, Germany, Italy and Spain) or non-existent (eastern Europe). As a result, a large productivity gap had developed across the continent.

These results have been confirmed by later studies (van Zanden, 1999). In around 1800 there was a significant difference between crop yields in different regions in Europe. According to the figures in Figure 5.1 the crop yield in England, the Netherlands and Belgium seems to have been around double the crop yield in the Mediterranean area, the Baltic area (Prussia, Poland and Lithuania) and Russia.

Figure 5.1: Estimated crop yields and yield ratio in four regions in around 1800 (Hectolitre per ha)

	North Sea	Mediterranean	Baltic	Russia
Crop yield	20	8 to 10	12	9
Yield ratio	10	5	4	3
Seed per ha	2	1.6 to 2	3	3

Source: van Zanden (1999)

The crop yield is equal to the yield ratio multiplied by the amount of seed used. The crop yield in the Baltic area and Russia was influenced by the fact that the seed sown per hectare was 50 per cent higher than in the North Sea area, so the crop yield underestimates the efficiency of agriculture in the north-western part of Europe compared with agriculture in eastern Europe.

The Netherlands is a special case in the sense that this region had not been under a feudal system since the Reformation. Friesland was not an attractive agricultural region and it was free from the interests of landlords. The rest of the land came into the hands of the rich bourgeoisie as the Netherlands developed into an important trading nation. The Netherlands became highly urbanised, and landowners introduced modern and profitable farming methods to satisfy the demand of the growing urban population (de Vries, 1997).

5.2 Britain

In the case of Britain, we must go further back in history than 1750. There were important changes in agriculture in the period 1500-1800. These changes were associated with Britain becoming first a leading commercial country, and then a leading commercial and industrial country.

The population increased from about 4 million in 1500 to 10 million in 1750 and to 21 million in 1820. In the same period, urbanisation started with London and in the eighteenth century other large cities grew up. The population of London is estimated to have been 40,000 in 1500, and it grew to 575,000 in 1700 and 865,000 in 1800 (de Vries, 1984).

These trends pulled agriculture up out of subsistence farming, and it became commercialised at an early stage. Food had to be supplied, especially to London. Textile products were needed, and the expansion of textile production from 1500 stimulated the demand for wool.

Two agricultural revolutions

It has been traditional to refer to the agricultural revolution in Britain in the eighteenth century. Recent studies suggest that it is more correct to speak about two agricultural revolutions, namely: the yeoman revolution 1500-1700 and the landlord revolution 1700-1800 (Allen, 1992).

The landlords were aristocrats and other large landowners. The yeomen were the class of farmers who owned or rented farms, and this was a relatively large group. A yeoman's holding was normally far smaller than the acreage of the landlord's estate, but a yeoman could own or rent as much as 200 acres of plough-land or 600 acres in grazing regions. "The yeoman was the country boy who practiced all the virtues lauded by Calvin" (Heaton, 1968). He was hard working, thrifty, land hungry, and when his business grew, he hired labour to help him.

The yeoman revolution 1500-1700 was prompted by the Black Death. The depopulation led to a concentration of land ownership. The large estate owners wanted to enclose the land and convert it into pasture, especially for wool production. As a result, in some cases, the open-field system based on small-scale agriculture disappeared. In most cases the open-field system continued, but the class of yeomen with larger holdings grew up, and the yeomen played a big role in introducing new crops and new farming techniques.

In the rural areas there were different classes. The large estate owners divided their interests between working their own lands and collecting rents from tenants. The yeomen were the bigger farmers who either owned or rented their land. There were still small-scale peasants in the village system, and landless agricultural labourers. A great amount of the cultivated land remained in open fields until the eighteenth century.

In the period 1500-1700 there was a rising demand for agricultural products. Prices were rising, and the large estate owners wanted to get more land and to raise the rents of their tenants. It was difficult to raise rents because they were fixed by custom, and it was not usually possible to terminate tenancies because the tenants were either copyholders or leaseholders. Copyholders had leases which were automatically transferred to the next generation, and leaseholders had life-long tenancies. During the period 1500-1700 the crown protected peasant farming. Freeholders who owned their own land were supported, and peasants' property rights were extended. The crown also supported tenants in their efforts to get long-term tenancies.

The landlord revolution took place in the eighteenth century as the open-field system disappeared and fields were enclosed. Landlords were eager to reorganise the farming system by taking more land in hand, especially village land, but the freedom to reorganise was restricted by the terms on which the peasants held their land. If a peasant was opposed to change, the only course open to the landlord was either to buy him out or to resort to an act of Parliament. Parliament was dominated by landlords and merchants who were interested in reforms. If a petition asking for permission to enclose land had been signed by landowners of a substantial majority of a district, permission by law was usually passed. The act would appoint commissioners whose task was to redistribute the land and to fix compensation to the satisfaction of all involved.

As a result of the eighteenth-century agricultural reforms, the class of yeomen disappeared, and a new farm structure arose in Britain. There were three classes: landlords, tenants and labourers. By around the middle of the nineteenth century, there were about 250,000 farmers and nearly 1 million hired labourers. The landlords owned most of the land. In 1873, half the land in England and Wales was owned by 2,250 persons in estates of 400 hectares and upwards, averaging 3,000 hectares apiece. The estates were split into medium-sized and large farms cultivated by tenants, who paid rents to the landlords. In 1910, tenants cultivated seven-eighths of the farms, and 90 per cent of the land (Heaton, 1968).

Political power and ideology

The political elite was interested in the agricultural reforms which took place in the eighteenth century, and which led to the concentration of land ownership in their hands. The landlords were interested in enlarging their properties because this gave them political power, social prestige and good rental income in prosperous years. Merchants, bankers and manufacturers were interested in acquiring land. The inheritance system favoured the concentration of land ownership. Once an estate had been acquired, it would pass undivided to the next generation, because the practice of primogeniture meant that only the eldest son inherited the estate. The "owner" would not be tempted to sell part of the estate, except under economic duress, because he did not enjoy unrestricted ownership, due to the entail system. He was obliged to pass his estate undivided to his son, and he could effectively be regarded as a life tenant.

The prevailing ideology also had an impact on agricultural development in Britain. Mercantilism, which is based on the idea of state intervention, was much less rooted in Britain than in France. Liberal ideas on economics were relatively well accepted, even before the liberal doctrine propounded in *The Wealth of Nations* by Adam Smith in 1776. According to the liberal philosophy, landlords and those who wanted to own land should be free to acquire as much land as they wanted. This attitude was reinforced by the belief that large-scale farming was most efficient. This opinion was influenced by Arthur Young (1741 – 1820), who wrote extensively on agriculture. Arthur Young travelled around Europe, and in France he met the physiocrats, among whom was F. Quesnay who made a distinction between *grande culture* and *petite culture*. Quesnay considered the *grande culture* in Britain to be a model for French agriculture. Young accepted Quesnay's idea about the efficiency of large farms. Large farmers had better access to finance than small farmers, so the amalgamation of farms led to increased capital intensity, greater employment, and higher yields. After travelling in France, and witnessing the inefficiency of small farms, Young's enthusiasm for large-scale farming turned into a rejection of peasant proprietorship.

Was the capitalist farming system necessary for agriculture to develop?

The development of British agriculture does not prove that the abandonment of the open-field system was a necessary pre-requisite for productivity growth. Crop yields and labour productivity doubled during the period 1500-1800, and recent studies have indicated that enclosures, as such, were not the main cause (Allen, 1992; Campbell and Overton, 1991; Overton, 1996). The performances of open-field farming and enclosed farming have been compared. Open-field villages did adopt the new farming methods and a large share of the increase in productivity took place in the period 1500-1700 when the yeoman revolution occurred. The yield was only slightly higher in the enclosed areas than in the open-field villages.

Half of the increase in labour productivity during the period 1500-1800 was due to higher output with a constant labour during the yeoman revolution in the seventeenth century. The other half occurred in the eighteenth century in the heyday of the landlord revolution. The enclosure movement brought about a shift from more labour-intensive cereal production to a less labour-intensive pattern of production based on pasturage. The increase in labour productivity was based on a decline in labour input without any significant increase in yields.

Enclosures changed the farm structure towards bigger farm units. This shift in structure did not in itself increase agricultural output. Small units produced more per hectare than the bigger units, but enclosures meant that the size of the agricultural labour force declined. When British agriculture was seen as the most advanced in Europe, this was due to high labour productivity.

Medium and smaller scale agriculture played an important role in Britain in the period 1500-1700. It made significant contributions to the increase in agricultural productivity. Enclosures and large-scale farming, which predominated in the 1700s, wiped out small-scale farming. On the basis of the evidence, it does not seem that the large-scale farming strategy was necessary for obtaining high yields and technological improvement.

Enclosures caused greater inequality

The enclosures of the eighteenth century caused increased inequality in income distribution, just like the industrial revolution. Tories and Marxists agreed on that point, although their explanations differed.

Marxists found two causes for the greater inequality, namely: the concentration of property ownership, and the falling demand for labour. Enclosures and farm amalgamations squeezed out small-scale farmers and deprived the peasantry of their land. The possibilities for obtaining alternative income were few. The demand for labour in agriculture decreased and industry could not absorb the unemployed.

The Tories did not accept the view that there was a falling demand for labour in agriculture, and they did not consider the concentration of land ownership to be problem, because it was legitimate and caused an increase in agricultural output. They explained the low wage rate by the Malthusian population theory.

Did large-scale farming contribute to industrialisation?

When agriculture is the dominant sector, it is obvious that other sectors, such as trade and industry, can only grow by receiving resources from agriculture.

Agricultural surpluses were necessary to feed the labour leaving agriculture. While labour was leaving agriculture, there are differing opinions about the absolute number of people working in agriculture.

The view of the landlords was expressed by Arthur Young (Mingay, 1975). The Tory view was that enclosures and large-scale farming contributed to an increase in employment in agriculture, and a large increase in production due to productivity gains. The increase of the total population was greater than the increase in agricultural employment, so labour from rural areas was leaving agriculture to work in the growing urban industries. Karl Marx, on the other hand, thought that the absolute level of agricultural employment fell due to enclosures. Marx found that large-scale, enclosed agriculture reduced employment per hectare (Marx, 1867). Capitalist farming reduced agricultural employment and the labour released could not find employment in the cities and joined the army of the unemployed.

According to the Tory view, large-scale farming made a positive contribution to industrialisation. Without the increased agricultural production and the migration of labour, industry could not have developed as positively as it did. The Marxist view was less positive, because the increased labour productivity in agriculture was due to a reduction of the size of the agricultural labour force, and the labour released was unable to find employment. The urban sector could not absorb the increased labour force. When small-scale farmers are capable of introducing new technology, the agricultural sector can increase production without releasing labour with no alternative employment possibilities.

In spite of the increased unemployment, Marx favoured large-scale farming, which he considered more efficient. Agricultural development in Britain was incorporated into his theory of historical development. Enclosures and large-scale farming were progressive and desirable because they created a society that would make socialism possible, and indeed inevitable.

Who were right, the Tories or the Marxists? The recent studies referred to above seem to support the Marxist view. Employment in agriculture did fall due to enclosures.

The importance of large-scale farming for the industrialisation in Britain can be questioned. A strategy based on smaller farm units and private ownership might have been a better solution. Agriculture delivered surplus production to the non-agricultural sector. Labour was released from agriculture, but all the labour could not be absorbed by industry.

The relationship between landlords and tenants

As a result of enclosures, the land was merged into relatively large farm units owned by the landlords but worked by tenants, so the relationship between landlords and tenants was important. This relationship was dominated by three aspects: the length of the lease, the amount of the rent, and the source from which capital for improvements was to be drawn. The relationships were mixed, as can be imagined, because the parties had both shared and opposing interests. They had shared interests in increasing earnings through higher productivity, because the landlords could get higher rents and the tenants could get higher living standards at the same time. If earnings stagnated or fell, due to falling prices, they would both be interested in getting as large a share as possible. During the period of enclosures, the landlords encouraged tenants to improve their holdings by giving them long leases and promising to compensate them for any capital and labour they sank into improvements. After the period of enclosures, tenancy agreements were made for shorter periods, which could be an advantage for tenants in times of falling prices, because rents was paid cash, not in kind.

5.3 France

Ownership and cultivation

In eighteenth century France, the land belonged to the crown, the church and landlords who were aristocrats or wealthy townspeople. Most landlords were not entrepreneurs but passive *rentiers*. Around one-third of the land was occupied by *censiers*, who were perpetual hereditary tenants, comparable to the English copyholders. A large part of the remaining land was leased to tenants called *métayers*. The holdings of the *métayers* were usually small and their farming was based on share-cropping, where the landlord often got one half of the produce and the tenant kept the rest. The *métayers* were smallholders, who lived under poor conditions similar to landless labourers.

The share-cropping system was inefficient because it induced peasants to produce less than they would have with a fixed rent. With decreasing marginal productivity, the variable marginal costs increase after a certain production level is reached. The increasing marginal curve constitutes the supply curve for the peasant. The optimal supply is reached when the marginal revenue, which is the price, is equal to the marginal costs. Share-cropping means that the peasant has to pay all the variable costs but gets only half the revenue when he has to deliver half the harvest as rent.

If the rent is fixed, there is an incentive to increase production. However, the share-cropping system has the advantage of reducing risk. If the harvest fails the rent paid to the landlord is automatically reduced, which would not be the case if the rent were fixed.

The limited influence of the physiocrats

Around 1750, the higher rate of population growth and rising agricultural prices stimulated the interest of some landlords in changing the open-field farming system to raise productivity. Agricultural improvements and reforms were discussed in French *salons*. The physiocrats believed agriculture to be the most important activity, and they wanted to increase production and productivity through agricultural reforms. They were greatly inspired by the enclosure movement in England.

Improved agricultural conditions offered two different courses for landlords to follow. The first course was the passive one, where landlords took advantage of the improved conditions by raising the rents and dues paid by the peasants. The second course was the more active one, where landlords could try to change farming conditions. They might try to abolish the common right to graze cattle after the harvest and to divide and enclose the common and waste lands, where new farms could be established. This latter strategy had some success from 1760-1780, when the state passed a series of decrees, one authorizing the abolition of common grazing rights, a second permitting the division of common land and a third encouraging the cultivation of waste land by exempting improved land from taxation. One of the leading physiocrats, Jacques Turgot, became Minister of Finance from 1774-76 and promoted agricultural reforms, but he was dismissed and the physiocrat ideas did not have a significant impact. Most landlords were only interested in getting higher rents, and the peasants, especially the *métayers*, resisted giving up their common rights.

The French Revolution

When the Revolution came in 1789, the peasants' demands were presented to the Assembly of the Estates. They wanted three things: 1) a limitation or reduction of the rights of landlords, 2) more land from the crown, the church and the large estates, 3) a ban on enclosures and a guarantee of pasture rights. The first demand was granted. The landlords were stripped of their judicial powers and lost the income derived from their positions as local judges. The *censiers* still had to pay rent, unless they took over ownership from the landlords. To obtain ownership, the censiers had to pay an amount equivalent to 20 - 25 times the annual rent. However, the *censiers* refused to pay either rent or the redemption amount. In the turmoil of 1793, the *censiers* were officially excused from

France

all payments of any kind, so they became proprietors of their farms (Bloch, 1931).

The second demand was not satisfactorily met. Land belonging to the crown, the church, and the emigrés passed to the state and was sold at auction in order to raise revenue. The largest purchasers were men with money, namely landlords wishing to add to their estates, large farmers and prosperous peasants. Landlords who did not emigrate retained their property and in many cases the emigrés bought back their own estates through friends and agents. Only some small proprietors got more land. There was no large-scale transfer of land to the peasants, and the great estates continued to exist.

The third demand was not well received by the legislative assembly which believed in individual freedom. Proprietors were given the right to work their land as they wished, enclosure was authorised, and pasture rights were restricted. The Revolution opened up for individual freedom in the cultivation of holdings in place of co-ordinated village management. However, the vast majority of peasants still had smallholdings fragmented into many small strips. In practice these decisions made little difference to the land use, because they were poorly and slowly implemented. There were several reasons for this. The peasants were strongly opposed to change, and the landlords were not as powerful as they were in Britain where they alone, or with the assistance of the enclosure commissioners, implemented the reforms.

It can be concluded that the result of the Revolution was more a modification than a transformation of rural society. As for the methods of cultivation, the pre-revolutionary system continued. The gainers were the *censiers*, who became owners of their farms, but the *metayers* and the landless labourers did not improve their lot.

Little progress during the nineteenth century

The enclosure movement in France was nearly at a standstill during the first half of the nineteenth century. The old open-field and strip system prevailed.

The period 1850-1875 was a generally prosperous one for agriculture, but French agriculture could not take full advantage of the positive trend. The reason was that French agriculture had not undertaken the necessary reforms. Progress in the second half of the nineteenth century was slow. Much of the French countryside was still dominated by subsistence farming. There was little contact with the market, the educational level was low and illiteracy was widespread. The farming methods were traditional and productivity was low (Weber, 1977).

From 1870, the domestic food market was influenced by the stagnating population. The French population did not grow from 1870 to 1940, and it has been argued that this hampered the modernisation of agriculture. The scarcity of hired labour was a constraint on the consolidation of smaller farms into larger units with higher productivity.

Small-scale farming in France

In contrast to Britain, French agriculture developed as *petite agriculture*. Before the Revolution, the primogeniture and entail systems, which were practised in Britain (as described above), did exist in France, but the practice of dividing property equally among heirs was widespread. The Revolution abolished the primogeniture and entail systems and made the equal division of property compulsory. This principle was kept in the Code Napoleon and, as a result, the farm structure in France became fragmented into a large number of small holdings. The small size of agricultural holdings in France was a social advantage because farming could absorb some of the population growth. Industrialisation started in around 1830 in Northern France, but it was much weaker than in Britain, so there was not a similar demand for labour in the industrial sector. When agricultural modernisation started in around 1850, most of the smallholdings were subsistence farms using traditional methods. The peasantry was uneducated and lacked the necessary capital resources for improvement.

Just before the First World War, France had about 5½ million farm units or almost the same as the USA at that time. A little less than 40 per cent of these were of 1 hectare or less and a little more than 40 per cent had a land area of between 1 and 10 hectares. Two-thirds of the land, comprising four-fifths of the holdings, was worked by the owners. The remainder was cultivated by tenants and *metayers*, and some tenants held large farms comparable to those in England (Heaton, 1968).

Differences between France and Britain

There were significant differences between agricultural development in France and in Britain. Firstly, in the eighteenth century new crops and new technology became available, but unlike Britain these were not widely introduced in France. Some reform-minded landowners, influenced by the physiocrat school, became aware of the disadvantages of the open-field and strip system in France. These people looked with envy to the English enclosures and English farming techniques. But many landlords were resident at the Court, and their interest in their land was limited to collecting rents and using their estates for pleasure.

Secondly, while there was a revolution in France, it did not have a significant impact on agriculture. The feudal privileges were swept away and one group of farmers, the *censiers*, obtained full ownership of their holdings. But the French Revolution did not change the farm structure significantly. The large estates and the land formerly owned by the crown, the church and the *emigrés* were still kept as large estates. Some rich bourgeoisie now became large estate owners together with the existing class of landlords. There was no profound change in the farm system. In the mid-nineteenth century, French agriculture was still characterised by having a few large estates and very many small and fragmented farms. There was little technological improvement in the first half of the nineteenth century. Productivity remained low and most of the population still worked on the land.

Thirdly, the inheritance system differed between Britain and France. In Britain, the inheritance system contributed to the concentration of land ownership in the hands of a small group of estate owners. In France, the inheritance system led to a parcelling out of the land to more smallholders.

5.4 Germany

Some landlords and public administrators in Germany were aware of the new ideas and agricultural reforms in Britain and France after 1750. However, very little action was taken until the French occupation of western Germany after 1793, and the French defeat of the Prussians at Jena in 1806.

Personal freedom and ownership in western Germany

In the French-occupied western part of Germany, the French improved the status of the peasants by securing their legal rights. Unlike the *censiers* in France, the peasants in western Germany did not become owners of their farms. The peasants were either perpetual or short-term tenants, and this system continued until the Revolution in 1848. The 1848 revolution started among urban workers and middle-class liberals, but the peasants joined them because of their desperate situation which was partly due to the failure of the potato crop in the previous years. The rulers wanted to split the alliance and decided to free the peasants from their landlords and to let them keep the whole of their holdings by paying compensation in a long series of small instalments. The peasants bought their own farms and the western and south-western part of Germany became, together with France, an area dominated by small peasant properties.

Personal freedom and ownership in eastern Germany

East of the Elbe, in Prussia, some reforms were also introduced after the defeat by Napoleon in 1806. It was recognised that the military strength of France was based on the liberated peasantry, while the Prussian army was made up of unfree peasant soldiers, lacking patriotic fighting spirit. Therefore, in 1807 an edict of emancipation proclaimed a comprehensive list of new freedoms. One of the most important changes was the abolition of personal serfdom. The personal rights of the peasants were improved, but there was no change in their economic position in relation to their landlords, because they still had to pay the old dues in labour services, in kind or in cash. In 1811, a decree made it possible for a tenant to become the owner of his farm and all his land if he paid a sum corresponding to twenty-five times the annual rent, or surrendered a share of the land to the landlord as compensation for keeping the rest. Hereditary tenants had to surrender one-third, and the non-hereditary tenants had to surrender one half of their land in payment. This meant that the large estates increased in size. The small and medium-sized holdings became so small after surrendering the share to the landlord that they could either not survive, or could only survive if the owner supplemented his income by working for the landlord.

Different size structures in western and eastern Germany

In the German area, it is important to distinguish between the area west of the Elbe, and the area east of the Elbe. In the western parts of Germany, many landlords were mainly interested in the rents they could obtain from the peasants. Often they did not live on their estates, but had posts in government service, the army or the church. Most of the land was worked by peasants on small farms. In the eastern part of Germany, the landlords ran their own estates, and relied on labour services from peasants and labourers. The landowners (*junkers*) and other large farmers succeeded in increasing the size of their holdings. The great mass of peasants either

Germany

became landless or workers with very small parcels of land. These peasants could either choose to work on the estate or to seek employment in the growing industrial sector. In around 1900, nearly half the arable land in Prussia was cultivated by the one per cent of landowners holding more than 100 hectares. In the rest of Germany, farms of more than 100 hectares only represented 10 per cent of the land (Tracy, 1982).

Farm consolidation was slow

The peasants' personal rights were improved when the French invaded western Germany and defeated Prussia. The transformation of peasants from tenants to owners was completed in around 1870 with very different size structures west and east of the Elbe. The consolidation of the scattered land, abolition of common pasture rights and the division of common land took even longer. Progress was slow. It took place chiefly during the nineteenth century, and it affected the east more than the west. At the outbreak of the First World War, much of the land was still cultivated in scattered strips, especially in the western part of Germany.

Early financial reforms in Germany

Agricultural reforms and agricultural development require investments and long-term financing. When agriculture moves from more or less subsistence farming to commercial farming, it is important that short-term credit is available at a reasonable interest rate.

The financial markets, created in connection with the industrialisation, do not necessarily serve the needs of the agricultural sector. It is important to create a rural credit market so that rural savings can be stimulated and allocated efficiently. It is also important to introduce credit instruments, which make it easy for farmers to get the necessary funds cheaply.

These general remarks are made in relation to Germany, because Germany was the first country to find ways out of the farm credit problem. Two new kinds of co-operative credit systems were introduced and the new methods of rural financing were copied throughout Europe, and later in the USA.

In 1770, the first Land Mortgage Credit Association was formed. The association was a co-operative in which the farmers were members. The purpose was to obtain loans for the members. The association issued bonds, which were backed by all the property of all the members. The credit system was a great advantage for borrowers and lenders. Borrowers could easily get credit for up to two-thirds of the value of their property. Lenders had greater security for their loans, because of the joint and several liability of the farmers, and the interest rate was low because the risk premium was nearly zero. And the margin between the interest rates of the borrower and the lender was small because the administrative costs were low.

In 1849 Friedrick Raiffeisen founded the first co-operative bank. The idea was to establish a co-operative in which the people of the district could deposit their savings and from which the local farmers could borrow. The members contributed only a small membership fee, but they accepted unlimited liability, which meant that they put all their property behind the bank as a guarantee of its solvency. Each bank was small and the members lived in the village. The lending decisions depended on an evaluation of the personal character of the applicant, his ability as a farmer, and his project.

5.5 Denmark

Personal freedom, ownership and farm consolidation

In around 1750, nearly all the land in Denmark belonged to large estates, which were owned by the crown and the aristocracy. The land belonging to an estate was divided into estate land, which was consolidated land worked on the estate owner's account by peasants and landless labourers, and village land, which was cultivated by peasants who were tenants using the open-field system.

The rise in agricultural prices from 1750 to 1815 was a strong incentive for landlords to increase production through higher productivity and by extending the cultivated area. The landlords were divided into two groups. One group wanted to extend the area of the land managed by themselves. This land was to be worked by squeezing as much service as possible out of the peasants. These landlords were only interested in technological changes that could directly improve productivity, and they were not interested in the emancipation of the peasants or in land ownership by the peasants. The peasants were against reducing the area of village land with the open-field system, and against the enclosure of common land by the landlords. Traditionally, the Danish monarchy protected the peasants and opposed integrating the village land and common land into the estates of the landlords.

Denmark

Another group of landlords was not only interested in improving productivity, but also in the emancipation of the peasants. Some of the families of the leading landlords originally came from Germany. They were inspired by the ideas of the Enlightenment, and they realised that every reform which contributed to increased productivity of the village land would be beneficial to them. The village land was owned by the landlord, and increased productivity would increase the rental of the land.

The first agricultural reforms were planned and implemented in the period 1755-1772. In the following period, 1772-1784, more conservative landlords were in power and the reforms were nearly brought to a halt. In 1784, progressive landlords took power, and up to the end of the century, there was a series of important decrees dealing with farming methods, peasant land-ownership, the limitation of labour service, and the legal protection of peasants. It took time to implement the reforms, and by around 1830 the open-field farming system had been replaced nearly everywhere by privately owned farms, where the land had been consolidated and farms had been moved out from the village and placed on the land belonging to them.

The content of the reforms

One group of landlords wanted the reforms to be limited to farming methods. Another group wanted the reforms also to include peasant ownership and improved legal rights for peasants. In the end, the reforms including all these elements.

The open-field system was abandoned. The land was consolidated, and the farms were moved out from the villages. The peasants took over ownership of the land, and this was financed by the landlords. They found that they could gain more by selling the land than by keeping the peasants as tenants. The instalments paid by the peasants to the landlords covered the redemption of the loans and the interest.

Nowhere in Europe were such comprehensive agricultural reforms decided on and implemented in such a relatively short time. The agricultural reforms were not the result of a well-conceived master plan, but they were decided pragmatically, bit by bit, as the problems arose.

Large peasant sector

The leading agricultural reformers had close ties with Germany. In some of the smaller principalities in western Germany, cameralist ideas were influential. The cameralists were interested in social matters, but they were also interested in purely technical matters. The agricultural sector could be developed either according to the philosophy of the cameralists or the physiocrats. The physiocrats were in favour of the *grande culture* as developed in Britain. Against this, the cameralists emphasised the importance of there being a multiplicity of individual farms. They wanted the land to be parcelled out from the large estates, labour services abolished and peasant ownership introduced. There is no doubt that the cameralist philosophy had an important impact on agricultural development in Denmark, which did not focus on the *grand culture*. In Demark the focus was on the middle-sized farm.

By and large, the agricultural reforms had been implemented by around 1830. The result was a bimodal production structure with few large estates on the one hand, and numerous medium-sized and small farms on the other. The large estates were more productive and were commercialised, whereas the smaller farmers were more or less subsistence farmers. However, the agricultural reforms had laid the foundations for future developments.

The period 1830-1875 is called the "grain sales" period because of the major exports of grain, especially to Britain. From 1850 there was a shift in the production pattern because from then on animal production increased more than arable production.

Early education

At a very early stage, the peasants in Denmark received education. In 1814, a school law was passed which introduced a compulsory 7 years of education for all children. The early introduction of general education played an important role in the development of Danish agriculture. During the grain sales period, 1830-1875, a new peasant culture, based on self-organisation, was developed. The peasants took a series of initiatives on cultural, socio-economic and political matters.

Culturally, the peasants took initiatives to form free congregations, independent schools and especially folk high schools. The folk high schools, which had no exams, were based on discussion and dialogue about all kind of spiritual and political matters, and engaged the interests of young rural people, who later became farmers.

Socio-economically, the peasants formed farmers' unions, agricultural schools, savings banks and mortgage associations. The farmers' unions arranged lectures and discussions, and they contributed to the dissemination of information about new production methods, just like agricultural schools. Farmers' unions also started to undertake research.

The peasants organised credit institutions such as saving banks and mortgage associations. From 1850 and in the following decades a wave of credit institutions were established.

Politically, the peasants manifested themselves through political parties and through the press.

In around 1850, British agriculture was the most efficient in Europe. Apart from Britain, Danish agriculture was second to none in Europe in the mid-nineteenth century. Danish agriculture was well equipped to take advantage of the prosperous period, 1850-1875, and to meet the challenges of the following period, 1875-1895, with its hard competition and falling prices.

The co-operative movement

Through the agricultural reforms and the self-organisation of farmers, a social capital was built up in Danish agriculture and society. This social capital was undoubtedly an important element behind the co-operative movement, which swept the country in the period 1875-1914. The co-operative movement took root in a period of rapid expansion of the dairy and pig sectors.

5.6 Mediterranean countries

In northern Europe, agricultural reforms changed the economic and social conditions of agriculture. The product range also changed. New crops were introduced already in the eighteenth century and new livestock products, such as dairy products, were produced on a large scale in the second half of the nineteenth century. In the Mediterranean countries there were neither agricultural reforms nor the introduction of new products. These countries were still producing the old staples, such as wheat, rice, fruit, wine, olive oil and silk, both for the domestic market and foreign markets. There were no great changes in the agrarian societies in Italy and Spain. Agricultural reform did not penetrate Southern Europe. Land was held in large estates by the rulers, the aristocracy, the church and rich townspeople. In regions with intensive and irrigated cultivation, the land was usually worked by tenants in smallholdings. They either enjoyed hereditary possession and paid fixed dues, or worked on a sharecropping basis. In northern Italy there were both bigger and smaller farms; there were hereditary tenants and sharecropping tenants. In central Italy, in the hill country, sharecropping tenants predominated, and in the south, large estates (*latifundia*) were cultivated by labourers.

In Savoy, in northern Italy, there were some reforms at an early stage. Already during the period 1760-1780, the peasants obtained their personal freedom. When northern Italy was conquered by Napoleon, the position of the peasants was strengthened. At the time of Italian unification in the 1860s, many of Italy's leaders were inspired by English agricultural practices and English economic development.

There was little agricultural change in Spain until the twentieth century. Large estates prevailed as great units in the central and southern part of the country, producing commodities such as wheat, grapes, olives or wool with a legion of labourers. In the North, the land was divided into small-holdings with scattered strips and with tenancies based on sharecropping.

5.7 Austria-Hungary and the Balkans

Product specialisation

The Austro-Hungarian Empire lasted until 1918. In the second half of the nineteenth century, its economic cohesion was based on the Danube and its tributaries, on a good railway system and on the commercial and financial services of Vienna. There was a high degree of specialisation between the different countries and regions of the Empire, so that economically it was a disadvantage when, after the First World War, the large free-trade area was broken up into a series of small national states, each protecting its own interests.

There was also a specialisation in agriculture. Austria did not have much cereal cultivation, but concentrated on livestock. Bohemia grew sugar beet and grain crops, and Hungary was the granary. The land in Hungary was a part of the great grassy plain which also covered large parts of Romania, and it proved to have rich arable soil, when ploughed up.

The Danube area

The ploughing up of the Danube prairie was stimulated when foreign markets were made accessible by the opening of the Black Sea to navigation. This happened in 1829, when Turkey was compelled to open the Bosporus and the Dardanelles to the merchant ships of all powers at peace with her. In 1856, navigation of the Danube was made free to the ships of all nations. When railways were built from the river to the plains, the work of converting much of the land in Hungary and Romania into large grain farms began.

Different farm structures

The agricultural structure before the First World War differed between Austria, Hungary, the central and western Balkans and Romania. In Austria the peasants had become proprietors of their land, and farms were generally small. In Hungary the land was held and farmed by large owners who hired labourers. There was a rural proletariat of about 4 million agricultural workers in Hungary, second only to Italy with 4.5 million rural labourers just before the First World War. In the central and western Balkans, villages combined individual cultivation of small plots with common use of the rest of the land for grazing of sheep, goats and pigs. They originally paid tribute, usually a part of the produce, to some Turkish lord, but when the Turks left, the peasants usually took over the land for themselves. On the rich Romanian plains the landlords managed large estates, and when the profitability of commercial grain growing increased, the landlords extended their domains by taking over more land from the peasants. The peasants and labourers lived under a system of serfdom and there were rural revolts. In 1864, a liberal minded king abolished serfdom, and it was decided that the peasants should retain their land, but compensate their landlords for the loss of their land and feudal dues. These reforms were not successful. In around 1900, approximately 40 per cent of the arable land belonged to estates of 500 hectares or more, and these were operated as large grain farms. Few peasants had enough land for their livelihood, and many had less (Basch, 1943).

5.8 Russia

Serfdom

In 1800, the population of Russia was about 40 million. Nearly all the population lived west of a line running from St. Petersburg to Moscow and then towards the south-east. About one-tenth of the population belonged to noble landowning families, the church and the small, but growing middle-class (Pokrovsky, 1933). Some of the rest were free farmers, but most were either crown peasants, who lived on state land and were personally free, or they were serfs on the estates owned by the landlords. Serfdom in Russia was serfdom in its most complete form. Serfdom is the state where one person is permanently subordinated to the authority of another person. The serf is bound to the land where he/she works. A serf is not free to choose occupation, spouse or to move away without the consent of the landlord. The landlord had jurisdiction over the serfs. A serf was not a slave who could be sold but a serf belonged to the estate. The peasants divided their time between cultivating their landlord's domain and cultivating their own share of the village land. Over most of Russia, the serfs were not so much individuals as members of a village community, where the village council shared out the arable fields in strips between families according to the number of people in the family. Redistribution of the land took place from time to time to take account of population changes.

Reforms came late

There was no change to the status of the peasants before 1861. The Crimean War 1854-1856 was lost, and this convinced the Czar that agricultural reforms were necessary for the development of the country. The Edict of Emancipation 1861, liberated the serfs from their landlords, but it did not liberate the land from the landlord. It was agreed among the landlords and the government that the peasants, or rather the village community, retained about half the land. The village community could either rent it or buy it from the landlords, who owned the village land. In the latter case, the government paid the owner in bonds, and the village community became responsible for collecting the money to repay the government in instalments spread over nearly 50 years. By 1880 about 85 per cent of the peasants had begun to buy, and in 1881 it became compulsory for the peasants to buy, but at reduced prices.

It was only in the second half of the nineteenth century that the peasants got their personal freedom and became owners of half the land. The period 1861-1905 was a difficult one for the peasants, in spite of their emancipation. In this period, the population increased by 80 per cent; the average farm-holding became smaller, and there were no great productivity gains in the village-community farming, because it was difficult to acquire the necessary capital.

Financing problems

Self-financing was difficult, because the peasants were squeezed economically. Agricultural prices were falling from 1875, and the peasants had to get cash to pay the instalments and taxes to the government. These resources were taken out of agriculture because the agricultural contribution to the fiscal budget was not returned as assistance for agricultural improvements. Domestic capital formation was so small that Russia had to import capital, and especially in the 1890s the available capital was invested in railway construction and on subsidising the growth of industry. Agricultural borrowing was difficult, and interest rates were high due to the lack of capital.

Improvements at the beginning of the twentieth century

Russia entered the twentieth century with its rural problem more acute than ever. Millions of peasants were land-hungry, food-hungry and in arrears with their instalments. The revolution in 1905 was mainly an urban revolt, but the peasants won some concessions. The remaining instalments were cancelled, and large areas of state land were made available for sale. In 1906, a more far-reaching reform was decided, aimed at emancipating the peasants from the village community. The prime minister decreed that any villager could withdraw his holding into a separate farm, and that the whole village could liquidate itself as land controller by a majority vote.

The situation of the peasants improved up to the First World War. Some peasants sold their land and went off to the cities, went to Siberia, or emigrated. Central and local government became more supportive of the farmers. A state land bank helped in the purchase of land, and by 1914 four-fifths of the arable land in European Russia was peasant property (Pokrovsky, 1933). Agricultural co-operation spread quickly and productivity increased due to the use of modern farm implements and better breeding and feeding practices in the livestock sector. The expansion of industrial centres provided larger domestic markets for food products.

However, these developments had not gone far enough to enable the country to cope with the situation in 1914. Production was well maintained, so the revolt in 1917 was not due to a collapse of the economy, but it was due to the inability of the Czar's autocratic administration to distribute the substantial supplies of food. So, Russian agriculture was well on its way to improvement when the Bolsheviks took over in 1917, followed by the turbulent period of civil war, 1917-1920.

Agricultural reforms in Europe 1750-1914

5.9 Summary

Over the last 250 years there have been tremendous agricultural developments in Europe and the USA. These developments were due to technological and institutional changes. There were two sets of important changes, namely: agricultural reforms and economic integration.

This chapter deals with agricultural reforms in different countries and different parts of Europe. It is interesting to compare different countries and different regions. Agricultural reforms encompass a series of reforms relating to farming techniques, land ownership and social relations between the different groups, especially the relationship between landlords and peasants.

The agricultural conditions differed in the different parts of Europe when the agricultural reforms started. Although the feudal system existed nearly everywhere in Europe, the peasantry was not equally oppressed in all countries. It seems that the position of the peasants was better in Britain than in France and western Germany. East of the Elbe, in the Baltic area and Russia, the peasants still lived under a system of serfdom. Productivity in Britain and the Low Countries was at least double the productivity elsewhere in Europe so the initial conditions for development were more favourable in Britain, when the population growth accelerated from around 1750.

The adjustment to the increased demand for food also differed in the different countries. In Britain the enclosure movement, driven by the desire of the landlords to acquire more land, eliminated the open-field system and the class of freeholders. The class of large estate owners owned nearly all the land, and it was divided into relatively large farm holdings cultivated by tenants, who paid rent.

The agricultural reforms in Britain were based on capitalist farming, and this contributed to a disproportionate distribution of income and wealth. It cannot be concluded that this strategy was necessary to support industrialisation. It has been argued that more people were released from agriculture than could be absorbed by the expansion of industry.

Agricultural reforms depended on the attitudes of the monarchs and the landlords, which were influenced by the prevailing ideology. The rulers of some of the smaller states in Germany, such as Bavaria, and the rulers in Denmark and in the Savoy in northern Italy were reform-minded. They wanted to restrain the desire of landlords to acquire land from the peasants; they supported the enforcement of the legal rights of peasants and the reduction of dues and labour services, which the peasants had to provide. They were inspired not only by the ideas of the Enlightenment, but also by cameralist thinking, which focused on the

Summary

strength and finances of the state. It was a kind of mercantilist thinking which emphasized the importance of a numerous and prosperous peasantry to ensure a strong state.

In France, in the last half of the eighteenth century, the landlords tried to benefit from rising prices by taking over land from the peasants and increasing the dues and labour services of the peasants. The king of France was an exception among the rulers in western Europe at the time. He was one of the few rulers who did not try to persuade the landlords to agree to reforms to improve the status and reduce the obligations of the peasants. The peasants took part in the Revolution, but the agricultural changes were modest. The landlords' rights were reduced; the *censiers* acquired private ownership and individual farming became possible, but the old open-field and strip cultivation system still prevailed.

Because of the inheritance system, the land was fragmented into an increasing number of ever smaller holdings. The farming methods were traditional and productivity was low. During the nineteenth century, French agriculture was initially stagnant and then developed very slowly. One reason was the slower industrialisation of France compared to England; another reason was the stagnation of the population from 1870.

In Germany, the agricultural conditions differed widely between western and eastern Germany. In western Germany the farming system was similar to the system in France with many small farms. In the west, the rulers supported the peasants against the landlords. In Prussia, the king, Frederick the Great, tried to restrain the landlords from taking over more peasant land, but without great success. As a result of the Napoleonic wars, the peasants in eastern Germany were emancipated. The peasants could become owners of their land if they surrendered a large share of it to the landlords. In western Germany, the large landowners refrained from taking over more peasant land, and after 1848 the peasants obtained ownership of their land. In eastern Germany the large estate owners succeeded in taking peasant land. The result was a class of landless labourers who had to work on the large estates, and a class of smallholders who often had to find additional income outside their farms.

The transformation from tenancy to ownership was completed by around 1870 with two different size structures in east and west. The consolidation of the scattered land had largely been completed in the east, but even by the outbreak of First World War land consolidation had not been completed in the west.

In France and Germany the peasants got personal rights at the time of the Revolution and the Napoleonic wars. It took longer to acquire ownership of the land and even longer to move from the open-field and strip system to the consolidated farm system. In contrast, all the different aspects of agricultural reforms were completed in Denmark in a very short time span.

Agriculture in Britain and eastern Germany was based on *la grande culture*, and agriculture in France and western Germany on *la petite culture*. In Denmark the peasant sector was characterised by an average farm size that was larger than the smallholdings in France and western Germany, but much smaller than farm sizes in Britain and eastern Germany. The result was a numerous class of middle-sized farmers who contributed to the development of the markets.

The agricultural reforms in western Europe were associated with technological progress, such as the use of new crops and later the growth of the dairy industry. These new products were not taken up in the Mediterranean area. The extent to which the introduction of new products stimulated interest in agricultural reforms can be debated, but it cannot be disputed that agricultural reforms occurred in the north but not in the south.

In eastern Europe and in Russia, the peasants only became personally free in the 1860s, and even then there was no individual farming among the class of peasants. In Russia, for example, the collective decisions of the village still played a major role.

It can be concluded that agricultural reforms were introduced in the northwest of Europe. The farming system was unchanged in the Mediterranean area, and the reforms came very late to eastern Europe and were at first limited to the issue of personal freedom.

In some countries reforms were implemented early, and in other countries it took a long time before they were all implemented. What was the importance of being early? It seems that there is some covariance between agricultural reforms and economic growth. However, it is not possible to give a precise estimate of the importance. Firstly, there are a number of elements in agricultural reforms, and there are interactions between the different elements. Secondly, other elements, such as industrialisation, also had an important impact. Thirdly, the effects of agricultural reforms are long-term.

Agricultural reforms at an early stage improved agricultural performance and thereby economic growth. When economic integration increased, it was an advantage to have a competitive agricultural sector, which could exploit the new commercial opportunities.

6. Trade policy and agricultural performance in different countries 1815-1914

Agricultural development is related to factors both within and without the agricultural sector. The agricultural reforms discussed in the previous chapter were changes which relied, at least to start with, on the internal resources of the agricultural sector.

Gradually agriculture became integrated into the economy through the increased "import" of inputs and "export" of outputs. This sectoral trade depended on the demand for agricultural products and the supply of inputs from outside, as well as the supply of agricultural products and the demand for inputs from within the agricultural sector.

Production specialisation can only take place if the commodities are traded. The volume of trade and of factor movements indicates the level of integration of the economy. Economic integration could only develop when markets were created and improved. The efficiency of the markets depended on the infrastructure and the enabling environment. Integration between the regions of a country and international integration between countries was developed through the reduction of transport and communication costs and through the establishment of institutions for research, extension services, credit, etc. In addition to these elements, international trade was also affected by political barriers in the form of varying degrees of protection.

This chapter deals with the nineteenth century and the beginning of the twentieth century up to the outbreak of the First World War. It is a period of significant economic integration.

The purpose of this chapter is to explain why the agricultural sector developed differently in the period when the economic integration occurred. Trade policy, which was shaped by ideology and the political struggle between class interests, differed from country to country. However, agricultural performance cannot be explained by trade policy alone. Other elements, such as the infrastructure, the enabling environment and the industrialisation of the urban sector, all contributed to the development of the agricultural sector.

The conditions differed from country to country, and all these different conditions have to be taken into consideration when explaining agricultural development. In the following, the trends in Britain, France, Germany, Denmark and the USA are analysed.

6.1 Britain

The economic ideology

At the end of the Napoleonic wars, Britain was the leading industrial country. The free trade doctrine had been developed by British economists, Adam Smith and David Ricardo, and it became the prevailing philosophy in Britain after 1815, because it suited British manufacturing interests. The remaining tariffs on manufactured goods were removed in the first half of the nineteenth century. Until the end of the nineteenth century there was no foreign threat to British industry. Even though France and Germany protected their industries, it was accepted that British industry should not be protected.

Agricultural intervention

For agriculture, the situation was different in 1815. There had been a long tradition of having Corn Laws in Britain, going back to the Middle Ages. Their purpose was to maintain fair prices and to avoid speculative and monopolistic practices. Internal trade was regulated, there were import tariffs and exports were restricted. Before the Napoleonic wars, Britain was normally a net exporter of grain, so import tariffs did not have any significant impact on the home market. The situation changed after the Napoleonic wars, when Britain became a normal net importer. A new protective Corn Law was passed in 1815, and it was changed in 1828, when a system of variable levy was introduced aiming at stabilising the home market price for grain.

Different interests

In the period from 1815 to 1846, when the Corn Laws were repealed, there was a heated debate about the Corn Laws, especially in the years of bad harvests, with high domestic grain prices. In 1838, the Anti-Corn Law League was formed under the leadership of Richard Cobden. He was a manufacturer and a Member of Parliament. As a representative of the manufacturing class, he was against the Corn Laws, because manufacturers were interested in low food prices and low raw material prices. Cereal was a wage good so high cereal prices increased labour costs and reduced the competitiveness of British industry.

The agricultural sector as such was not united in opposition to the manufacturers. Agricultural labourers had an interest in low food prices. Tenant farmers were not strong advocates for the Corn Laws, because the rent they paid to the landlords depended on the cereal price. The landlords were in favour of the Corn Laws, but even here some of them were reluctant in their support, because they also derived income from other sources such as coal mines and manufacturing.

The Corn Law question divided the country between urban and rural interests, but the landed interest was relatively weak because not all the rural population shared a common interest. Politically, the landed interest was weakened by the Reform Act of 1832, when the power of the landed aristocracy was reduced. The Reform Act increased the number of electors to Parliament, and these new electors came mostly from the urban areas. In 1846 the Tory leader, Robert Peel, repealed the Corn Laws so that foreign grain could enter Britain duty free.

The Golden Age 1846-1875

What were the economic consequences of the repeal of the Corn Laws in 1846? For the following 30 years there were no negative consequences. British agriculture had no difficulty in surviving without protection, because foreign exports to Britain were relatively limited. Demand grew, and cereal prices rose. British agriculture prospered, the cultivated area expanded and land values rose. The period 1846-1875 was a Golden Age, especially compared to the last quarter of the nineteenth century.

The agricultural crisis 1875-1895

The agricultural crisis from 1875 to 1895, which hit landowners especially hard, was not sufficient to create a protectionist alliance between farmers and industrialists. Industrialists were still in favour of cheap food and cheap raw materials, and the agricultural sector was politically further weakened by the decline in agriculture's share of total employment. In 1880, only 16 per cent of the male work force was occupied in agriculture. The landlords were interested in getting cereal price protection, but the prevalence of the landlord-tenant system made it difficult to form a united agricultural front. There was also a division of interests between arable and livestock farmers. The small livestock producers in the north and the west of Britain were interested in low feedstuff prices, and they were not interested in forming a coalition with the landlords.

There were changes in the production pattern of agriculture. The arable land was reduced by 15 per cent from 1870 to 1900; the wheat acreage in particular was reduced. This land was turned into permanent pasture for beef production. The cattle stock was increased by 25 per cent, whereas the pig stock was increased by only 10 per cent from 1870 to 1900.

The economic crisis was concentrated on the larger estates, which had to reduce the rents payable by the tenants. The small farmers benefited from the rent reduction if they were tenants, and they benefited from the changes in the relative prices of cereal and livestock products, because livestock production is relatively more important for small farmers.

Because of economic hardship, landowners had to sell their land, often to the sitting tenant, to obtain sufficient funds to finance their obligations. There was thus the start of the break-up of the landlord-tenant system, as many tenants became owners of the land they had previously rented. Nevertheless, in 1914 around 90 per cent of the holdings were still rented

The debate about the agricultural crisis was focused on the cereal sector and the economic problems of the big landowners. Therefore, the crisis may have been perceived as being more severe than it really was, when the farming sector is looked at as a whole. The crisis seemed more severe in south-east England than in England, Scotland and Ireland as a whole.

No significant shift in production

Britain continued to pursue a free-trade policy for agricultural products in spite of the economic crisis of 1875-1895, but there was no deliberate strategy for shifting production from cereal growing to livestock, as in the case of Denmark. There are several reasons for the rather modest adjustment in British agriculture. Firstly, there was a lack of understanding at the time of the permanent shift in the relation between arable and livestock prices. At the time it was widely believed in Britain that the economic distress was mainly caused by bad harvests. The focus on a series of bad harvests distracted from the important long-term shift in relative prices. There was insufficient attention paid to the fact that the income elasticity of livestock products was much higher than the income elasticity of cereals. Secondly, the interests of the landowners, being cereal growers, received much more attention in society than the interests of small farmers in the west and north, producing livestock. There was not a large class of freeholders who could organise themselves to initiate the transition to animal production. Thirdly, the co-operative movement which lay behind the successful transition of Danish agriculture from cereal to livestock production never had similar success in Britain, although some co-operatives were created. The lack of an independent class of freeholders may be the reason why the co-operative idea did not catch on in British agriculture.

The idea of fair trade

From around 1875 up to the First World War, a new attitude towards tariffs appeared under the name of 'fair trade'. The USA and Germany were building up their industries behind tariff walls. British industrialists felt the competition from these newly industrialised countries. Britain was no longer the dominant industrial country. Many people regarded a one-sided free trade policy in Britain as absurd. Under the heading of 'fair trade' they wanted Britain to introduce tariffs on manufactured goods imported from countries which refused reciprocity for British goods. Joseph Chamberlain became the spokesman of the fair traders, and in 1903 he began a campaign for tariff reform based on imperial preference. The fair traders wanted moderate duties on foodstuffs from outside the British Empire. The idea of a preferential free trade area consisting of Britain and the rest of the Empire won support. The overseas countries of the Empire should furnish Britain with foodstuffs, and Britain should deliver industrial goods to the overseas markets. However, there was some concern about dependence on food imports to Britain, as it was felt that Britain was losing its command of the seas when Germany started to build a powerful navy.

Even though ideas about fair trade won some political support, it was not sufficient to change British trade policy, which maintained a unilateral free trade policy until the 1930s.

6.2 France

The economic ideology

In France, protectionism had its roots way back in history. Mercantilism was founded in France in the seventeenth century, and it was the dominant philosophy in the eighteenth century. During the Napoleonic era the Continental System meant that British goods were either prohibited or subject to high tariffs

The trade issue in France was not dominated by economic theory as in Britain and Germany. In Britain there was a school of free trade, which emphasised the idea of comparative advantage. In Germany there was an important protectionist school, based on the idea of protecting infant industries.

Most French economists supported protectionism. This policy was adopted more in response to practical and immediate needs than in accordance with some well-conceived doctrine. The arguments in favour of protectionism were similar to the arguments of the mercantilists. Its basis was the belief that imports diminish employment in the importing country. The idea was that the prosperity of a country increases if it imports less than it exports. At the very least there should be self-sufficiency.

Protectionism 1815-1850

French industry was accustomed to high protection, and there were vested interests. During the Restoration Monarchy, 1814-1830, imports of manufactured goods of any origin were liable to be prohibited, and this protection was extended to agriculture. In 1819, a sliding scale of duties on grain, similar to the British Corn Laws, was introduced.

In the period of 1830-1848, a free-trade association was formed in France along the lines of the Cobden Anti-Corn Law League in Britain, but this movement gained little public support. The parliament opposed tariff reforms, and it rejected a proposal to remove duties on food and raw materials.

Liberalisation 1850-1875

When Napoleon III became Emperor in 1852, the free-traders gained an important supporter. He was impressed by the Peel reforms in Britain, and he presented a free-trade proposal to the French parliament, but the proposal was rejected. Napoleon III pursued his aims by agreeing the Anglo-French commercial treaty of 1860. As an emperor he had the right to make treaties with other nations without the approval of the parliament.

The so-called 'Cobden Treaty' of 1860 was a free-trade treaty. Britain gave France concessions by reducing duties on wines and spirits. France made greater changes by reducing the tariffs on manufactured goods to moderate levels and by removing duties on nearly all foodstuffs and raw materials. The sliding scale of duties on grain was also removed. After

France

the Cobden Treaty in 1860, France signed ten other commercial treaties with different countries during the 1860s. The Cobden Treaty and the other treaties included most-favoured-nation clauses, so that the lower duties resulting from these bilateral treaties were extended to a greater part of European trade.

Return to protectionism 1875-1914

The free trade in France obtained by the Cobden and other treaties was subject to attack after the Franco-Prussian war, 1870-71. The Third Republic had a heavy burden of debt, and the government wanted to raise import duties for fiscal reasons. This attempt failed, and it was first in around 1878, when the commercial treaties were due to expire, that France entered a new period of protectionism. The preparation of new treaties began in 1875, and a strong protectionist movement initiated by the iron and textile industries made itself felt. Agriculture was not in the forefront of this movement, but the industrialists needed to make an alliance with agriculture. Soon, the principal agricultural organisation adopted a protectionist stance by demanding equal treatment with industry. In 1881, a new tariff was adopted. The tariffs on manufactured goods were higher than before, but still moderate, and there were some increases in the duties on cereals and livestock products.

The revival of protectionism was initiated by the industrialists, but when the agricultural crisis was felt in the following two decades, agriculture joined industry in its efforts to get increased protection for both agricultural and industrial products. The protection level for agricultural products increased during the 1880s and 1890s. The duties on agricultural products generally ranged from 10 to 25 per cent; those on industrial products were mostly over 25 per cent (Tracy, 1982). The protection of manufactured goods was increased, but most agricultural raw materials for industry such as wool, hides, cotton and flax, continued to enter freely. The interests of the manufacturers prevailed over those of the farmers. In spite of the improvement in the agricultural situation after 1900, the increased tariffs on foodstuffs remained unchanged up to the First World War.

Protectionism a partial success

What was the impact of protectionism on agriculture? For wheat, which was the most important commodity, and which was of special interest to the farmers' association dominated by the big landowners, the tariff increases in the 1880s and 1890s meant that prices fell less than in Britain. Protectionism was successful in the sense that the wheat area under cultivation tended to increase in the last decade of the nineteenth century. The increased imports of cattle and beef in the late 1870s were checked by increased duties, and after 1900 France became self-sufficient in beef. Wine was the next most important product of French agriculture after cereals. Import duties on wine reduced imports and increased French production, but the countries exporting to France diverted their exports to other markets where they competed with French exports. Algerian wine got a foothold in France, and under the cover of protection there was an artificial expansion of the vineyards in France leading to over-production and difficulty in finding markets. Sugar-beet producers were supported by export subsidies. Other sugar-beet producing countries were forced to increase their subsidies until in 1902 it was agreed between these countries to refrain from granting subsidies. French protection was successful for grain, cattle and dairy producers but not for wine and sugar-beet producers.

Land reforms, the development of infrastructure and the enabling environment came late

The most serious objection to the protectionist trade policy was that it diverted attention away from the need for a constructive long-term policy for French agriculture. In around 1875, the structure of French agriculture remained almost unchanged. There was a huge number of fragmented smallholdings. In 1892, around 40 per cent of the holdings were of 1 hectare or less; 85 per cent of the holdings were of 10 hectares or less (Heaton, 1968). There was still a large number of tenants without any guarantee that they would be compensated for making improvements to their holdings. Agriculture was bound by tradition and inertia and there was a high rate of illiteracy in rural areas.

The lack of a long-term policy was due to two factors. Firstly, governments did too little to bring about improvements. A Ministry of Agriculture was established in 1881 for the first time. There was political polarisation between republicans and conservatives, and between 1881 and 1914, there were 42 different governments. Secondly, the voice of agriculture was dominated by the interests of the cereal growing landlords, and the peasants were weak because they were not organised.

However, some changes did take place between 1880 and 1914. Rural France increasingly came into contact with the outside world. After 1880, the construction of roads in rural areas was officially promoted, and the spread of the railways brought hitherto remote regions into contact with urban markets. Basic education began to make significant progress in the countryside after the introduction of universal education in the 1880s. Illiteracy was reduced and the French identity was strengthened. From 1870, compulsory military service also contributed to a change of attitude. Many young peasants discovered other ways of life and higher living standards for the first time.

In 1884 associations for the defence of economic interests were legalised, and farmer's syndicates were set up throughout the country, mostly by the aristocracy or the bourgeoisie to insulate the peasantry from the spread of republican ideology. These syndicates concentrated on the joint purchase of inputs, but in some cases they undertook collective sales of farm produce. Later, the republicans introduced the co-operative idea to the areas of insurance and credit. The rural credit movement was largely inspired by the Raiffeisen example in Germany.

French agricultural performance

There was a slow rate of modernisation of French agriculture from 1875 to 1914. During the two decades of crisis 1880-1900, French agricultural production only increased by 10 per cent. The low productivity and the absence of dynamic growth in French agriculture can be seen from the data (see Section 3.4). In 1880 the outputs per male worker in Britain, the USA and Denmark were, respectively, 100 per cent, 80 per cent and 40 per cent above the output per male worker in France. The increase in productivity from 1880 to 1900 was around 10 per cent in France, 10 per cent in Britain, 25 per cent in USA, and 33 per cent in Denmark.

In spite of the low production increase, France turned from being a net importer to a position of almost self-sufficiency in many products, and a net exporter of some other products before the First World War. From a mercantilist point of view, which was the traditional idea behind the protectionist policy, this change was considered as proof of the success of the protectionist policy. The need to be self-sufficient in case of war was also an argument used by the supporters of protectionism. A modest production increase could be combined with increased self-sufficiency, because of the stagnation of the French population from 1870 to 1940.

The protection of agriculture cushioned the effect of the price falls on the world market during the last two decades of the nineteenth century. This protection was beneficial to the cereal growers. Animal production, also being protected, was exposed to smaller price falls than arable products, but it did not benefit from the steep falls in the world market prices for cereals. There was no important shift from cereal to animal production.

It cannot be concluded that the failure to adjust from cereal production to animal husbandry was caused by the agricultural protection which raised feed costs for animal producers. In Britain, which had a more efficient agriculture, the free trade policy did not induce a large shift from cereal growing to animal husbandry, as was the case in Denmark.

In Britain, with free trade, total agricultural production stagnated during the period, 1880-1900. In France, with increased agricultural protection in the same period, production increased by 10 per cent. Free trade, as an alternative to agricultural protection, might have caused stagnation or even a fall in agricultural production. This does not seem unlikely, when the lack of dynamics in French agriculture is taken into consideration. There is no doubt that free trade would immediately have reduced incomes, especially for large landowners, but also among peasants selling cereals or among smallholders, who also worked as agricultural labourers.

The lack of dynamic growth may have had a variety causes. Firstly, as has been pointed out, there were structural problems such as the lack of land reforms, lack of education and lack of infrastructure. Secondly, the French economy grew relatively slowly, compared to Britain and Germany, during the period 1870-1914. GDP per capita grew at a lower rate in France than in Germany, but at a higher rate than in Britain. However, the total economy grew less in France because the population stagnated, whereas it increased significantly in Germany and Britain. Thirdly, the slow progress of agriculture has been related to lack of productive investments. The lack of investment was also a problem for industrial development. It is argued that French capitalists were more interested in overseas investments than in domestic industrial expansion (Duby and Wallen, 1975-76).

British agriculture had great problems in the last quarter of the nineteenth century. This was not a big problem for a country where agriculture provided only 15 per cent of total employment, but it was a problem in France where half the work force was employed in agriculture.

6.3 Germany

Moderate protection 1815-1850

In 1815 the German region consisted of a multiplicity of kingdoms, principalities and duchies. The leading country was Prussia, which was the prime mover in uniting the countries into the German Empire in 1871.

Prussia reduced its tariff rates after the Napoleonic Wars. The duties were moderate and they formed the basis of the external tariff barrier when the German customs union was formed in 1834. This common tariff included tariffs on grain.

Liberalisation 1850-1875

The period 1850-1875 was a prosperous one for agriculture, and at that time agricultural opinion in Germany was strongly in favour of free trade. Germany was a net exporter of grain, and agriculture did not need protection. Agriculture was also against the protection of German industry, because this would cause higher input prices for agriculture, and because protection for German industry might lead to Britain opposing imports of German grain. The industrialists were in favour of protection, and they strongly supported the ideas of Friedrich List about infant industry protection. The farmers' opposition to industrial protection prevented the industrialists from obtaining the protection they wanted. Therefore, the industrialists tried to form a coalition with the landlords to convert them to protectionism, but without success at first. Import duties on grain were abolished in 1853. The first major change in the tariff rates occurred when the German Customs Union negotiated a treaty with the France in 1862. This was followed by similar treaties with other countries, substantially reducing the tariff rates on manufactured goods.

Varying degrees of protection 1875-1914

German agriculture was confronted with difficulties in the period 1875-1895, both on the export and the home markets. German exports of grain to France and Britain were squeezed out by supplies from the USA, and on the growing home market German agriculture was confronted with increasing imports from Russia, Austria-Hungary and the USA. The farmers, led by the Prussian landlords and industrialists, joined in a common effort to return to protection for both agriculture and industry. A new tariff law was passed in 1879. It included moderate duties on grain and increased duties on livestock products. The duties on grain were too low to prevent a fall in grain prices in the 1880s. The farmers demanded further protection. In 1885 and 1887, further protection of grain and livestock products was agreed by the parliament. The coalition between farmers and industrialists was not as strong as in France. The coalition broke down in 1890 when Otto Bismarck was dismissed as chancellor and replaced by a chancellor without ties to agriculture. The government came under pressure from industrialists, who no longer had common interests with agriculture. German industry had developed and was now internationally competitive, so industrial protection was no longer needed as before. At the same time, German industry wanted agricultural protection eliminated. German industry wanted to keep food costs down to achieve lower wage costs, and industrialists wanted greater access to foreign markets, which could be more easily obtained if German tariff concessions were given on foodstuffs. Industrialisation had also led to a greatly increased urban population which was interested in low food prices.

At the beginning of the 1890s, several commercial treaties between Germany and its trading partners expired. Germany wanted to obtain advantages for its exports of manufactured goods in return for concessions on agricultural tariffs. Treaties were signed with Austria-Hungary, Romania and Russia, all exporters of grain for which the German tariffs were lowered.

The political climate had changed again when a new tariff was enacted in 1902 in preparation for the renewal of the commercial treaties. Higher duties were levied on all agricultural products as well as on many manufactured goods. Germany was arming itself, and sought a greater degree of economic self-sufficiency. Politically there was more responsiveness to the demand from farmers for higher protection of agricultural products, although the agricultural conditions had improved from the end of the nineteenth century.

Shifting opinions

This short historical description shows that at different times there were different opinions on the question of more or less protection. These shifts reflected the political debate in Germany. From 1880 to 1914 the total population of Germany grew rapidly, but the rural population declined as a proportion of the total population. This gave rise to discussions among politicians and academics about whether Germany should be an agrarian or an industrial state. Was the relative decline of agriculture desirable for social, strategic and economic reasons? Originally, the industrialists favoured List's infant industry argument. Later, many of them became free-traders like the industrials in Britain. Some of the grain producing landlords were in favour of temporary agricultural supports during times of severe foreign competition, others were in favour of more permanent protection because they considered a high degree of self-sufficiency important in the event of war, and because they were afraid of Germany losing its social and political stability if it became a purely industrial state.

Policy instruments

German protection policy was not only a question of tariffs. The livestock trade was protected through trade regulations, officially for sanitary reasons. At one time all imports of live animals were prohibited, and at other times cattle and pigs could only be imported from certain countries on restrictive conditions. There were also restrictions on imports of meat products. The restrictive rules either prohibited or impeded imports. Some of these measures would today probably have been considered to be non-tariff barriers.

An import certificate system was also applied. There had been a long tradition for Russian wheat and rye to pass through eastern German ports, where it was mixed with local grain of inferior quality. Thereby the eastern German producers obtained increased demand. When the grain duty was re-introduced in 1879, this transit trade was allowed to continue under an import certificate arrangement. The re-export of foreign grain, or of foreign grain mixed with German grain, gave the right to import a similar quantity of grain without duty.

Eastern Germany exported a large part of its cereal production, especially rye, whereas western Germany imported a great part of the cereal it needed. The reason for this was that transport from eastern German ports to Nordic consumers was cheaper than transport by rail to western Germany. Also, western German consumers were used to a higher quality than the poor quality grain from eastern Germany.

Later, the import certificate system was extended to cover the different trade patterns of western and eastern Germany. Exports of foreign or home produced cereals from Germany entitled the exporters to a certificate that allowed imports of grain without duty. These import certificates became negotiable, which meant that certificates obtained by exporting grain from eastern Germany could be used to import grain into western Germany. The certificates could obtain a price slightly below the duty on grain imports. An eastern German rye exporter could then obtain an export price equal to the world market price plus the value of the import certificate, and when this artificially high export price was higher than the domestic price there was an incentive to export. The import certificate worked as an export subsidy.

The German *Junkers* also launched the idea of a state import monopoly for grain. According to this proposal, all imports of grain should be undertaken by the state and resold on the domestic market at a price corresponding to the average of prices in the previous years. The earnings obtained when import prices fell below this level should go to a fund, which could cover the losses when import prices rose above the resale price on the domestic market. When grain prices fell, it would support the domestic price level. The proposal was rejected by the government, but the core of the idea was realised when the National Socialists came to power in 1933, and it was continued in German agricultural policy after 1949.

German agricultural performance

Agricultural reforms did not take place rapidly in western Germany. The legal position of the peasants was improved at the beginning of the nineteenth century, but it was only from 1848 that the peasants started to become owners of their holdings. The abolition of the open-field system and the consolidation of landholdings also started at around the same time in western Germany. In eastern Germany land consolidation had started earlier and by around 1850, most of the landowners had consolidated their holdings, which had become larger because the peasants had to give up a large part of their land in order to obtain private ownership of their land.

From the start of the German Empire in 1871 up to the First World War, there was significant technological progress. A comparison with France shows much stronger productivity increases in Germany. In 1800, the productivity index in both Germany and in France was 6.5. It was nearly twice as high in 1860 when it was 12.2 in France and Germany. During the period 1860-1914, productivity increased slowly in France, but strongly in Germany. In 1910, the productivity index was 17.7 in France but nearly double that in Germany, at 30.6 (Bairoch, 1999).

The productivity increases were especially strong in eastern Germany, while in western Germany productivity increased as the obstacles to individual initiative were removed.

Institutional changes played a big role in Germany. Research and education were important elements. Agricultural sciences flourished, especially in agricultural chemistry, where Germany played a leading role in the world. Justus von Liebig (1803-1873) laid the foundation for the chemical study of soil and the use of chemical fertilizers to rectify soils by the replacement of constituents abstracted from the soil by various crops. Much of the German soil was of poor quality, so artificial fertilizers became widely used. Agricultural colleges were transferred to the universities, and equipped with experimental stations. Below the university level, agricultural schools were established. The dissemination of know-how was facilitated by basic education becoming compulsory, and the peasants learned to read and write.

The production of new crops, such as sugar beet and potatoes, played an important role in the development of agriculture. A German chemist discovered the sugar in beet, and in 1815 production began in earnest. New machinery came into use because of the new crops. Britain became the model for much of the technical progress, including drainage. Albrecht Thaer (1752 - 1828) had introduced knowledge of English agriculture, and he wrote about the "Principles of rational agriculture".

The removal of internal trade barriers started with the *Zollverein* in 1834 and continued as the German area gradually expanded into the German Empire. The different regions were linked together through an extensive network of railways. The demand for agricultural products increased significantly from 1870. During the period 1870-1914, the German population increased by 70 per cent. It was also the period when Germany became truly industrialised.

There was good availability of finance for the agricultural investments because the rural credit system was well developed.

What was the effect of the protectionist policy on agriculture? Tariff protection could not prevent the fall in the world market prices for grain causing a fall in prices on the German market in the period 1880-1900. But, due to protection, the price fall on the German market was less than the price fall on the world market.

Tariff protection did stimulate domestic production. In the period 1880-1914, the area under cereals grew slightly and the yield increased significantly, due to improved techniques. The production of rye doubled and the production of wheat increased two-thirds during the period (Tracy, 1982). First, the increased protection caused a decline in imports of cereal, but from the end of the 1880s, the domestic demand for fodder for the expansion of livestock production caused a large increase in imports of barley. The tariff protection of wheat and rye was the same, but the expansion of rye production was greater. It was easier to grow rye than wheat in the soil and climatic conditions of eastern Germany. The import certificate system, which acted as an export subsidy, caused a large increase in the exports of rye.

The livestock sector was also protected through tariffs and import restrictions. Behind these import barriers, the rising demand due to the increased population and economic growth of Germany caused a significant increase in the stock of cattle and pigs and a sharp decline in the number of sheep (Tracy, 1882).

In spite of a significant increase in agricultural production, Germany gradually moved from being a net exporter of agricultural products before 1870 to a net importer, partly due to a high growth in per capita income and partly to the rapid increase in population.

During the protectionist period, 1880-1914, there were important developments in German agriculture. In spite of the protection, people moved out of the rural areas and into the industrialised centres in the Ruhr, Berlin and Saxony. However, this migration was more determined by the pull factors of industry than the push factors of agriculture. During this period, the German economy grew by approximately 2 per cent per capita per year, so it is difficult to conclude that the protectionist policy had significant negative effects on the economy.

6.4 Denmark

Agricultural reforms created a bimodal structure

Denmark, like other European countries, was dominated by mercantilist ideas from the beginning of the seventeenth to the end of the eighteenth centuries. Industries were protected and manufacturers were supported by the state. In 1797, new tariff regulations were implemented, based on free-trade ideas. Industry was not considered a natural activity for Denmark, and it was thought better to focus on agriculture.

Most of the regulations behind the agricultural reforms were issued from 1784 to the end of the eighteenth century, and the new farm system, with consolidated and enclosed farms, was largely in place by 1830. Most of the farmers became owners of their holdings, but there were still many tenant farmers after 1815. The agrarian reforms were not the result of some master plan. The reforms consisted of a series of regulations which were decided upon piecemeal, as the need arose during the transformation process. Until 1815, the transformation was facilitated by the high agricultural prices before and during the Napoleonic wars. The post-war period, 1815-1830, was one with general economic problems, not least for agriculture. Firstly, agricultural prices were low and, as a cereal exporter, Denmark could not compensate by introducing tariff protection. Secondly, Denmark had difficulties in exporting. Before 1814, Denmark had a privileged position exporting cereals to Norway in spite of the low quality of cereal, but this market was lost as Norway was no longer under the Danish crown. Exports to Britain were also hampered by the corn laws of 1815.

By around 1830, when the situation improved, the farm structure in Denmark was bimodal. There was a commercial sector of large estates with much higher productivity than the relatively small peasant farms, which were to a large extent based on subsistence or semi-subsistence farming.

Increasing exports 1830-1875

During the period 1830-1875, there were increasing exports of agricultural products, especially to Britain. In 1830 only 18 per cent of the agricultural production value was exported, but in 1875 this share had increased to 38 per cent (Christensen, 1983). To start with, the exports were mainly cereals, but from 1850 the export value of animal products increased more than the export value of grain exports. From 1850, the prices of animal products increased more than cereal prices, and the focus started to shift towards animal production, such as butter, initially among the big estate owners.

The start of self-organisation

Especially from around 1850 the peasants organised themselves at various levels. Politically they engaged in party politics. Culturally they participated in building schools, especially the folk high schools. Education, in its many aspects, was considered important. In 1814, a school reform introduced by the government made it compulsory for all children to receive 7 years of education. Socio-economically, the peasants formed farmers unions, and established agricultural schools and credit institutions, such as savings banks and mortgage lending associations.

Because of these factors, Danish agriculture was well prepared when the agricultural crisis, with falling grain prices, started around 1875. The agricultural reforms had been realised long before, the peasants had already started the shift from cereal to animal production, and they were already trained in self-organisation, which meant they were active in changing their conditions.

Trade policy and agricultural performance 1815 - 1914

The co-operative movement

The years 1875-1914 saw the development of the co-operative movement. Some of the estate owners specialising in cereal growing were in favour of cereal protection, but the small and medium sized farmers were interested in taking advantage of the low cereal prices by shifting to dairy and meat production. In the mid-1880s, there was a proposal to impose tariffs on grains, but the proposal was rejected due to opposition from the left, the farmers' party. The landlords were not as powerful as in France or Germany, and the farmers were so numerous and so well organised that the free-trade stance was maintained. The technical innovation of the cream separator in 1879 combined with the social innovation of co-operative production, enabled the farmers to establish dairy co-operatives. The first dairy co-operative was started in 1882, and the idea spread quickly. By 1890 there were around 700 dairy co-operatives. The idea also spread to the meat sector where the first co-operative slaughterhouse was started in 1887, and it then spread to the input sector, where feedstuff and fertiliser purchasing co-operatives bought the necessary inputs as cheaply as possible (Jensen, 1937). The main idea behind the co-operative movement was to prevent traders outside agriculture exploiting a local monopsony or a local monopoly. Through the co-operative movement, Danish farmers succeeded in establishing an efficient and integrated structure of production, processing, distribution, and marketing of homogeneous products of high quality.

The transition from cereal to animal production was greatly favoured by the export opportunities of the expanding British market. Britain was an open market close by, and there were established trading channels because exports of animal products had already started before 1875. The real income of British wage earners increased and the income elasticity of dairy and meat products were high. Before the agricultural crisis, Denmark also had important exports to the German market, but these were hampered by the German protectionist policy. For disease control reasons Germany introduced a ban on imports of live pigs, which were of great importance to Danish farmers. This blow gave a strong impetus to the switch to meat exports in the form of bacon to the British market.

Large increases in the animal produce

From 1870 to 1914 there was a large increase in animal production in Denmark. It was partly driven by the favourable export opportunities of the British market, and partly driven by the ability of Danish agriculture to adjust to the new opportunities brought about by falling cereal costs. In 1914, the Danish production of butter was four times the level of 1870, and the production of pork and bacon was five and a half times as high. The production increase was not only due to an increase in the size of animal stocks, but also to productivity increases, especially in the dairy sector, where the yield per cow increased from 1200 kg to 1700 kg of milk per year (Skrubbeltrang, 1953). The re-orientation of Danish agriculture meant that it shifted from being a net exporter of grain to a net importer of grain and other feedstuffs and fertilisers. In 1914 nearly two-thirds of agricultural production by value was exported.

The strong focus on animal production meant that smallholders and medium sized farms could make a living from their activities. The average farm size was significantly smaller than in Britain, but larger than in France or western Germany. The maintenance of a reasonable farm size structure in Denmark was the result of the custom whereby the eldest son, or the son best suited, inherited the farm and compensated the other heirs in cash, or more often by a mortgage.

6.5 The USA

The frontier movement

The agricultural situation in the USA was totally different from that in Europe. In Europe, the farming and ownership structure had developed gradually, as described in Chapter 5. The history of the USA in the nineteenth century is the history of how the frontier moved from the east coast westwards. Technically, a frontier area is defined as a region in which there are more than two and fewer than six inhabitants per square mile, and the frontier line is the line separating areas with more and with fewer than six people per square mile. In 1790, the frontier line was the Allegheny Mountains, and the USA was co-extensive with the East Coast states. By 1830 the frontier had moved to the Mississippi river, by 1860 it extended along the 97th meridian and it finally closed around 1890. In the nineteenth century the vast American plains were occupied by settlers coming from Europe. This large immigration is reflected in the population increase. In 1790 the population of the USA was 3.9 million, in 1830 12.9 million, in 1860 31.4 million, and in 1910 91.9 million.

According to the predominant occupation, it is reasonable to speak of the miners' frontier (1840-60) and the ranchers' frontier (1860-90). These were closed by the farmers' frontier moving westwards from Mississippi and eastwards from the West Coast. The miners' frontier consisted of scattered settlements in California and the Rocky Mountains where they searched for metals, especially gold and silver. The ranchers' frontier was the area between the 97th meridian and the Rocky Mountains, where cattle were raised. The area was grassland, and because of the low rainfall it was believed to be unfit for cultivation. In the 1860s it was found that cattle could be raised on the pastures and a cattle industry grew up. The mining activities dwindled and the miners and new immigrants turned to agriculture. Cattle ranching also disappeared, and the land was taken over by farmers cultivating the land. This all happened in the period of 1860-1890.

What was the effect of this movement of the farmers' frontier? The number of farms grew from 2 million in 1860 to 6 million in 1910. During this half century 2 million km^2 of new land was brought under cultivation, corresponding to an area as large as western Europe (Scheiber et al., 1976).

The forces behind the farmer's frontier

What were the forces behind this huge settlement and extension of farm land? Firstly, the construction of transcontinental railways allowed surplus production to be sent to the East Coast, from where it was exported to Europe. Secondly, legislation, especially the 1862 Homestead Act, permitted settlers to take over the land either without charge, by fulfilling certain criteria, or by paying a small fee per acre. These land laws made it possible for financiers to buy up large areas of land. Thirdly, a series of innovations made it possible to take in the new areas and cultivate them on a much larger scale than was known in Europe. The ranchers' frontier was taken over by the farmers with the help of the production of windmills and barbed wire which could be bought at feasible prices. Windmills were necessary for pumping up ground water for irrigation, which was necessary due to the lack of rain. The farmers also had to enclose their fields against the ranchers' cattle which roamed the prairie. The type of land occupied was suitable for large-scale farming and this was made possible by the mechanical revolution in USA, which came in the half-century following 1860. Machinery for land preparation, sowing and harvesting greatly increased labour productivity.

The USA

Agricultural prices 1860-1895

What were the economic conditions for the farmers? The farmers benefited from the Civil War, 1861-1865, because of high agricultural prices, partly due to the reduced supply of agricultural products, and partly to general inflation. As a result, farmers extended their holdings and equipment. After the war, farmers suffered from sharply declining prices. This was the beginning of a period, 1870-1895, with economic difficulties and discontent among the farmers because of falling prices and other problems. The falling prices of agricultural products were caused by increased supply and by a deflationary policy. Money supply was reduced because the government wanted the paper currency to be on a parity with gold. The relative price of gold went up, because of high demand for gold. Keeping a fixed gold price meant that the prices of other commodities had to fall. The farmers fought the deflationary policy of the federal government from the late 1860s to the end of the century. American farmers were predominantly borrowers and so were hurt by a decline in the general price level. In addition, there was no rural credit system after the Civil War, so there was a lack of credit at reasonable interest rates. Falling prices, fixed nominal interest payments on borrowings, lack of credit facilities and falling land prices all contributed to the hardship. Farmers were often forced to see their mortgages foreclosed, and the alternatives were to go into industry, to become tenants or agricultural labourers, or to move to the frontier.

Imperfect competition

Another problem was the strong market power of the actors on whom the welfare of the farmers depended. The railroads belonged to private companies which charged relatively high rates and discriminated in favour of industry at the expense of agricultural interests. Big business and monopolies developed rapidly during the last decades of the nineteenth century. Monopolists in meat packing and other processing industries were often able to hold the prices paid to farmers artificially low, while they profited from the high prices charged to consumers. The farmers felt that the middlemen buying up the farm commodities were taking an undue share of the profit. Monopolists or oligopolists on such important farm inputs as barbed wire and machinery were often able to overcharge the farmers.

Tariff policy

There was also dissatisfaction with the government's tariff policy. After the Civil War, the general level of tariffs was raised partly for fiscal reasons, and the tariff laws increased protection. As exporters, farmers did not benefit from agricultural tariff protection, but they suffered from the high tariff protection of manufactured goods. The high industrial protection in the USA made it difficult for European manufacturers to compete on the US market, and for balance of payment reasons this prompted moves for agricultural protection in Europe, from which the American farmers suffered.

Regional problems in the West and the South

These problems were general, but there were also some regional problems in the West at the frontier and in the South. In the West, there was a conflict between land-hungry farmers and cattle ranchers, and a conflict between homestead farmers and financiers and companies wanting land for speculation and profit. The Homestead Act of 1862 was criticised for not taking more care of the interests of the first group. In the South the abolition of slavery was a blow to the existing farming system of large landholdings and this had to be transformed.

Farmers' initiatives

How did the farmers react to improve their situation? They took initiatives to apply political pressure through farmers' organisations and political parties, and to overcome some of the market problems by various co-operative efforts. The farmers did not succeed in changing the deflationary monetary policy, nor in changing the tariff policy.

Farmers were influential in initiating anti-railroad and anti-monopoly laws in the states and, eventually, in the federal government. The farmers were among the first to fight the abuses of monopolies and the discriminatory behaviour of the railroad companies.

Farmers were also in favour of legislation against the increasing concentration of power in industry. The half century following the Civil War saw the culmination of economic *laissez faire* and the reaction against it. The American industrial revolution was speeded up by the Civil War. The golden age of small manufacturing businesses owned by a single or a few entrepreneurs was before the Civil War. After the war, big business took over. Economic power was concentrated through mergers, trusts and pools, which created monopolies and oligopolies. The general discontent of farmers, small business owners and consumers resulted in anti-monopoly legislation at state level, and later at federal level in 1890 with the Sherman Antitrust Act, which was later supplemented by new legislation.

Inadequate credit system

For decades farmers had complained about the inadequate credit facilities, but this attracted little interest before 1900. The West had largely been developed on borrowed money, and in its early years it was a debtor region. Farmers could only get loans from eastern moneylenders at significantly higher interest rates than eastern borrowers. The higher interest rates were partly due to the greater risks of frontier loans and partly due to the inadequate banking facilities in the West. The national bank system established in 1863 was criticised by the farmers. It did not adequately serve small communities, because the minimum capital required was too high and encouraged the flow of capital from rural areas to the cities. In around 1900, government circles became familiar with the agricultural credit system in Europe, especially in Germany. Under the Federal Reserve Act of 1913, establishing the Federal Reserve System, the national banks were, for the first time, permitted to lend money on farm mortgages, and agricultural papers running for six months could be re-discounted at the Federal Reserve banks. The Federal Farm Loan Act of 1916 authorised the establishment of Federal Land Banks with the objective of making it easier to obtain short and long-term loans and ensuring that loans could be obtained at lower interest rates. The problem was that the farm credit system did not exist in the period 1865-1895 when it had been needed most. It was only established after 1895, when the agricultural situation had improved due to rising agricultural prices.

Scientific farming

From its beginning American farming was characterised by being extensive. Mechanisation had already begun before the Civil War and it spread in the half century following the war. The invention of new machinery and the use of existing technology were stimulated by the establishment of agricultural colleges and agricultural mechanical schools. The Homestead Act of 1862 gave away some of the best land to the states, and the income from this land was devoted to the establishment and operation of agricultural colleges and agricultural and mechanical schools. Mechanisation to improve labour productivity was one part of scientific farming. The other part of scientific farming, concerning increasing yields, improving product quality and preserving the fertility of the soil, did not attract much attention before 1880. At this time, there was increased interest in obtaining higher yields and reducing production costs at a time when agricultural prices were low. Greater competition also prompted an interest in improving the quality of products. As the farmers' frontier was closing, the gradual disappearance of unoccupied arable land stimulated an interest in preserving soil fertility.

Crop production and large farms

The vast areas of arable land, combined with increased mechanisation, meant that US agriculture developed into a mainly cereal producing sector. Naturally, there was also production of livestock products, especially at the ranchers' frontier, but relatively speaking the livestock sector was not as important as it was in Europe. This specialisation favoured financially strong farmers, also because of the inadequate farm credit system. Smallholders and financially weak farmers had to give up and find alternative employment in the cities or become agricultural labourers. All these factors meant that the average farm size became much larger than the average peasant farm in Europe.

Increasing prices from the end of the frontier

The rapid occupation of the West, made possible by the building of the railroads and stimulated by the Homestead Act, increased agricultural production beyond normal needs, and from the end of the Civil War until the late 1890s, US farmers suffered from falling nominal prices due to the too rapid expansion of production and the deflationary monetary policy. This situation changed in around 1895. From that time, increasing demand not only kept up with supply but grew faster, so that real agricultural prices and land prices rose. 1895-1920 was the heyday of US agriculture.

Interrelationship between Europe and the USA

The rapid expansion of US agriculture was conditioned by the existence of the European market. This market speeded up the advance of the frontier, the occupation of new land, the flow of immigration and the improvement and extension of the transport system. Foreign exchange revenue from agricultural exports, together with large-scale borrowing in Europe, made an important contribution to the financing of the imports necessary for the American industrialisation which took place behind highly protective tariff wall. When exports of agricultural commodities started to decline after 1900, the increased urban demand in the USA was able to substitute for the decreasing European demand. It was the artificial expansion of US agriculture during the First World War, to meet increased European demands that caused the problems for US agriculture in the 1920s.

As described above, the rapid expansion of US agriculture had a significant impact on economic developments in Europe, although different countries adjusted in different ways as analysed in this chapter.

6.6 Summary

There were some general trends in trade policy, as described in Chapter 2, but there were also some important differences between countries. Britain was the front-runner on trade liberalisation, and Britain stuck to its free-trade policy until 1914. France and Germany followed the liberalisation trend during 1850-1875, but returned to protectionism during the period 1875-1914. The tariff histories of Austria, Russia and Italy ran on similar lines. This means that five of the six great powers in Europe followed the same line. Some of the smaller countries such as Denmark and the Netherlands followed the British pattern.

Britain was the first country to introduce agricultural reforms and its agricultural productivity was higher than elsewhere. These agricultural reforms played an important role in economic development, as they started before the start of industrialisation. The rapid population growth combined with urbanisation and industrialisation stimulated agricultural development. The infrastructure and the markets were established at an early stage.

From 1846, agricultural imports to Britain were free from tariffs, but as British agriculture was the most productive in Europe, it flourished until 1875. Britain kept its free-trade policy and agriculture suffered. The shift to animal production was only made by the smallholders but not by the large tenants and the landlords. From 1875 to 1914, agricultural output was constant. The output per hectare was constant and labour productivity only increased by around 10 per cent.

There were no land reforms in France in the first half of the nineteenth century, so when the prosperous period 1850-1875 arrived, French agriculture was not well equipped to take advantage of the improved prices.

When the agricultural crisis started in around 1875, French agriculture was still relatively backward. The size structure of French agriculture was still predominantly one in which most peasants only had very little land, and this was still scattered in strips. Because of the size of their smallholdings, many of the peasants were still more or less subsistence farmers. The poor infrastructure and the poor enabling environment were also barriers to the development of commercial farming. The infrastructure in many rural areas was poor; basic education in the countryside was insufficient and illiteracy was widespread. There were significant improvement in infrastructure and education from 1880 up to 1914.

An important part of the enabling environment was still missing, namely research and extension service systems. The French agricultural research system was only established after the First World War and was closed down in the 1930s, so it only became effective after the Second World War. Likewise, in the 1920s, an effort to establish an agricultural extension service was unsuccessful, and again it was only after the Second World War that such a system was available for smallholders.

The lack of dynamics in agriculture was the reason for the slow development. The population in France was stagnant. There is no reason to believe that a free trade policy would have induced a strong shift from cereal to animal production. A free-trade policy would probably only have caused social distress without much development. French agriculture was not in a condition to be able to exploit the opportunities of shifting to animal production.

In Germany and France, labour productivity was the same in around 1800, and it increased at the same pace up to 1860. From 1860 to 1914, productivity increased in Germany by 150 per cent, but in France by only 45 per cent.

Agriculture in western Germany was dominated by smallholders, who only acquired private ownership in 1848. In western Germany, the division of the common land, the abolition of common rights and the consolidation of land holdings were slow in the first half of the nineteenth century. The change of cultivation methods in eastern Germany took place earlier. Eastern Germany was dominated by the landlords, who managed the land themselves, with labour services provided by peasants and landless labourers. By 1850, the large landowners in the east had nearly completed the consolidation of their land, and they were in a position to carry out agricultural improvements.

From the beginning of the German Empire in 1871, there was a large increase in the agricultural production. The land area sown with cereals

Summary

increased slightly in Germany, whereas in Britain it declined by 20 per cent. The number of cattle and especially pigs increased significantly. As already mentioned, there was a large productivity increase.

After 1871, Germany constituted a large market with a good infrastructure. Agricultural demand expanded because of a large population increase and a high growth in per capita income, stimulated by industrialisation.

German agriculture was able to respond by increasing production, because the agricultural sector could benefit from institutional developments. Agricultural research was at a high level, especially in chemistry. Universities with experimental stations and agricultural schools were established. Basic education was improved. Farmers had good access to finance, thanks to the rural credit system based on the co-operative ideal.

Germany moved from being a net exporter of agricultural products before 1870 to a net importer, despite the return to tariff protection. The sharp increase in demand could not be satisfied by the increase in domestic arable and livestock production.

During the period 1875-1914, Britain continued its free-trade policy whereas Germany returned to protection. In 1870, agricultural labour productivity in Britain was 25 per cent higher than in Germany. In 1910 agricultural productivity in Germany was 25 per cent higher than in Britain. So there is no clear evidence that agricultural protection in Germany was harmful to the agricultural sector, and there is no clear evidence that the general tariff policy in Germany harmed the performance of the German economy.

Important agricultural reforms took place in Denmark relatively rapidly in the period 1784-1815. Peasants' legal rights were strengthened and the open-field system with scattered strips of land was replaced by consolidated and enclosed farms. Most of the peasants became owners of their farms in this period. As a result, an independent class of farmers sprang up. The educational level was relatively high, thanks to the school law of 1814 which introduced seven years of compulsory education for all children.

The self-organisation of the peasants and the co-operative movement played a major role in the development of Danish agriculture. The government supported agricultural research and education and the construction of infrastructure. In the first half of the nineteenth century, large-scale farming on large estates and peasant farming existed side by side. Productivity on the large estates was higher, but the peasants gradually learned how to improve their production methods.

Danish agriculture was able to benefit from the prosperous economic trends in the period 1850-1875. The prices of livestock products increased more than cereal prices, and livestock production increased more than cereal production. When agricultural prices declined during the period 1875-1895, Denmark continued its free-trade policy. Despite the lower prices agricultural production, and especially the production of dairy products and pig meat, increased significantly. Agricultural labour productivity increased by two thirds from 1870 to 1910, and during this period Denmark, as an agricultural society, experienced the same rise in living standards as Germany, and its economic growth was higher than Britain's.

The agricultural situation in USA was different from that in Europe. Because of railway construction, the Great Plains in the west could be brought into agricultural production, despite the relatively low supply of manpower. American agriculture became highly mechanised, with large farms, where the land was cultivated extensively. It was only in around 1890, when the farmers' frontier was closed, that the focus of interest moved from land extension to land productivity.

In spite of the large exports of grain to Europe during the period 1875-1895, this was not a prosperous period for American farmers. In general, price levels fell due to the deflationary monetary policy, and the real burden of their debts increased because the interest and instalment payments were fixed in nominal terms. There does not seem to have been a steeper decline in agricultural wholesale prices than in wholesale prices in general (Historical Statistics of the United states, 1789 - 1945, 1949).

The deflationary policy was not the only issue to provoke discontent among the farmers. Farmers were also discontented with the tariff policy. Manufactured goods as well as agricultural products were protected through high tariffs. The farmers did not benefit from agricultural protection because USA exported agricultural products, but the farmers suffered from the protection of manufactured goods. Industrial protection increased the prices of agricultural inputs and consumer goods.

The farmers were also discontented with the lack of cheap credit. A rural credit system was lacking in the period 1865-1900, when the major expansion of agricultural production took place. Farmers had to rely on East Coast financiers who charged high interest rates.

The period 1865-1914 was the era of big business, when large corporations were built up. The markets were characterised by monopolies and oligopolies that exploited or abused their market power. The farmers suffered from high railway freight rates and low farm prices when delivering their outputs to the monopsonists for further processing.

Summary

The period 1895-1914 was a prosperous one for US farmers. The real prices of agricultural products rose. Domestic demand increased due to the increased population and the increased GDP per capita, and the growth in cereal supply levelled out when the frontier was closed.

7. Agricultural markets and public intervention 1914 – 1945

7.1 The First World War and the restoration of peace 1914-1929

During the First World War, food prices rose sharply, as they always do in war time. Farmers in Europe and overseas benefited from the high prices, which persisted for a few years after the war, due to the shortage of food.

The problem was to keep food prices down for the benefit of consumers. The existing tariff protection was suspended and in many countries rationing was introduced to ensure the fair distribution of limited supplies.

Overseas production expanded greatly during the war and it continued to expand during the 1920s. Agricultural production in Europe had fallen during the war, because of reduced soil fertility, loss of livestock and lack of investment. After the war, production recovered and the pre-war level was first reached and then surpassed. Before the war, Russia had been a major exporter, especially to Germany, but its exports ceased after the war.

At the outbreak of the First World War, Britain was heavily dependent on agricultural imports. In the first years of the war imports were not threatened, and it was only in 1917 that initiatives were taken to stimulate domestic production through guaranteed minimum prices for cereals. During the 1920s, Britain continued its free trade tradition and its farmers suffered from the British foreign exchange policy. Britain wanted the pound to return to its pre-war gold parity, in spite of the large increases in domestic prices which had occurred since the outbreak of the war.

French agriculture was severely hit from the beginning of the war. The battlefields of northern France included some of its most productive land; this was put out of production and livestock was depleted. A great part of the agricultural labour force was called up for military service, fertilisers were in short supply, transport was lacking and the necessary investments could not be made. The production of wheat declined significantly during the war, and on average imports of wheat and flour were three times as high as before the war. The existing duties on food products were suspended during the war to facilitate imports and moderate the rise in food prices. The government took over the purchase and distribution of the major food products. Gradually, during the 1920s, the pre-war tariff protection was reinstated. Agricultural production recovered relatively quickly, considering the extent of war damage, and by 1925, cereal production reached its pre-war level.

At the beginning of the war, Germany was dependent on imports of large quantities of foods, particularly bread grain, and considerable quantities of animal feedstuffs. During the war, these imports were cut off to a far greater extent than those of Britain. Food shortages were serious, and there were major obstacles to increased production. There was a sharp fall in crop yields and a decline in livestock production due to the shortage of feedstuffs. Price controls were introduced to restrict the rise in food prices, but they were not accompanied by measures to encourage production.

After the war, German agriculture was exposed to international competition, since tariffs on food products had been suspended at the outbreak of war. In 1925, Germany recovered its right to determine its own tariffs, and there was a revival of the old controversy between those who wanted agricultural protection, particularly the landowners, and those who were opposed to it. The reintroduction of moderate tariff protection and the import certificate system stemmed the fall in prices, but agricultural prosperity was by no means restored. The government had an overriding preoccupation with promoting exports of manufactured goods, especially because of the obligation to pay war reparations.

The First World War provided a stimulus for exports of US farm products to Europe. US industry also benefited from the war, first by the elimination of competition from European manufactured goods, and then from increased European demand and America's participation in the war.

During the war, US agricultural production was over-expanded to meet wartime export demand. When European agriculture recovered in the 1920s, there was a general oversupply of food products. Important European importers tried to moderate the fall of domestic agricultural prices by returning to pre-war tariff protection, which restricted US exports.

Over the period 1924-1928 the agricultural situation in the USA did stabilise, more due to internal economic growth than to the recovery of foreign demand. The European markets were still slack, and US wheat exports faced increased competition from Canada, Australia and Argentina.

Exceptionally good harvests in 1928 in Europe and overseas added to cereal stocks. By the middle of 1929, world stocks of wheat were equivalent to more than a year's exports of all the exporting countries. In June 1929, the USA passed the Agricultural Marketing Act. One objective of this was to initiate and assist in the establishment of marketing co-operatives to give farmers greater bargaining power. Another objective was to stabilise market prices by setting up publicly financed stabilisation corporations to purchase commodities on depressed markets and store the commodities until they could be sold on more buoyant markets.

When prices fell after the start of the Great Depression in October 1929, the stabilisation corporations tried to keep prices up by purchases. However, the crisis became so acute and the funds were so limited that the initiative failed and the scheme had to be abandoned.

7.2 The introduction of agricultural support policies in Europe 1929-1939

In the USA, October 1929 saw the Wall Street Crash and the start of the Great Depression. The stock market collapse was not the cause of the depression, but it was the event that triggered it. Prices fell, industrial production fell and unemployment rose in the years 1929-1932. Then the economic situation was stabilised and there was some recovery during the rest of the 1930s.

The depression started in the USA, but it soon spread to Europe where Germany was especially badly hit. In June 1930, the US Congress passed the Smoot-Hawley Tariff Act. This Act raised tariff rates significantly, and for many products the tariff levels became prohibitive. European exports were hit by the high protection level, and with rising unemployment and balance of payments problems, European countries felt they had to respond by increasing their tariff rates. This beggar-my-neighbour policy caused the spread of the depression from one country to another, and it deepened the crisis.

Agricultural markets were especially hard hit by the depression. Agricultural prices fell more than industrial prices. Farm incomes fell, and because of the economic importance of the agricultural sector, this contributed to the economic depression.

Britain

When the crisis broke, in 1929, the dramatic fall in world grain prices was immediately reflected on the British market. Other countries protected and supported their agricultural sectors, and as the British market became the only non-protected market, it was flooded with dumped imports.

Britain had to give up its free trade policy. In 1931 and 1932, laws were passed which allowed the government to impose tariffs. Manufactured goods in particular were protected, whereas major foodstuffs and raw materials were exempt from tariffs. The government was authorised to discriminate between countries. It could allow imports from specific countries to enter duty free or at a reduced tariff, and it could increase import duties on products from countries which discriminated against British products.

The tariff policy of Britain followed the principle that domestic goods should have first priority; goods from the Dominions (self-governing countries belonging to the British Empire) and the colonies should have second priority; and goods from other countries should have third priority. This principle lay behind the imperial preference negotiated between Britain and the Dominions in Ottawa in 1932.

The Ottawa Agreement gave imperial products, mainly agricultural products, preference on the British market, and gave British manufactured goods preference in the Empire. Imperial products imported to Britain were exempt from import duties. For a series of agricultural products such as wheat, cheese, fruit, etc., British tariffs on goods from third countries were increased, thus increasing the preference for Empire imports.

Since imperial preferences exempted most agricultural products from duties, British farmers benefited little from the raised tariffs on foreign products. Support for British farmers was given by a series of different measures for different products. The support measurers were introduced piecemeal for the different products, and were not part of an overall plan.

For wheat, a deficiency payment system was used. Farmers were guaranteed a price which was above the market price, and the price difference was paid by the government.

For milk, there was intervention in the organisation of the markets. Milk marketing boards were set up in 1933. They had the exclusive right to buy and sell milk, and they allocated the milk between different users to obtain the best return. The revenue was paid back to the farmers as an average milk price, regardless of the use of the milk. The boards were able to pursue a price differentiation policy because they had a monopoly.

The introduction of agricultural support policies in Europe 1929-1939

They charged a high price for milk sold for liquid consumption, and a low wholesale price for milk sold for manufacturing dairy products. The price differentiation was logical, because there was foreign competition on the markets for dairy products but not on the liquid milk market. Dairy products from the Dominions could enter Britain free of duties, as import restrictions were precluded under the Ottawa Agreement.

Beef and cattle were mainly imported from Ireland, Argentina, Australia and New Zealand. British beef producers were hit by a substantial fall in prices. The government tried to solve the price problem by restricting foreign imports, but this was not enough, and subsidies were given in the form of a flat rate per animal as a supplementary measure.

Pig producers were also in a critical position, and a quota system was introduced. British producers and each of the countries exporting to Britain were allocated quotas, limiting overall supply and creating a better balance in the market. The share of British suppliers was increased at the expense of foreign suppliers and a voluntary agreement with exporters to the British market reduced British imports.

Minimum prices for home-produced bacon were fixed at such a high level that it caused a big increase in supply. Britain gave up the voluntary agreements and enforced further restrictions on imports. Imports from foreign countries other than the Dominions were cut by about half. A big exporter like Denmark, which depended on exports of bacon, was severely hit. Imports to Britain were organised on the basis of export licences given to the exporting countries, so that exporters did benefit from the higher prices caused by the restriction on imports.

Market interventions in Britain neutralised the most severe effects of the crisis for British producers. These interventions also led to a striking shift in the import pattern for food products. In the ten years up to 1938, import volumes from the Empire increased by 43 per cent, whereas imports from other foreign countries declined by 17 per cent. Total imports were nearly stagnant, increasing by only 6 per cent over these 10 years.

France

In France, different kinds of intervention in the agricultural markets were taken step by step. The first step was to increase tariff protection for agricultural products, but because of the continuing fall in world market prices, the protection from tariff increases was not considered sufficient. The second step was to introduce systematic import restrictions to support prices. Such restrictions do not work when a country shifts from being a net-importer to a potential net-exporter. France was a potential net-exporter of wheat and wine in years with plentiful harvests. The third step was a more fundamental intervention in the organisation of the markets, in an attempt to bring about a balance between supply and demand.

When the crisis broke, in 1929, the first reaction was to increase tariff protection. Duties on agricultural products were raised not only in 1929, but also in 1930 and 1931. The end result was a very high protection level, but the support of tariff protection was not considered sufficient, as the increased tariff rates on agricultural imports were neutralised by falling prices on the world market. Also, tariffs on some agricultural products and on many manufactured products could not be increased, because they were bound by agreements in trade treaties which France had entered into.

Therefore, as a second step, import quotas were introduced as a new general protection measure. Previously, import quotas had been related to tariff concessions. These concessions were limited to the import quota (tariff quota). France was the first country to make systematic use of import restrictions as a means of protecting industry and agriculture. To start with, the quotas were only intended to be temporary, but the quota system remained in force until France joined the European Economic Community.

The administrative system for import restrictions changed during the thirties. Originally the import quotas were global, which meant that every country could export as long as the quota had not been used up. The problem with this system was that all the permitted imports were made immediately after the opening of the quota. The system of global quotas was replaced by a system based on import licences, which were allocated to French importers according to their past imports. It is always difficult to find the 'right' allocation of import licences between importers, and the system neutralises competition between them. Because of these difficulties, a system of export quotas was tried. Each exporting country got a quota, and was responsible for the distribution of licences between its exporters. Exporters were then in a strong bargaining position in relation to French buyers, so it was the foreign exporters who earned the quota rent. French traders complained, so the export quota system was replaced by a new import licence system, under which importers had to pay for import licences. For some agricultural products the system developed into a variable levy system. The tax payable was calculated as the difference between a desired domestic price and the world market

The introduction of agricultural support policies in Europe 1929-1939

price, which fluctuated. As time went on, the administration of the quota system not only served to protect domestic producers, but it also became an instrument for discriminating between different exporting countries in trade negotiations. When entering into trade treaties with other countries, France gave specific concessions on imports if French exports received reciprocal concessions on the foreign market. The quota system did not apply to imports from French North Africa and the colonies.

Import restrictions are not enough to raise price levels when domestic production, plus the permitted imports, exceeds domestic consumption. In such cases a third step, involving more far-reaching market intervention, was needed. The aim was to create a better balance between supply and demand in order to support prices. There were such interventions for wheat and wine.

To stimulate the demand for domestic wheat, the French minister for agriculture had powers to prescribe the minimum percentage of domestic wheat which millers had to use in flour. This percentage was often close to 100 per cent, but it varied according to the size of the harvest.

In the 1930s, even the milling ration system was not enough to bring about a market balance which could create price stability. Public purchases of wheat were tried in order to secure a minimum price for farmers. However, the intervention costs were too high, and the public price guarantee was replaced by an obligation on millers to buy wheat at a minimum price. Other measures were used to reduce supplies, such as restrictions on the cultivated area and the right of the government to claim a part of the harvest stored on the farm, but these did not have long-term effects. The government also relieved the market by subsidising exports.

The political situation in France was unstable. One government succeeded another after a short period in power. Under these conditions it was difficult to establish a more coherent long-term agricultural policy. At any given time, the policy was marked by piecemeal initiatives to solve specific acute commodity problems. When the Popular Front government came to power in 1936, there was a more systematic attempt to insulate the market from the forces of supply and demand. A wheat board was established, which gained monopolistic control over all foreign trade in wheat. It could also decide on measures necessary to absorb surpluses.

During the 1930s, there was an increasing surplus of wine. Wine from French North Africa could enter the French market unhindered, and increased imports contributed to the fall of wine prices on the French market. Several measures were taken in an attempt to create a better market balance by reducing supply. If the total supply on the market exceeded a certain level, wine producers were compelled to deliver part of their production to a public organisation for distillation. Large producers were prohibited from planting new vineyards. Later, a system of marketing permits was introduced. Each producer was only allowed to sell a certain quantity on the market, and he could be forced to sell the rest of his produce at a very low price for distillation.

Germany

The Weimar Republic tried various means to solve the agricultural crisis of the years 1929-1932.

Already in 1929, Germany introduced a compulsory milling ratio for domestic wheat in flour. The ratio was increased as the market price fell until it was nearly 100 per cent in 1931. Tariffs were also extensively applied. The government was empowered to adjust tariff rates by decree. The aim of the tariff policy was to keep consumer prices stable, but this became impossible.

A state monopoly for all trade in maize was introduced. Since the domestic production was very small, it was effectively an import monopoly. Rye was the most important cereal and already in the 1920s Germany tried to keep up the price of rye through market interventions. Government support was given to private bodies storing surpluses, and later the government itself intervened in the market. It was difficult to dispose of the government stocks, so part of the rye stock was rendered unfit for human consumption and sold as animal feed.

Germany did not use import quotas in the same way as France. In Germany, import quotas were used as bargaining tools for granting trading partners tariff concessions on limited quantities.

The increased protection of the agricultural sector in the period 1929-1932 prevented prices on the domestic market from falling to anything like the same extent as prices on the world market. Prices were kept up by reducing imports. There was a nominal fall in farm incomes, but this was a period of deflation and the prices of manufactured goods fell by about as much as the prices of agricultural products. For farmers with large debts, the nominal price fall was disastrous, and they were hit by bankruptcy. For other farmers the situation was acceptable, especially compared with the economic distress in the manufacturing sector where there was huge unemployment.

State intervention became much more comprehensive when the national socialists came into power in 1933. The agricultural policy of the

The introduction of agricultural support policies in Europe 1929-1939

national socialists was based on some fundamental ideas which had previously been current in Germany and were current elsewhere in Europe at the time. Different elements were combined into a coherent philosophy with an overall policy which was systematically carried out. The agricultural policy was based on the ideas of: 1. The importance of a large agricultural sector. 2. Corporatist organisation. 3. Regulation of agricultural markets to ensure fair prices.

The national socialists were interested in structural policy. Their goal was to create farms of a minimum size, sufficient to support a family. These new farms could not be sold without permission, they could not be mortgaged, and they should be passed intact to a single heir. Farm ownership was strongly regulated. The agricultural population was an important factor in preserving German culture and social stability. Politically it was important for there to be substantial agricultural production to ensure a high degree of self-sufficiency in case of war.

The State Food Corporation comprehensively organised food production and distribution. It was based on the corporatist idea of unifying all the participants in food production and distribution in one organisation. All farmers, all agricultural workers, all processors and traders dealing with agricultural produce and agricultural inputs were equally obliged to belong to the State Food Corporation.

The internal administration was hierarchical, allowing total party control of the apparatus. For example, farmers could be required to deliver a specified percentage of their crops on a specific date via a specific intermediary. It was a very bureaucratic system and heavily staffed, because the sector was so closely regulated and supervised.

This organisation also implemented the new regulation of agricultural markets. The main objective was to ensure fair and stable prices for agricultural products. Farm prices were to be at a level which would provide farmers with a fair income. Price intervention was also used to guard against price fluctuations. There was a deliberate attempt to replace the law of supply and demand by administrative pricing.

The pricing policy was the central aspect of agricultural intervention. Import controls and trade policy were also important elements in implementing the pricing policy. State import boards were set up for all important commodities. Private importers had to obtain import licences from the state import boards. If a board found that the necessary demand existed, the import was allowed upon payment of a levy, which corresponded to the difference between the desired domestic price level and the import price. In reality, this was a variable levy system. The import boards could also buy the produce from the importers and resell it at a higher price on the domestic market or they could import on their own account, and they could intervene on the domestic market by buying and selling commodities and keeping stocks. This buffer stock role was important for smoothing out the price fluctuations which would otherwise be caused by supply fluctuations.

Not only did the boards control the total volume of imports, they also played an important role in relation to German trade policy. The state import boards were required to favour imports from countries which were prepared to buy German goods. The former system of trade treaties, in which the most-favoured-nation principle was an integral part, was abandoned and replaced by bilateral arrangements, involving reciprocal guarantees of import quotas and preferential tariffs.

German trade was diverted away from western Europe and North America and towards Italy, southeast Europe and Latin America.

European exporters

In western Europe, Denmark and the Netherlands were important exporters. Countries in central and eastern Europe, such as Poland, Hungary, Romania, Bulgaria, and Yugoslavia were also exporters of agricultural products.

The exporting countries in central and eastern Europe were in a difficult situation in the 1930s. The agricultural sector played a dominant role in these countries, but they were poor, so they could not afford to support their agricultural sectors. These countries tried to co-ordinate their exports and to obtain preferential treatment from the countries of western Europe. In 1931, France offered some preferential treatment for exports of wheat from Hungary, Romania and Yugoslavia. For a while, Germany had a similar agreement to import wheat from Hungary and Romania, but it was only after the national socialists came to power in 1933 that more extensive trade preference schemes were established with countries in south-eastern Europe. These preferential trade agreements did not solve the agricultural problems of the exporting countries, but they did give some limited benefits to exporters.

In Denmark, at the start of the crisis, 80 per cent of export revenue came from agriculture. Around two-thirds of agricultural production was exported, so it was clear that the fall in world market prices could not be neutralised by protection, but it could be neutralised to some extent by foreign exchange policy. When Britain left the Gold Standard and devalued the pound in 1931, Denmark also left the Gold Standard and devalued. This passive adjustment was followed by an active devaluation strategy; in 1933 the Danish currency was devalued against the currencies of Britain and Germany, its two main export markets. Another problem was the imposition of import quotas by countries importing Danish farm products. Various commodity-specific marketing boards were set up. Their purpose was to allocate export licences and facilitate price equalisation through the pooling of the prices obtained in different export markets.

A series of measures was taken to support prices on the domestic market. A high price for sugar-beet was fixed, causing a high price for refined sugar. A tax on domestic butter consumption was introduced to fund a butter price subsidy for farmers. A grain price subsidy was financed through an import duty. Exports of pork were reduced, because of foreign import quotas, and if pork production had not been reduced there would have been a fall in the domestic pork price. Therefore, production quotas for individual producers were imposed to bring about a major cut in pig production. These domestic price-support measures depended on import controls, which were enforced through the allocation of the scarce foreign currency.

The Netherlands was in a similar position to that of Denmark, and some of the instruments applied were similar. Domestic marketing and external trade in agricultural products were regulated through commodity-specific marketing boards. Direct subsidies were used to maintain domestic producer prices and export subsidies were used to maintain exports.

7.3 The Great Depression and agricultural policy in the USA 1929-1939

The Great Depression and Agriculture

The US agricultural sector had adjustment problems during the 1920s. US agriculture expanded during the First World War, and it was over-expanded when agriculture in western Europe recovered. During the 1920s, production grew by around 15 per cent and labour productivity by nearly 25 per cent. Large areas of land, which had formerly been used to grow fodder for horses, were now released for commercial production as tractors replaced horses. Following good harvests, cereal stocks were exceptionally high when the stock market crash came in October 1929.

The farmers were not financially well consolidated when the crisis came. The agricultural sector was hit especially hard from 1929 to 1932.

The index of farm prices fell by 56 per cent, and the net nominal income of agriculture fell by a little less than 70 per cent, from $6.7 billion in 1929 to $2.3 billion in 1932. The general price level also fell so that, in real terms, farm income fell by 50 per cent. Out of 6.5 million farms, 2.5 million were mortgaged, and half the mortgaged farms were so distressed that the farmers lost their farms (Benedict, 1955).

The collapse of agricultural prices in 1929-1930 was a major factor helping to turn a slump into a deep depression. Falling prices had a negative influence on economic expectations, making businesses more reluctant to invest. Although the relative importance of US agriculture was declining, the agricultural sector still played an important economic role in 1930. 25 per cent of the male labour force worked in agriculture. The distress of agriculture reduced agricultural demand and spread the crisis, as the farmers' inability to repay loans caused a spate of bank failures, which had independent deflationary effects. Money supply was reduced because bank failures destroyed money and encouraged currency hoarding. Business confidence was further weakened, discouraging investment.

The lower demand of the agricultural sector had a knock-on effect, increasing unemployment in urban industries. High unemployment and lower incomes in the cities depressed demand for agricultural products, which further aggravated the crisis in agriculture, pushing prices lower.

The fall in agricultural prices in the period 1930-1934 was not the result of increased production but of shrinking demand. The average level of agricultural production in the period 1930-1934 was 2 per cent below the average for the preceding five years (USDA, 1942). The overproduction was caused by shrinking demand, both at home and abroad. The fall in prices was primarily determined by shrinking domestic demand due to falling incomes. A more appropriate demand-oriented macroeconomic policy could have cushioned the sharp fall in agricultural prices (Friedman, 1963).

Price stabilisation schemes under the Agricultural Marketing Act of June 1929, referred to above, could not cope with the dramatic fall of prices. The government did not react because the Hoover administration, 1929-1933, believed in a non-interventionist policy. To start with, the crisis was thought to be similar to previous crises, being a normal part of the economic cycle. This view was supported by the mainstream economists who believed in the self-regulating forces of the economy. It was only after Franklin D. Roosevelt became President in March 1933 that the policy changed. During his presidential election campaign, he had promoted the New Deal programme.

The Great Depression and agricultural policy in the USA 1929-1939

The New Deal programme

The New Deal was a comprehensive programme, dealing both with foreign affairs and internal affairs, including the roles of the federal and state governments vis-à-vis the economy. The economic part of the New Deal programme was based on the idea that economic intervention was necessary to alleviate the social distress caused by the economic crisis. Its objectives were recovery, reform and relief. The economic programme encompassed nearly all parts of economic life including industrial policy, labour market policy, agricultural policy, and recovery policy.

The industrial policy was concerned with prices and wages. Before the First World War there had been a strong anti-big business movement, trying to encourage competition through anti-trust legislation. The National Industrial Recovery Act of June 1933 tried to dampen too strong competition, because the problem now was depressed prices. A code of business practice, designed to ensure fair competition, had to be worked out for each industry. These codes included the regulation of labour conditions. Nearly every code restricted the working hours of manual workers to 40 hours per week and fixed minimum wages. They contributed to the organisation of the labour market by stimulating collective bargaining.

The New Deal introduced an agricultural price and income support policy to the USA for the first time. During the period 1860-1914, land settlement, research and education, and farm credit programmes had been initiated and expanded. Within the legal, technological and credit framework, resource allocation, production and returns to producers were largely determined by the state of domestic and foreign markets. There was little direct government support for farm products, in contrast to the policy of high levels of protection for manufacturers.

The agricultural policy was designed to improve the relative prices and incomes of the farm sector by direct government intervention. The direct intervention in agriculture was more pronounced than in other sectors of the economy.

The recovery policy was also new, and it can be considered as a forerunner for Keynesian theories about an active fiscal policy. Employment was stimulated through public work projects. The federal budget, which balanced in 1930, was expanded and it showed an increasing deficit after the Roosevelt administration came into office. Increased social security provided under the Social Security Act 1935, promoted unemployment insurance and retirement pension schemes.

Macroeconomic stabilisation policy was unknown before 1933 because the market economy was considered to be self-regulating with no need for intervention. This attitude was changed dramatically by the New Deal philosophy. Active fiscal policy was introduced as an instrument and new legislation allowed for an active monetary policy. The President acquired the right to require the Federal Reserve Bank to expand credit, and to conduct an active foreign exchange policy. In April 1933 the US dollar came off the Gold Standard and the dollar was significantly devalued.

Agricultural policy

The Roosevelt administration responded quickly to the desperate financial conditions in agriculture. Because of the low prices many farmers defaulted on their loans, and private lenders would neither give loans nor renew loans.

In May 1933 two acts were passed to relieve the economic distress of farmers. The first act, the Agricultural Adjustment Act, introduced measures for raising agricultural prices and giving income support. The second act, the Emergency Farm Mortgage Act, provided refinancing of farm mortgages held by private lenders through federal land bank loans. There was a lower interest rate on land bank loans.

The idea behind the Agricultural Adjustment Act was to restore agricultural prices to the same level as in the period 1910-1914 when the agricultural economic situation had been considered satisfactory. Indexes for agricultural output prices, agricultural input prices and consumer prices were calculated for the base period 1910-1914. If input and consumer prices had risen 30 per cent since the base period, then agricultural output prices should also be raised 30 per cent to preserve the parity between the prices paid and received by farmers.

The main instrument for achieving this was the control of supply. The Secretary of Agriculture could reduce the acreage or the marketed volume of any basic agricultural product. A base acreage for each crop was determined for each grower who was obliged to grow no more than an agreed percentage of his base acreage. Farmers received compensatory payments for the land set-aside.

The rental payments on set-aside land were supplemented by other compensatory payments. For some products, growers received "parity payments", depending on the gap between the parity price and the price actually received from the market. The parity price could be considered as the target price and the parity payments as a form of deficiency payment. Parity payments were partly financed by levying processing taxes, which were ultimately paid by consumers, and partly by the government. The measures in the Agricultural Adjustment Act could not bring immediate relief to the farm sector, as there were large stock overhangs in the markets for the major storable products. Therefore, the Commodity Credit Corporation was established to make loans to farmers against stored products. The commodity stored acted as collateral for the loan. The loans were based on a fixed rate, the loan rate, per unit of the commodity. The loan could be repaid either in cash or in kind by passing the ownership of the commodity to the Commodity Credit Corporation, regardless of the market price. This system provided farmers with liquidity, and it also set a floor price for the commodity. If the market price was above the loan rate, the farmer could sell the crop and repay the loan. If the market price was below the loan rate, the loans could be repaid in kind.

Another important institution, the Federal Surplus Relief Corporation (FSRC) was set up to buy farm commodities at the market price and to distribute them to state relief agencies for the benefit of the unemployed and the poor. A school lunch programme was initiated, and later a Food Stamp programme was introduced. People with below a certain income level received food stamps which could be used to buy food. These initiatives created extra demand for food products in a situation where farm-prices had fallen because of depressed demand. So the Federal Surplus Relief Corporation helped farmers by creating extra demand, and it was also an important relief measure for low-income households. The FSRC ran a deficit, and its activities amounted to a food subsidy scheme.

A main element of the agricultural policy was to raise domestic agricultural prices through the loan rate mechanism. A loan rate above the world market price would create problems, because it would stimulate foreign imports and make it difficult for US exports. A couple of amendments to the Agricultural Adjustment Act in 1935 took care of these problems. The President was authorised to impose quotas on imports if foreign supplies impeded programmes for raising the prices of farm products. Another provision was that thirty per cent of all import duty revenues should be made available for programmes to expand domestic and foreign demand for US farm products through consumption and export subsidies.

Change in trade policy

During Roosevelt's first term as President there was a change in US trade policy. The Smoot-Hawley Tariff Act of 1930 had raised tariffs to a record level. The Act was criticised by economists because it prompted European countries to retaliate. Agricultural imports to the USA were relatively unimportant, so high tariffs did not benefit agriculture. High protection of manufactures did hurt European exporters, who retaliated by protecting their agriculture against US exports.

This was the background to Roosevelt's sharp reversal of trade policy towards lower tariffs. The Reciprocal Trade Agreement Act of 1934 authorised the President to pursue a policy of tariff reductions and quota increases through reciprocal trade agreements. These agreements were based on the most-favoured-nation principle. A series of agreements was made, and there is some evidence that they led to a modest expansion of trade, also for farm exports (Saloutos, 1982). As US farm exports were relatively small, the impact on the economic conditions of agriculture was small.

7.4 Lack of international co-operation

During the Great Depression, policies for giving agricultural support were introduced in Europe. Agriculture was first regulated by trade interventions and then by domestic interventions.

Protection hurts exporters. In the USA, the agricultural sector was regulated first through domestic intervention and then, to some extent, by trade intervention. Raising import duties on agricultural products does not help an exporting agricultural sector unless they are necessary for introducing domestic support schemes. At the time, US agricultural exports, as a share of total US production, were relatively small, and the difficulties of US agriculture were mainly caused by the fall in the domestic demand for agricultural produce.

In most European countries the agricultural sector had economic difficulties in the period 1875-1895. It was a period when bilateral trade treaties were made and tariff protection returned, together with discrimination between imports from different countries. There was no international co-operation seeking to limit the escalation of tariff protection, though there were international meetings at which the agricultural difficulties were discussed. The one exception to this picture of non-cooperation was the Brussels Sugar Convention of 1902, by which the sugar exporting countries agreed to refrain from using export subsidies.

In the inter-war period, 1919-1939, international cooperation was more wanting than ever, although international conferences, especially under the auspices of the League of Nations, were held to discuss the problems of agriculture. During the crisis in the 1930s, protection against imports and other market interventions spread from country to country. There was no international system that was able stop the spread of this beggar-my-neighbour policy. However, there were a couple of exceptions in the form of international commodity agreements.

International Wheat Agreement was signed in 1933. In the first instance it was a two-year agreement. With some exceptions, exporters undertook to limit their exports to certain quotas, and to reduce wheat production. Importers committed themselves not to increase their output of wheat and agreed to adopt measures to increase consumption. They also agreed to reduce tariffs and relax import restrictions on wheat once there was a sustained rise in world market prices from a low level. The agreement was not successful because importers did not take the necessary steps to increase imports, and exporters did not reduce their production and exports as intended. After two years, the agreement was not renewed.

An International Sugar Agreement was signed in 1931 between seven exporting countries. They agreed on a system of export quotas to achieve a certain price level on the world market. Their goal was not achieved, and the agreement failed because it was not comprehensive enough. Only seven exporters signed the agreement, and the large importers were not involved. In 1937 a successor agreement included most of the exporting countries and the large importers of sugar. The agreement seemed to be a more effective arrangement, but this could not be tested because of the outbreak of war in 1939.

These international commodity agreements were based on the idea of market regulation, so the idea of regulation spread from national markets to international markets. International market regulation is justified in periods of low international prices, but the problem is that it does not work when there is widespread economic distress.

7.5 *How did agriculture perform?*

Agriculture benefits from high prices during wars. The task of governments is to keep agricultural prices down in times of war for the benefit of consumers.

In wartime, prices will be high in spite of public interventions, and farm incomes will be high. However, agriculture will have problems in belligerent countries because, like other civilian industries, agriculture will have problems in getting the necessary resources which are otherwise allocated for military purposes.

In between the two world wars, the conditions for agriculture were difficult. In Europe, agriculture had to recover from reduced soil fertility, reduced livestock and worn out buildings and machinery. In the USA, agriculture had been over-expanded during the war, and production had to be adjusted. Economically, the 1920s were not a prosperous period and it was followed by the Great Depression of the 1930s, which hit agriculture hard with drastic price falls.

Despite the bleak economic conditions of agriculture, there were important changes in the period 1920-1945. This is illustrated in Table 7.1, which shows the changes in agricultural output, employment and labour productivity in the period 1920-1945, compared with the previous period 1880-1920, and the subsequent period 1945-1980.

The figures show that there were important production increases in the period 1920-1945. This was the case for the USA, Denmark and the UK, whereas output declined in France, as northern France was one of the battlefields at the end of the Second World War.

The number of male workers in agriculture increased in the period 1880-1920 in the USA and Denmark, but there was a slight decline in France and the UK. From 1920 onwards there was a decline in the agricultural labour force in all countries. It is interesting to note that the decline in employment seems to have accelerated in the period 1920-1980.

The output per male worker, which is an indication of labour productivity, increased more in the period 1920-1945 than in the previous period. Again, there is clearly an accelerating increase in labour productivity.

The ratio between the agricultural land area and the agricultural labour force also changed. In the UK, France and Denmark, the area of agricultural land increased slightly from 1880 to the 1920s, since when it has been either stagnant or slightly decreasing. Since 1920 there has been a large decline in the agricultural labour force, so the land area per male worker has increased. This is shown in Table 7.2

The number of hectares per male worker in the USA is much larger than in Europe. In the USA the land is cultivated less intensively than in Europe, and the labour-intensive livestock production is relatively smaller in the USA than in Europe. In Europe, in the period 1920-1945, there was only a slight increase in the land area per male worker. It has only been since 1945, and especially since 1960, that the land area per male worker has increased significantly in Europe, as mechanisation has substituted machinery for labour.

How did agriculture perform?

Table 7.1: The percentage change in agricultural output, employment and labour productivity 1880-1980 for the USA, Denmark, France and the UK

	USA			Denmark		
	Agri-cultural output	Number of male workers	Output per male worker	Agri-cultural output	Number of male workers	Output per male worker
1880-1920	83	28	66	83	21	55
1920-1945	47	-27	100	36	-6	44
1945-1960	28	-44	138	67	-18	104
1960-1980	46	-55	224	28	-60	219
	France			United Kingdom		
1880-1920	26	-9	36	4	-11	17
1920-1945	-4	-15	17	36	-10	50
1945-1960	92	-33	185	32	-17	59
1960-1980	67	-49	235	49	-45	165

Source: Calculations based on data from Hayami and Ruttan (1985)

Table 7.2: The land area in hectares per male worker in agriculture 1880-1980 in the USA, Denmark, France and the UK

	USA	Denmark	France	United Kingdom
1880	26.0	8.8	6.7	14.3
1920	36.6	8.1	7.8	16.6
1945	61.5	8.7	8.3	18.5
1960	111.0	10.3	13.3	23.2
1980	239.8	24.2	24.1	38.9

Source: See Table 7.1

During the 1930s, policies for agricultural support were introduced in Europe and USA. The direct cause was the need to relieve the economic distress of the agricultural sector. Particularly in the USA, the problem was not the agricultural policy itself, but the fact that it was introduced too late.

The aim of the policy was to relieve the economic distress caused by the Great Depression, but as demonstrated in Chapter 8, the agricultural policies were maintained in the post-war period in spite of the fact that economic activity was high.

Were the agricultural policies in Europe and the USA successful? Given the circumstances of the Great Depression, there is no doubt that the agricultural interventions temporarily relieved distress. However, these interventions should have been made earlier and it would have been better if there had been some kind of international coordination.

The longer-term problems were not solved. The main agricultural producers in western Europe tried to solve their agricultural problems through trade intervention, because they were net importers. This pushed the problem onto the exporting countries. The USA tried to solve its agricultural problems by reducing supply, but this was not successful in the long run. From 1930-1940, agricultural output increased even though the agricultural labour force decreased. The aim of reducing supply could not be realised due to increased labour productivity. Because of general unemployment, the reduction of the agricultural labour force was so slight that it could not neutralise the increase in production from labour productivity gains.

The long-term problem of agricultural surpluses first arose in the USA during the 1920s. It continued as an underlying problem in the 1930s, although the low agricultural prices in the period 1929-1932 were caused by large stocks and decreased demand due to the depression.

7.6 Agriculture in the Soviet Union 1917-1939

The economic performance of the Soviet Union

Industrialisation started in Russia before the First World War. Nevertheless, it was still predominantly an agricultural society, with around 70 per cent of the workforce involved in agriculture.

The period 1914-1920 was disastrous for the Russian economy. From September 1914 to October 1917, Russia was a belligerent in the First World War. In October 1917, the Bolsheviks took over and there was civil war between the red armies and the white armies, ending in November 1920 with victory for the red armies.

The economic collapse in Russia was even more catastrophic than the collapse in Germany, Austria and other countries hit by the war. In those countries the main problem was inflation, but production did not decline greatly and it soon recovered. In Russia, hyperinflation was accompanied by a dramatic fall in production. In 1920, industrial production was only 20 per cent of the level in 1913, and the crop yield in 1920 was only around half the yield in 1913. Industrial production returned to its pre-war level by 1926, but agricultural production had not yet reached the pre-war level because the yield had declined. The areas sown in 1926 were already somewhat larger than before the war (Baykov, 1946).

The First Five Year Plan started in 1927-1928 and gave priority to heavy industry. According to the official figures, the average annual increase during the First Five Year Plan was 29 per cent. Although the increase in industrial production was lower during the subsequent plans, according to the official statistics, in 1939 industrial production was a little less than 5 times the level in 1929. This gives a cumulative rate of increase of 17 per cent per year. The official figures seem to overestimate the actual production increases, and a more careful estimate indicates a cumulative growth rate of 13.5 per cent per year (Lewis, 1953). This increase in industrial production took place while the deep economic crisis of the 1930s hit the rest of Europe and the USA.

The number of people dependant on industry increased from 15 million in 1926 to 45 million in 1939. However, this enormous increase was only slightly higher than the total population increase from 147 to 170 millions (Lorimer, 1946).

Agricultural production had reached its pre-war level by around 1929 when forced collectivisation began. The immediate results of this were catastrophic. Production fell, and there was famine in parts of the Soviet Union in the years 1931-1933. Once collectivisation was established, there was an increase in agricultural production. In 1939, a smaller agricultural population cultivated a larger area than in 1929 and produced a harvest about 20 per cent larger. This was a dramatic transformation of agriculture in a short time, but at huge human cost. However, from a purely production point of view, the transformation cannot be considered a great success. The production increase was only a little higher than the population increase.

After the Second World War, all the problems connected with state farms and collective farms led to very slow growth in agricultural production. This was in contrast to the very high production increases in western Europe and the USA.

The economic policy 1917-1939

At the time of the revolution in 1917, it was Lenin's intention to nationalise the means of production gradually. Because of the civil war, Lenin found it necessary to take more drastic steps to control the economy than he originally intended. Nationalisation was pushed through during the civil war period, 1917-1920. Factories, credit institutions, internal and external trade were all nationalised. Workers were forced to accept the work they were offered and a system of equal earnings was adopted. The market was neglected and replaced by a system of requisitioning supply and rationing demand. This period of nationalisation, requisitioning and rationing, was called the period of War Communism.

War Communism created problems, especially in rural areas. During the revolution, the peasants took over the large estates and redistributed the land, and this caused output to fall. The government needed food for the cities, but the prices it was willing to pay were so low that the peasants were unwilling to deliver. There was a vicious circle. The government tried to requisition grain; the peasants reduced their sowings; the cities suffered from shortages of food and agricultural raw materials; the workers returned to their villages in search of food; factory output declined; the peasants became increasingly unwilling to part with their crops, as the industrial production offered in exchange got smaller and smaller. Rationing in the cities became more severe and there was famine. Livestock holdings were also greatly reduced.

In 1920, industrial and agricultural production nearly collapsed, as illustrated by the figures referred to above. The country was unable to feed itself. It was realised that a new policy was needed to deal with the situation.

In 1921 the New Economic Policy (NEP) restored private trading and allowed private ownership in some cases. The state retained a monopoly of production in the most important industries, while allowing small private factories to operate in less important industries. The financial sector was controlled by the state. The government relaxed almost all controls over trade. State factories sold their output to private traders, who distributed it to consumers. The requisitioning of grain was stopped and the peasants sold their grain on the open market. The government taxed the peasants in money, rather than by forcing them to deliver goods at low prices.

The results of the NEP were positive. The peasants increased supplies of food and agricultural raw materials to the cities and to industry. By 1926, industrial production was back to the level of 1913, and the area under cultivation was somewhat larger than it had been before the war.

During the years 1924-1926 there was a lively academic debate about future development strategy, which will be discussed in more detail in the following section. The objective was to create a strong, economically developed country in which state property played a decisive role. All agreed that this objective should be realised by industrialisation, and that industrialisation should be based on the extraction of resources from agriculture. But there was disagreement about how it should be done, and how quickly it could be done.

To start with the NEP, which was based on the market mechanism, had the upper hand, but gradually there was a shift away from the NEP. The role of private traders was gradually reduced. Collective and state trading associations were organised, and the private traders' share of retail trade fell from 75 per cent in 1922-1923 to 22 per cent in 1927-1928 (Baykov, 1946).

The policy of rapid industrialisation based on heavy industry triumphed over the policy of gradual industrialisation based on consumer-oriented industries. The First Five Year Plan began in 1927-1928. The high investment level needed for industry demanded a high rate of savings, which was difficult to realise in a country with a low GDP per capita. The funds necessary for industrialisation had to be obtained from agriculture through forced savings. One method was the "scissors" strategy, squeezing resources out of agriculture by fixing low farm output prices and high input prices and consumer prices. The other method was heavy taxation. Both methods were applied.

The farmers were forced to save and they would be the last to benefit from the results. In a predominantly rural society, opposition was to be expected. In summer 1928, it became evident that the peasants were unwilling to suffer the high rate of savings imposed on them. They did not deliver the grain necessary for feeding the growing urban population, so rationing had to be reintroduced.

The resentment of the government was focused on the "kulaks", who were the farmers with marketable supplies. The kulaks were not at all large landowners; they belonged to the upper stratum of peasants, being sufficiently large to need to hire labour. Millions of the poorest farmers were net purchasers of food, and the middle peasants had only very little to spare. Only the kulaks had the marketable surpluses needed for the urban population.

In 1929 the decision was taken to eliminate the kulaks by extending collectivisation and taking their land into the collective farms. Collectives had existed since the revolution, but they were only viewed with favour by the very poorest farmers. In June 1929, only 4 per cent of the farmers were in collectives, by March 1930, this share had gone up to 55 per cent. The collectivisation process then slowed, but by 1936 as many as 90 per cent of peasants belonged to collectives.

Collectivisation was resisted not only by the kulaks but also by other peasants, and the immediate results were catastrophic. Peasants preferred to slaughter their cattle rather than having them collectivised. In 1935, the number of cattle was only half the level it had been in 1928, and the same was true for horses. Food shortages were acute, and there was famine in parts of Russia in the years 1931-1933.

In some circles, the collectivisation was considered a success. First, it solved the immediate problem of securing the whole of the marketable surplus for very little outlay. Loyal communists were put in charge of the collectives and they neither hid the grain nor tolerated a reduction in output. It was easier to get access to the production of large collectives and to enforce delivery. Second, agriculture became integrated into the general planning. The activities of millions of individual farmers could not be controlled by the planning authorities. Now the collectives could be told what to produce and how to produce. Third, collectivisation increased labour productivity, because the larger units facilitated mechanisation and it became easier to apply scientific methods. The number of tractors in 1939 was around 7 times the level of 10 years before, and agronomists and others with university degrees were employed by the collectives.

All the disadvantages of collectivisation became clear after the Second World War.

7.7 The debate about development strategy in the Soviet Union

Two different sets of options

The socialist regime which took over in 1917 was based on the theories of Karl Marx, in which social ownership and the equal income distribution were key points. So, all agreed that the main industries and the financial institutions should be nationalised, together with the main trading companies.

However, a more detailed description of how a socialist economy should be organised was never worked out by Marx, nor later by Lenin or Stalin. So there was room for different ideas which were vigorously debated, especially in the years 1924-1926 (Cohen, 1974).

Marx predicted that, according to the 'social laws', socialism would first occur in the most industrialised country, which at the time was Britain. Marx's prediction was confounded. The first socialist state became the Soviet Union, which was a society in which 70 per cent of the population worked in agriculture in 1914.

The debate about development strategy in the Soviet Union

Among those who participated in the development strategy debate, there was agreement on two issues. The socialist state should be based on industrialisation, and the industrialisation should be realised by an inward-looking strategy. Industrialisation should not rely on participation in international trade, but it should be based on the extraction of resources from agriculture.

The disagreements were about how these resources should be extracted, and how quickly this could be done. N. Bukharin was the leader of the school of thought which argued that the extraction of resources should be undertaken in co-operation with the peasants, by using the market mechanism (Bukharin, 1920). E. Preobrazhensky, a leader of the opposing school of thought, did not care about cooperation with the peasants; he favoured quick industrialisation by a massive extraction of resources through the planning mechanism (Preobrazhensky, 1926).

Political and moral issues

These disagreements encompassed political, moral and economic questions. Politically, Bukharin emphasized the great importance of the alliance between the workers and the peasants during the October Revolution in 1917 and the following civil war. He argued that this alliance should still be the backbone of the socialist society, and he feared that socialism could fail if the peasants opposed the regime. Preobrazhensky, on the other hand, did not regard this alliance as important.

Morally, it seems that Bukharin opposed any systematic political and economic oppression of the peasantry. He was against using force, and he was against forced collectivisation when that was decided upon. For Preobrazhensky and other traditional Marxists, moral values did not play any role in the social judgement of policies. The attitude inherited from Marx was that moral judgements were irrelevant. Scientific socialism contained a set of laws for social and economic development based on class and economic structures. Social judgements should only be based on this scientific socialism. Right and wrong should only refer to what would promote the realization of a society shaped by the inherent forces behind the inevitable progress towards socialism. Marx did not accept any law in his social model other than that of cause and effect. Moral questions were irrelevant to the choice of means, as long as the means supported the goal.

There seem to be some moral values in Bukharin's distinction between capitalist and socialist industrialisation. According to Bukharin, an essential feature of capitalist industrialisation was its parasitic impact on agriculture and the peasants. Together, the bourgeoisie in the cities and the landlords in rural areas exploited the workers and the peasants. Socialist industrialisation, by contrast, should not be a parasitic process in relation to the rural areas but should be the means of transforming and uplifting them.

Different opinions about economics

The economic theories behind the two schools of thought were totally different. According to Bukharin, development should be driven by the demand side, using the market as an instrument. When the great mass of people, including the peasants, got higher incomes, there would be a demand for consumer goods which would increase the demand for capital goods. According to Preobrazhensky, development should be driven by the supply side through the central planning mechanism. First, the capital goods sector had to be developed, which would then make it possible to produce consumer goods. Resources should be allocated by planning, so consumers should not have any influence on the production pattern through the market. In the economy there are important linkages between different productions which can be described by an input-output model. In a market economy, when one sector such as agriculture needs more input from another sector, e.g. the fertiliser industry, this will be reflected in the market, first through price increases and then by supply increases. In a planned economy, there will be no response if the planners are not aware of the need or if they consider the need to be less important than other needs.

In short, Bukharin believed in relying on demand, the market and linkages between sectors. Preobrazhensky was in favour of the scissors' policy, squeezing resources out of agriculture through unfavourable terms of trade between agriculture and industry. With low agricultural prices, the urban population would get cheap food, and with high industrial prices, industry should be able to save for further capital accumulation.

Bukharin was against the idea of forced savings. He believed that the necessary savings should be made voluntarily, as far as possible. He was against unfavourable terms of trade for agriculture. The peasants still constituted by far the largest population group. It was important that the peasants got reasonable prices for their products. Reasonable prices would increase incomes, and then rural savings would increase. The kulaks were able to save, and in the longer term he expected all peasants to be able to save.

Savings should be obtained from three sources: the first was agriculture; the second was industry, where the surplus could be saved; and the third was an income tax paid by those who earned higher incomes. For Bukharin it was a bad strategy "to feed the hen so badly that it was not able to lay eggs". People should have an incentive to work, and after they had earned money they should be taxed.

Bukharin was also against high industrial prices. He feared that high industrial prices would have a negative effect on production volumes, because the price elasticities were high. High prices would decrease the quantity of goods demanded and this would hurt consumers, especially the poorest consumers.

There were two other reasons why Bukharin was against high industrial prices. First, high production levels would ensure higher savings. High industrial prices cause low sales volumes, and the turnover will be lower when price elasticities are high. When fixed costs are high, unit-costs will fall when production volumes increase. Therefore, Bukharin argued, the total savings will be higher when capacity utilisation is high. Second, Bukharin feared that high industrial prices would promote "monopolistic parasitism" and "bureaucratic degeneration". Bukharin thought that any monopoly conceals within itself the seeds of decay. Bukharin believed in the competition that firms were exposed to in market economies. He believed that the managers of the state firms should be under permanent pressure to produce more rationally and more cheaply to satisfy the needs of the masses. He feared that high industrial prices would neutralise such efforts.

In short, Bukharin was in favour of inducing the peasants to increase their production and savings by paying them reasonable prices, whereas Preobrazhensky believed in forcing the peasants to fulfil their goals. Bukharin foresaw that Soviet industry might degenerate into a sector with state monopolies, lacking inner dynamics.

Attitudes towards ownership also differed. Preobrazhensky was in favour of public ownership in all sectors, whereas Bukharin was in favour of a mixed economy in which the large manufacturing companies, the financial companies, the transport sector, and foreign trade should be in public ownership. However, there should be room for private ownership in farming, in skilled trades, in retail and wholesale trading, and in the service sector.

The debate between these two schools of thought also concerned the structural composition of the economy and the tempo of industrialisation.

Bukharin believed in the importance of having the right proportions between various sectors of industry, as well as the correct relations between industry and agriculture. Planning should respect the necessary proportions of the different sectors. Planning should have nothing to do with systematically breaking down the socially necessary proportions, which Bukharin believed would be the case if Preobrazhensky's ideas were followed. In modern terms, Bukharin believed in balanced growth, whereas Preobrazhensky believed in unbalanced growth.

There was also a debate about the tempo of industrialisation. Preobrazhensky was in favour of speeding up the industrialisation process by a pumping resources out of the agricultural sector. Bukharin found this strategy destructive, and he was willing to accept a slower pace to start with, because it would create a better foundation for a higher growth rate in the longer term. In 1928, one of the earliest rigorous models of growth, by G.A. Feldman, was published (Feldman, 1928; Domar, 1957). It was a Marxian model in which investments were split between the production of capital goods for the capital goods sector and the production of capital goods for the consumer goods sector. This model showed that, in the longer term, a higher level of consumption would be attained, if a bigger share of total investments were allocated to the capital goods sector. A similar model was elaborated by P.C. Mahalanobis, who was the chief architect of the planning model of India in the 1950s.

According to Preobrazhensky's thinking, there were two effects of turning the terms of trade against the peasants. First, it would lead to increased capital accumulation. Second, accumulation based on deteriorated terms of trade for the peasants would be possible without deteriorating the economic position of the industrial workers.

The first proposition is correct, but the second one is wrong. Under market conditions, a lower farm price will reduce the supply of farm products. If the food supply is lower, there will be fewer supplies for the industrial workers (Sah and Stiglitz, 1984).

7.8 Summary

The period 1914-1945 was a turbulent one in which economic performance was severely affected by a world war at the start of the period, another world war at the end of it, and the most severe economic depression ever seen in between.

During the two world wars, agricultural products were in short supply and agricultural prices rose sharply. Politically, the challenges were to

Summary

keep prices down and to ensure the fair distribution of food between consumers.

During the Great Depression, agricultural prices fell drastically and farmers' incomes, after the payment of interest and instalments, fell even further. The challenge was to curb the number of bankruptcies among farmers. This was why agricultural policy, defined as the establishment of market organizations for the different commodities, was widely used for the first time.

In the USA, the agricultural sector was an important factor first in causing the depression and then in deepening it. In 1929, the stocks of agricultural products were high, and when confidence in the economy dissolved, selling out of stocks contributed significantly to the fall in prices. During the Great Depression, agriculture was still an important activity, accounting for 25 per cent of the total labour force. When farmers' incomes fell, the demand for consumer and investment goods also fell. Widespread defaults on interest and debt repayments by farmers forced many banks and other credit institutions to close. The financial crisis spread, and in combination with an inadequate monetary policy, this severely aggravated the depression.

The political response, in the form of a supportive agricultural policy from 1933, came too late. As a net exporter of agricultural products, the USA could not maintain farm incomes through a protectionist trade policy. US agricultural policy was based on reducing supply on the one hand and price and income support on the other hand. The price support took the form of a target price, combined with a minimum price through the loan rate system. The demand for agricultural products was also stimulated by government intervention.

Agricultural interventions came earlier in western Europe. As net importers, France and Germany protected their markets through tariff protection, and this was followed up by a series of other interventions such as import quotas, the introduction of market organizations, such as marketing boards, and initiatives for increasing demand and decreasing supply. France and Germany wanted to support market prices for agricultural products.

Britain tried to overcome some of its problems through a system of imperial preferences. Agricultural exports from the Dominions and colonies were allowed to enter free of customs duties, which were only levied on imports from third countries, such as Denmark and the Netherlands. This meant that British farmers could not be supported through high market prices, and they were supported instead through a deficiency payment system. When the depression deepened, a comprehensive set of discriminatory import quotas was introduced. The idea was to reduce supply so as to keep prices up, giving first priority to domestic producers, and then to exporters from the Dominions and colonies.

The new countries which were formed in central and eastern Europe after the war had major economic problems during the 1920s and 1930s. In Russia, the Soviet Union was formed in 1917, and in the period 1917-1929, its agricultural sector was initially subjected to War Communism, then to the New Economic Policy, and finally to forced collectivisation from 1929. The important debate about development strategy ended in victory for those who favoured the comprehensive extraction of resources from agriculture through a totally new farm system based on large collective and state farms. Industrial production expanded rapidly, but the growth in agricultural production was very modest.

The period 1914-1945 was characterized by the lack of international cooperation. There was no co-operation on trade policy, agricultural policy or foreign exchange policy. Each country acted autonomously and did not seem to take account of the fact that its pursuit of a beggar-my-neighbour policy would only hurt the international division of labour without solving its domestic problems.

Behind the turbulent events of wars and depression in the period 1914-1945, some important agricultural trends can be detected. Agricultural productivity increased at a higher rate than before the First World War, especially in the USA. Technological innovations and improvements continued to be made, and they built on earlier improvements, having a cumulative effect. The absolute number of people working in agriculture started to decline. There was also stagnation or a slight decline of the area in agricultural use. Investments are difficult in wartime and in times of depression, but in the 1920s there was an increase in capital stock, especially in the USA.

Agricultural supply continued to increase, apart from during the wars when some of the belligerent countries suffered from reduced supply. Demand continued to increase due to the increase in population, though the rate of population increase was lower than before the First World War. The demand for food products was also influenced by a slower growth in GDP per capita. For example, when the average GDP fell in the USA during the Great Depression, it had a negative impact on food demand.

During the 1920s, there were some signs of over-production in agriculture. The agricultural supply in the USA and other overseas areas continued to expand due to productivity gains. In Europe, agricultural supply first recovered and then surpassed the pre-war level. In the 1930s

Summary

the agricultural situation was abnormal due to the Great Depression, so that it was only after the Second World War that a more permanent trend toward agricultural over-production could be recognized.

8. Adjustment and agricultural policies 1945-2000

After the start of the Second World War there was general concern, throughout Europe, to ensure the availability of sufficient food supplies for consumers at reasonable prices, especially in the importing countries. International trade was disrupted by the war. Import volumes of food products were reduced to a greater or lesser extent, as were the imports of inputs, such as fuel, feedstuffs, and fertilisers, which were important for maintaining domestic production. Production capacity was also reduced because the supplies of primary production factors were reduced. Battlefields could not be used for farm production, the labour force was reduced and farm buildings and farm machinery were not adequately maintained.

In most cases, the supply problem was due to the lack of variable inputs, capital and labour. The reduced supply led to higher consumer prices, and in order to avoid soaring prices, maximum prices were introduced for food products. Maximum prices were often combined with rationing schemes to ensure the fair distribution of limited supplies.

8.1 The immediate post war period 1945-1950

The immediate post-war years were characterised by the lack of food supplies in Europe. In Britain, domestic production was above the pre-war level, but this was necessary to substitute for the shortfall of imports. In nearly all the other countries in Europe, agricultural production was far below the pre-war level. It was difficult to make up the shortfall through imports, because there was a shortage of foreign currency. The food situation after the war was especially difficult in West Germany because it was cut off from food supplies from East Germany. The most acute problems were solved by the United Nations Relief and Rehabilitation Administration (UNRRA) which provided emergency post-war relief and aid. The USA was the principal contributor to UNRRA. In 1948, the Organisation of European Economic Cooperation (OEEC) was founded, and this was the organisation that administered the Marshall Plan, allocating US aid and loans to western European countries.

In the immediate post-war period, the general aim was to expand agricultural production as quickly as possible. These efforts were successful. Agricultural production in the OEEC countries had already reached pre-war levels by 1949/51.

During the war and the post-war period, US agricultural production expanded, but this did not create a problem of surpluses until 1954. Domestic consumption grew less than production, but exports increased and remained at a high level until 1954. The agricultural policy of the 1930s was based on price parity, acreage programmes, and the loan rate system. The wartime agricultural policy of high parity prices was continued after the war until 1954.

Theodore W. Schultz analysed the farm income problem and predicted that there would be falling real prices for agricultural products (Schultz, 1945). The feeling in the USA was that there would be a new agricultural crisis with falling prices. The experiences of the post First World War period and the Great Depression supported this expectation, which influenced the US position on international trade in agricultural products.

8.2 GATT and agriculture

The Great Depression had a major impact on economic and political thinking. People realised that the Great Depression had developed and spread due to inadequate economic policies and the lack of international co-operation. John Maynard Keynes formalised the theory behind the macroeconomic stabilisation policy which became widely accepted after the war (Keynes, 1936). International co-operation was to be facilitated through the UN system. International economic institutions such as the International Bank for Reconstruction and Development (IBRD) and the International Monetary Fund (IMF) were established. The IBRD (also known as the World Bank) became the channel for providing development assistance to developing countries, and the IMF established a pegged exchange rate system, in which the exchange rate of a country was fixed, but was adjustable if a fundamental balance of payments disequilibrium arose. It was also intended that a third institution, the International Trade Organisation (ITO) should promote international trade discipline and trade liberalisation, but the treaty founding this organisation was never ratified by the United States.

In place of the ITO, international trade co-operation developed around the General Agreement on Tariffs and Trade (GATT) which was signed by 23 nations in 1947. The GATT contained a set of rules on trade intervention which the contracting parties had to follow. The GATT also provided for the gradual liberalisation of international trade through a series of conferences, called "rounds".

The GATT trade rules did not cover agriculture, which made it possible for some countries to conduct protectionist agricultural policies.

According to GATT Article XVI, export subsidies are prohibited for all products except primary products. The contracting parties are required to try to avoid the use of export subsidies for primary products because they hurt domestic producers in importing countries and producers in other exporting countries. If used, export subsidies should be applied in such a way that the country only obtained "an equitable share of world export trade in that product" compared to "a previous representative period". This rule is framed in such vague terms that it allows for different interpretations and it has been the cause of many disputes.

According to GATT Article XI, quantitative restrictions on imports are prohibited, though foodstuffs are exempted in some cases. If quantitative restrictions are applied to imports of foodstuffs, restrictions should also be applied to domestic production, so that the ratio of imports to domestic production remains unchanged. According to GATT Article XIII, any import quotas must be applied so that the shares of imports from different countries correspond as closely as possible to the shares which existed prior to the import restrictions. These rules reflect the non-discrimination principle which is one of the basic principles of the GATT.

Even these rules on quantitative restrictions did not satisfy the USA, so in 1955 the USA got a "temporary waiver" from the rules. The USA obtained the right to apply quantitative restrictions to imports in accordance with what it considered to be necessary for the implementation of its own agricultural policy. This temporary waiver lasted until the agricultural agreement of the Uruguay Round entered into force.

Agriculture was exempted from the GATT rules on some very important issues. This allowed countries to conduct uncoordinated agricultural policies which supported domestic agricultural production in the industrialised countries and discriminated against imports.

The idea behind the GATT rules was to bind the trade policy of each of the signatory countries so as to open up for international trade without discrimination. But in agriculture there was the opposite result. Due to resistance, especially from the USA, there were almost no restrictions on the agricultural policies which countries could adopt.

Adjustment and agricultural policies 1945 - 2000

For industry, the rules on free trade restricted the autonomy of each country to pursue its own trade policy. For agriculture, the main aim of many countries was to retain their freedom to support domestic producers, and this prevented the creation of international rules to eliminate protectionist policies in agriculture.

8.3   Agricultural policies 1950-1960

Western Europe

There was a shift in the goal of agricultural policy in Europe. Just after the war, in the period 1945-1950, the goal was to expand agricultural production to eliminate food shortages and to improve the balance of payments. From the beginning of the 1950s, shortages had been eliminated, and the problem became increasingly one of how to ensure farmers' incomes at a level which was acceptable to other groups in society.

In Britain, during the war farmers had obtained some price guarantees for the post-war period. The goal in Britain was to promote a stable and efficient agricultural industry, capable of producing part of the nation's food needs. It was recognised that Britain would still have to rely on imports, but that there should be support schemes to ensure a reasonable level of employment and incomes in the agricultural sector.

State trading was gradually abandoned, and in 1953 fixed guaranteed prices for cereals were replaced by minimum guaranteed prices, backed by deficiency payments. Markets became decontrolled to allow prices to be determined by the market to the minimum guaranteed level. For other products, such as milk products, marketing boards regulated trade.

In France, the goal was to expand the agricultural production by developing the agricultural sector to relieve food shortages and the balance of payments problem. State boards were established for the different commodities. Their aim was to insulate the domestic markets so that farmers could get higher prices than world market prices. Imports were controlled, either by import licences or through state controlled import monopolies. When domestic supply exceeded domestic demand, the surplus was exported. The difference between the domestic price and the world market price amounted to an export subsidy for French farmers.

In the period 1880-1945, the productivity levels of French agriculture had been relatively low and had increased only slowly. This pattern changed after the war, when productivity increases were equal to those of countries with the highest productivity gains. France became an important exporter, especially of grain.

When the German Federal Republic was constituted in 1949, the German government aimed to ensure stable prices for producers at a level which could cover production costs, even for small farms, and enable the poorer parts of society to afford to pay for their food needs. Import and storage boards were set up as important instruments for stabilising prices at the target level. These boards not only controlled imports, they could also intervene on the domestic market by buying, selling and building up stocks. As world market prices fell during the 1950s, the import and storage boards were used, together with other import control measures, to maintain German prices at levels which were well above world market prices.

There was a general trend towards increased protection for agricultural products in Europe in the 1950s, in contrast to the tariff reductions for industrial products. As a result, the net import level in the 1950s was below the level in the 1930s before the outbreak of the war. Protection took the form of domestic production supports, export subsidies, and import barriers of various kinds (GATT, 1958).

Important exporters suffered from this trend. In Europe, Denmark and the Netherlands were small countries which suffered from this protectionism. Outside Europe, the USA, Canada, Australia, and Argentina were important exporters which all suffered from European protectionism.

USA

In the USA, labour productivity nearly doubled from 1940 to 1950 and nearly doubled again from 1950 to 1960. However, agricultural output only increased by around one-third in the period 1940-1960, because the number of male workers in agriculture fell by more than 50 per cent.

It was expected that there would be agricultural surpluses leading to falling prices after the Second World War, and that this would necessitate a post-war adjustment of US agriculture and agricultural policy. This adjustment was postponed for nearly a decade by a combination of special circumstances. After the war there was strong demand for US agricultural produce to relieve food shortages in Europe and in other parts of the world. In 1950, the Korean War broke out and lasted until 1953. High demand for farm commodities during this war alleviated the problems of farm incomes and surpluses in the USA.

From 1954 and for the rest of the decade, there were increasing signs of production surpluses and excess capacity, which showed up as growing commodity stocks from 1954.

The Republican Eisenhower administration came to power in 1953, and it proposed a reorientation of agricultural policy in a more market-oriented direction. The idea was to introduce a system of flexible price supports. The support should range from 75 to 90 per cent of parity, with the level of support declining as supplies increased. The plan was also to expand agricultural exports.

The Agricultural Act of 1954 did not go as far as the original proposal, but compared with the high fixed-price supports of previous administrations, the Eisenhower administration succeeded in making price supports more flexible and generally lower.

The Agricultural Trade Development and Assistance Act, better known as PL 480, was also passed in 1954. It had two combined objectives, namely: the foreign policy objective and the agricultural policy aim of reducing surplus production. Agricultural commodities were sold abroad in exchange for foreign currencies in order to circumvent the problem of dollar scarcities in aid-recipient countries.

Stocks remained high and farm incomes fell. The Agricultural Act of 1956 contained a cropland diversion programme and a soil bank programme. Farmers were paid to take land out of the production of surplus commodities and to practise soil conservation measures. The soil conservation programme of 1956 had its roots in a similar act of 1936, which had the aim of combating soil erosion in connection with serious dust storms.

In spite of these political initiatives, the end of the 1950s was characterised by agricultural distress and discontent. The Commodity Credit Corporation stocks were very high, and there was a need for further adjustment.

8.4 The foundation of the European Economic Community and the Common Agricultural Policy

The idea of European integration

After the war there was a widespread desire to avoid future hostilities in Europe, especially between Germany and France. Political and economic co-operation between the European nations was seen as the path to stability and progress. The 1950s were the decade when important

The foundation of the European Economic community and the CAP

decisions were taken. The creation of a common market for agricultural products was an important element in European integration.

In 1950, France proposed the establishment of a "high authority" for agriculture, with supranational powers to create a common European agricultural market where production was controlled, prices were fixed, and internal agricultural trade barriers were removed. Britain was generally opposed to the supranational concept, and preferred the idea of an intergovernmental body which should reconcile the differences between national agricultural policies. While France favoured a supranational authority, Britain wanted to maintain its links with the Commonwealth from which it still got an important part of its food imports. Because of these diverging interests no agreement was reached.

In parallel with the idea of creating a common market for agricultural products there was a proposal to create a common market for coal, steel and iron. Negotiations resulted in the foundation of the European Coal and Steel Community (ECSC) by France, West Germany, Italy and the Benelux countries in 1951. The French idea of a "high authority" with supranational powers was introduced in the ECSC. The high authority was to decide on the removal of customs duties, quotas and subsidies, and to fix common prices. The high authority consisted of technocrats and became a powerful institution. Before decisions were taken, a Council of Ministers had to be consulted, and a European Assembly, appointed from among the members of the national parliaments, convened from time to time.

These attempts to create a common market for these two sectors put into practice the idea of bringing about integration gradually. Political integration was to be brought about by establishing economic integration, sector by sector. This was the philosophy of the leading politicians in the six countries participating in the ECSC.

Instead of creating a common market in steps, by taking in new sectors, the idea of creating a common market in one step for all sectors took root. The six members of the ECSC convened at an intergovernmental conference in Messina in 1955. The conference resulted in a report in 1956, which formed the basis on which the Treaty founding the European Economic Community (EEC) was built. The idea behind the ECSC was to be extended to all sectors.

Britain and the Scandinavian countries were not interested in participating, and Britain came up with an alternative proposal for creating a free trade area between the OEEC countries.

The EEC Treaty 1957

In March 1957, the Treaty of Rome was signed, establishing the European Economic Community (the EEC Treaty). It was a comprehensive treaty including the establishment of a customs union for industrial products, a common agricultural policy, free movement of labour, services and capital, common policy rules and rules for the common institutions.

The EEC Treaty had specific rules for the foundation of a common market for industrial products, but the chapters dealing with agriculture were less specific. There was no specific statement of the principles on which the common agricultural policy should be based, and there were no indications of the intended support level.

The agricultural sector did not play an important role in the negotiations leading up to the EEC Treaty, although the establishment of a common agricultural policy was considered to be a cornerstone of the European integration process. The negotiators did not want conflicts about how to create a common market for agricultural products to hamper the idea of creating a community with common institutions. It was evident that the creation of a common agricultural market would cause tensions. Interventions in the agricultural sector varied between the six partners, and it was no easy task to dismantle national policies and replace them with a common policy, with shared principles and common support levels.

Articles 38-47 of the EEC Treaty dealt with agriculture and indicated some broad goals for the future. Agriculture should be a part of the common market so that international duties and restrictions on trade between Member States were to be removed. It was also stated that the common market for agricultural products was to be accompanied by a common agricultural policy, and the objectives of this policy were listed. Market organizations were to be established for different products, and their terms could vary from product to product according to the specific conditions of their markets. The Commission was to convene a conference at which the Member States should determine the guidelines for the Common Agricultural Policy (CAP). This conference was held in Stresa in July 1958, and the Member States' delegations included representatives of the main farming organisations and the food industry. On the basis of the decisions of the Stresa conference, the Commission came up with a proposal for the CAP.

The Common Agricultural Policy was implemented during the years 1958-1967. This period can be divided into two sub-periods. In the first, 1958-1962, the main task was to agree on the principles behind the CAP.

The foundation of the European Economic community and the CAP

In the second, 1962-1967, the task was mainly to agree on common price levels, and to harmonise the different national price levels. In short, the task was to put the principles into practice.

The choice of principles 1958-1962

When a common agricultural policy is to be decided, there are a number of important questions to be dealt with. Should agricultural markets be strictly regulated, or should they rely more on market forces? How large should the preference margins be for products from other Member States? Should the farm-income problem be solved by price support or through structural change?

Different countries had different views, especially on the degree of market regulation and internal preference levels vis-à-vis third countries. France and Italy favoured a high degree of market regulation, whereas the Netherlands was against too strict a regulation of the market. France and Italy stressed the importance of high levels of mutual preferences, whereas the Netherlands emphasized the importance of continued trade links with third countries.

In January 1962, the Council agreed on a package of regulations. The agreement of 1962 is often considered to be the birth of the CAP because it instituted the three basis principles of the CAP, namely:

- *unity of market*, to be achieved by removing internal restrictions and barriers and the gradual harmonisation of farm prices in the Member States,
- *community preference*, to be implemented through a system of variable levies,
- *common financing*, by the establishment of the European Agricultural Guidance and Guarantee Fund (EAGGF).

The cereal support model, which was agreed in 1962, illustrates the idea behind the Common Agricultural Policy, as shown in Figure 8.1. The support scheme is based on three institutional prices, decided each year by the Council, namely: the indicative price (R_P), the threshold price (T_P) and the intervention price (I_P). The indicative price is what is considered to be the appropriate price. The threshold price (T_P), fixed just below the indicative price, is the minimum price of the commodity imported from outside the European Community (EC). The intervention price (I_P) is the minimum market price within the EC. Farmers can always obtain the minimum price by selling to the public stocks (intervention stocks).

Figure 8.1: The cereal support scheme

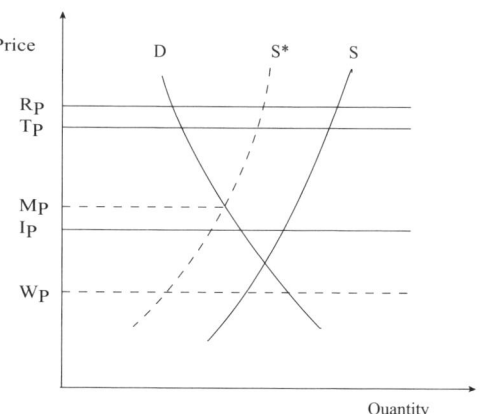

The two prices indicated by dashed lines are determined by market forces, namely: the world market price (W_P) and the internal market price (M_P), which is determined by domestic demand (D) and domestic supply (S^*), which is equal to the total supply (S) minus the exported quantity.

The domestic price level is maintained through market protection, export subsidies and buying into intervention stocks. Market access is not possible at a price below T_P, because the difference between T_P and W_P, which fluctuates, has to be paid as a variable levy. Farmers will not export unless they get the same price on the export markets as on the domestic market. So the exported quantity, equal to the horizontal difference between S and S^* will receive export restitutions (subsidies) equal to M_P minus W_P.

Because of the artificially high domestic prices, there are high costs associated with the CAP. Export restitutions and spending on intervention stocks have to be financed, together with any non-price supports which may be paid to the farmers. It was decided that these expenditures should be financed jointly by the Community, but there was no agreement about how the Community's expenditures should be covered by the Member States.

The implementation of the principles 1962-1968

The Member States had to agree on the level of the institutional prices, see Figure 8.1. The price level for cereal, for example, differed in the different national markets. In Germany and Italy, which had the highest cereal prices, the price levels were around 35-40 per cent above the price level in France, where the prices were the lowest. The price levels in the Netherlands and Belgium were around 15 per cent higher than in France. The negotiations were difficult. As an exporter of cereal, France was interested in finding a quick solution to facilitate its exports to the other Member States. In Germany, the Farmers' Union succeeded in influencing the official German position not to accept a lower common price than the existing high price level in Germany. The result was an agreement where the intervention price was fixed at a level very close to the German and Italian domestic price levels. When the cereal market organisation started in 1967/68, the wheat intervention price was around 100 per cent higher than the world market price.

In 1965-1966, there was a serious dispute between France and the Commission in particular about the supranational powers of the common institutions. The dispute was about two questions. The first was about abandoning the rule on unanimous decision-making in relation to the CAP. The other was about how to finance the EC budget, where CAP expenditures were more than half the total budget.

In 1965, the EC had come to the point where qualified majority voting had to be substituted for unanimous decision-making for the implementation of the CAP. The French president, Charles de Gaulle, was against giving up the veto right.

The other point of conflict was whether the Community should have its own financial means. The Commission proposed that the Member States should surrender their controls over tariff and levy revenues and transfer these to the Community, where the European Parliament controlled the common budget. President de Gaulle was opposed to the idea of strengthening the supranational power of the institutions.

These conflicts were solved in 1966 by the Luxembourg Agreement. The Council agreed to declare that if, in future, a Member State found that its vital interests were at stake, then negotiations should continue until a unanimously agreed solution was found. The financing problem was solved, temporarily, by the Member States agreeing to share the budgetary expenditures according to a fixed scheme of distribution. In 1970 it was decided that Community expenditures should be financed from three sources, namely: customs duties, variable levies, and up to 1 percentage point of value added tax. Since then the Community has had its own financial resources.

8.5 Agricultural policy problems 1968-1973

By 1 July 1968, the customs union for industrial products was completed, and a common agricultural policy, with market organisations for most agricultural products was established. Very soon two new important agricultural issues were put on the agenda.

Structural policy

Already in the period 1958-1962, when the principles behind the CAP were laid down, Sicco Mansholt, the Commissioner for Agriculture 1958-72, feared that a high price level would create over-production. In 1968, there was even more reason to fear that the CAP would lead to surplus production. Mansholt's idea was that over-production could only be controlled effectively by reducing the area of agricultural land and the number of people working in agriculture. This should ensure that the remaining farms would be efficient enough to earn a living from a lower price level. In 1968, the Commission published the Mansholt Plan, based on the idea of reducing agricultural resources. The reduction was to be voluntary, but the EC should stimulate the process by providing a variety of financial incentives, such as giving financial support for the early retirement of farmers, re-training farmers and the merger of farms.

The question of structural policy in the agricultural sector was a sensitive one. In northern Europe, structural changes would be easier than in southern Europe, where many less developed regions were heavily dependent on agriculture.

The EC ended up by adopting three socio-structural directives in 1972. These directives concerned support to encourage: (a) the modernisation of farms; (b) the cessation of farming and reallocation of agricultural areas for structural improvements; (c) the acquisition of alternative occupational skills by the farm population.

The three directives fell short of the original Mansholt Plan. The limited scope of the three directives, which had tried to introduce a common structural policy with a longer-term perspective, confirmed that pricing policy would remain at the core of the EC's agricultural support policy.

Foreign exchange problems

One of the three cornerstones of the CAP was the unity of the market. Institutional prices were fixed in 'units of account', which were converted

The agricultural trend of falling real prices

to national currencies at pegged exchange rates, i.e. fixed but adjustable exchange rates, according to the IMF system.

In 1969 the German mark was revalued and the French franc was devalued. This meant that the institutional agricultural prices had to be increased in France and decreased in Germany. France would not accept a rise in food prices, and Germany would not accept a fall in farm prices, so the agreed solution was to introduce the green currency system. For agricultural products, the French and German institutional prices should still be calculated on the basis of the previous exchange rates. In the market, agricultural imports were paid for in the currency of the importing country and converted to the currency of the exporting country at the new exchange rate. So the green currency system had to be supplemented by a system of border taxes and subsidies called monetary compensatory amounts.

Because the consequences of foreign exchange rate changes were not followed for agricultural products, the unity of the market in the EC broke down. From this point on, there were three different price levels for agricultural products. In devaluing countries the price level was artificially low. In revaluing countries, the price level was artificially high. In countries where the green currency was equal to the official currency, the price level was unaffected.

This green currency system became more important when the Bretton Woods fixed exchange rate system broke down in 1973, and it only lost its importance when the euro was introduced in 1999.

8.6 The agricultural trend of falling real prices

During the 1920s, over-production in US agriculture caused real agricultural prices to fall. These unfavourable agricultural conditions became disastrous in the 1930s in the USA and Europe during the Great Depression. These extraordinary conditions, with decreased food demand, obscured the fact that the world was entering an era of agricultural over-production.

Already in 1945 Theodore W. Schultz predicted that agricultural prices would fall in the post-war period (Schulz, 1945). Agricultural developments since the beginning of the 1950s have proved that he was right. Figure 8.2 illustrates the developments in Europe and the USA.

From period 1 to period 2 the demand curve for agricultural products has moved only slightly to the right. The increase in demand has been low because the population increase has been low and the income elasticity, which was already low in 1950s, is close to zero today. The increase in the average income per capita has not increased the total demand for food, but it has shifted the demand from poorer quality to better quality products.

The supply curve has moved strongly to the right from S_1 to S_2 because of large production increases. The supply increase, due to increased production, will be reduced if resources (land, capital and labour) are taken out of agriculture. This has happened to a large extent for labour.

Figure 8.2: Falling real agricultural prices

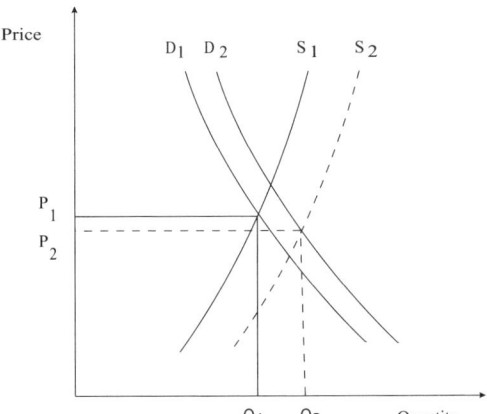

The change in turnover of the agricultural sector depends on the amount of the price decrease and of the production increase. The income in the period 2 $P_2 \cdot Q_2$ is not necessarily lower than the turnover in the previous period $P_1 \cdot Q_1$. So the average income of farmers is not necessarily reduced. Even if the total income of the agricultural sector is reduced, the average income will increase if the percentage decline in the labour force in agriculture is more than the percentage decline in total agricultural income.

This analysis is based on a closed economy without trade and assumes that agriculture is only producing one commodity. When more agricultural products are produced, some will have higher income elasticities than others. Normally, animal products have higher income elasticities than cereals. Higher quality goods have higher income elasticities than lower quality goods, which emphasises the importance of the product mix.

In an open economy with a fixed world market price, the agricultural price will not fall if the domestic price is at the level of the world market

The agricultural trend of falling real prices

price. As shown in Figure 8.3, the price will still be P_1 even if the supply increases more than the domestic demand, because the excess supply can be sold on the world market.

This case is based on the assumption of a constant world market price. However, this assumption is not valid if the supply increases more than the domestic demand in all industrial countries. In this case there will be a falling world market price, unless there is a corresponding increase of net imports to developing countries.

When agricultural prices fall, there will be structural changes in the agricultural sector. Farmers can be split into three categories: pioneers, followers and laggards (Cochrane, 1958). The pioneers are the farmers who are the first to invest in new and more productive methods. The followers are the main body of farmers who later invest in the improved technology when they realise that it may be profitable. The laggards are those who stick to the old technology.

Figure 8.3: Agriculture in an open economy

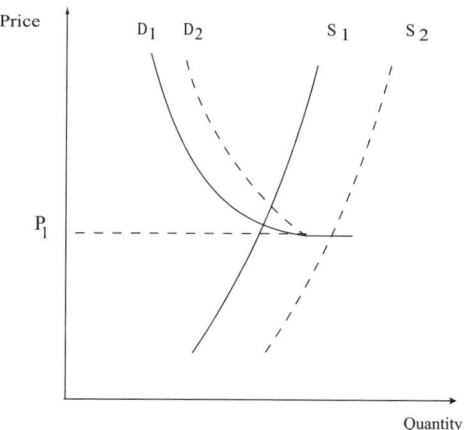

The pioneers are relatively few in number. They benefit from lower costs due to improved productivity, and from a constant price level which is not influenced by the slight increase in supply. The followers also benefit from the lower costs resulting from their investments, but they are faced with a falling market price as their numbers mean that the total supply is increased so the price level falls.

The pioneers gain because they reap an extra profit by being the first. The followers will be unhurt because they compensate for lower prices with productivity gains. The laggards are the great losers because they will suffer from lower prices without having lower costs. They will be squeezed out, and their farms will be taken over by other farmers

This process will stop if technological progress stops or if farmers are unable to invest in improved technology because they are over-indebted.

The agricultural supply depends not only on the labour productivity but also on the size of the labour force. Large productivity increases will cause large production increases, unless there is a rapid migration of labour away from agriculture. When there has been sufficient migration and the necessary restructuring of agricultural resources, it should be possible to reach equilibrium where the average farm income is satisfactory in relation to the average income in society.

It is easier for farm employees to leave agriculture than it is for farmers. When most of the employees have left, the total labour force in agriculture can only be reduced if farmers leave the industry. The necessary adjustment of the number of farmers may take time, and there are good economic reasons to give support during the adjustment period.

However, there are several problems if such support extends beyond a reasonable period. It is a problem if agricultural support makes it more difficult to reach equilibrium, with reasonable farm incomes without support. It is a problem when support, which is conceived as being temporary, becomes permanent.

8.7 The Common Agricultural Policy 1973-1990

When the CAP was initiated in around 1960, the six EC Member States were net importers of nearly all agricultural products. The self-sufficiency ratio increased during the 1960s but in 1970 the self-sufficiency ratio was still only above 100 for very few products. The rapid increase in agricultural production continued during the 1970s, in spite of the continued large migration of labour from agriculture which had started after the Second World War. By around 1980, the self-sufficiency ratio in the EC, which had been enlarged in 1973 with the accession of the UK, Denmark and Ireland, was above 100 for several important products. So the EC had moved from being a net importer to an important net exporter, and this trend continued throughout the 1980s.

This trend was the result of the economic forces which caused real prices to fall, as illustrated in the Section 8.6, combined with the impact of the CAP.

The Common Agricultural Policy 1973-1990

When the CAP started to work in 1967/68, the institutional prices were fixed at high levels, well above world market prices. For wheat, the intervention price was around twice the world market price.

Figure 8.4 shows the development of the institutional prices, which were fixed annually, from 1973 to 1992. The common prices in European Currency Units (ecu) doubled from 1973 to 1984, but from then on, they were nearly constant. The same prices in nominal currencies nearly trebled from 1973 to 1984, but from then on the nominal price increases were very small. The nominal prices in national currencies are converted from the common prices in ecu by using the green currency rates. The green currency rates were devalued in relation to ecu, which explains the much larger price increases in national currencies.

The real prices in national currencies have been calculated on the basis of the nominal prices, adjusted for inflation using the GDP deflator. The real prices were constant from 1973 to 1984, and it has only been since then that the real institutional prices have been reduced.

Figure 8.4: CAP institutional prices 1973-1992

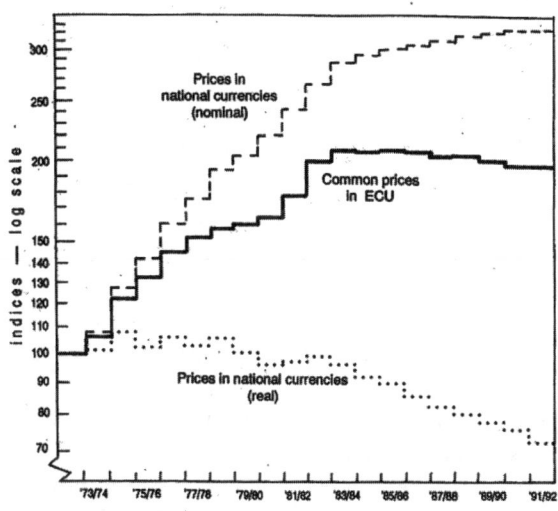

Source: Tracy (1996)

There was an increase in production volumes due to technological progress, and the high price levels also encouraged higher production levels. High prices in themselves encourage more intensive farm production, and they also make it possible for farmers to finance investments in new machinery and new inputs, so they benefit from technological progress. It is not easy to compare internal EC prices with world market prices because of world market price fluctuations and foreign exchange rate fluctuations, but comparisons show that for most commodities, the ratio exceeded 1.5. In some years the ratio went as high as 4 for some products, especially milk products.

From 1984, the EC realised that the CAP had to be adjusted to avoid the problem of growing agricultural surpluses. The high agricultural price levels in the EC led to high costs for consumers and tax payers, although the high dollar exchange rate in the first half of the 1980s temporarily relieved budgetary problems.

Apart from conducting a more prudent price policy from 1984, the EC has tried to curb agricultural surpluses through different policy interventions, such as disguised price reductions, the reduction of the use of inputs and the application of quotas.

Farmers have had to pay co-responsibility levies on some products, such as milk and cereals. These are a kind of production tax which should contribute to the financing of the CAP. Set-aside programmes for land and retirement schemes for farmers were introduced. Production quotas were introduced in the milk sector in 1984, because of the need for a quick reduction of the production surplus.

The high price levels in the EC were not the only problem. There was also a problem of the distortion of relative prices. There was a price distortion between cereals, where the EC price was high, and non-cereal feed substitutes such as oilcake, tapioca, and residues such as maize gluten feed and citrus residues from the juice industry. These feedstuffs could enter the EC duty free, under agreements made during the Dillon Round (see next section). Vegetable oil crops in the EC were supported through a deficiency payment system. There was also a price distortion between butter (milk fat) and vegetable oils, such as rapeseed oil, soybean oil and olive oil. Again, oil products were supported through deficiency payments, and milk through the price. To avoid these distortions, there were plans to tax cereal substitutes and vegetable oil products, but these plans came to nothing.

The main concern in the EC was the high costs of production surpluses. There were no official plans for integrating the EC agricultural sector into the world market. Most of the interventions referred to above were inefficient short-term solutions with no long-term perspective.

8.8 Why was the CAP allowed to be developed?

The Dillon round 1960-1961

When the EC was founded, the question arose as to whether the EC's regional economic arrangement was compatible with the GATT rules (Article XXIV). This was the direct motive for the Dillon round, 1960-1961. In relation to agriculture, the USA was concerned about the choice of policy instruments and the level of protection. The USA was especially worried about the use of variable levies to ensure a given target price level in the EC. The USA argued that the system of variable levies was contrary to the GATT rule that all tariffs should be bound. There was no specific ban on the use of variable levies in the GATT agreement, but they were contrary to the spirit of the GATT.

The USA was not successful in these negotiations, apart from obtaining a zero tariff binding for oilseed and other non-grain feed, giving duty-free access for these products to the EC. However meagre this concession may have seemed at the time, it turned out to have major consequences for the future of the CAP, due to the price distortions which developed between competing products.

The USA did not accept that the CAP was compatible with the GATT agreement, but it did not veto the CAP for political reasons. The USA was interested in the success of western European integration, and did not want to cause internal problems for the EC Member States in their efforts to integrate. It was also difficult for the USA to argue against the CAP, because the USA itself had been the cause of the exclusion of agriculture from the GATT when it had been set up.

The Kennedy Round 1964-1967

The USA initiated the Kennedy Round in order to ensure that a united Europe would be outward looking. The USA tried to secure its agricultural exports to Europe, because this would ease the financial position of farmers in the USA and help the balance of payments, which was deteriorating during the 1960s.

From the start of the negotiations, the USA proposed that the existing EC protection of agricultural products should be halved. The USA also proposed that the Community should give minimum access commitments, equivalent to the existing levels of imports for the products for which the Community was evolving common regulations and prices (Josling et al., 1996).

The position of the Community was that it chose to defend all the essential elements of its first common economic policy. The Community wanted to maintain the freedom to choose its agricultural policy and to decide its common price levels without interference. Nothing came of the Round in relation to agriculture.

The Tokyo Round 1973-1979

International trade co-operation continued and the negotiations of the Tokyo Round took place in the period 1973-1979. Agricultural issues were again on the agenda, but there were no changes in the stances of the USA and the EC.

The USA, and other exporting countries, wanted to improve their access to the EC market. The EC, on the other hand, continued to defend the CAP, and the EC negotiating mandate stated that the CAP principles and mechanisms could not be called into question and were therefore not a matter for negotiation. To solve the problems of trade, the EC again proposed to stabilize commodity prices and to expand agricultural trade through international agreements. The idea was to manage markets while leaving domestic agricultural policies intact. The world market had become more important for the US farm economy, and exports played a more significant role in US agricultural policies. The EC still considered the agricultural sector to be a closed economy, where exports were a residual matter. The EC exports were of minor importance, and the sporadic supply surpluses should be dealt with in an ad hoc manner. The reason why the US conceded on this may be explained by the flourishing state of the world market, where the US farm sector could expand its exports without trade liberalisation.

8.9 US agricultural policy 1960-1990

The principles behind the US policy of agricultural support remained very much the same from its start in 1933 up to 1990. Agricultural support was implemented through three sets of instruments, namely: supply management, the loan rate mechanism, and a kind of farm price support. However, the relative importance of the three sets of instruments varied from period to period, as did the level of supply restrictions and the level of the loan rate and the farm price.

Figure 8.5 illustrates the application of the US policy instruments. D is the demand curve and S the farmers' supply if there were no set-aside programme. Because of supply restrictions, the current supply is S*. P_L is the loan rate and P_T the target price. Farmers are sure to receive the price P_T, because the difference between the target price and the market price will be paid by the government as a deficiency payment. In figure 8.5 the market price is equal to P_L, which is the minimum price on the market. The supply will be OB, but only OA will be sold on the domestic market, so the residual AB must either to be stocked or exported.

Figure 8.5: US agricultural policy

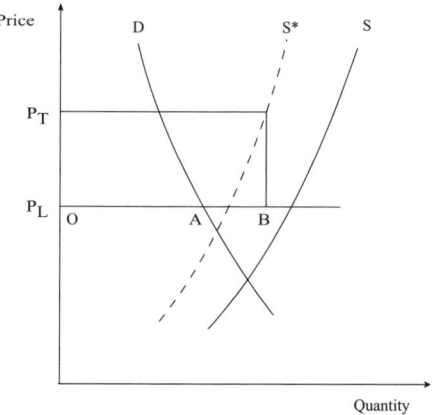

The loan rate and the target price varied more in the USA than the corresponding prices (the intervention price and the threshold price) in the EC. The USA was a net exporter, especially of cereals, which was why the USA had to take more account of the international market in planning its agricultural policy.

During the period 1954-1960, there was an excess supply, and the attempts to adjust production levels were not wholly successful. It has been estimated that the excess supply was about 8 per cent in around 1960 (Johnson, 1963). The loan rate was relatively high, because the market price was either at the loan rate level or below. Public stocks grew rapidly because of the high loan rate.

Adjustment in the 1960s

When the Kennedy Administration came to power in 1961, it had three priorities for agricultural policy. First, it aimed to increase farm incomes. Second, it wanted to reduce public stocks. Third, it wanted to eliminate the problem of surpluses by implementing a comprehensive supply-management programme. The goal of reducing stocks was attained by lowering the loan rate to the world market price level. During the 1960s world market prices were sluggish. The aim of increasing farm incomes was achieved by giving price supports in what was effectively a deficiency payment system, though this term was first officially used in 1973.

American agricultural policy during the 1960s can be considered as a success in the sense that the over-production which existed at the beginning of the decade had nearly disappeared by its end (Johnson, 1973).

The prosperous 1970s

At the beginning of the 1970s, the Nixon Administration had two goals. The first was to expand American agricultural exports. During the Tokyo Round, the USA tried to make international markets more open, but without success. The second goal was to ensure a reasonable income level for farmers through deficiency payments which were formally introduced in 1973, though in reality the system had already been applied. The 1970s was a prosperous period for American farmers. Agricultural prices were generally high, though there were wide price fluctuations. The domestic prices for cereals and oilseed in 1972-1974 were influenced by the sky-high world market prices due to bad harvests in several parts of the world. Because of the high prices, the US stocks were nearly exhausted, so stocks were not available to moderate price fluctuations. It was argued that an effective reserve stock programme was needed.

Except for a couple of years, the market price was well above the loan rate and the target rate. Distortions of relative prices were also felt in the USA. In some years, the target price for wheat was above the market price, whereas the market price for maize was above the target price. So fixing the target rates distorted production and relative market prices.

As an alternative to government stocks, a system of farmer-owned reserves was established. The idea was that these stocks should help to moderate price fluctuations.

The turbulent 1980s

The Agriculture and Food Act of 1981 was passed at a time when most analysts expected that the strong demand for American exports would continue. The scarcities of the 1970s were reflected in the expectation of rising commodity prices, and this had a particular impact on agricultural policy at the beginning of the 1980s.

The 1981 Act increased the target rates and loan rates for the first year, followed by 3-5 per cent annual increases for 1982-1985, based on the assumption that inflation would continue. In spite of the increases in the institutional prices, it was expected that there would be no major deficiency payments in the future.

The events of the following years were very different from the expectations behind the 1981 Act. International demand for grain fell and the dollar appreciated, causing American exports to decline for the first time since the 1960s.

Public expenditure increased dramatically. Export promotion programmes were instituted, the loan rates were kept high to assure farm incomes, and stocks grew rapidly. To re-establish market balance, farmers had to participate in a comprehensive set-aside programme in which they were not paid in cash but in kind, with the aim of reducing stocks. From 1981/1982 to 1983/1984, the area sown with wheat and coarse grain was reduced by 25 per cent.

The goals for the new farm bill in 1985 were: to increase farm incomes; to increase US exports; to reduce public stocks; to reduce budgetary costs; and to deal with environmental problems.

An ex-post evaluation of the 1985 agricultural bill should be mainly positive, although the support level was relatively high. Farm incomes increased, but there can always be a debate about the extent to which such improvements are caused by changes in market conditions or by agricultural policy.

Changes in the world market 1970-1990

Of the world markets for agricultural products, the cereal market is by far the most important for the USA. During the 1970s and 1980s, there were great changes in the price levels for cereals and wide fluctuations. In nominal terms, the price level in the 1970s was much higher than in the 1960s. In the first half of the 1980s, the nominal price level fell before it recovered to some extent in the second half. There was a significant decline in real prices of cereals from the 1970s to the 1980s. On the world market, the 1970s was a boom period, whereas the 1980s was a period of depression.

The 1970s and 1980s were characterised by wide price fluctuations. During the years 1972-1974, the world market prices for wheat and maize were three times the level they had been at the beginning of the 1970s. In

1980, the price level for wheat, in dollars, corresponded to the price level in 1972-1974, before a steep price fall in 1981-1985. In dollars, the price fall for wheat was around 40 per cent. The price recovered in the years 1986-1988.

There were also big changes in the volumes traded. Table 8.1 shows the total volume of cereal traded on the world market and US exports. During the 1970s, the world trade volume more than doubled, and two-thirds of the increase came from US exports. During the first half of the 1980s, world trade declined by 45 million tons, and US exports declined even more, by 51 million tons. The main cause was the appreciation of the dollar which made US agriculture less competitive. The EC was self-sufficient in cereals in 1980, but it became an important net- exporter during the first half of the 1980s. In the second half of the 1980s, international trade and especially US exports recovered.

Table 8.1: Trade in wheat and coarse grain on the world market

	Total trade	US exports	US share
	Million metric tons		Percentage
1961-62	77	35	45
1971-72	101	40	40
1980-81	213	112	53
1985-86	168	61	36
1989-90	198	102	52

Source: Based on data from Wisner (1990)

8.10 Agriculture more dependent on world markets and macroeconomic policies

The agricultural situation changed in the 1970s and 1980s compared with the previous period 1950-1970. The agricultural economy became more dependent on world market conditions and macroeconomic policies.

Exports became more important

The domestic demand for agricultural products was stable and not sensitive to changes in economic activity. Foreign demand became more important to the USA in the 1970s. US agricultural export revenues increased from 15 billion dollars in 1970 to 20 billion dollars in 1973 and 41 billion dollars in 1980. The value of agricultural exports, as a proportion of gross farm income, rose from 12 per cent in 1970 to over 25 per cent in 1980. The exports consisted mainly of cereals, oilseed and oilseed products which together amounted to two-thirds of total agricultural exports in 1980. American producers of these products became heavily dependent on export markets. From 1976-1980, exports provided over half the cash receipts of wheat and rice growers, nearly half the cash receipts of soybean growers and 40 per cent of the cash receipts of feed grain growers (Ingersent and Rayner, 1999).

US agriculture had become heavily dependent on exports, so US farmers were severely hit when the world market for cereals shifted in 1980s. The traded volume fell and prices dropped.

The EC also became more dependent on the world market. In 1950s and 1960s the EC was a net-importer, but it gradually increased its exports and reduced its imports to become an important net-exporter. Farmers were not hit directly, because the excess supply was either stocked at the intervention price or exported at the domestic market price, due to export subsidies. But the increasing costs of exports and intervention stocks involved expenditures which influenced the price policy in the long run.

The agricultural economy, especially in the USA, had become much more dependent on exports and this lead to increasing interdependence between the agricultural policy in the USA and the agricultural policies of other countries, not least in the EC.

Macroeconomic policy became more important

Because of the increasing importance of exports, either directly as in the case of the USA or indirectly as in the case of the EC, farmers became more dependent on foreign exchange rates, which were in turn influenced by macroeconomic policy. This was clearly seen in the case of US agriculture. After the Bretton Woods system broke down in 1973, there was a significant depreciation of the dollar up to the end of the 1970s. This depreciation contributed to the large expansion of agricultural exports from the USA, because US farmers improved their international competitiveness.

This situation was reversed in the first half of the 1980s when the dollar appreciated strongly due to the macroeconomic policy of the Reagan Administration. American farmers lost competitiveness in a shrinking world market.

Agriculture also became more sensitive to macroeconomic policy on the cost side. During the 1970s, agriculture became more capital intensive, and new farmers had to pay much higher prices for their farms. The increased indebtedness of investing farmers and young farmers meant that they were more vulnerable to increases in interest rates. Farmers had become more specialized, which meant that a greater share of their inputs was bought-in. This in turn meant that their costs were more dependent on the general level of inflation in society.

At the end of the 1970s and the beginning of the 1980s, interest rates and the inflation rate rose. As a result, in this period US farmers were hit by a double squeeze, both from an appreciating dollar and increased costs. EC farmers were only hit by cost increases. The dollar appreciation relieved the pressure on the budget, so that EC price increases could be higher without causing budgetary problems.

Why policy changes in the 1990s?

There were two important new trends in the 1970s and 1980s. The first was the increasing dependence of the agricultural economy on international markets. The implication of this was increased interdependence between the agricultural policy in the USA and the agricultural policies in other countries, not least in the EC. The second trend was towards a broader interface between the agricultural economy and the general economy in the country, which meant that there was a deeper interaction between agricultural policy and macroeconomic policy.

When the next GATT Round, the Uruguay Round, started in 1986, the agricultural situation, especially in the USA, was totally changed. During the 1970s, US agriculture had become more integrated in international markets, and then in the first half of the 1980s there was a significant fall in traded volumes and in prices. US agriculture suffered from the most severe crisis since the Great Depression of the 1930s. This explains the US attitude in the Uruguay Round. Now it was vital for US agriculture to secure the liberalization of international trade in agricultural products. The USA would only sign up to a new GATT agreement if agriculture was included.

8.11 Agricultural reforms since 1990

The American threat, that no new GATT agreement would be reached without an agreement on agriculture, prompted a reform of the agricultural policy of the EC.

The MacSharry Reform was agreed in 1992, and was gradually implemented in the years 1992-1995. It did not cover all commodities, as it was only a reform of the support for the cereal and beef sectors. The high intervention prices for cereals were significantly reduced, so market prices for cereals within the EC were closer to world market prices. As compensation for this price fall, farmers were given support per hectare so that their total incomes from cereal growing were unchanged. In the beef sector, the intervention price was also reduced and farmers received annual premiums as compensation. The reform was a shift towards a more market-orientated agricultural policy, away from price supports and towards supports tied to inputs, such as land and animals.

The MacSharry Reform opened the door to an agreement on agriculture between the EC and the USA which later became the first GATT agreement on agriculture, dealing with market access, internal support and export subsidies. The agreement was implemented during the period 1995-2000.

Market access was to be improved by converting all kinds of import barriers into tariff equivalents, which should then be gradually reduced. This meant that the EC's variable levy system had to be replaced by bound tariff rates. A system of tariff quotas, whereby the tariff on a given import volume would be reduced or totally removed, was also agreed.

All the internal agricultural support measures were split into categories. One category, such as extension services and research support, did not distort trade, so these were considered acceptable. Trade distorting measures were split into two categories: one in which there were some restrictions on support expenditures; and the other in which there were no restrictions. It was agreed that total support for the latter category should be reduced.

It was also agreed that export subsidies should be reduced. A maximum level of export subsidies would put pressure on the internal price policy to reduce the risk of producing a large surplus to be exported.

In 1996, a new Agriculture Improvement and Reform Act was passed in the USA. Most agricultural support became totally decoupled from production. The deficiency payment system was abandoned, and the entitlements now received by farmers were calculated on the basis of a farmer's past production. The support was to be given without any obligation to produce.

In 1999, the EU adopted Agenda 2000, which was a continuation of the policies of the MacSharry Reform. Discussions started about a new agricultural agreement to be part of a new WTO Round. In 2001, the Doha Round was launched.

In 2003, the internal support system of the EU agricultural policy was changed. The hectare support was converted to entitlements on the basis of past production, along the same lines as in the US legislation of 1996. The support was conditional on the farmer's compliance with environmental, animal welfare, and food safety regulations. Also the land district policy, with the purpose of creating higher economic activity in the land districts in general, was upgraded. It was decided that the new EU Member States should gradually receive the same hectare support and the same annual premiums as the farmers in existing Member States.

8.12 Summary

Since the recovery after the Second World War, agriculture has been marked by the farm-income problem. It has been difficult for farmers to obtain income increases corresponding to the average increases in incomes outside agriculture. The increase in productivity has been spectacular, and there has also been a spectacular fall in the real price of agricultural products. First, farm-workers left agriculture and since then there has been a more or less continuous decline in the number of farmers. The average farm size has increased, farms have become specialised, the agricultural capital stock and investment in human capital have increased, and the use of bought inputs such as feedstuffs, fertilizers and pesticides has increased. Agriculture has become a capital-intensive industry with intensive production, especially in Europe.

During the period 1950-1970, the farm-income problem was the main problem. This was the period when the highly protective agricultural policy of the EC was founded. Subsequently, new problems relating to agriculture have arisen. Highly intensive agricultural production has caused environmental problems, which have increasingly attracted public attention. Intensive animal production has prompted concerns about animal welfare. There have been demands for new production methods to ensure a pollution-free environment, to preserve amenities, and to address animal welfare concerns. The trend towards mass production has also raised questions about food quality and food safety. It is clear that the migration of labour away from agriculture has been an important part of the solution to the farm-income problem. However, there is a problem if farmers who quit agriculture, cannot get new jobs in the thinly populated regions in which agriculture is the dominant occupation. If alternative occupations do not exist in rural districts, there is a risk that these regions will become depopulated. In the EU, the rural district problem has attracted increased attention since the enlargement with the accession of the eight new central and eastern European countries.

Summary

A policy of agricultural support was first applied during the Great Depression in the 1930s to alleviate social distress. Policies of agricultural support continued after the Second World War. After the post-war recovery the problem was not social distress, but that the farm incomes could not keep up with the general increase of incomes in society. The aim of the agricultural policies was to increase the level of farm incomes and to moderate the volatility of agricultural prices.

The agricultural policies of the USA and the EU in the period 1960-1990 were marked by the legacy of the past. All the instruments applied in US agricultural policy were derived from the Agricultural Adjustment Act of 1933. The CAP led to internal liberalisation of agricultural trade between the EC Member States, but the market organizations for the different commodities, which were inherited from the agricultural policies of Germany and France during the 1930s, created a high protection barrier.

The 1947 GATT agreement, with the amendments in 1955, exempted agriculture from the general GATT principles. As a result, the USA and the EC were free to conduct their own agricultural policies without being subject to international discipline.

The initial support price level chosen by the EC was far too high, as long-term productivity increases were stimulated by the high price policy. For political reasons, the EC was allowed to build up its protectionist agricultural policy so that no significant positive results came out of the Dillon Round 1960-1961, the Kennedy Round 1964-1967 and the Tokyo round 1973-1979.

During the period 1973-1984, nominal support price levels tripled and real prices were constant in the EC. During the 1970s, US agriculture became much more integrated into the world market. World market prices were high, and US agriculture benefited from the depreciation of the dollar after the Bretton Woods system was abandoned.

During the first half of the 1980s, US agriculture suffered its worst crisis since the Great Depression. World market prices fell, and US agriculture was squeezed between a strongly appreciated dollar and a high interest rate, caused by the USA's macroeconomic policy.

It can be concluded from the economic analysis that the trend of agricultural overproduction in the industrialised countries did not have any significant impact on agricultural policies until around 1985. The price policy of the CAP was less flexible than the US price policy, which varied a great deal from period to period. The US price support policy was much more influenced by world market conditions than the support policy of the CAP. This reflects the fact that the USA was a net exporter, whereas the EC was originally a net importer. The agricultural policies in the USA and the EC were decided independently, but they became indirectly more and more interlinked through the increasing importance of international trade in agricultural products.

The severe crisis in US agriculture in the first half of the 1980s brought about a firm stand from the USA during the Uruguay Round 1986-1993. The USA would only accept a new GATT agreement if it included an agricultural agreement. This paved the way for the MacSharry Reforms of 1992 and the successful conclusion of the Uruguay Round.

III Lessons from the past

9. The determinants of agricultural development

9.1 A development model

On the basis of the previous chapters, it is possible to set up a model for economic development, which is illustrated in Figure 9.1. In the middle of the figure there is a very simple description of the economy. It is divided into a rural sector and an urban sector. It is assumed that the rural sector is more or less identical with agriculture, and the urban sector is more or less identical with industry. In reality there is also a service sector delivering trading, transport and financial services. This tertiary sector is important because it is only due to these services that a market economy based on specialisation is able to function.

Figure 9.1: Factors influencing economic development

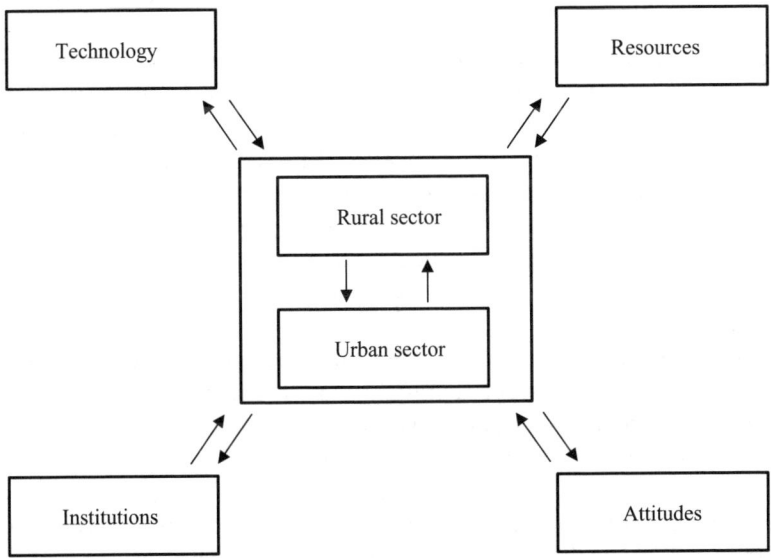

The determinants of agricultural development

Linkages and terms of trade in a two-sector model

There are important linkages between the rural and the urban sectors. Agriculture delivers foodstuffs to the urban sector, both for direct consumption and for processing. In return, the urban sector delivers inputs and consumer goods to the rural sector. These exchanges take place through the markets.

There will also be factor movements between the rural and urban sectors. When there is an excess supply of labour in rural areas this labour tends to migrate to the urban sector to find employment. With specialisation between agriculture, on one hand, and craft and industry, on the other hand, productivity increases. The increase in the GDP per capita makes it easier for consumers to save, and this facilitates an increase in investment.

The development of commodity, labour and capital markets creates more transparency, reduces transaction costs, and allows for the more efficient allocation of resources.

The income which agriculture earns from the urban sector depends on the prices of the agricultural products sold and the prices of the inputs bought. Some of the income earned by agriculture is spent on consumption, and the rest is saved. Consumption expenditures depend on consumer prices. The higher they are, the less is left for savings. If agricultural savings determine agricultural investment, it is clear that low agricultural income, due to a combination of low commodity prices, high input prices, and high consumer prices, will reduce agricultural investment. The volume sold depends on the price level of the goods and the income level of the buyers. It is important to realise that the earnings of agriculture and industry are interrelated. Low agricultural prices benefit the urban sector, but if they reduce agricultural incomes so that agricultural demand for industrial products is reduced, industry will suffer.

In the urban sector, it can be argued that savings for investments will be high if the price level of industrial goods is high and the price level of agricultural products is low. This would be correct if the volume of industrial products sold was not affected by prices, but of course this is not the case.

The conclusion is that the terms of trade between the rural and the urban sectors are extremely important. The ideal situation is a system in which relative prices reflect relative scarcities, and where the economic system induces changes which overcome the scarcities.

A development model

Factors influencing development

In Figure 9.1, there are four boxes surrounding the economy; each box contains the name of a factor of critical importance. Resources, technology, institutions and attitudes together form a framework around the economy. They determine how the economy works and how it performs, but they are also influenced by the economy. This is why there are arrows pointing in both directions between the four corner boxes and the economy.

The resources are the primary production factors such as labour, capital and natural resources. The resource endowment changes when the population increases, when the capital stock is augmented by investment, when new land is cultivated, or when new mineral deposits are exploited. Population changes are, of course, of special interest. A population increase will not only increase the supply of labour, it will also create a demand for food which may lead to investments in clearing new land or induce new farming systems, increasing productivity.

In agriculture it is not only the total amount of labour, capital and land that matter, but also the distribution of land. Wealth distribution in agriculture may be skewed so that only a limited number of large estate owners own most of the land. In this case, most of the labour force will either have no land or only small plots of land. Alternatively, there may be a more equal distribution of land between farmers. Agricultural development will be very different in these two cases.

Technological improvements take place when innovations occur. Formerly, many innovations were 'accidental', and were due to individual inventors who combined ingenuity with luck. More recently, technological improvements have been institutionalised in research centres, either private or public. Here, the needs of the producers play an important role. If there are bottlenecks in the production chain, or if some production factors are scarce, there are incentives to search for solutions to eliminate the bottlenecks or to reduce the use of scarce and expensive production factors. In this case, one can speak about 'induced' innovations.

The concept of an institution is not clearly defined. In daily life an institution is often synonymous with an organisation. Schools are educational institutions, universities are educational and research institutions, banks and mortgage lending associations are financial institutions, and trade unions and employers' associations are labour market institutions.

Institutions can also be understood as a set of existing rules and conventions in a society, such as the system of property rights, the system of trading, and the rules on lawful and unlawful behaviour. Rules and conventions influence behaviour. They govern behaviour within economic units, such as families, firms and bureaucracies. They govern behaviour between economic units when there are rules for market relationships, such as trading laws. They govern behaviour between economic units and their environment, for example the relationship between a firm and a regulatory agency.

In the present context, the concept of an institution is used in its wider sense, including both institutions as organisations and institutions as rules and conventions. In brief, institutions encompass not only physical entities, but also the rules and conventions of society.

Markets, as such, can be considered as the result of a given institutional set-up. The way the market functions depends on the system of property rights, formal and informal rules, and the physical institutions that are part of the whole market complex. The market can be considered as a signal system through which information is transmitted from the demand side to the supply side and vice versa. The better the market works, the more efficiently will resources be allocated, and the more will innovations be made and disseminated.

Finally, attitudes matter in a society. Individual beliefs determine the behaviour and preferences of each person. Beliefs at group level can be described as attitudes. In different societies, different behaviours are considered meritorious. People normally want prestige and respect from others. Such different norms will influence society, because personal energy will be directed towards obtaining prestige. The entrepreneurial spirit will be stimulated when it is prestigious to earn money, to possess great wealth and to start new productions. The coherence of society is important. When a society is harmonious, with shared attitudes, it is easier to co-operate within the society. Co-operation also depends on mutual trust, and this depends on the existence of legally enforceable rules.

A dynamic model set in motion by shocks

The economic development model illustrated in Figure 9.1 shows the mutual interrelationships between resources, technology, institutions, and attitudes on the one hand, and the economic system on the other. The model should be considered as a dynamic sequence. At a given moment there is a given framework around the economy. The amount of resources is given and so is the technological level. There is a set of institutions and some prevailing attitudes. These factors determine economic performance.

A development model

If the framework is fixed, the economy will be stationary, but when the framework changes, the economy will develop. Some of the changes in resources, technology, institutions and attitudes may arise independently of the economy. These are 'exogenous' changes. Other changes may be the result of deliberate efforts to overcome some of the existing economic problems. These are 'induced' changes.

It is very seldom that economies are totally stationary, as there will always be some minor changes in the framework. Minor changes will cause minor adjustments, but the simple reproduction of the existing economic pattern will prevail. When there are important exogenous changes which induce other changes, the conditions are created for an evolutionary development.

Population changes are a factor of major importance. There was a significant decline in the population during the period 1350-1450 due to the Black Death. From 1750 on, there was a sharp increase in population, which was to some extent due to medical improvements. The economy is deeply influenced by such an exogenous change, and the new economic conditions can induce changes in technology, institutions and attitudes, which again have an impact on the economy. The whole economy is set in motion and new bottlenecks are created. There will be pressure to overcome these obstacles.

The main point is that exogenous changes influence the economy and induce new changes in the framework. This new framework will create new economic conditions which will in turn induce new changes in the framework. The model describes a dynamic sequence over time. External shocks initiate economic changes. Disequilibrium occurs in the system in the form of bottlenecks, and the attention of scientists, inventors, entrepreneurs and public administrators will be focused on overcoming these bottlenecks. Overcoming bottlenecks creates new possibilities.

Interrelationships between the framework and the economy

The interrelationship between each of the factors – resources, technology, institutions and attitudes – on the one hand, and the economy on the other hand is clear. The changes may either be exogenous or induced. An exogenous increase in the population influences the GDP per capita, and a change in the GDP per capita influences the number of children per family. Exogenous investments due to technological progress will increase the GDP and the rise in GDP will induce changes in investments which determine the increase of the capital shock. For example, oil deposits are natural resources, and the supply of oil can be increased when new deposits are discovered and exploited. Increased oil production can also be induced by higher oil prices, which makes it profitable to drill off-shore.

It is clear that new technology can either be exogenous, or it can be the result of research activity induced by the relative scarcity of production factors. If there is a lack of a special category of workers, there is an incentive to innovate machinery which can substitute for the workers.

Institutional changes can also be exogenous or induced, although the distinction is not always clear in practice. The introduction of savings banks or mortgage lending institutions may be considered exogenous changes. The introduction of property rights over common land may be an induced change, which is intended to avoid the over-exploitation of the common land.

It is clear that attitudes are determined by the past, though they may change over time. The educational level and the spread of information have an impact on common beliefs. For example, new scientific discoveries can change attitudes towards traditional religion. Technological and institutional changes which transform economic conditions can also change attitudes. It is not only economic development that can be influenced by attitudes; attitudes can also be influenced by economic development.

Development policy, just like any other kind of economic policy, is heavily influenced by attitudes. Attitudes towards public intervention differ in different societies. Attitudes towards the outside world may differ. Some countries want to protect their industries, whereas others are against protection. A change in development strategy may be prompted by new ideas about development published by researchers. Here there is an exogenous change, whereas a change provoked by a bad experience can be regarded as an induced change.

Direct links between the development factors

Resources, technology, institutions and attitudes are interlinked through the economic system. But there are also some direct links. Some examples will illustrate the point.

Technology determines which production factors are in short supplies. Historically, with low technology in agriculture, land was in short supply, and the size of the harvest determined how many people could be fed. Today, in the industrialised countries, agricultural land is in ample supply.

A development model

Karl Marx considered the ownership of the means of production to be the most important factor driving social and economic development. The reason for this was that the proprietorial class was the ruling class, which determined the structure of society, including its institutions and ruling attitudes. Karl Marx did not realise that skewed income distribution would induce the formation of trade unions and political parties, which would gradually change societies without revolutions.

A large part of institutions relates to existing laws which are influenced by attitudes. When there are different classes with different interests, the power structure and the way in which political decisions are made is extremely important. Some countries are governed autocratically, others are governed democratically. For example, the prevailing attitudes to democracy and human rights have had a great impact on institutions. There is an important interrelationship between institutions and attitudes. In the past, attitudes have to a large extent been determined by the church, but with scientific discoveries the power of the church has gradually been reduced.

Development economics is a special discipline

The content of a theory varies according to its purpose, so it is not surprising that development theory differs from growth theory, or that growth theory differs from short-term neoclassical theory.

Short-term neoclassical theory assumes a given amount of resources, a given distribution of assets, a given technology and a given preference structure on the demand side. It is a static equilibrium model. Institutions and attitudes are effectively ignored because it is a short-term model. The markets are normally assumed to be perfect and the agents are assumed to maximise profit in the case of the producers, or utility in the case of consumers.

Growth models are long-term models which normally focus on the dynamic impact of increases in the labour force and capital stock and the impact of technological progress. In such models, resources and technology change, in contrast to the neoclassical theory. Neoclassical theory focuses on resource allocation, whereas growth theory focuses on how the economy develops when resources are increased and technology is improved. Institutions and attitudes are not taken into account. It is often assumed that demand will ensure full use of all the production factors. All the institutions necessary for perfect markets exist, and there is perfect competition on the markets.

Traditional neoclassical theory and growth theory do not look at institutions and attitudes. However, institutions and attitudes should be included in the development theory because development involves changes in institutions and attitudes, combined with factor accumulation and improved technology.

9.2 Common characteristics of feudal societies

There were some common features in most of the European countries before the modern era. The societies were static and they were characterised by a clear division of people into classes. There was a class of landlords, a class of clergy, a burgher class of artisans, traders and merchants, and a class of peasants. Some people owned the production factors, others were the producers. There was a ruler in the form of a king and his court, the ruling class – often the landlords – and the lower classes.

There were different social relationships between the individuals of the different classes, for example between the rulers and the ruling classes on the one hand, and the subordinate classes on the other hand. In agriculture there were social relationships between those who owned the land, the king, the clergy and the landlords on the one hand, and the producers – the peasants – on the other hand.

These social relationships had an impact on individual behaviour, which in turn influenced the way society functioned. Such relations exist in every society, and they define the basic constraints – the possibilities and the limits – on individual economic actions. Social relations, based on ownership of property, form constraints, because they define the resources at the disposal of individuals and the way in which individuals have access to those resources. Social relations established the communities which maintained and reproduced the resources at the disposal of individuals, and the manner of the individuals' access to those resources. This was done at the level of society, in other words it was beyond the control of any one individual.

In the farming system, the peasants were producing for subsistence and not for exchange. The peasants themselves more or less produced all they needed. They did not have to respond to market opportunities, and they were not under pressure to match the technical improvements adopted by others.

The peasants were not compelled to sell on the market, and they were not interested in becoming dependent of the market. It was a risky business to become dependent of the market. If the peasants bought and sold on the market, problems could easily arise because food prices were very volatile, depending on the size of the harvest. The peasants who depended on the market were extremely vulnerable. If a peasant specialised in non-food crops or pre-industrial home production, such as textiles, he would no longer be self-sufficient in food products. He would have to buy on the market and he would be in trouble if there was a bad harvest. In times of food scarcity those who relied on buying food through exchange might not be able to get enough through the market. If food was available, it might only be at a very high price, which could be beyond the means of the specialised peasant. Market-dependant peasants, producing non-food products, had to sell their specialised production at low prices when purchasing power was low. Consumers who had to buy food at high prices only had a smaller part of their income available for the consumption of other commodities.

While traditional peasants did buy and sell in markets, the important point was that they avoided becoming dependent on the market. Their main goal was to avoid risks, and this had a pervasive influence on their behaviour. The peasants wanted to diversify their production to become independent of the outside world and they wanted to have large families as insurance against illness and for their old age. In this case, profit maximisation was not equal to utility maximisation.

Like the peasants, the landlords who owned the large estates were free from the necessity of responding to trading opportunities. They owned land and controlled sufficient labour to provide their households with sufficient goods. They were not compelled to produce competitively in order to survive. However, the estate owner might be induced to maximise his income by increased specialisation, reinvesting surpluses in the means of production and introduce new techniques, but his relationship with the peasants working on his estate was an obstacle. The peasants were obliged to work on their landlord's estate free of charge, so there was no need for investment. If investments were undertaken, there was no guarantee that they would be profitable. The peasants were in charge of production and they were working under coercion, with no incentive to increase production.

The surpluses of the landlords were spent on weaponry and luxury goods, especially textiles. In other words, the surpluses were not invested but consumed. When the landlords wanted to increase their surpluses, they tried to force the peasants to work more, and they had the opportunity to supplement their incomes by acquiring office under the crown.

The determinants of agricultural development

Most people lived in rural areas, and even in early modern times in around 1750 only 10-12 per cent of the population lived in towns (de Vries, 1984). Artisans produced on a small scale, and they typically based their production on personal orders, typically from the landowning class, and not on the demands of an impersonal market. Production for an impersonal market must be stimulated by the purchasing power of ordinary people as potential customers.

The artisan producers and the merchant middlemen in the towns protected their incomes by forming communities. They organised themselves into guilds whose chief purpose was to secure the incomes of their members by regulating prices, trading conditions and the number of actors in specific trades. These communities wanted to eliminate any competition which could have benefited the most efficient producers. The artisan and merchant communities were also successful in influencing public regulations. Artisan and merchant activities were not allowed outside the towns, so the citizens of the towns had a monopoly on these activities. The bigger craft guilds and trading companies were often granted a charter which bestowed privileges, such as the exclusive right to produce or the exclusive right to trade with a foreign country, for example. The best way for manufacturers and merchants to increase their profits was often to increase their privileges.

Under the pressure of the growing population, the land was divided into smaller units, and a growing number of peasants had problems surviving. They increased their labour efforts in cultivating the land, so that land productivity increased while labour productivity decreased. Those with access to urban markets could make more intensive use of family labour, especially wives and children. They could cultivate more labour-intensive commercial crops such as flax, garden vegetables and plants for producing dyes. Others produced textile products for sale. Peasants turned to commercial agriculture and to non-agricultural productions, which were industrialised later, but this was not a profit-maximising response to growing opportunities. It was a secondary choice, dictated by the needs of survival.

The feudal system was a conservative system, without the dynamics that characterised the market economy which started to develop during the eighteenth century, especially the second half of it. The peasants were fighting for the right to use the land, for lower dues and reduced labour services on the estates of the landlords. The landlords, on the other hand, tried to get as high a surplus from the peasants as they possibly could. The system lasted for centuries and it did not seem to matter whether the landlords or the peasants had the upper hand at any given time.

9.3 The different stages of agricultural development

The feudal system was established during the Middle Ages and continued until the start of the agricultural revolution. There were changes during the feudal period, but they were minor compared to the changes which took place after the start of the agricultural revolution.

The feudal system reproduced itself without generating much development. There was a dual economy in which the rural sector constituted 80 per cent or more of the population. The economy was based on self-sufficiency and coercion by the ruling classes.

There is some debate about exactly when the agricultural revolution started. It is evident that the first changes occurred before they gained sufficient momentum to have an economic impact. The start is often dated to the period around 1750, though it is recognised that it started at different times in different countries.

According to a study made by Bairoch, the approximate dates for the onset of the agricultural revolution in various countries were the following: Britain 1690-1700; France 1750-60; United States 1760-70; Switzerland 1780-90; Germany, and Denmark 1790-1800; Austria, Italy and Sweden 1820-30; Russia and Spain 1860-70 (Bairoch, 1969).

Development is associated with productivity increases. In the longer perspective, there seems to have been an increase in the rate of productivity gains in western developed countries when the feudal system began to disappear. According to the labour productivity data in Chapter 3, productivity increased 50 per cent during the period 1800-1850, 100 per cent during the period 1850-1910, nearly 200 per cent during the period 1910-1960, and 300 per cent during the period 1960-1990 (Bairoch, 1999).

It seems reasonable to split agricultural development into four stages:
First stage	1750-1850
Second stage	1850-1914
Third stage	1914-1950
Fourth stage	1950-2000

There are different characteristics associated with each stage.

The first stage was characterised by technical and institutional changes which involved important investments in the agricultural sector. The institutional changes were the agricultural reforms which involved the emancipation of the peasants, who started to interact with the market.

The second stage was the one in which the economic integration was a dominant feature. Within each country there was integration between regions and between rural and urban areas. Internationally, countries were linked by trade, investments and migration. It was the period when the infrastructure and institutions necessary for establishing markets were put in place. The extensive network of railways began to be constructed in around 1850.

The third stage was a period of disruption with two world wars and the unprecedented economic crisis of the 1930s. During the first two stages, the agricultural labour force was growing. During the third stage up to 1950 there was a slight decrease in the agricultural labour force. During the 1930s, when agriculture was severely hit by the Depression, interventionist agricultural policies were introduced for the first time.

The fourth stage was the period when there were large decreases both in the agricultural labour force and in the number of farms. During the 1950s, the migration of agricultural workers to industry increased, but the number of farms and farmers did not change notably. It was only from around 1960 that the sharp decline in the number of farms started in most Western European countries. Average farms became much larger, and production became specialised and increasingly dependent on inputs bought-in from outside. The number of full-time farmers decreased more than the number of farms, because the number of part-time farmers increased.

During the third stage, real agricultural prices were heavily influenced by the adjustment after the First World War and the Great Depression, so it is not easy to identify a long-term trend. The idea of a long-term deterioration of real agricultural prices first arose in the third stage, but it was only during the fourth stage this long-term trend became absolutely clear. The interventionist agricultural policies, which had been introduced during the 1930s were continued in order to compensate for the falling real prices.

It is difficult to put specific dates on the different stages. Development is a gradual process which does not start in a specific year and then suddenly stop at the end of the period. Also, what is characteristic for one period can also apply to other periods. Agrarian reforms continued after 1850, and there were investments in infrastructure and markets before 1850. Moreover, agricultural development was far from synchronous between the countries. Agrarian reforms started in some countries, before others. In the first stage in particular, which was characterised by agrarian reforms, there were major differences in the timing of this stage in different countries.

9.4 The first stage of agricultural development

In societies where up to 80 per cent of the population is engaged in agriculture, no economic development is possible without agricultural development.

Normally, economic development is assumed to have started in around 1750 and this means that agricultural development must have started at around the same period. People speak about the 'agricultural revolution', but the idea of revolution is at odds with the reality of gradual transition. In around 1750, when the agricultural changes started to take place, there were significant changes in resources, technology, institutions and attitudes.

From 1750 there was a significant increase in the population, and this created increased demand for food products. Agricultural prices rose from 1750 to 1815, and this was an incentive to increase production.

At the same time, technological improvements contributed to changes in production methods and to institutional changes. The technological changes can be described as the crop-livestock husbandry model.

New crops, such as turnips and clover, had been known before 1750, but it was at around that time these new crops were used more extensively in British agriculture. The system of letting land lie fallow could be abandoned and feed production could be increased without exhausting the soil. This laid the foundation for increased livestock production. The manure from the increased livestock was used as fertiliser to maintain soil fertility. This crop-livestock cycle was a closed agricultural cycle which did not rely on inputs from outside the agricultural sector.

The technological changes were based on the crop-livestock husbandry model, but there were additional technical changes which improved productivity. There was an extension and improvement of arable land. The common lands were integrated into more intensive production. Land was cleared and new techniques were used to drain marshy areas.

This was also the period when more scientific selection of seed and breeding materials started. There were improvements to traditional farm implements, such as ploughs. Wooden ploughs were replaced by iron ploughs. New implements were also introduced. The scythe replaced the sickle and the seed drill replaced broadcast sowing.

The institutional changes involved important agricultural reforms which dismantled the feudal system. These institutional changes were interwoven not only with technological changes but also with ideological changes.

The mid-eighteenth century was the Age of Enlightenment, when there were some important ideological shifts. Philosophers were influenced by the ideas of reason and of human rights. It was the task of enlightened people with power to contribute to improved production methods. The foundations of agricultural reforms were also influenced by the idea of the emancipation of the peasants. This ideology supported technical and institutional change. In 1776 Adam Smith published his work "The Wealth of Nations", in which he emphasized the importance of the market and declared that labour rather than nature was the only source of wealth. This was an attack on mercantilism, which was the ruling idea. According to mercantilism, wealth was to be acquired by protecting trade and by public support for manufacturers.

The agricultural reforms involved a series of different changes. The open-field system, based on collective decision making, was replaced by individual farming. The vast numbers of scattered strips of land were consolidated into enclosed fields. In several cases, the farmhouses and farm buildings were moved out from the village into the centre of the land holding. These reforms had a direct positive impact on agricultural productivity.

The peasant class was emancipated in the sense that their legal rights were enforced. The labour services they had to deliver under the feudal system were fixed, reduced or removed. In most cases the peasants became owners of their own farms. In many cases the distribution of land was associated with a more equal distribution of income. These reforms contributed to the creation of a class of independent farmers. The farmers did not have to obey their landlords, and they were exposed to an incentive system which rewarded activity and initiative. These reforms improved agricultural productivity in the short and, especially, in the long run.

It took time to implement these technical and institutional changes, which not only required major investments but also involved political conflicts because of the differing opinions and opposing interests of the landlords. So it is not surprising that the positive impact on agricultural production was spread over a long period.

The technical and institutional changes should be considered as a composite, as it is not possible to identify the economic impact of each piece of the reform complex.

In the first stage, technical changes in the form of the crop-livestock husbandry system, combined with the extension of the arable area, and institutional changes in the form of agricultural reforms got the agricultural sector moving. The crop-livestock husbandry system involved a more intensive use of the land. The crop increase was partly due to taking in more land and partly due to higher yields on the land already used.

The agricultural changes made in the first stage were based on internal resources. The investments associated with the technical and institutional changes came from agriculture itself. Agriculture delivered both the necessary labour and the necessary capital. Many of the resources which were generated by agricultural production were spent on agricultural investments. The resources which were taken out of agriculture were to a large extent used in textile and iron production.

9.5 The second stage of agricultural development

The process of integration

When the initial changes in the first stage had been made, the economy continued to develop in the second stage. This was due to the dynamic effects associated with the division of labour and the creation of markets.

Firstly, markets were gradually created and improved. To start with, markets were either non-existent or they were rather rudimentary. It was the landlords who used the markets, and they were limited because they mostly only served the local rural area and nearby towns that could be reached in a day. Gradually markets were extended and their performance improved.

Secondly, the peasants became increasingly integrated into the markets, and this had a dynamic effect in itself. There were new technological improvements, and the peasants wanted to apply the new methods because they gave them better incomes. They had the possibility of financing the necessary investments when a credit market was established. There was a more or less continuous stream of technical improvements, and these became integrated into agriculture because the peasants made the necessary investments. The inherently stagnant characteristics of the feudal system were replaced by the dynamics of the markets.

Thirdly, agricultural development paved the way for the division of labour leading to industrialisation, which was stimulated by technical innovations. When both agriculture and industry developed, there were important interrelationships between the rural and urban sectors, and these stimulated further development.

The determinants of agricultural development

In the second stage, agricultural productivity increased more than in the previous period. It was the stage when the rural and urban sectors became more integrated, combined with a sharp increase in the relative importance of the urban sector. Agriculture became increasingly dependent on the rest of the economy, and an increasing share of its inputs came from outside agriculture.

During the second stage, labour and capital were released from agriculture and invested in the development of markets and industrialisation.

The development of markets not only required the construction of a transport infrastructure, it also involved the development of a distribution system, a human resource development system, a research and know-how system, and a financial and labour market system.

Industrialisation was linked to agriculture by forward linkages, backward linkages and income linkages. The forward linkages consisted of agricultural deliveries of cereals, sugar beet, potatoes, milk, farm animals and wool for processing in mills, breweries, distilleries, sugar refineries, dairies, slaughterhouses, meat processing and textile industry, etc.

The backward linkages were established by the agricultural demand for tools, implements, machinery, processed feedstuffs and fertilizers.

Income linkages are concerned with the relationship between the income in one sector and the expenditure on products from other sectors. When the peasants increased their income, they were able to buy industrially manufactured consumer goods. The textile industry replaced home produced clothes at an early stage.

In the first part of the second stage, a large part of the released agricultural resources was invested in the development of markets. The remaining resources were invested in industrialisation, which was mostly based on forward and backward linkages. During the second part of the second stage, relatively more was invested in industrialisation and less on the development of markets, where the need for resources was reduced. The pattern of industrialisation became more influenced by income linkages than previously.

The transport and distribution systems

To move from a self-sufficiency economy to a market economy is a big step. If surplus production, above the self-sufficiency level, is to be profitable, it has to be sold. Transforming potential markets into actual markets depends on transport costs. Before the railway network began to

The second stage of agricultural development

be constructed in around 1850, water transport by sea, river or canal was the most important means of long-distance transport.

Without an infrastructure it is impossible to develop a market economy. The infrastructural investments were heavily dependent on technological progress. The invention of the railways and the improved marine transport technology – when steam replaced sail, and iron ships replaced wooden ships – involved major investments. The railways needed rail networks and rolling stock. Improved marine transport needed harbours and ships.

Markets bring together actual and potential buyers and sellers, so they cannot fulfil their purpose unless buyers and sellers can communicate with each other at a reasonable cost. The establishment of communication systems, such as a telegraph system or a telephone system needs large resources.

A distribution system which is able to deliver products from farmers to consumers and farm inputs from producers to farmers also had to be established. Farm products have to be collected for further processing before the processed goods are distributed to wholesalers and then to retailers. Improved productivity was associated with improved inputs and new inputs, but new and improved inputs were only useful to the peasants when they were available on the market. Seed selection improved the quality of seed, but the improved seed could only increase productivity when it became available on the market. From 1840 manure was supplemented by imported guano and later by chemical fertilisers. Farm-produced fodder for animal feed was supplemented with bought-in concentrates, such as oil cake. The availability of these inputs depended on the distribution system being able to deliver the inputs at the right time.

The gradual development of the markets was a resource-intensive activity, which was of crucial importance for agricultural development in stage two.

Human resource development

The existence of a market and a distribution system is a necessary but not sufficient condition for development. In addition, the peasants had to be willing and able to be integrated into the market.

There were markets even in feudal times and in the first stage of agricultural development, but it was only the landlords who bought and sold in the market, whereas the peasants were self-sufficient.

It is risky to be dependent on the market if prices are volatile, but if institutional changes are introduced which reduce the risk, the peasants will be more interested in taking advantage of the market.

It will be difficult for a farmer to become a market-oriented decision-maker unless he has received a general education. He has to understand the relevant information and to take decisions based on it. The farmer is an entrepreneur. He has to allocate resources between different crops and different animal production, he has to combine the different inputs profitably, and he has to choose between different productions methods which involve different levels of investment.

A general education, combined with some specialist agricultural education, will make it easier for the farmer to receive and evaluate advice and information. Education will not only make him a better farmer, but also a citizen who will be more open to co-operation and political activity. When farmers are educated they are more aware and better able to take joint initiatives through self-organised co-operatives and institutions. Educated farmers are also better equipped to take part in politics, where they have the opportunity to promote public investments which can stimulate agricultural development.

Innovation and diffusion systems

The flow of innovations and the diffusion of new production possibilities also explains why agricultural development continued in stage two, after the sector started to move in stage one.

New farm practices involve the introduction of new products or improved products. New farm practices are also concerned with the use of new or improved inputs, together with the introduction of new or improved production processes.

The way in which new farm practices are discovered has changed. Originally, innovations in cultivation methods were made by farmers themselves. Young, who wrote about the agricultural changes in Britain in the late eighteenth century, considered that improved farm practices, for example the introduction of the seed drill, were important contributions to the productivity increase.

Later, experimental stations were established. Their task was to test different farm practices to find out which method was best. By their experiments, the stations contributed actively to the innovation of new methods.

Then agricultural universities were established. Their purpose was to educate specialists and to initiate research. They trained veterinary

The second stage of agricultural development

surgeons, agronomists and others who could assist farmers on the basis of the latest research results. The agricultural universities specialised mainly in applied sciences, though there was a clear understanding of the relevance of more basic research, which tended to be undertaken in the general universities.

When improved farm practices were initiated by individual farmers, as was the case originally, they were very much determined by the needs of the farmer. When there were bottlenecks in production, efforts were directed towards removing those bottlenecks. Experimental stations, agricultural universities and research institutes have been regionally based, with close ties to the farming sector. This has been important, because the innovations have mainly been responsive to the needs of the agricultural sector, and these vary from region to region.

The diffusion of existing know-how and innovations takes time, but this time can be shortened when the flow of information is improved and when the peasants are better equipped to receive and understand the information. The establishment of farmers' associations for transmitting information through meetings and publications is very useful when the peasants are motivated to take part. Extension services to the peasants are very important to the efforts to increase agricultural productivity.

Agricultural associations were established, and they helped farmers in improving the quality of the crop and measuring the yield. Similar assistance was given to livestock producers, e.g. dairy farmers. When extension service systems began to be established in the second half of the nineteenth century, the focus was on technical matters. In many cases it was implicitly assumed that the production methods which could increase yields and improve quality would also ensure higher farm income.

It was only at a much later stage in the twentieth century, with the introduction of the discipline of farm economics, that it was emphasised that maximisation of profit does not follow automatically from maximisation of yields. At that later stage, farm accounting became the instrument by which the economic performance of individual farmers was measured. Economic analyses of farm accounting data showed that there could be wide variations in economic performance. It was realised that the quality of farm management had an important impact on the economic result.

The rationale behind the extension services was the improvement of productivity in agriculture. This could be achieved by improving the general productivity of all farmers by the rapid dissemination of innovations and best farm practice throughout the farming sector.

The determinants of agricultural development

Average productivity would also be increased if the laggards among the farmers were able to catch up with the front runners.

The capital and labour markets

In addition to establishing markets for products, it was also important to establish markets for capital and labour. The creation of markets for products is resource-intensive. Finance is necessary and this can be acquired through public taxation and private savings. Public taxation needs a public administration and private savings need a financial system consisting of savings banks, banks and mortgage-lending institutions.

During the second stage a capital market was created. Saving banks were established in rural areas. They were important in many respects. They induced the peasants to save and they allocated savings to investors who were known locally. Because the investors were known, the administration costs were small and the proportion of loan defaults was low. The establishment of a credit system also had a risk-reducing effect. Investments were risky when harvests could fail and when prices were low. When borrowing on an unorganised market, the borrower becomes dependent on a personal lender, and the costs are high. The peasants were very risk-averse and this hampered initiatives and investments. The risks were reduced once the capital market was organised. The possibility of getting a loan when needed increased, and the costs were reduced.

During the second stage, labour was released from agriculture through productivity gains. The agricultural sector did not need the whole of the increase in population and the development of markets and industrialisation demanded labour. During the first part of the second stage the labour markets were not well-organised. Employers were in a strong position, and they could more or less dictate the terms of employment, including the wages.

During the last decades of the nineteenth century, labour unions started to be organised in industry and gradually labour conditions improved and real wages increased.

A more organised labour market was a great step forward from a development point of view. Collective wage bargaining between employers' associations and trade unions was an advantage, because the employers were willing to accept higher wage increases than was the case with unorganised markets. When all employers in a given trade have to pay higher wages, wage competition between them is eliminated. The higher wage increases gave employers an incentive to rationalise and mechanize industrial production, which led to lower prices for industrial products. The industrial working class expanded and real labour wages increased, and both these factors contributed to an increase in the demand for food, especially for animal products where the income elasticity was higher than for cereal products.

9.6 The third stage of agricultural development

By the end of the second stage and the beginning of the third stage, agriculture had completed two great tasks. It had contributed to the development of markets and to the integration of the rural and the urban sectors.

The third stage of agricultural development in Western Europe and the USA started in around 1914. The start of the third stage concerned both the absolute size and the relative size of agriculture. The absolute size of the agricultural sector, measured by the size of the agricultural labour force, had reached its maximum at the start of the third stage, apart from Britain where the decline had started earlier. However, in the more industrialised countries, agriculture was no longer the dominant sector measured in terms of employment. In Britain, employment in agriculture was a quarter of the employment in the secondary sector. In the USA and Germany, the numbers employed in agriculture were fewer than in industrial employment.

Food consumption, as a share of total consumption, was at a much lower level than during the previous stages. In 1914 around one third of total consumption was spent on food and beverages in Western Europe and the USA. By 1960 this share had fallen to around a quarter.

During the first and second stages, agricultural development was crucial for the overall economic development of a society. This was no longer the case in the third and fourth stages, though agriculture was still an important sector, especially during the third stage.

During the third stage there were still important changes in technology, institutions, attitudes and resources, but they were not generally as fundamental as in the second stage.

The third stage coincided with a very turbulent period. There were two world wars separated by the worst depression ever seen. The general economic and the agricultural economic conditions were very much influenced by these events.

Nevertheless, there was still technological progress in agriculture, and productivity continued to increase except during the war years. There were still institutional changes in the sense that the markets continued to develop, but the changes in the commodity markets were relatively minor compared to the dramatic changes which had taken place in the previous stage. The institutional changes were more marked in the capital and labour markets.

There were also important changes in attitudes. At the beginning of the second stage, the idea of free trade was realised in Europe, and the former trade protection, both internal and external, was removed. At the end of the nineteenth century it was realised that the raw social consequences of industrialisation were unacceptable. The socialist movement grew and gradually became more important. As a result, the workers set up trade unions and governments, especially the government in Germany, introduced social laws and labour market laws to ameliorate the living and working conditions of the working class.

During the third stage, the Great Depression gave rise to social distress, not only among workers, but also among farmers. To alleviate some of these problems, far more comprehensive social and labour market policies were introduced. The distress of farmers gave rise to the introduction of interventionist agricultural policies.

Social policy, labour market policy and agricultural policy were remedies for the social distress which came after the event. Many of the problems could have been avoided if the right interventions had been made to deal with the economic crisis at an earlier stage. The idea of macroeconomic stabilisation policy, which was given its theoretical foundation by J.M. Keynes in 1936, was introduced, and became a fundamental element of economic policy after the Second World War (Keynes, 1936).

During the second stage, the amount of resources had been increased significantly. The size of the labour force had increased, as had the capital accumulation. In agriculture, the area of arable land had been increased. During the third stage, the total labour force continued to increase, but at a lower rate than previously. The capital accumulation suffered from the two world wars and the Great Depression. The area of agricultural land was either stagnant or slightly decreasing.

The interrelationships between the rural and the urban sectors were still important. When the agricultural sector received low farm prices at the beginning of the Great Depression, the reduced farm incomes had a direct negative impact on the demand for industrial products. There was also an indirect effect, as many farmers defaulted their loans. Many banks went bankrupt and bank depositors lost their deposits, contributing to the development of the crisis. High unemployment also had a negative impact on the agricultural sector as the reduced incomes led to a decline in the demand for food and contributed to the downward spiral of agricultural prices. Had the agricultural sector been supported at an earlier stage, the crisis might not have been so severe.

During the third stage, the agricultural labour force was reduced. The reduction during the period 1914-1945 was relatively modest compared to the reduction during the period 1945-1960, when the movement of labour away from agriculture accelerated. The number of farms and the number of farmers remained fairly constant or declined only slightly at the end of the period. The decrease in the labour force was due to the migration of farm workers. The agricultural and non-agricultural labour markets had become more integrated, so the barriers between the markets were reduced. Responsiveness to income disparities and employment possibilities increased.

Agricultural output increased and the labour force was reduced, so agricultural labour productivity increased, especially after the Second World War. During the 1950s there was a trend towards substituting capital for labour, especially in the USA, which was around 20 years ahead of agriculture in Western Europe.

Interventionist agricultural policies were introduced for the first time during the Great Depression. This support was thought of as a relief measure, which would be removed when normal economic conditions were restored, but these agricultural policies continued after the Second World War.

9.7 The fourth stage of development

The fourth stage started in around 1960 in Western Europe and earlier, in around 1940, in the USA. It started when the number of farmers and farms started to decline.

Technology continued to improve. Known machinery was improved and new machinery was invented. High yielding cereal seed, responsive to the use of fertilisers, was introduced, causing a dramatic increase in the yield ratio. Plant infestations were avoided by a large increase in the use of pesticides. Animal breeding programmes were continued, so the efficiency of animal production was improved.

The result was a very large increase in labour productivity. The capital-labour ratio increased because capital in the form of machinery replaced labour. The use of inputs such as fertilisers, pesticides and feedstuffs, bought from outside, increased. Agriculture became more dependent on deliveries from outside. Farms became larger and more specialised. There was horizontal specialisation as mixed farms, simultaneously producing cereals, milk, pigs and poultry, disappeared. Farms now specialised either in cereal, dairy, pig or poultry production. There was also vertical specialisation as the value added in the food processing industry increased in relation to the value added in the primary sector. Today, employment in the food-processing industry is about the same size as employment in the primary agricultural sector.

The relative importance of agriculture fell from about 20 per cent of GDP in 1960 to about 5 per cent or even less in 2000. The share of food consumption of total consumption fell from 25 per cent in 1960 to about half of this in 2000.

There was a release of labour from agriculture, which was easily absorbed by the urban sector, especially during the period 1960-1973, when there was a high growth rate, particularly in Western Europe. The net flow of funds went from society at large to agriculture, because of the agricultural support policies.

There were some changes in attitudes. The creation of the welfare state was the great goal in western Europe. The idea was that no social group should be left behind the general improvement in living standards. This attitude contributed to the acceptance of agricultural support as long as farmers were confronted with an income problem. There were also new topics on the agenda, including the protection of the environment, conservation, the survival of rural communities and food standards.

These ideological changes had some impact on the institutional framework for agriculture in the form of the legislation. There were important interventions in the market mechanism, not least through agricultural policy. However, the trend towards still bigger farms with industrial-style production was allowed to continue.

Until the fourth stage, the family farm was considered to be the only type of farm on which agriculture should be based. Most farms were of small or medium size, so the farming structure could be considered unimodal. During the fourth stage, the size structure changed significantly. Firstly, there has been a division between part-time farmers on the one hand, and full-time farmers on the other hand. Secondly, full-time farmers have been divided into medium-sized farms and industrial farms, which employ a greater or lesser number of workers. The question is whether the medium-sized family farms will disappear, as they develop either into industrial farms or part-time farms.

There will be a farm-income problem when average agricultural real incomes fall behind the average real incomes in alternative occupations. When real agricultural prices fall, farmers may have an income problem. Real agricultural prices fall when price levels for agricultural products rise less than the rise in general price levels in the society.

The fourth stage of development

There were falling real agricultural prices in the USA during the 1920s. In the years 1929-1933, there was a further significant fall before real agricultural prices were restored during the remainder of the 1930s. It was only after the Second World War that it became clear that there was a long-term trend towards lower real agricultural prices. The demand for agricultural products increased only a little in Europe and the USA. The population increased more slowly and the income elasticity was small and declining when the income level rose. On the other hand, supplies increased due to productivity gains, in spite of the reduction in the agricultural labour force. If the percentage increase in production is greater than the percentage fall in real prices, agricultural turnover will increase. How farm incomes develop will depend on the costs, which will increase due to the greater use of variable inputs and the larger capital stock which has to be financed. The agricultural turnover minus the costs equals the income of the agricultural sector. If the income of the sector falls, the average farm income will only rise if the number of farmers falls more than the fall in the sector income.

The development of average farm incomes depends on the degree of the fall in real agricultural prices, the rise of agricultural productivity, the rise in costs, especially the capital costs, and the reduction in the number of farmers.

It seems evident that there was a farm-income problem after the Second World War. In a free market economy one would expect the relative fall in farm incomes to induce farmers to leave agriculture until a new equilibrium with income parity is reached.

The question is why the income problem seems to be permanent and why farmers continue to invest when there is an income problem.

The traditional answer to this question has been given by Cochrane (Cochrane, 1958). Farmers are divided into three groups: pioneers, followers and laggards. When agricultural innovations are made, some pioneers invest in the new methods to reduce their variable production costs. The pioneers' production level will increase, but the price level will not fall because the pioneers are relatively few in number. The pioneers will gain because their costs are reduced.

When, after an interval, the followers, who are greater in number, follow the pioneers by investing in the cost-reducing methods, the price level will fall. The followers will neither gain nor lose, because their cost reduction will more or less correspond to the fall in prices. The losers will be the laggards, who do not invest; they encounter falling prices without getting the benefit of the cost reductions associated with innovations. Sooner or later the laggards will be squeezed out, and their assets will be sold to the farmers who are able to stay in business. This adjustment will often take place when old farmers, who are not as dynamic as younger farmers, retire from business.

The process just described is a description of the dynamics of the market mechanism. Through the market mechanism, innovations are incorporated into the production process through investments.

In other sectors, the market mechanism is similar, but the result will not be an ever lower income level as seems to be the case in the agricultural sector. The investments which channel the innovations into the production process do not seem to ensure an increase in agricultural incomes corresponding to the increase in incomes elsewhere in society. Why then does the process continue?

One answer is that some kind of income parity will be established when the adjustment has taken place. The problem here is that the adjustment seems to have been taking place since the end of the Second World War, and it is not yet finished.

Another answer is that farmers have to invest if they want to stay in business, regardless of the farm income. But the problem is that the low farm incomes are not reflected in land prices and the prices of farms themselves. When the earnings in a sector are low, the prices of the production factors should be correspondingly low, so that a reasonable income level can be achieved. Does each new generation of farmers perpetually overestimate agricultural income potential? Do they underestimate the fall in real agricultural prices? Do they underestimate the capital costs or overestimate their management skills? Are farmers not profit-maximisers? Are they more interested in large farms and impressive machinery? Do they expect the public to alleviate their problems through a continuation of substantial agricultural support?

9.8 What will happen in the fifth stage?

In European countries, where agricultural labour productivity is highest, and in the USA, the agricultural labour force has reached such a low level that it is reasonable to assume that there will be no significant further reductions. This can be considered as the start of the fifth stage, here at the beginning of the twenty-first century.

What will be the trends in this coming stage? How will the resources, technology, attitudes and institutions develop in the agricultural sector?

As already mentioned, no further decline in the labour force can be expected. The capital stock will most probably be constant. The number of part-time farmers with a relative low amount of capital will increase.

What will happen in the fifth stage?

The number of full-time farmers will slightly decrease, and the capital-intensity of production will increase correspondingly. The number of farms with employees will increase, but it is far from certain that the number of very large 'industrialised' farms will increase due to the negative attitudes towards that kind of farming. Farm specialisation will remain, but farming methods will be adjusted to meet changing requirements. Public attitudes towards agriculture are already changing, and these trends will be reinforced during the fifth stage. The public will focus more on food quality and on agricultural production methods.

Consumers with high and increasing incomes will focus more and more on the quality of food products. One quality aspect is food safety, which will be a fundamental requirement. Food products have to be produced under hygienic conditions and they must not contain harmful residues such as antibiotics. Another quality aspect concerns the nutritional value of food products. With the increasing levels of obesity in the population there is no doubt that nutritional considerations will play a big role in the future.

The public will be increasingly concerned about the negative externalities caused by the present farming methods. The environment suffers from the intensive use of fertilisers and pesticides which cause pollution of the ground water, rivers and the sea. The landscape and wild animals and plants are harmed by the present production methods. Intensive livestock production raises concerns about animal welfare.

These attitudes will change existing production methods as new regulations will be introduced. These attitudes will also influence technological innovations and how these innovations are applied. There is no doubt that the technique of genetically modifying organisms could have an important impact on agricultural production methods, but it is unclear to what extent it will be applied commercially. The new technology raises a number of important and complex ethical questions.

The institutions will also be influenced by the new attitudes. The food processing industry will have to deliver differentiated food products of high quality. Therefore, the food industry needs raw materials delivered by the farmers, which fulfil specific requirements. So it can be envisaged that, in the future, an increasing share of production will be based on specific contracts between individual farmers and processing firms. Systems will be introduced to ensure that the specific requirements are fulfilled. When food safety is important, it is important to be able to trace a product through its different production stages. Only in this way is it possible to find the source of a problem if a food item does not fulfil food safety requirements.

When negative externalities, in the form of pollution, landscape deterioration, lack of biodiversity and lack of animal welfare, are no longer acceptable, the role of the farmer will change. He will no longer be merely a businessman, producing the largest volume at the lowest price, he will also be a steward of the natural resources under his control. In other words, agriculture has a multifunctional role in society.

During the fourth stage, interventionist agricultural policy has become an important and permanent feature. At the end of the fourth stage, there has been a change in the composition of agricultural support, even though the total value of the support has remained more or less constant. There has been a move away from a price support policy towards a more decoupled support in the form of income support. This trend will continue as the focus moves away from pure production to the multifunctional tasks of agriculture. Support will either be directly linked to new tasks, or it will depend on cross-compliance with the new demands.

There are other elements which may influence the trend from price to income support. Income support is less trade-distorting, so if there is international pressure to reduce trade distortion, this pressure will influence the changes. Also, there has been a change in the relative transaction costs between price and income supports. In the past, the transaction costs per farmer have been higher for income supports than for price supports. There are direct transaction costs related to the different kinds of agricultural supports. However, the higher administrative costs of income supports compared to price supports have to some extent been reduced by administrative improvements based on information technology. Even if the transaction costs are still higher for income supports, the total costs have been markedly reduced because of the reduced number of farmers. There are indirect transaction costs associated with the financing of the outlays. Price supports are financed by consumers through the market, whereas income supports are financed through the public budget. Higher taxes due to income support may be difficult to accept politically, and higher marginal taxes may have a negative effect on labour supply. When the number of farmers is reduced, the political and economic problems associated with financing income supports through taxes are also reduced.

In the fifth stage, food demand in the industrialised countries will be more or less stagnant, when the population is also stagnant. The increase in supply will depend on the amount of resources in agriculture and productivity. With technological progress it will still be possible to make productivity gains, but the opposite trend may be at work if farming methods become less intensive, perhaps due to environmental concerns.

If food demand is stagnant, and if the supply increases only moderately in the industrialised countries, there should be a continued decline in real agricultural prices, unless there is an excess demand for agricultural products in the developing countries. Due to population increases, income increases and diet changes, a significant increase in food demand in developing countries can be expected. If local increases in supply in the developing countries cannot keep pace with demand, there will be excess demand in developing countries which will have to be satisfied by the industrialised countries.

There are widely differing opinions about the future trend of real prices for agricultural products. Some expect increasing real prices; others expect that the past trend of falling real prices will continue.

9.9 Summary

Economic development is a highly complex process which cannot be properly understood if one focuses on only one aspect of it. Economic development depends on a series of factors which can be grouped under four headings, namely resources, technology, institutions and attitudes. These four factors can be considered as the framework surrounding the economy.

There is mutual interrelationship between the surrounding framework and the economic system. Resources, technology, institutions and attitudes may change due to exogenous influences, or the changes may be induced by the economic system.

There are also direct links between the four factors constituting the framework. Through the legislation, attitudes influence the institutions of a society, and the impact of technological changes depends on the nature of the existing institutions. The relative scarcity of a given resource such as labour, capital or land, depends on the existing technology.

As illustrated in the previous chapters, economic development in Europe and the USA has been characterised by an increase in resources, technological progress, institutional innovations and the emergence of new attitudes. Economic development has also been characterised by a dramatic change in the economic structure. Societies were originally dominated by agriculture, but they have gradually been transformed into societies in which nearly all economic activity takes place in the urban sector in industry and services. To understand development it is important to look not only at the total economy, but to split up the economy into rural and urban sectors. There are very important interrelationships between the two sectors, which should not be disregarded. Economic development is also concerned with resource allocations.

The description of the economic development process presented in section 9.1 is not at all precise. Nevertheless, it gives some understanding of the complexity of economic development. It also gives a survey of all the different elements which have influenced economic development in the past, so it may give a better understanding of the past.

Past agricultural development is divided into four different stages, each with specific characteristics. This way of looking at the past as a series of stages has to some extent been inspired by the development theory of W.W. Rostow (Rostow, 1960). Rostow works with five different stages for a society, and he supposes that all societies, sooner or later, move through the five stages. The five stages are: 1. the traditional society; 2. the transitional stage or the preconditions for take-off; 3. the take-off; 4. the drive to maturity, and 5. the stage of high mass consumption.

Before agricultural development started in the eighteenth century in the western part of Europe, societies were feudal, corresponding to traditional society in the terminology of Rostow. The peasants were partly subsistence farmers, and partly forced to work for the estates of their landlords. This stagnant society reproduced itself without any significant changes.

The first stage of agricultural development corresponds to Rostow's transitional stage. This was the stage when agricultural productivity started to increase. There were technological changes when the crop-livestock husbandry concept became the normal farming system. There were important institutional changes in the form of agricultural reforms which were stimulated by the new attitudes of the Age of Enlightenment. These agricultural changes demanded resources which came from within agriculture. Labour supply increased due to the population increase.

The productivity increase was crucial for several reasons. Firstly, higher productivity decreased the risk of famine in years with bad harvests. Secondly, it improved the nutritional standard of the population. Thirdly, it made it possible for the population to grow at a higher rate. Fourthly, higher productivity made it possible to feed those who left agriculture to work in non-agricultural activities.

The second stage of agricultural development corresponds to the take-off stage of Rostow. At this stage markets were developed and the necessary economic structures were established. Markets only work satisfactorily when the necessary infrastructure exists, when inputs are

Summary

available, when innovations are made, when information is disseminated, and when the necessary institutions are established.

Economic development depends on productivity increases, which are a product of the division of labour, which needs economic integration, which again depends on well-functioning markets. The creation of economic integration is resource-demanding, because a series of steps must be taken. Transport and distribution systems are needed; human resources have to be developed through education; an innovation and diffusion system is necessary to create dynamic markets; and labour and capital markets are necessary to enable the realisation of the new opportunities.

If the process of gradual economic integration gets started because the markets and economic environment are improved, it seems that agricultural development becomes sustained. Progress breeds further progress.

During the first two stages, agriculture was the backbone of economic development. Agriculture was the main sector in the economy and in spite of the gradual rise in the rate of productivity increase during the first two stages, the absolute number of people working in agriculture continued to increase.

When the third stage started, society had become heavily industrialised, and the absolute number of people working in agriculture started to decline. During the fourth stage, there was a large substitution of capital for labour and labour productivity increases reached unprecedented heights. Real agricultural prices fell, and the number of farms declined dramatically. In spite of the increased farm sizes, agricultural support remained substantial. Once agricultural support had been introduced, and then gradually increased, it became difficult to dismantle.

The stage theory presented in this chapter is useful for giving an overview of agricultural development during the period 1750-2000. In order to give this overview, each stage has been referred to as occupying a fixed period in time. The first stage started when agricultural development started, and ended in the mid-nineteenth century when railway construction changed the face of transport. The second stage was from the mid-nineteenth century to the First World War, and during this stage there was interregional integration in each country and international integration between countries. The third stage was the turbulent period 1914-1950 with two world wars and the Great Depression, and the fourth stage was the post war period.

It is clear that such a fixed chronological classification is problematic as different countries may be at different stages at any given time, and because the economic development was far from synchronous.

The stage theory presented here has been developed on the basis of the historical experiences of the countries which are industrialised today. It is not claimed that this stage theory can be applied without modification to developing countries today. However, it is suggested that many of the problems which the Western countries experienced in the past exist today in many developing countries. It may be useful for today's developing countries to draw the lessons from the past, even though their conditions may be quite different from the conditions of the past.

10. Agriculture in the early stage of economic development

10.1 Agriculture or industry as the engine of growth

The economic development of Western Europe started in the eighteenth century. What was the role of agriculture in the development process? Was it in agriculture or was it in industry that economic development started? On the basis of historical studies it seems reasonable to conclude that agricultural development preceded industrial development.

The start of the agricultural revolution

Agriculture was already highly developed before 1700 in the Low Countries (present day Netherlands and Flanders). Most of the ideas on which the agricultural revolution was based came from the Low Countries, where there was a continuous development, which makes it quite difficult to date the start of the agricultural changes (de Vries et al., 1997).

In England, too, it is difficult to set a date for the start of the agricultural revolution. There were already important changes in English agriculture in the period 1500-1700, described as the 'yeoman revolution'. However, there is broad agreement about the date of the start of the second revolution, called the 'landlord revolution'. On the basis of his own studies and the studies of others, Bairoch concludes that it can be stated with reasonable confidence that the second agricultural revolution started in England in around 1700 or at most within a quarter of a century prior to this (Bairoch, 1969).

He finds it more difficult to establish a chronology for the start of the agricultural revolution in other countries. There are fewer studies of the subject for other countries than there are for England, and the regional differences in most of the other countries are much more marked.

However, Bairoch does suggest some approximate dates for the onset of the agricultural revolution in various countries. These dates are: England 1690-1700; France 1750-90; Germany and Denmark 1790-1800; Austria, Italy and Sweden 1820-30; Russia and Spain 1860-70.

Agriculture in the early stage of economic development

To emphasise that these dates are only approximate, Bairoch refers to the case of Italy. It can be misleading to date the start of the agricultural revolution in Italy to 1820-30, when agricultural development differed so widely between Northern and Southern Italy. Agriculture was already highly developed in the densely populated Po valley in the seventeenth century, whereas in the South, agriculture was underdeveloped in the nineteenth and in large parts into the twentieth century.

The industrial revolution came later

According to Bairoch, the traditional and generally accepted date for the start of the industrial revolution in Britain is 1750-60 (Bairoch, 1969; Bairoch, 1982). In Britain, the agricultural revolution, which started around 1700, preceded the industrial revolution by half a century.

Bairoch also dates the start of the industrial revolution in other Western European countries on the basis of his own studies and studies of others. In France the industrial revolution started around 1780-1790, which was 20-30 years after the start of the agricultural revolution.

Britain and France are the two main countries for which the most data and studies are available on this early period of development. This interest is justified by the important role played by these countries. Britain was the cradle of the industrial revolution and France was the first great continental European country to follow. Both Germany and Italy only became unified countries in the nineteenth century. In the case of Germany, agricultural development started in around 1800. Its industrial advance was very slow, and it was only by 1850 that industry really began to develop. Belgium, together with Northern France, was the area where industrialisation started on the continent. Also in the case of Belgium, agricultural development preceded the start of industrialisation.

As already mentioned, it is difficult to establish chronologies for the start of the agricultural revolution or for the industrial revolution. In spite of these uncertainties, it seems reasonable to conclude that the agricultural revolution preceded the industrial revolution.

A priori reasoning

A priori, one should expect economic development to be based on agricultural development. Before industrialisation started, around 80 per cent of the population was working in agriculture. In the traditional societies agriculture was quite different from agriculture in a modern society.

Agriculture or industry as the engine of growth

In pre-industrial society agricultural work included making textiles, which was mainly done at home on the farm. The same was true, though perhaps to a lesser extent, of building activities and transport and distribution. In most cases the peasant delivered and sold his surplus produce himself. These other activities were generally subsidiary activities, and they represented only a smaller proportion of the total work of the peasant family. The production of agricultural products was the main activity, but increased productivity through specialisation between households was inhibited by the risk of famine. If a former peasant specialised in textile production, he might have great difficulty in getting the necessary food in years with bad harvests.

When 80 per cent of the labour force is engaged in agriculture, it is difficult to imagine how economic development could start without agricultural development.

The population increase opened the way for the intensification of agricultural production by replacing the fallow system with an annual cropping system. It also opened the way for the extension and improvement of arable land, for example, by taking in the common land for more intensive production.

The increased productivity reduced the risk of famine and opened the way for specialisation between food production, textile production and other activities. Specialisation will in itself increase productivity in textile, building, transport and distribution activities. The increased earnings from farming, derived from increased productivity, made it possible for the peasants to give up producing their own textiles and instead buy from producers who specialised in textile production.

Industrialisation will only be successful if the products can be sold, and they can only be sold if there is a market. Domestic demand depends on the income level which in turn depends on productivity. Agriculture was the largest sector and if there had been no productivity increase in agriculture, there would have been no increase in real income, and there would have been no increase in demand.

Purchasing power is a prerequisite for selling industrial products. There must also be a physical framework around the market in the form of transport and distribution systems.

Industrialisation depended on the economic conditions in agriculture, where 80 per cent of the labour force worked. If industrialisation attracts labour from agriculture which is needed in agriculture, agricultural production will stagnate or decrease, and it will not be possible to release labour from agriculture in the long run.

An agricultural surplus was necessary

In traditional societies, before the agricultural revolution, the average agricultural worker produced a surplus of foodstuffs of around 20 to 30 per cent more than the needed for his family's consumption. This surplus was consumed by the 20 per cent of the population outside agriculture.

There were annual fluctuations in agricultural yields, so that subsistence crises occurred from time to time, and more or less serious famines were inevitable.

The profound changes in the agricultural production system, which started in the eighteenth century, broke out of this cycle. The increase in productivity in the space of around 50 years augmented the average surplus of the agricultural workers. The average surplus of around 25 per cent in traditional society was now increased to a surplus of 50 per cent or more. This meant that the threat of famine was more or less eliminated, and this made it possible for development to be based on specialisation.

10.2 Agricultural demand stimulated industrialisation

The increase in the productivity of agriculture led to a higher income level which stimulated agricultural demand for industrial products.

Households gave up the home production of textile products and other consumer products as they concentrated more on purely agricultural activities. Higher income levels made it possible for the peasants to buy in textiles, clothing and other consumer goods from outside.

Agricultural demand was not only important for the development of the textile industry but also for the development of the iron and steel industry. The iron industry started to develop in Britain during the first half of the eighteenth century. Available data from England show that, between 1720 and 1760, iron consumption increased by 50 per cent, whereas the population only increased by 10 per cent and total industrial production by 15 per cent, including coal mining (Hoffmann, 1955).

There were no major technological changes in the non-agricultural sectors, such as railway construction or iron shipbuilding, which could explain the large increase in the demand for iron. This increase in demand for iron seemed to stem from agriculture.

Britain embarked on the agricultural revolution during the first half of the eighteenth century. This involved the gradual elimination of fallow land, the clearance and improvement of neglected land, improved equipment, new types of implements and the wider use of horses and horse-shoeing. All these elements had an important impact on the demand for iron.

The elimination of fallow land involved a considerable increase in farm work, especially ploughing. The clearance of waste land also led to an increase in the area cultivated. So the need for tools and equipment increased.

Improvements in agricultural implements essentially consisted of the gradual replacement of the wooden parts of implements by iron. This was especially so in the case of the plough, in which more and more iron was incorporated from the end of the seventeenth century, until by the middle of the nineteenth century it was made wholly of iron (Fussell, 1952).

The combined effect of these various factors resulted in a great increase in the agricultural demand for iron. The constantly rising demand from agriculture put pressure on the iron industry. This demand provided a powerful stimulus towards eliminating the main bottleneck in the domestic iron industry, which was the shortage of fuel, especially wood. The use of coal, rather than wood or charcoal, as the basic fuel for blast-furnaces was the technical innovation which removed this bottleneck.

The agricultural revolution had an important impact on the early development of the iron industry. The economic role of the iron industry was not as important as that of the textile industry at the earliest stage of the industrial revolution. Nevertheless, iron played a major and decisive role in enabling technical innovations in all kinds of activities. The supply of low-cost iron made possible the widespread use of machines in which iron played an important part.

Through a backward linkage, agriculture contributed significantly to the development of the iron industry, which was a vital part of mechanisation during industrialisation.

10.3 Agriculture supplied resources

The agricultural sector delivered food supplies, labour, entrepreneurship and capital to the non-agricultural sector. The productivity gains in agriculture made available an agricultural surplus which made it possible to support the labour force which moved from agriculture to industry. The income from the sales of food supplies was spent on consumer and investment goods produced in the industrial sector.

The increase in agricultural productivity during the eighteenth century meant that the population gradually obtained better nutrition, and it meant that labour could gradually be released from agricultural production. One part of the released labour took care of the extensive agricultural investments which were involved in the agricultural reforms. These reforms were a prerequisite for the continuous increase in agricultural productivity. Another part of the released labour was employed in industry, especially in textile production which was now separated from agriculture. The specialisation of textile production, combined with the technological improvements in the textile sector, really improved labour productivity. The increased productivity in agriculture made it possible for the peasants to deliver an agricultural surplus as payment for the supply of textile products from the newly established textile sector.

Historical evidence seems to indicate that both entrepreneurship and capital initially came from agriculture. Industrialisation in Britain and in other countries started when textile production was separated from agriculture through the division of labour. When agricultural purchasing power increased, due to productivity increases, some of the rural population specialised in textile production. An investigation of the origins of textile manufacturers in Britain shows that at the beginning of industrialisation they nearly always came from the rural areas, and mostly from the class of yeomen (Mantoux, 1928). Mantoux found that in the case of metallurgy, such as iron production, many of the entrepreneurs came from small local workshops, and further back, their families originally came from the countryside and the peasantry. A series of studies of agriculture and economic growth in England confirm that nearly all the resources on which industrialisation was based came from agriculture (Jones, 1967). Other studies of the start of industrialisation in France, Switzerland and Russia show the same picture. Both in the textile industry and in other industrial sectors, the great majority of entrepreneurs were people of modest backgrounds, especially former farmers (Mantoux, 1928; Braun, 1967; Yatsunsky, 1962).

The studies also show that nearly all the capital on which early industrialisation was based came from agriculture. There were no great problems in financing early industrialisation. The demand of capital was limited and it could quite easily be delivered by agriculture. The quantity of tools and machinery necessary to start industrial production was limited. The technology was relatively simple and labour-intensive, and it was not necessary to produce on a large scale in order to be competitive.

Estimates show that much greater investment was needed to put a man to work in agriculture than in industry. It seems that the investment needed to employ one person in agriculture, was eight times the investment needed to employ one person in industry (Bairoch, 1969). These figures are the average figures for Britain, France and Belgium in the first half of the nineteenth century. The value of the land represented the major part of the investment needed to employ labour in agriculture. It is obvious that the difference between the investments needed in agriculture and in industry varied according to the degree of development in agriculture and industry. The availability of land, and thereby the price of land, also influenced the difference.

The sale of an average farm unit employing one labourer would produce enough funds to establish an industrial unit employing eight persons. When the agricultural revolution started, some peasants sold their farms, and because they were already acquainted with the production of textiles which took place on the farm, it was relatively easy, both technically and financially, for them to shift from agricultural activities, including textile production, to specialised and industrialised textile production based on hired labour.

Indirectly, the landlords contributed to the financing of industrialisation. The peasants sold their farms to the landlords, so the funds of the landlords were indirectly channelled into industry. However, the landlords also invested directly in industry as the agricultural revolution gave them increased income through higher rents.

It is notable that the capital and the entrepreneurs who started industrialisation came from agriculture and not from the urban capitalist class. Merchants and traders made up the urban capitalist class at the start of industrialisation. At different times there seem to have been different classes of capitalists, each playing an important role, such as landlords, merchants, industrialists, bankers, etc. Just prior to industrialisation, the capitalist class consisted of merchants, and when industrialisation started and developed this class was replaced by industrialists. The new class of capitalists, the industrialists, did not spring from the capitalists of the preceding period. When a group of people encounters new opportunities, and when they have the ability to exploit the new opportunities, they become the new rich. The merchants in the cities did not encounter the new opportunities in the same way as people in agriculture. Even if they were aware of the new opportunities, there was no great incentive for them to shift from trade to industry. The merchants already had sufficient resources at their disposal from their traditional trading activities to enable them to live comfortably.

Agriculture in the early stage of economic development

10.4 Interrelationship between agriculture and industry

There is no doubt that agricultural development played a major role for the overall economy and for industrialisation. On the other hand it is also true that agricultural conditions depended on industrial development. There were important interrelationships between agriculture and industry.

Agriculture supplied resources and constituted a market

When agricultural productivity increased, the peasants could buy industrial products and this stimulated the development of the textile industry and the iron industry at the beginning of the industrial revolution.

The textile industry was based on resources coming from agriculture, namely labour, entrepreneurship and capital. It became more profitable for peasants to give up household production of textiles and to concentrate on agricultural production, and increased incomes from agricultural specialisation made it possible for them to buy textile products.

The iron industry was developed on the basis of demand from agriculture. The agricultural revolution increased the demand for more and better tools and implements to cultivate the land more intensively. The improvements consisted largely in the gradual replacement of wooden parts by iron parts, as typified by the plough.

Industry supplied commodities and constituted a market

The industrial revolution meant mechanisation and improved production techniques, which increased productivity in the textile and iron industries. The prices of industrial goods fell, and this increased the demand for textiles and iron in the agricultural sector. The greater penetration of improved tools and implements in agriculture contributed to further increases in agricultural productivity.

The industrial revolution meant there was an increase in the supply of consumer goods and investment goods. Industrial development also increased the demand for agricultural products. When the wages increased, the demand for food products, especially animal products, increased. When the textile industry expanded, there was an increased demand for agricultural raw materials such as wool and textile fibres.

Interrelationship between agriculture and industry

The early industrialisation took place in somewhat closed economies

Industrial development depends on resources, technology, institutions, attitudes and interrelationships with agriculture, as illustrated in Figure 9.1 in the previous chapter.

Industrialisation depended on technological innovations such as the construction of machinery and the use of steam power, which in turn relied on iron ore and coal deposits. The early industrialisation was located in those areas where these natural resources were available. However, these natural resources were a necessary but not a sufficient condition for industrial development.

Industrial production also depended on the existence of a potential market and such a market was only to be found in the domestic economy, which mainly consisted of the agricultural sector.

Without agricultural development, industrialisation would only have been possible if the industrial products could have been exported and exchanged for agricultural imports. At the time when industrialisation started in Western Europe such development was not possible. International trade is only profitable if the advantages of trade, due to differences in the relative productivities between the agricultural and industrial productions in the two countries, are so great that they outweigh the disadvantages of transport and other trading costs.

The economies in the early period of industrialisation were not totally closed. There were contacts across borders, which meant that knowledge of technological inventions was spread through publications and personal contacts. However, in the beginning the spread of know-how was restrained by bans on the export of new machinery and bans on the emigration of skilled workers, who might start industrialisation abroad. It took time before all these mercantilist ideas about the need for restrictions were overcome.

The economies were closed in the sense that industrialisation could not be based on foreign demand. The transport and the communication barriers were so great that industrialisation could only be based on domestic demand. Even at a later stage, when the infrastructure had improved so that exports and imports started to be significant, continued industrialisation was determined by domestic needs. In Europe and the USA industrialisation was based on the domestic markets. When agriculture is the dominant sector it is clear that agricultural needs have a large impact on the pattern of industrial development.

Once markets have been established and gradually improved, there are important backward, forward and income linkages originating in agriculture, which determine the path of industrialisation. The need for agricultural inputs, the supply of agricultural raw materials for processing and the demand for consumer goods when agricultural incomes increase, are all opportunities for industrialisation.

The needs of agriculture opened the way for industrial development. Once the interrelationships between agriculture and industry had been established, the path was open for a harmonious development in which living standards increased in each sector. These interrelationships were established through markets. Gradually, more and more of the new production resources moved to the industry, adding to the capital stock and the labour force. Agricultural resources still increased, but at a much lower rate than industrial resources.

Economic development depends on the efficient allocation of capital and labour. It also depends on income distribution. An equal income distribution creates better social and economic conditions for further development. During the earlier development stages, a high growth rate per capita for the whole of society is often a result of a relatively high growth rate, both in industry and agriculture, whereas a low growth rate per capita often is associated with low growth in both sectors.

10.5 Agricultural development and population growth

Agricultural development in Western Europe started at a time when the population also started to grow at a higher rate than before. This raises the question of the relationship between agricultural productivity and population growth.

In 1798 Thomas Malthus published his essay on population. According to Malthus, the population tends to grow faster than the supply of food, so the production of food determines the level of the population. If agricultural productivity increases, the population can increase at a faster rate. In this theory, agricultural productivity is an exogenous factor, determining the size of the population. The Malthusian population theory led to the income distribution theory and the belief that in the long run the wage rate could not be raised above subsistence level.

Gradually the Malthusian theory lost support. The average per capita consumption of calories increased, indicating that food production, measured in calories, increased more than the population.

Ester Boserup has studied different forms of land use through history (Boserup, 1965). The history of land use shows that the existing land resources have been used more and more intensively. It is her thesis that it is population pressure that causes agricultural development, in the sense that a population increase induces more intensive use of the land resources. A larger population needs increased food supplies, and this is obtained by changing land use. According to Boserup, the causation runs from population increase to food supply increase. The population increase is the exogenous factor determining agricultural development. This theory is directly contrary to the Malthusian theory.

It is evident that the population increase from the middle of the eighteenth century played a role in the agricultural revolution which took place at the same time.

Firstly, it can be concluded that the most advanced agriculture was found in strongly urbanised areas. The most advanced agriculture at the time was found in the Low Countries, where several larger cities had grown up based on trade. Advanced agriculture was found in other urban areas in Europe. This was the case in France around Paris, in the Rhine valley in Germany and in the Po valley in Northern Italy. London also became an urban centre with a highly developed agricultural hinterland.

Secondly, the population increase in the north-western part of Europe caused food prices to rise, which induced a change in the farming system. The technology change involved a shift from a short fallow cultivation system, where one half or one third of the arable land lay fallow every year, to an annual cropping system without fallow. These technological changes were followed by institutional changes in the form of agricultural reforms.

The shift in north-western Europe from short fallow cultivation to annual cropping has often been described as the result of an autonomous technical revolution. Cropping the land without fallow was made possible by the use of crop rotation with fodder plants, of which some were leguminous. Economic historians have emphasized that the new crops had been known for some time, so the change was brought about by the application of an already known technology, and was induced by the increased demand for food products (Campbell and Overton, 1991).

However, population increase, as such, cannot explain the start of agricultural development. It is only one element among the others.

The population increased at a higher rate than before, not only in north-western Europe, it also increased at a higher rate than before in southern and in eastern Europe, including Russia, but there were no similar technological and institutional changes in these countries as a response to the population increase.

While technological and institutional changes started in north-western Europe, they did not occur at the same rate in Britain, France, Germany and Denmark. Also, the changes, especially the institutional changes, were quite different in the different countries. For example, the farm size structure became very different in the different countries.

Outside Europe there were also much larger increases in the population during the period 1750 – 1914 than in the previous period, but these population increases did not induce agricultural developments corresponding to the European development. It was the era of colonialism, so this may be a part of the explanation why the agricultural sector did not respond to the population increase with technical and institutional changes.

Nevertheless, it is clear that the population increase did have a positive impact on the demand side. The larger population and rising agricultural prices stimulated interest in increasing supply, which became possible due to the increased labour force. There was a need for a larger labour force when annual cropping replaced the short fallow system. There was also a need for a larger labour force to undertake all the investments connected with the enclosure of the common land and the technical and institutional changes which took place. When the necessary labour was available, it was easier to carry out the agricultural reforms.

Population growth made agricultural development possible, but there will only be agricultural development if the necessary investments are made. How can one ensure that these investments will be made? Here it is very important to have an incentive system so that all parties have an interest in the long-term benefits, and can work together to realise the investments.

10.6 Agricultural reforms and farm size structure

Agricultural development in Western Europe was heavily influenced by agricultural reforms involving technical and institutional changes. The open-field farming system was abandoned and replaced by individual farming. The peasants acquired new legal rights, and the tenancy system was either improved or replaced by private ownership.

When these agricultural reforms were made in Western Europe, they were implemented differently in the different countries. In Britain and in Eastern Germany, the agricultural sector became dominated by large farms, whereas in France and Western Germany farm size structure was characterised by the multiplicity of smallholders. In Denmark the reforms brought about a great number of medium-sized farms, which were smaller than the farms in Britain, but larger than the smallholdings in France and Western Germany.

Agricultural reforms and farm size structure

Which size structure is best?

When planning agricultural reforms, it is reasonable to ask which size structure is best. Before the agricultural reforms, there were two different kinds of farming. One was farming the land of large estates managed by landlords and the other was the open-field farming system. The large estate owners were better educated and had the means of financing innovations. The large estates had economies of scale so that machinery could be better utilized.

When considering the optimal structure in relation to agricultural reforms, it is problematic to base conclusion on experiences which pre-date the agricultural reforms. The agricultural reforms were so fundamental that they may have changed the relative productivity of farms of different sizes. Experience shows that after the agricultural reforms, small farmers cultivated their land more intensively than large farmers, and they were also more interested in starting and enlarging livestock production.

The farm structure which existed after the agricultural reforms was different in different countries in Western Europe. Is it possible to draw any conclusions from the experiences of the different countries? The agricultural performance in Britain and Eastern Germany, with large farms, differed from the performance in France and Western Germany with small farms, and from Denmark with medium-sized farms. Agricultural performance depends not only on the size structure, but on a series of other factors. The efficiency of the markets is crucial for agricultural performance, as is the extent to which a satisfactory economic environment has been established. Infrastructure, inputs, innovations, information and institutions are all important factors determining agricultural performance.

At an early stage, when the markets and the economic environment are not yet fully effective, it can be easier to improve agricultural output in the short term by focusing on larger farms, but the social consequences of former peasants becoming landless labourers may be great. In the longer term, once the markets and the economic environment have been improved, it may be an advantage to have relatively small farms.

The size structure itself may influence the creation of markets and the necessary economic environment. When farmers organize themselves in co-operatives, they can establish distribution channels and credit institutions. When they get involved in politics, for example by forming a political party, they will be able to influence the political debate on the development of the economy.

The ability to organise and to promote policies which are accepted by most farmers will often depend on the farm structure. When there is a class of large estate owners and large farmers, they will normally take the lead and promote initiatives which are beneficial to themselves but not necessarily to the other farmers, including smallholders. When there are many smallholders, it may be difficult for them to organize and to win political influence. When there is a large class of peasants owning medium-sized farms, it may be easier for them to organise themselves economically and politically.

Whatever the mechanisms are, it is important to stimulate the self-organisation of the peasants. In Western Europe the highest level of self-organisation took place in Denmark, where the large class of medium-sized farmers, often together with smallholders, established co-operatives dealing with economic factors, political parties, and cultural institutions dealing with education and spiritual values. Popular movements, such as the peasants' movement, the smallholders' movement and labour movement, became important elements in the economic development of Denmark.

The production pattern was also related to the farm size structure. In Europe the large farms focused on growing arable crops, whereas the small farmers were more interested in livestock production.

A comparison between agriculture in the USA and Europe also shows a relationship between farm size and the production pattern. In the USA, the average farm size has been much larger than the average farm size in Europe, and in the USA, arable crop production has been relatively much more important than in Europe.

Path dependence

When public bodies intervene in structural changes, such as agricultural reforms, it is important to realise that future developments depend on present choices. Some of the consequences can be foreseen, but others are difficult to predict.

The shaping of future possibilities by past decisions can be called 'path dependence'. When a country has made important choices, the path of the future development is determined, and in practice it cannot be changed.

Agricultural development in Denmark can be used as an example. The most comprehensive agricultural reform in Europe took place in Denmark in the last two decades of the eighteenth century. As a result, the farmland was consolidated and the subsequent size structure was characterised by there being predominantly farms of medium size.

Summary

This size structure, together with the general school reform of 1814, meant that a class of independent and well-educated peasants grew up during the first half of the nineteenth century. They were able to organize themselves economically, politically and culturally. When the agricultural terms of trade improved in the period 1850-1875, Danish agriculture was able to benefit from the improved opportunities. Grain exports had started earlier, but a shift towards increased livestock exports started in this period. This shift took advantage of a change in the relative prices of cereals and livestock in favour of livestock products.

When the agricultural crisis came, with falling agricultural prices, especially for cereals, Denmark decided not to protect the agricultural sector by setting up tariff barriers. The owners of large farms tried to get a cereal tariff bill through parliament, but they failed due to the peasants' party which favoured free trade. They wanted cheap cereals which could be used as inputs in livestock production. At the same time, the peasants organised themselves in co-operatives, which became very successful.

The agricultural changes and the farm structure which came out of the agricultural reforms of the eighteenth century were a prerequisite for the advance of the new class of peasants. The agricultural development of the nineteenth century was a result of the previous agricultural reforms.

The free trade policy and the co-operative movement of the last decades of the nineteenth century determined the success of Danish agriculture, which continued in the twentieth century.

The existence of a relatively powerful class of peasants explains the Danish tariff policy and the co-operative movement. After 1846, Britain was a free market, open to food imports. Why was it Danish agriculture, and not French or British agriculture that was so successful in exploiting the opportunity? Why did the co-operative movement not become popular in Britain? The answer may be the absence of a large class of medium-sized farmers owning their own land.

10.7 Summary

Economic development is often associated with industrialisation. This is also the case when looking at the economic history of Europe and the USA.

It is difficult to give a precise date for the start of the agricultural and industrial revolutions because their development was gradual. However, the evidence indicates that agricultural changes preceded the start of industrialisation. If agricultural changes had not taken place, industrialisation could not have taken place.

The evidence also shows that the agricultural changes which gave rise to industrialisation started in England and then spread to other Western European countries. Agricultural changes occurred much later in southern and eastern Europe, including Russia.

A priori considerations also lead to the conclusion that economic development would not have been possible without gains in agricultural productivity, because agriculture so completely dominated the economy at the start of the modern era.

For several reasons an agricultural surplus was necessary for economic development. The nutritional levels rose and improved the health of society. An increased agricultural surplus reduced the risk of famine, which enabled people to move from agriculture into other activities, such as industry. Economic development was greatly stimulated by the division of labour. There were static gains from specialisation, but there were also dynamic gains from technological and institutional changes which increased productivity.

Agricultural development was important because it paved the way for industrialisation from both the demand and the supply sides. Agricultural productivity gains increased agricultural income, which was spent on consumer goods, such as textile products, and on investment goods, such as improved tools and implements, in which iron parts were substituted for wooden parts. To start with the iron and coal industries in England were based on agricultural demand.

On the supply side, agriculture delivered the necessary food for the increasing urban population. Agriculture delivered labour, capital and entrepreneurship. Investment in industrialisation, for example in the textile sector, was easier than investment in agriculture because the capital need was limited. The technology was simple and not very capital demanding, and the labour costs were small.

Entrepreneurship for textile production was available from agriculture, because textile production was part of agriculture before industrialisation. The rich merchants in the urban areas did not encounter and were not interested in the new opportunities to the same extent as the farmers.

There were some very important interrelationships between agricultural development and industrialisation. Agriculture supplied resources and constituted a market for industrial products. Industrialisation and urbanisation led to an increased demand for agricultural products and the urban sector delivered goods and services to the rural sector.

To start with, industrialisation took place in closed economies. Even if there was some potential foreign demand, trade was not profitable due to the high transport and communication costs.

Summary

The agricultural reforms started at a time when the population grew at a higher rate than previously. This raises the question of causality. Did the agricultural improvements make it possible to feed a larger population, or did the population increase generate demands which induced the agricultural changes? The first explanation is in accordance with the Malthusian population theory, whereas the second explanation is in accordance with Boserup's theory. It is also possible that there was an iterative process so that the two theories together can explain the simultaneous increase in population and agricultural production. Boserup's theory is not universally applicable. The population in southern and eastern Europe, and in other parts of the world, increased just as much as in western Europe without prompting a similar change in the agricultural sector.

The agricultural reforms influenced the farm size structure differently in different countries. The question of the optimal size structure is not purely technological, as efficiency depends on existing institutions. Before the agricultural reforms, the large estates were often more productive than the open-field farming system, but when the agricultural reforms took place, relative productivity may have changed. Land productivity is often higher on small farms than on large farms, whereas the reverse is the case for labour productivity.

It is important to realise that the farm size structure may influence the ability of the farming sector to organize itself. When the peasants themselves participate in the development process, progress will be realised more rapidly, and it is more certain that the initiatives taken will comply with the more relevant needs.

When path dependency is taken into consideration, it is reasonable to conclude that pervasive agricultural reforms have an important long-term effect. It is also reasonable to conclude that a farm size structure which facilitates self-organisation in the agricultural sector will have far-reaching effects.

11. Markets and institutions for further development

11.1 The market mechanism and development

The development of markets is an important element in the process of economic development. Firstly, the market mechanism contributes to development by absorbing dynamic changes and transmitting them to producers, who are induced to take initiatives to adapt to the changes. Secondly, the market mechanism helps to identify bottlenecks, which can slow down or stop the development process. Bottlenecks highlight problems which have to be dealt with by the private and the public sectors.

The market induces initiatives through competition

The market mechanism is based on competition between producers. The market mechanism has two different effects, a static effect and a dynamic effect.

When an economy moves from being a self-sufficiency economy to a market economy with a given technology, there will be a division of labour. The reallocation of resources will lead to a rise in living standards.

Even if there is no technological progress, the market mechanism will have a dynamic effect because competition induces producers to increase their productive investments to increase profits and to stay in business.

When there are technological innovations, and when information about the new possibilities is diffused through the economic system, the market mechanism will induce further investments, which will improve profitability. When there is a more or less continuous flow of innovations, the market mechanism will ensure that both disembodied and embodied technological progress will be incorporated into production processes and the development effect of the market mechanism will be increased when innovations are diffused through the economic system.

The market mechanism has a much wider impact when it is combined with technical and institutional changes which improve productivity. If there is an exogenous flow of technical and institutional changes, an effective market mechanism will ensure that these changes are incorporated in production processes. Market prices, which reflect scarcities of resources, may also induce innovations to overcome bottlenecks.

Revealing the bottlenecks

At any given moment, the markets can be used as an instrument for identifying the bottlenecks that are hampering development. The bottlenecks are revealed either through high prices or through lack of availability.

If the information system of a market is rudimentary, there can be a question as to whether a bottleneck will stimulate some private or public initiative to develop an educational or extension service system. If the necessary inputs, such as fertilisers, are not available, the demand for them may create an opportunity for imports, which may later be replaced by domestic production.

The scarcity of a given resource can induce innovations to overcome the scarcity. If land is the factor in relatively short supply, then innovations will be concentrated around yield-increasing innovations, such as the use of fertilisers and pesticides. When labour is in short supply and land is abundant, then there will be incentives to develop machinery which can substitute for labour.

The idea is simple. The market identifies the bottlenecks and initiatives are undertaken either by the private or the public sectors to overcome the bottlenecks. Bottlenecks can take the form of the lack of a given output or input, or there may be deficiencies in the market system and the enabling environment.

When bottlenecks occur and are not removed they will become hindrances to development. The time dimension is important. If bottlenecks can be removed quickly, development can continue unchecked. If they are not removed quickly, they will hamper development. As long as the bottlenecks exist, they put a brake on the development process, so when there are bottlenecks, the way they are dealt with is important.

It takes time to develop and improve markets. If they are imperfect, they should not be neglected; the task then is to improve the market mechanisms through appropriate interventions. Agents who rely on the market act in response to market signals, so if a market is sending false or inadequate signals, it will influence the development process negatively.

When there are market deficiencies and market failures, there is a need for appropriate remedies. If the market mechanism is working well, there should be reluctance to intervene, as any intervention may not be for the better.

11.2 The implementation of the market economy

The development of markets requires investment

Markets are developed gradually. It is a resource-demanding task to develop markets. Investments in infrastructure, distribution systems, education, research, information systems and institutions are necessary.

The physical structure of the market, such as the infrastructure and the distribution systems, determines the transport, communication and trading costs.

The way a market works depends on the educational level and attitudes of the people in it. The decision-makers should be able to take advantage of the market opportunities. The people have to be given a general education supplemented by a more specific, vocational education. The willingness and ability to co-operate is important, because it allows for development which is based on self-organisation. The willingness and ability to participate in the political process improves the ability to identify bottlenecks in the economy and to reduce or eliminate them through public investments.

Market performance depends on the existence of innovation and diffusion systems. Universities and research institutes should promote innovations, which are then disseminated through the information and education system.

Besides commodity markets, there should also be factor markets. Well-functioning capital and labour markets not only allocate resources more efficiently, they also induce less risk-averse attitudes among investors and induce people to improve their skills.

It is important to emphasize that the effects of investments in infrastructure, distribution, education, research, information and institutions are interlinked. The cumulative effect of implementing all the elements is greater than the sum of the parts. It is not possible to implement all the elements at once. The investments are time-consuming and they demand substantial resources, so it is important to find the right priority for the sequence of investments. The level of investments in the different areas should be geared to each area so that they all contribute to the best economic result with the lowest use of resources.

Who takes the initiative?

Markets and the enabling environment should be based on both private and public initiatives. For example, the establishment of the agricultural distribution system in a market economy is typically a task for the private sector. The initiatives can either be taken by people outside agriculture or by the farmers themselves. The self-organisation model is based on the idea of co-operation between farmers to solve some of the problems which arise in the course of the development process.

The self-organisation model can only work if the general educational level is sufficiently high. Those who take the initiative should be able to analyse a problem and to come up with a viable solution to it. Those who co-operate should have a common goal and common interests; otherwise it will be difficult to find viable solutions. Mutual interest, mutual trust, and the ability to organise without too high costs are necessary ingredients of the self-organisation model.

The self-organisation model can be used in relation to purely economic issues such as the establishment of a co-operative entity which sells farm products, or which buys farm inputs, sells consumer goods, or borrows and lends financial funds. The self-organisation model can also be used to form professional agricultural associations which contribute to finding the best farming practices, which are then diffused to the members. Agricultural associations can run extension services and experimental stations where new inputs, new farming practices and new management ideas are applied in practice. Self-organisation initiatives can also be related to education, either vocational training or more general education.

The self-organisation model can be used for establishing political groups which can influence legislation, and thereby the development strategy for society.

In theory, investments in infrastructure can be undertaken either on public or private initiative. However, the scale of such tasks is so big that it is normally considered a task for public authorities, publicly financed. Infrastructural investments create natural monopolies, and private ownership of such monopolies can lead to abuses of monopoly power. If the fees charged for services are too high, the use of the infrastructural investments will be reduced and this will hamper market integration.

Such investments can only be undertaken gradually when public resources are limited in an undeveloped economy. Public funds will be relatively small because it is difficult to collect taxes when the economy is undeveloped. A large proportion of transactions will be carried out by barter trade where money is not involved, and there will be no efficient administration for the collection of taxes.

In these circumstances, it would be advantageous to mobilise private resources and to stimulate interest in self-organisation.

A development strategy is needed

Economic development in Europe and the USA was based on the market. This was also the case in Russia until 1917 when the Bolsheviks took over and introduced development through planning, which eliminated the market mechanism.

Even in a market economy there is a need for important public investments and for interventions in the market, for example in relation to trade policy

It is not possible to come up with a general development plan with the 'correct' sequence of all the necessary public investments and economic interventions in the market. Nor is it possible to make recommendations for a given country without a thorough study of its specific conditions.

Even for a specific country, it is difficult to make a detailed long term master plan for public investments and legislation.

A country should have a clear idea about its development goals. The kind of public investments and legislation required should be decided on the basis of the existing constraints on development. The identification of existing bottlenecks, which can be revealed by looking at the performance of the markets, should have a decisive influence on the policy of the country.

There are different groups in society with different goals and different interests, so it is not always easy to agree on a common development strategy. There may be disputes which delay reforms or the transformation process. So the legislation which determines the development path very much depends on the decision-making system and the attitudes in society.

Legislation and public investments should be based on the present needs which are identified through the markets. The development benefits of research will be reduced if the research is not adjusted to the needs of the society. When the labour supply is relatively abundant, new labour-saving technology will not be appropriate. If a research institute comes up with a new high-yielding seed variety, it will not be of much use if there is no dissemination of the innovation, because of the lack of an extension service. If the yield of the new variety is crucially dependent on the use of fertilisers and water, it will not be sensible to sow the new variety unless these inputs are available. The introduction of new and complicated machinery will not be successful if its users do not know how to operate it, or if people with the skills to service and repair the machinery are not available.

Public investments should be determined by needs, and the sequence of investments should be determined by the bottlenecks that occur. When one bottleneck is removed, a new one arises. There are important complementarities between different investments, for example, between research, education and information.

There is a need for an overall philosophy for the development strategy. Should the emphasis be on agriculture or on industry? Should the trade policy be protectionist or liberal?

Agricultural development emphasises the importance of markets

As analysed in Chapter 10, when the agricultural sector employs most of the population, it is impossible to initiate general economic development without there being agricultural development. Agriculture is the engine of growth which stimulates industrial development.

In the next stage, economic development is associated with economic integration between the rural and urban sectors. In this stage, agricultural and industrial developments support each other once the markets have been improved and the enabling environment has been established. Thus, in this stage it is important to improve and enlarge the markets. It is a challenge to develop the economic environment so that markets will perform better. The neglect of markets and the enabling environment will be an obstacle to further development.

It is still important to focus on agricultural development so as to avoid the risk of neglecting the formation of markets, as agriculture cannot be developed without markets and an adequate institutional environment, see section 11.3. If efforts are focused on industrialisation, it is easier to forget the importance of national markets and of the overall economic environment.

If agriculture is focused on as a development target, it will not be possible to overlook the importance of creating markets. Agriculture can be considered as the sector which stimulates interest in building an overall market economy for the whole country.

11.3 Markets are of special importance to agriculture

Many decision-makers in agriculture

For several reasons, the existences of markets and of a well-functioning economic environment are of special importance for agriculture. Markets are important because of the great number of farmers each of whom is a decision-maker. The sum of all their decisions should generate a supply which, under normal weather conditions, will correspond to the demand of the society.

Because of the great number of decision-makers in agriculture, such a result can only be obtained through some kind of price mechanism. In agriculture, there are many small producers, whereas there are only few producers in each sector of industry.

In agriculture, the production unit is also a household. Unless the farmers are 100 per cent commercialised, some of the production will be consumed in the household.

Because of the great number of farmers and because only a share of their production is sold on the market, it is impossible for an economic planning committee to command a given supply of agricultural products. In industry, where there are only a few firms in each sector, it is relatively easy to tell the few managers how much to produce and to impose sanctions if they do not obey orders. In agriculture it is impossible to monitor all the producers. Planning is possible at an early stage of industrialisation, but this is not the case in agriculture. Here a market mechanism is needed.

Agricultural production geographically dispersed

In agriculture, land is an important production factor which means that agricultural production is geographically dispersed, in contrast to industrial production which is geographically concentrated.

When production is geographically dispersed, it is important for there to be an infrastructure which makes it possible for farmers to buy and sell commodities. An infrastructure is necessary but not sufficient. There should also be distribution channels to ensure the flow of outputs from the farmers to the consumers and the flow of inputs from the suppliers to the farmers. The distribution channels for agricultural outputs and inputs consist of links between a series of activities, such as wholesaling, retailing, agricultural processing, the industrial production of inputs, transport and storage.

Well-functioning distribution channels demand markets between the different links and operators on the different markets.

11.4 Agriculture is a biological production

Agriculture differs from most industries in that agricultural production is based on biological processes which cannot be controlled by man. In agriculture, the manager has to adjust to changing natural conditions. This means that timely performance is important, and this can more easily be ensured if the manager is also the operator and if the operator also has a direct economic interest in the farm earnings.

Seasons in agricultural production

In industry, the production conditions are constant throughout the year. In agriculture, the production conditions change from season to season as the temperature and precipitation vary according to the season. High temperatures in summer alternate with low temperatures in winter, and rainy seasons follow dry seasons.

Planning for agricultural production is more difficult than for most other productions due to its seasonality. Even where there is a fixed seasonal pattern, unvarying from year to year, seasonality creates some special conditions. In arable production there are peak seasons when the soil has to be prepared for sowing and when the crop is ripe for harvesting. During the peak seasons there is a greater need for labour. How should this labour bottleneck be overcome?

It can be overcome by seasonal contracts with local labour or by migrant labour which moves to the region in peak seasons. It can also be overcome by mechanizing some of the more labour-intensive tasks, such as ploughing and harvesting. Buying a tractor can speed up the activity and remove some of the bottlenecks. A tractor may also save labour in other operations. Mechanisation will often be profitable from a private point of view. The question is whether it is beneficial from a social point of view, if it leaves people unemployed. The immediate effect of mechanisation is the substitution of capital for labour, but the long-term effect can be positive. If mechanisation eliminates peak season problems, farmers may be able to get a second or third annual crop. Agricultural production will be increased, which is positive, also from a social point of view. The agricultural labour force will have a more evenly spread annual work load. The increased agricultural production has to be traded,

Agriculture is a biological production

transported and further processed, all of which provide further employment possibilities.

There are other examples where the negative impacts of seasonality can either be avoided or reduced by different kinds of investments. In the dry season, crops cannot be cultivated due to the lack of rain. If there is investment in an irrigation system, this bottleneck can be eliminated. In wet seasons, some land cannot be cultivated because the soil becomes waterlogged, and this can be prevented by investment in draining the land.

The variability of agricultural production

The problem of seasonality is exacerbated by the fact that the seasons do not necessarily follow a fixed schedule. The right time for ploughing, sowing and harvesting changes from year to year. Yields depend heavily on the timely performance of these activities.

The time for harvesting is decided by the farmer, who has to evaluate benefits and risks of different alternatives. A good decision not only depends on the judgement of the farmer, it also depends on the availability of reliable local weather forecasts.

There can only be timely performance when the necessary inputs are available. When the soil needs to be fertilized, the necessary fertilisers have to be available on the market, and the necessary seed has to be available for sowing. The availability of the right inputs at the right time depends on the efficiency of the market and the distribution chain. If the seed arrives three weeks after the optimal sowing time, the seed may still be sown, but the harvest will be small and the quality poor.

Crops and livestock can be hit by disease, influencing the quantity and quality of agricultural production. To avoid disease or to limit the impact of disease, it is important to monitor the arable production and the livestock. It is also important for farmers to be able to get information about diseases and advice about treatment by contact with agronomists and veterinary surgeons.

Some production factors are not homogenous

Farmers have to take into consideration that some of their important inputs are not homogenous. Even within a single farm, the soil quality will vary from place to place. This means that the choice of crop and fertilisation has to be adjusted to the soil quality of different plots of land. The livestock consists of individual animals each of which has to be treated differently, for example in relation to feeding, to obtain the optimal result.

11.5 The institutional framework and agriculture

Decision-making and institutions

Agricultural production cannot be fully controlled by farmers because it involves biological processes. Agricultural output is highly dependent on the weather and the incidence of diseases.

Some problems can be avoided or reduced by farmers and society through preventive actions. The impact of droughts can be avoided by irrigation; the impact of heavy rain can be reduced by drainage; flooding from rivers can be avoided by building dams, regulating the flow of water; the outbreak and spread of animal diseases can be avoided through vaccination programmes. Investments are needed to prevent the damaging impacts of these factors.

In most cases farmers have to accept the weather and the risks of the outbreak of diseases and try to obtain the best possible result by timely performance. The farmers have to plough, to sow and to harvest when the weather is favourable. A farmer has to avoid diseases and prevent them from spreading by monitoring his crops and livestock. Timely performance is very important in agriculture. So the farmer is not dealing with a predetermined agenda. He has to decide the important tasks of the day, determined by exogenous factors such as the weather.

Agricultural performance depends on the willingness and ability of the farmer to take the right decisions, and to perform the right tasks at the right time. The farmer will only be willing to take care to perform the right tasks at the right time if he benefits personally from his extra efforts. And the farmer will only be able to take the right decisions at the right time if he has sufficient knowledge, and if the environment allows him to implement his decisions.

For each farmer and for the agricultural sector as a whole, the institutions have a decisive influence on performance. Because of the varying production conditions in agriculture, each farmer has to take a series of decisions. The quality of the decisions will be better if the farm manager is also the farm operator, and the farm manager will be more engaged in the decision-making when his own income depends on his decisions.

The institutional framework and agriculture

The decisions depend on the economic environment. If markets and distribution channels do not exist, the farmer can only rely on inputs from the farm or the near neighbourhood. If the markets are imperfect, the necessary inputs may not be available at the right time or they may be very expensive. How the markets function, and how the economic environment around the markets works, influence the decision-making.

The decisions taken by a farmer depend on his possibilities, and these possibilities depend on the situation in which the farmer finds himself. It should be the goal to establish an environment around the farmer which induces and enables him to take decisions that are beneficial from both a private and a social point of view.

Climate risks and institutions

Agriculture is more exposed to risks and uncertainties than industry because it is affected by the changing weather and by fluctuating agricultural prices. The risks and uncertainties of the weather can be reduced through investments and institutional changes.

Different varieties of a given crop will often be more or less resistant to extremes of weather. The traditional local seed varieties are often better adapted to a broader range of weather conditions than newly developed varieties, which are more dependent on "normal" production conditions. If the production conditions are normal, high-yielding varieties give a much higher yield than the local varieties, whereas the local varieties give a higher yield under abnormal conditions.

The choice of seed variety depends on the level of risk aversion, which in turn depends on the farm income level. When farmers are poor, a harvest failure can be fatal. If the farmer has to service a debt, he may default on his loans and be forced to sell his farm. A wealthy farmer has greater leeway and is less affected by a bad harvest, so he will typically be less risk averse.

When poor farmers are risk averse, they may prefer local varieties of seed to high-yielding varieties, in spite of the fact that high-yielding varieties perform much better under optimal conditions. High-yielding varieties need complementary inputs such as fertilisers and water. If these inputs are not available, the high-yielding varieties may perform worse than the local varieties. If fertilisers are available and irrigation is possible, the risks of using high-yielding varieties will be eliminated.

When markets have been developed, so that fertilizers are available, and when investments in irrigation have been realised, the risks associated with choosing high-yielding varieties will be diminished.

If insurance schemes are introduced, the peasants will have the possibility of covering their risks, which will make them less risk averse. A disaster insurance scheme will eliminate the worst consequences of a drought.

Another possibility for reducing risks is to implement a share-cropping system. Share-cropping is an institution which is inefficient from an income maximization point of view, but it can be preferred because it is risk-reducing, see below.

Market risks and institutions

Agricultural prices fluctuate more than other prices when supply and demand change. In poorer countries, the food demand of households is highly sensitive to income levels, and the income levels of the peasants depend on agricultural prices and the size of the harvest.

For a subsistence farmer, it is risky to specialise in non-food production such as textile production. If the harvest fails, it can be difficult for a family without its own source of food to acquire the necessary food or to acquire food at reasonable prices. Once the agricultural production of a society is well above subsistence level, there is less risk that food will not be available if the harvest fails.

So increased agricultural productivity will raise the production level and reduce the risk of famine. In such a society it will be less risky for farmers to abandon subsistence farming and turn to commercial farming, and it will be less risky to specialise in non-food production.

There are several ways in which the uncertainties and risks can be reduced. Price uncertainty for farmers can be reduced by providing information about future expected prices. By introducing an agricultural pricing policy, the government can eliminate some of the price uncertainty. The government can promise farmers that it will reduce price fluctuations to within a certain band of prices with upper and lower limits. Such a scheme can be realised by a policy of import and export interventions. An alternative would be to stabilize prices by establishing a buffer stock programme, where a public body buys and sells stocks to keep domestic prices within the band.

An example: why use the share-cropping system?

In Europe, before the agricultural reforms, a large part of the land was cultivated by tenants on a share-cropping basis. Under this system, a share of the harvest was given to the landlord as payment for the use of the land.

Why was the share-cropping system so widely used in Europe and in the developing countries, even after the Second World War? It can easily be demonstrated in Figure 11.1 that the share-cropping system is inefficient because the optimal production level will not be reached. Private ownership or a tenant system where the rent is a fixed monetary amount is more efficient.

The peasant is confronted with the supply curve SS. If the market price is P_o, a private owner or a tenant, who has to pay a fixed rent, will supply the volume Q_o. Under a share-cropping arrangement, the peasant has to deliver, for example, half his output to the landowner. The peasant will only get the price P_s, which is half of the market price P_o, and will only supply the volume Q_s.

Figure 11.1: Share-cropping reduces the production volume

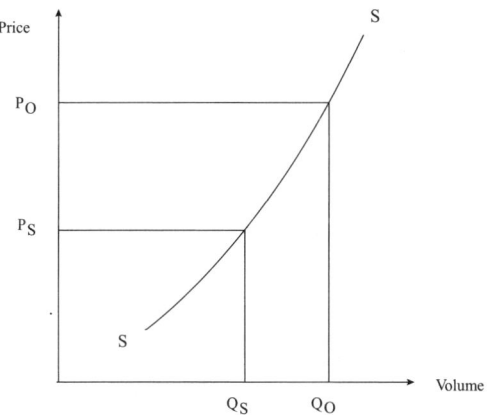

The share-cropping system was developed in a society with an economy based on barter. Why did the share-cropping system continue after money became more widely used? If the peasant bought the land from the landowner, he would be exposed to risks which he had not had before. He had to sell some of his output in order to be able to service his debt. If the harvest failed or if the price level was low, he might be unable to get enough money and he might default his loan and so be obliged to sell his land. Private ownership was a more efficient institution, but it was also more risky for the peasant. Risk perception depends on the economic position of the person perceiving. If a person is relatively poor, and if the possibility of covering the risk is small, the risk aversion will be high. When there is a trade-off between profit and risk, it is understandable that the less risky option will be chosen.

Another alternative to the share-cropping system would be to integrate the land into a large estate managed by a landlord. Then decisions about production would be taken by a manager, and the problem would be how to implement those decisions. The land had to be cultivated by labourers or peasants who had to deliver labour services, and they had no personal financial interest in the farming. So the integration of the land into a large estate led to other inefficiencies which made it a less profitable solution than share-cropping. There were efficiency costs associated with the separation of labour and management in farming.

11.6 The experience of the Soviet planned economy

The Russian economy had started to develop relatively successfully in the last two decades before the First World War. Industrialisation had started and there was clear progress in the agricultural sector. Agricultural productivity, measured as millions of net calories produced per male worker, increased from 5.6 in 1800 to 6.0 in 1890, which is only an increase of 7 per cent in nearly a whole century. From 1890 to 1914, there was an increase from 6.0 to 7.4, which is nearly 25 per cent (Bairoch, 1999). Agricultural progress, combined with increased industrialisation during the period 1890-1914, led to a significant increase in the GDP per capita compared to the period 1820-1890.

When the Soviet Union was established in 1917, it ushered in a new economic system based on planning. From 1929 there was forced collectivisation of Soviet agriculture. Private individual farms were replaced by collective and state farms. Agricultural labourers on the collective and state farms were only allowed to cultivate a small plot of land of their own.

The introduction of the socialist system meant that all economic activity was planned, and there was no longer any reliance on the market mechanism. Supply was to be planned according to needs which were politically determined. The prices were fixed bureaucratically, and demand had to adjust to the planned supply. The planning system determined what each factory should produce, to whom the output was to be delivered, and from whom the inputs were to be obtained. The terms of trade between the agricultural and industrial sectors were politically determined. After the Second World War, this socialist farming system

The experience of the Soviet planned economy

was also applied to the Central and Eastern European countries which were under communist rule.

Agricultural performance 1950-1990

How did Soviet agriculture perform after the Second World War? There was a large increase in agricultural output, and a significant improvement in the diet of the average citizen. However, when agricultural performance is measured as labour productivity, the improvements in the Soviet Union lagged far behind developments in the USA and Western Europe.

Table 11.1 shows labour productivity in the USSR, the USA, and Denmark, which throughout this period was the country in Western Europe with the highest labour productivity. In 1950, labour productivity in the USSR was only around one fourth and one third of the productivity in the USA and Denmark, respectively. Up to 1970, the rate of growth in the USSR kept pace with the USA and Denmark, but without narrowing the significant gap. Since 1970, the USSR has performed worse than the USA and Denmark in spite of its much lower productivity level. It can be concluded that the agricultural performance in the USSR has been unsatisfactory by comparison with the USA and Denmark.

Table 11.1: An index of agricultural productivity in USSR, USA and Denmark 1950 -1990[1]

	USSR	USA	Denmark	USSR:USA Per cent	USSR:DK Per cent
1950	21.3	94.6	58.9	22.5	36.2
1960	38.3	184.1	90.4	20.8	42.4
1970	55.8	226.3	146.4	24.7	38.1
1980	58.8	291.5	225.8	20.2	26.0
1990	63.4	332.7	346.7	19.1	18.3

[1] The index reflects labour productivity in agriculture, measured as millions of net calories produced per male worker.
Source: Based on Bairoch (1999)

One factor behind the lower labour productivity in the USSR has to do with its different philosophy on employment. In a market-oriented economy, private firms employ labour until the wage rate equals the value of the marginal product. The firm is only concerned with the private costs, because the social costs of unemployment are considered to be an externality. In a socialist economy, the firm has to employ a given labour force all the time. Workers are employed even if the value of their marginal product is less than what they are paid. Those who are unemployed in a market economy will be employed in a socialist economy, which leads to a bias in favour of labour productivity in non-socialist countries.

Another factor concerns the natural conditions for production. These conditions will be good if the soil is fertile and there is the necessary precipitation. In the Ukraine, the soil is very fertile, but the precipitation is low. In other areas with sufficient precipitation, the soil is poor (Ellman, 1981). It is debatable how far natural conditions should be taken into consideration in measuring labour productivity when it is possible to compensate for unfavourable natural conditions through irrigation and fertilisation.

A third set of factors concerns the institutional set up in a socialist economy. There are three problems for agriculture in a socialist economy. Firstly, there is the problem of the planning system, when decisions are taken by politicians and bureaucrats with insufficient information. Secondly, socialist farming is based on large-scale production units, such as collective and state farms with a large work force. Thirdly, it is difficult to establish an incentive system for farm workers.

The planning system

There are some general problems connected with a planning system from which agriculture also suffered. The market mechanism is replaced by planning and there are great costs associated with such a system.

Firstly, an extensive class of bureaucrats is needed to generate and implement the plans at the central, regional and production unit levels. At the central level there is a central planning committee which deals with the overall planning, and there are sectoral planning committees which deal with the planning in each sector. At the regional level there are similar committees dealing with regional planning in the different sectors. In each region and in each sector there are a great number of production units which have to participate in the planning process. The planning process is very demanding on labour resources, involving high direct costs.

Secondly, the planning system involves a series of indirect costs because the replacement of the market by planning means that production is for the plan rather than for use.

In the Soviet Union, the supply of commodities was decided politically, and consumers and investors had to accept the produced

The experience of the Soviet planned economy

volume of each commodity. If, at the fixed price, demand exceeded supply there would be queues, but queues would not induce an increase in supply unless political decisions were taken. At the administratively fixed prices there was excess supply of some products, and for others there was excess demand.

Political decisions about production volumes and production quality were taken without any feedback from the end users. As a result, consumers and investors did not get the product quality they wanted and needed. In such a system, product development and product innovation can easily be neglected, and when politicians and bureaucrats take the initiative to innovate, the new products may not meet the needs of the end users because they were not involved in the innovation process.

In a planning system, it is not only difficult to set appropriate production volumes and appropriate product qualities, it is also difficult to ensure the efficient use of production factors. For example, the maintenance of investment goods may be neglected because it is easier to demand new investment goods from the planning agencies. Instead of repairing tractors and other machinery, the collective and state farms demanded new tractors and new machinery, even when the repair costs were low.

It is difficult for the planners to take decisions about volumes and qualities without guidance from a market in which prices reflect what is needed and what is not needed.

It is also a problem for the central planners that they have to take far-reaching decisions without being able to predict the unintended responses of bureaucrats at lower levels and of the producers. If it is decided that meat production should be increased, bureaucrats at a lower level may be tempted to obtain some political credit by choosing methods which hurt production in the long run. If the increased supply of meat is obtained by slaughtering dairy cows and breeding stock, it is evident that milk production and the future generation of livestock will be diminished.

In many socialist countries politicians have tried to obtain supplies by a procurement system, where the peasants have to deliver a certain quota at a low price. If there is an increased need, it would seem to be an obvious solution to increase the procurement quota. However, experience shows that such a policy may be counter-productive because the peasants become less interested in producing the wanted product. They will shift to other activities which are of greater benefit to themselves. Such adverse behaviour is difficult to avoid in planned economies, especially if there are many production units, as in the agricultural sector.

Economies of size

Socialist farming, as practised in the Soviet Union and later in the Central and Eastern European countries, was based on large-scale farming in collective and state farms. It is assumed that there are benefits associated with large-scale farming just as there are in industry, but this does not take into consideration the major differences between industrial and agricultural production.

In agriculture, production is a sequential process where different activities are in focus at different times of the year. In industry, the different production processes take place simultaneously. Therefore, it is easier to obtain economic benefits from the division of labour in industry than it is in agriculture.

All production processes in industry are of a technical nature, which means that there is a fixed relationship between the input and the output when a given technique is applied. Agriculture is characterized by biological processes where natural inputs, such as soil conditions, temperature, precipitation and diseases, all play an important role. Monitoring the production process is much more demanding in agriculture than in industry.

It is easier to get a disciplined and highly efficient labour force in industry than in agriculture. In industry, the labour force is concentrated, whereas in agriculture it is geographically dispersed, so it is easier to supervise the labour force in industry. The work of each worker in industry is more uniform than in agriculture, so it is easier for managers to give orders in industry than it is in agriculture. Because of the erratic elements in agricultural production, it is more difficult for a manager in agriculture to oversee the whole production process than it is in industry. Because it is difficult to manage the labour force on a collective or state farm, the labour force has to show more self-discipline and take initiatives. This might be expected if there were some incentives, but because it is difficult to evaluate agricultural work performance adequately, it has been difficult to apply satisfactory incentive schemes.

There are managerial diseconomies of scale in agriculture. The efficient large-scale organisation of labour requires efficient planning, administration and bookkeeping which are not necessary in smaller farms where each farmer organises his own work. The managerial diseconomies of scale increase with the size of the farm, and they depend on the educational level of the workforce. The diseconomies are greater where the labour force is more or less illiterate.

It is often assumed that there are economies of size in agriculture in relation to transport, marketing and financing. It is reasonable to assume that the unit costs of these activities will decrease when the size of the agricultural production unit increases. But it should not be forgotten that small and medium size farms, as known in Western Europe, can compensate by co-operation. They can set up co-operatives, which can provide services on a large scale and deliver the services at a price which is no higher than the unit costs of large production units.

Also, it should not be forgotten that the economies of size in agriculture in any given country are not only technological; they also depend on the existing resources and institutions.

The land-labour ratio is important. If labour is relatively abundant, which shows up either as open or disguised unemployment, it is more reasonable to focus on agricultural development which aims to increase output with a fixed or even increased labour force rather than obtaining a constant output with a smaller labour force. In other words, it is more important to focus on increasing land productivity than labour productivity. In this case, the economies of size will be small, because it will be reasonable to base agricultural development on smaller farm units where the labour intensity in production is higher.

It is also evident that economies of size vary from product to product. For example, today there are greater economies of size in poultry production than in milk production in Western Europe. It is clear that economies of size also depend on the available technology.

Economies of size also depend on the availability of inputs. In the old days, when the animal production on a farm depended on the feed produced on the farm, there was a limit to the expansion of animal production. This limit no longer exists, since feedstuffs can be bought in from outside. It is clear that the availability of transport facilities at a low price increases the possibility of selling products over greater distances, and so has an impact on the economies of size.

Labour incentives

According to socialist beliefs, the replacement of the capitalist system by a socialist system would in itself increase labour productivity. According to this belief, the workers would be induced to work harder because they would no longer be exploited by the capitalists who owned the means of production. In a socialist state, the means of production are owned by the people, so they should have a greater interest in working harder. In real life this expectation was not fulfilled because the workers did not feel that much was gained by replacing a class of managers in private firms by a class of bureaucrats controlling publicly owned firms.

In agriculture there were special problems associated with the shift to collective and state farming. Firstly, there were large transition costs in the introduction of socialist farming, because the peasants were against giving up private proprietorship. Secondly, the individual farming system was replaced by a system where a class of managers took the decisions and the operators had the responsibility for implementing them. Thirdly, it was not possible to develop an incentive scheme, taking into consideration the special production conditions of agriculture. The individual farming system, where the owner, the manager and the operator are one and the same person, is far better adapted to the special production conditions of agriculture.

In efficient farming, the workers should be disciplined; they should be able to adjust to the changing conditions so that timely performance is ensured; they should be able to take initiatives based on quick decisions. These qualities are important, given the specific production conditions of agriculture. When the owner is the manager, who is also the operator, there is no problem. However, if these three activities are shared between different people, it is necessary to introduce an incentive scheme, but this is complicated by the specific production conditions in agriculture.

Agricultural production is geographically dispersed, and the larger the production unit, the more it is dispersed. Soil fertility varies from plot to plot, so the use of inputs should be adjusted accordingly. The erratic and seasonal nature of natural inputs, such as varying temperatures and precipitation, make it important to plough, to sow and to harvest at the right time. The operator has to monitor how the arable crops are growing and whether the animals are thriving. Otherwise the operator has to take quick decisions about different kinds of intervention.

Some farm activities are more industrialized than others. Poultry production is such a case, and it seems that the economies of size are greater here than in other agricultural productions.

11.7 Summary

Economic development depends on markets. Once agricultural development has started, economic integration between the rural and the urban sectors is decisive for further economic development, and economic integration cannot be realised without markets. Technological and institutional changes open up for the creation of markets in the first stage, and enable the development of the necessary economic environment in the second stage.

Summary

Markets not only provide for some static effects associated with the improved allocation of resources, there are also dynamic effects connected with the market mechanism. With a given technological and institutional framework, markets will create competition which will induce entrepreneurs to invest and to improve their performance to stay in business. When technological and institutional changes occur, either exogenously or induced by the markets, further gains will be obtained by the dissemination of information and by the availability of improved products, improved inputs and new production methods.

The market mechanism is also a useful indicator of bottlenecks. If there is demand for commodities, services, production factors, improved technology and new institutions, this will be revealed by the market, either through high prices or through the lack of availability. When private agents and public authorities become aware of the bottlenecks and remove them, this will open the way for new opportunities and new bottlenecks will be revealed.

The economy cannot be developed by a once-and-for-all master plan. Economic development can only be realised by gradually removing the most severe constraints. The market mechanism is a good means for revealing the bottlenecks or constraints which hamper further development.

The establishment of efficient markets requires a series of important investments. Markets are created by investments in infrastructure and by establishing distribution channels. Investments in information systems, education, and research, together with institutional changes, are important for creating the necessary conditions for markets to contribute to economic development.

Who should take the initiative to create the markets and the enabling environment? The tasks are so big that it is not enough to rely on the initiatives of the public authorities. Economic progress will be slow unless private people also contribute. When groups of people, such as peasants, are able to organize themselves to solve problems of common interest, there can be rapid progress. Existing attitudes and legislation determine whether initiatives are taken and to what extent the co-operation will be successful.

There will only be economic integration if markets are established, but the importance of creating national markets and an adequate economic environment can easily be forgotten if a country focuses only on the urban sector and industrialisation. Agricultural development gives a much more insistent reminder of the importance of markets, because agricultural development is impossible without investment in markets.

Why is agricultural development not possible without markets and an enabling environment? There are many more producers in agriculture than in industry. Agricultural production is geographically dispersed. The infrastructure and distribution channels are decisive, and price signals are necessary for the adjustment of supply to demand. In industry, there are few producers and geographical concentration, so national markets are not so necessary. In industry, marketing can be performed by the individual producer, whereas in agriculture this task has to be undertaken by some organisation. Research can be undertaken by an individual industrial firm, but the testing of new crops and the introduction of new inputs and production methods has to be done by agricultural research institutes.

As well as the markets, institutions play a central role in the development of agriculture. Careful management is necessary if farming is to be successful. Each farmer has to make a series of decisions unlike those taken in industry, because agricultural production is exposed to the seasons, the variability of the weather and the risk of diseases. Each farmer has to adjust to the variables of farming conditions. Timely performance is important, and this can more easily be ensured if the manager is also the operator and if the operator also has a direct economic interest in the farm earnings.

There are more risks in agriculture than in industry. There are risks from the weather and risks of plant and animal diseases. Some of the risks can be avoided or reduced by different kinds of investments, others cannot be avoided. The institutional framework influences the risks. High-yielding varieties of seed can give a much larger harvest than local varieties, if water and fertilisers are available. However, the local varieties can be much more resistant to the lack of rain or fertiliser than the high-yielding varieties. So the choice between high-yielding and local varieties depends on the choice between profitability and risk. The ready availability of fertilizers and irrigation will affect the choice.

Different systems of land holding can also affect the trade-off between profitability and risk. A farm can be cultivated by a freeholder; it can be cultivated by a share-cropping tenant, who shares his output with the landowner; or the farm can be a part of a large estate, where the peasant has to deliver labour services. Private ownership ensures higher profitability than a share-cropping system, but if there is a bad harvest, the private owner is more vulnerable. Risk-reducing institutions, such as a credit system, will stimulate interest in private ownership rather than share-cropping. Although share-cropping is not efficient, it may be a better solution than incorporating the farm into a large estate. A sharecropper may nevertheless be more efficient than the labourer who is forced to work.

The importance of the market and the family farm can be illustrated by looking at the experience of the Soviet Union. The market was replaced by a planning system, and family farms were replaced by large collective farms. There are a number of general problems in a planned economy, and these became even more acute in agriculture because of the large number of producers and the special production conditions in agriculture.

It was difficult for the state to get the necessary agricultural supplies from the farms by command, so private ownership was replaced by collective and state farms. New problems arose because there are not economies of size in agriculture, as there are in industry. Agriculture is characterised by having sequential production processes, by having no fixed relationship between inputs and outputs, and by having geographically dispersed production. Given these characteristics, the family farm has a great advantage, because the owner is also the manager and the operator of the farm. There are substantial managerial diseconomies in farming, and it is extremely difficult to implement an incentive scheme which can ensure high productivity when the ownership, management and operation of the farm are in the hands of different groups of people.

12. Economic policy intervention

Governmental decisions have always had important impacts on conditions in society. The attitudes of the rulers and the ruling circles have influenced how society has functioned and the relations between the different classes in society.

The modern era, which started around 1750, has been characterized by technological and institutional changes. These changes were made more easily in some countries than in others. Agricultural reforms were a precondition for increases in productivity in agriculture, and the establishment of markets and the institutional framework were a precondition for continuing economic development.

Before the start of the modern era, societies were static. While these traditional societies could not be transformed into evolutionary societies by government alone, the attitudes of governments and the initiatives taken by them were important for creating the framework for economic development. Legislation and the political and economic support of the government for the transformation of society constituted the development policy.

Development policy is concerned with structural changes, whereas economic policy is concerned with the stabilisation of employment, income and prices.

The period 1750-1914 was one in which government interventions can be considered as development policy. Public interventions focused on the structural changes which were necessary to develop societies. Before 1914, the only kind of stabilisation policy was trade policy intervention to ensure greater price stability.

The period 1914-1945 was one with two world wars, an adjustment period in the 1920s and a Great Depression in the 1930s. The two wars were characterised by heavy public interventions to manage military production and the production necessary for civilian purposes. The 1920s was a period of return to more normal conditions.

It was only after 1929, and the onset of the Great Depression, that a series of policy interventions was made in the form of trade policy, exchange rate policy, fiscal policy, monetary policy and agricultural policy. Their purpose was to repair the damage which had already occurred.

The true period of economic policy intervention first occurred after the Second World War. The purpose of this economic policy was to stabilise economic development, so as to avoid both high unemployment and high inflation. The goals were to secure full employment, price stability and stable real incomes which should gradually be increased by economic growth.

This chapter deals with economic policy in the form of trade policy, agricultural policy and macroeconomic policy.

12.1 Trade policy

Trade policy can either be used as a structural policy instrument or as a stabilisation policy instrument. According to the theory of comparative advantage, free trade leads to a better allocation of resources than trade protection. According to the infant industry argument, it is possible to obtain a better structure in the longer term by protecting industry initially, until it can resist foreign competition.

However, trade policy can also be used in the short term to influence prices by varying supplies to the domestic market. Agricultural prices fluctuate because the harvest changes from year to year due to changing weather conditions and the incidence of disease. If domestic prices are high, a country can lower its trade barriers to improve market access for foreign produce, and if prices are low, the country can reduce imports by raising trade barriers. If a country is an exporter of agricultural products, it can lower domestic prices either through an export tax or an export ban.

Trade policy 1750-1875

Trade policy did not initially play an important role. When economic development began, industrial production was so small that there was no great difference between the relative productivities of agriculture and industry. The natural barriers to international trade, such as transport costs, were so high that they neutralised the comparative advantages which could be obtained by product specialisation between agriculture and industry. Economic development started in closed economies.

It was only later, as industrialisation progressed, that the ratio between agricultural and industrial productivity developed differently in different countries. When the differences in relative productivities grew between countries which had industrialised to greater or lesser degree, and when

Trade policy

transport costs fell, the door was opened for increased international trade. This development started after the Napoleonic Wars, and accelerated when railway construction started in earnest in around 1850.

In around 1750, mercantilism was the ruling economic philosophy in nearly all Europe, apart from in Britain where it never gained a foothold as on the Continent. The idea of free trade started in Britain and was supported by the work of Adam Smith, but the policy of free trade only won ultimate recognition with the repeal of the Corn Laws in 1846. Until then, the Corn Laws had been used as an instrument for stabilising the domestic prices of cereals. The supporters of free trade argued that it would lead to a more favourable economic structure in Britain.

The acceptance of free trade, based on structural considerations, spread throughout Europe during the economically prosperous period 1850-1875.

Different trade policies in Europe 1875-1914

Economic conditions deteriorated in around 1875 and trade protection was reintroduced. When Western Europe was flooded with agricultural products, especially cereals from the USA and Russia, the different European countries responded differently.

Britain continued its free trade policy, so agricultural prices fell. However, British agriculture did not suffer from the repeal of the Corn Laws. During the period 1846-1875, British agriculture prospered because the demand for cereals in general in Europe was high, due to the population increase and the increasing GDP per capita. In 1850, productivity in British agriculture was the highest in Europe. From 1875 there was agricultural decline in Britain and land was taken out of production. There was no co-operative movement which could have eased the transition from cereal growing to livestock production.

The free trade policy was continued because its main purpose was to keep food prices down so that the competitiveness of British industry would not suffer.

France shifted towards a protectionist trade policy for both agricultural and industrial products in the 1870s. Agricultural prices fell because the increase in tariff protection was less than the fall in import prices, including the freight costs. In spite of the protectionist policy, French agricultural performance was weaker than in Germany where agriculture was also supported. There are several explanations for this poor performance. First of all, at the time French agriculture suffered from general backwardness. The economic environment which is so important for agricultural development was lacking. The infrastructure in the rural areas was inadequate, the educational level was not high, there was no agricultural research of importance, nor a system for extension services. Furthermore, there was no pressure from the demand side which could have stimulated agricultural development, as the population in France was stagnant from 1870 to 1945.

Under these conditions it seemed reasonable to moderate the price fall for agricultural products. A further fall in prices would have caused social distress in the rural areas because of the lack of alternative employment possibilities. Industrialisation in France was slower than in Britain, so there was less scope for absorbing people from the rural areas in times of social distress. It is doubtful whether a further decline in cereal prices in the case of free trade would have caused a shift towards livestock production. The ability of French agriculture to adjust was poor at the time.

When the economic crisis came in the second half of the 1870s, Germany also departed from the free trade policy and replaced it with agricultural and industrial protection. Behind the protective tariff walls German agriculture increased its productivity. This positive German performance was stimulated by population growth and industrialisation on the demand side, and by well-functioning markets and a positive economic environment, due to agricultural research and a co-operative tradition, on the supply side. Production increases were lower than the increase in demand, so Germany became a net importer of agricultural products, in spite of agricultural protection.

Due to the agricultural protection, the price falls in Germany were moderate, as in France. The tariff protection in Germany can be regarded as an economic success. German agriculture was able to develop behind moderate protection barriers. Agricultural labour productivity doubled from 1860 to 1900. On the other hand, the protection was not so high as to make it difficult for German industry to attract labour from the rural areas.

In Denmark, the free trade policy was continued after 1875. All agricultural prices fell, but the decline in cereal prices was much greater than the decline in prices for livestock products, so Danish farmers adjusted to the new conditions by expanding their livestock production. When the crisis began in around 1875, Danish agriculture and the economic environment around agriculture were sufficiently well developed to enable adjustment to be made to the new conditions.

The free trade policy and the adjustment to the new conditions were a great success in Denmark. In Germany there was strong industrialisation

Trade policy

and the GDP per capita increased 71 per cent from 1875 to 1913, but in Denmark which had only weak industrialisation, the increase in the GDP per capita was 85 per cent, due to the agricultural development.

The positive development in Denmark was not only a result of the initial conditions in 1875 and the free trade policy, it was also conditioned by the ability to link agricultural development to the industrial development in two neighbouring countries, Britain and Germany. British and French agriculture could, in principle, have obtained the same advantages as Danish agriculture by selling to the expanding British markets. The fact that British and French agriculture did not grasp this opportunity was a great advantage to Danish agriculture.

Table 12.1: Trade policy and agricultural performance 1875-1914

Agricultural performance \ Trade policy	Free trade	Protection
Positive	Denmark	Germany
Negative	Britain	France

During the period 1875-1914 there was no correlation between the choice of trade policy and economic performance as illustrated in Table 12.1. In Britain and Denmark the agricultural sectors were not supported, whereas France and Germany supported their agricultural sectors. In France, agricultural production increased 15 per cent, but in Britain production stagnated.

This pattern confirms that agricultural performance cannot be explained by the choice of trade policy. Agricultural performance depends on a series of different elements, which influence the ability to adjust to new conditions.

Similar trade policy for agriculture and industry 1875-1914

During the period 1875-1914, the trade policy for agriculture and industry was similar in the sense that a country either pursued a free trade policy for both agriculture and industry, or it followed a protective policy for both sectors. Britain and Denmark conducted a general free trade policy, whereas France and Germany protected industry as well as agriculture.

In the countries that chose trade protection, the protection level was not the same for each sector or for each product in each sector, so the trade protection distorted the price structure. However, the resource allocation between agriculture and industry was not systematically distorted in favour of one of the sectors, which would have been the case if only one of the sectors had been protected.

After 1875, tariff protection was a response to the lower prices resulting from the lower transport costs. As a proportion of the consumer price, transport costs are greater for agricultural products than for most industrial products, so a reduction in transport costs has a greater effect on agriculture than on industry, and one could expect agricultural prices to fall relative to industrial prices. If, on the other hand, productivity growth in industry is higher than in agriculture, the relative prices of agricultural and industrial products will not necessarily change.

When the agricultural and industrial sectors in general are protected by the same percentage tariff rate, the intention is not to favour one sector at the expense of the other. Such a strategy can be considered as inward-looking strategy which stimulates activity in both agriculture and industry, compared to the activities in the non-tradable sector, such as the service sector. Today, such a shift in the relative attractiveness of the import competing sectors compared with the non-tradable sectors can be obtained by changing the nominal foreign exchange rate.

This could not be done in the period 1875-1914, because the foreign exchange regime had fixed exchange rates based on the gold standard. A general tariff protection can be considered as an instrument with some of the same properties as a change in the foreign exchange rate. The import competing sectors were favoured, whereas the exporting sectors suffered because trade protection increased the cost levels.

Agriculture and industry treated differently after the Second World War

After the onset of the Great Depression in 1929, each industrialised country tried to solve its economic and social problems through trade protection, both for industrial and agricultural products. In the case of agriculture, trade policy became an integrated part of a comprehensive agricultural policy which involved a series of different instruments, only some of which were related to trade. There were no international rules

Agricultural policy

constraining the beggar-my-neighbour protectionist policies. Each country acted on its own without any international co-operation.

After the Second World War there was international co-operation on trade and tariffs under the auspices of the GATT. Until the GATT was replaced by the World Trade Organisation (WTO) there was no international agreement on agriculture. In the industrial sector, the average protection level in the industrialised countries was gradually reduced from around 40 per cent after the Second World War to around 4 per cent today. In the agricultural sector, the agricultural support policy including high trade protection, which started during the 1930s, continued after the Second World War, and in several cases it was even extended.

This illustrates the great difference between agricultural protection in the period 1875-1914 and agricultural protection in the period 1950-2000. In the first period, some countries followed a free trade policy for all products, while others followed a protective policy for both agricultural and industrial products. In the second period, the trade policies of the industrialised countries severely distorted the relative prices of agriculture and industry, because agricultural support was extended while industrial protection was removed.

12.2 *Agricultural policy*

No agricultural policy before the Great Depression

As shown in the previous section, different countries pursued different trade policies during the period 1875-1914. Trade policy was a part of development policy which differed in different countries.

Agricultural policy can be defined as a sector-specific policy, applying a comprehensive set of interventions to agricultural markets to obtain a series of goals, mainly the goal of reasonable farm incomes. Agricultural policy was only introduced in Europe and the USA during the Great Depression, and was continued after the Second World War.

Up to the time of the Great Depression, agricultural development was based on market forces, which were only modified in some periods and in some countries by trade policy which consisted mostly of tariff policy. When agricultural policy was introduced, the interventions became so extensive that the basic mechanism for ensuring market equilibrium was more or less eliminated. The agricultural markets became managed markets where free market forces no longer worked, due to the interventions. Agricultural policy influenced the terms of trade between agricultural and non-agricultural products.

Agricultural policy in the 1930s

The Great Depression caused massive unemployment in the urban sector and low incomes in the rural sector, due to low agricultural prices.

In the USA, the government responded to the crisis by implementing the protective Smoot-Hawley Tariff Act in 1930, but nothing else was done before 1933 when the new president, Roosevelt, launched his New Deal programme. Its purpose was reform, relief and recovery.

Agricultural policy, in the form of a set of market schemes for different products, was introduced for the first time, with the aim of increasing farm incomes. There were several significant elements in the US agricultural policy. Firstly, farm-gate prices were considered to be too low, so they were increased by production subsidies in the form of deficiency payments financed through the federal budget. Secondly, minimum price levels were instituted by the loan rate system. Such price interventions would have caused surpluses, which would have increased stocks significantly if measures had not been undertaken to control supply and demand. Thirdly, supply was reduced by a supply management programme in the form of either acreage or production reduction. Fourthly, the demand for food products was stimulated by a food relief programme in which the government bought food products which were distributed to those in the urban areas who were worst hit by the Depression.

When US agricultural policy was introduced in 1933, it consisted of a comprehensive and coherent set of measures whose purpose was to relieve the economic problems from which agriculture had suffered during the years 1929-1933.

It was a problem that the agricultural policy was introduced after the economic crisis had arisen. It should have been introduced much earlier to prevent the crisis. Economic confidence was shaken by the collapse on the stock market in Wall Street Crash of October 1929. The problem was that no interventions had been made to prevent the cumulative processes which created the Great Depression. The fall in farm incomes reduced consumption and investment in farming, and the social distress in the cities reduced the demand for food products.

Unlike the situation in the USA, the larger European countries, such as Britain, Germany and France were net importers of agricultural products. When domestic agricultural prices fell, because of falling world market prices, the natural initial response was to raise tariff protection. Because of the continuing decline in world market prices, tariff protection was supplemented by import restrictions and by market organisations for different agricultural products. The different market organisations implemented a number of different instruments, such as minimum price schemes, state monopoly bodies, marketing boards, milling obligations to stimulate domestic demand, and measures to reduce supply.

In France and Germany the approach adopted was to support the farmers through high market prices which were obtained by different kinds of interventions. High farm-gate prices were obtained through high market prices paid by consumers. There was some discrimination between different imports. The French colonies, especially Algeria, had import quotas and Germany did the same in relation to some central and eastern European countries. Discriminatory tariff rates were also used as a lever for obtaining benefits for the country's own exporters.

The agricultural policy of Britain differed from the policies of France and Germany, due to the Imperial Preference System. Britain wanted to support British farmers who were hit by the low world market prices, but it did not want to raise domestic prices by a general level of high protection. Britain also wanted its Dominions to have free access to the British market, whereas it aimed to reduce imports from third countries by trade protection. As a result, British farmers did not benefit from high domestic prices because the Dominions could export without tariffs. The farmers were supported through a deficiency payment system instead.

The agricultural policies introduced in the USA and in the larger countries in Europe differed from each other due to the different conditions of each. The USA was a net exporter and could not solve its farm income problem through trade protection. From the beginning, supply management played an important role in US agricultural policy.

The bigger countries in Europe were net importers, so they could raise domestic price levels by trade protection, squeezing out imports. France and Germany built up elaborate agricultural policies based on having higher domestic consumer prices than world market prices. The agricultural policy in Britain was different because it wanted the Dominions to have free access to its domestic market, so British agricultural support for cereals was based on deficiency payments.

The agricultural policies of the 1930s were aimed at relieving the social distress caused by the Great Depression, but these policies were continued in the post-war period in spite of the general economic prosperity. The instruments used during the 1930s were also applied after the war, so the agricultural policies applied in the second half of the twentieth century inherited all the main characteristics of the 1930s.

Agricultural policy 1950-1990

The main instruments of US agricultural policy were a minimum price system in the form of the loan rate system, production subsidies in the form of a deficiency payment system, and supply management in the form of set-aside programmes.

From its inception the Common Agricultural Policy (CAP) which was established in the period 1958-1967 was considered to be a cornerstone of the European integration process, which explains why it was tacitly accepted by the USA. The CAP was based on limiting market access through protection, internal price supports and export subsidies. The farmers benefited from high consumer prices which were obtained by a high level of protection against imports. On the domestic market, prices could not fall below a minimum level, which was ensured by the public purchase and storage of surpluses. When there was excess supply, exports were subsidised.

There were different market organisations for the different product sectors, each based on a set of instruments. The various instruments influenced international trade differently. Some of the instruments were intended to regulate foreign trade, whereas others were intended to regulate domestic production, consumption and farm incomes.

The agricultural policies in the USA and in Western Europe in the period 1950-1990 were more or less a continuation of the agricultural policies of the 1930s. The USA applied the same policy instruments, and the CAP inherited a series of elements, especially from the agricultural policies of France and Germany.

Agricultural policy was continued in the post-war period, even though the general economic conditions were totally different. In the 1930s agricultural policy was a response to the social distress in the farming sector when the whole economy was suffering from the Great Depression. In contrast, the post-war period was characterised by overall prosperity with economic growth and high employment. The problem was that increases in farm incomes could not keep pace with the general increase in incomes. The agricultural policies of the 1930s were continued in order to solve the farm income problem while adjustments were made. In spite of a large fall in the farm population and the number of farms, agricultural policies continued more or less unchanged until the 1990s. The lesson is that once a support policy has been introduced it is

Agricultural policy

very difficult to change. There are strong elements of the ratchet effect in agricultural policy, especially when vested interests are created.

When looking at the differences between the agricultural policies of the USA and the EC, the legacy of the past is evident. The differences reflect the fact that the USA was a net exporter, especially of arable products, and the EC countries were originally net importers of agricultural products. The fact that the EC has become a net exporter of some agricultural products raised new problems, but it did not bring about any profound change in policy.

When the CAP was established in 1967, the EC chose a policy based on high domestic prices compared to world market prices. From the start of the CAP and up to around 1984, real agricultural support prices were constant, and it was only after 1984 that a more prudent price policy caused real agricultural prices to decline. The high domestic price level was obtained by high variable levies on imports.

Agricultural support can be split into price supports obtained through trade protection, and other supports, such as production subsidies, input subsidies and direct income support. Price supports are more trade-distorting than other supports which distort trade to lesser and varying degrees.

The CAP was mainly based on price supports, whereas US agricultural policy was more based on production subsidies and income payments, which are less trade-distorting. From the start, US agricultural policy was based on supply management, which was first introduced in earnest in the EC in 1984 with the milk quota system.

The US agricultural policy involved greater price variations than the CAP. The US policy was more market-oriented, and therefore more flexible. US agriculture was more integrated into the world market for cereals, so the USA had to adjust its agricultural policy to changing world market conditions.

Agricultural policy since 1990

Agricultural policy was only able to support and protect agriculture in the industrialised countries because agriculture was exempted from the GATT co-operation in the period 1950-1990.

This situation was changed by the Uruguay Round of the GATT (1986-93). US agriculture had suffered from low world market prices in the first half of the 1980s. As a consequence, the USA wanted liberalisation of international trade in agricultural products. The USA threatened the EC by declaring that the USA would not sign a new trade agreement unless it

Economic policy intervention

included an international agreement to liberalise trade in agricultural products.

The EC was forced to change its policy, which it did with the MacSharry reform in 1992. The reform did not lower the support level but changed the support mechanisms. In the cereal sector, price support was replaced by hectare support. Because of the MacSharry reform, the Uruguay Round could be successfully concluded in 1993. For the first time, there was a comprehensive international agreement on trade in agriculture. Foreign market access was to be made easier, export subsidies were to be reduced, and the most trade-distorting support was to be reduced. This was considered the first step towards agricultural trade liberalisation, and was to be followed up by further steps in future rounds. Currently, the WTO countries are trying to reach a new agreement in the Doha Round.

12.3 Problems caused by agricultural policy

Short-term consequences for consumers, producers and taxpayers

An artificially high price level stimulates supply and reduces the demand for a given product. The effect of this can be illustrated in a simple partial equilibrium model of the comparative static kind, where welfare is measured by using the terms consumer surplus and producer surplus. Figure 12.1 illustrates the effect when the domestic price is P_D and the world market price is P_W. Table 12.2 shows that consumers will be hurt by the higher consumer price, whereas the producers will benefit from a higher farm-gate price. Taxpayers will benefit if the public revenues are increased and they will lose if the agricultural policy involves larger expenditures.

If the welfare loss to consumers and taxpayers from paying one dollar more is equal to the welfare gained by producers from earning one dollar more, the total welfare loss associated with the agricultural price support will be b plus d.

If the average farmer has a lower income than the average consumer, it could be argued that the one dollar extra earned by producers, increases their welfare more than the welfare loss of the richer consumers.

Figure 12.1: Comparison between free trade and protection in an importing and an exporting country

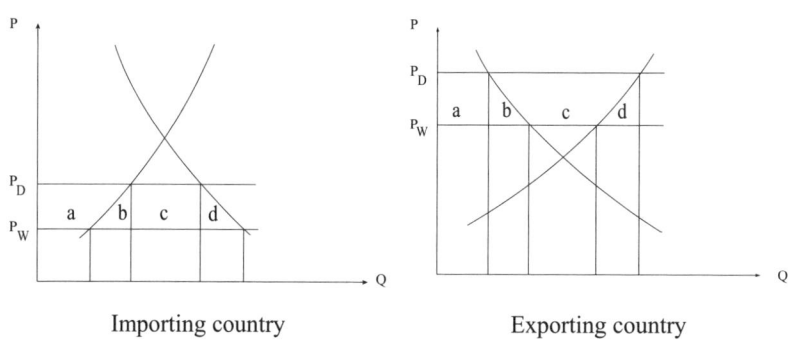

Importing country   Exporting country

Table 12.2: The welfare effects of a price support policy

	Importing country	Exporting country
Consumer surplus decrease	a+b+c+d	a+b
Producer surplus increase	a	a+b+c
Budgetary revenue	c	− (b+c+d)
Total decrease	b+d	b+d

In the short term, it is also a problem that relative prices will often be distorted. There are different market schemes and different support levels for different products. If the support level for a product is too high, there will often be surplus production which will either lead to increased stocks or it will be dumped on the export markets. If the support level for another product is too low, there can be excess demand which can only be satisfied by imports.

Because of price distortion, the allocation of consumption and of available production resources will not be optimal.

Fluctuations and risks

Figure 12.1 illustrates the market situation at a given moment, but the market situation changes when demand, supply and world market prices change. The prices in agricultural markets fluctuate more than in markets for industrial goods. This has been used as an argument in favour of agricultural price support.

For poorer consumers, there is no doubt that stable food prices are an advantage. The same conclusion is not so clear for farmers, because farmers are more interested in income stabilisation than in price stabilisation.

Farmers are exposed to price risks and the risks of bad weather and diseases, etc. Is it an advantage to have minimum farm-gate prices? Does it not make it easier to plan and to make investment decisions?

The answer is not a clear "Yes". It is true that a minimum price reduces the price risk, but it is replaced by a political risk, namely the risk that the minimum price cannot be maintained because it has been set too high.

A minimum price can stimulate interest in product specialisation. Instead of having farms with diversified production, such as different arable crops, pigs, beef cattle and dairy cows, farmers may specialise in one or a few products. Product diversification is a risk-reducing measure, which is no longer necessary when other risks are reduced.

If a farmer specialises because of the introduction of a minimum price, he has to buy more inputs from outside, so he is exposed to new risks because input prices can fluctuate.

If the farmer's response to pricing policy intervention is to increase investments he will expose himself to new risks. The larger capital stock will increase the fixed costs, and this investment will be more sensitive to the other risks. The debt service payments will depend on interest rate fluctuations.

All private business is associated with risk. It can be argued that an entrepreneur exposes himself to a given sum of risks. If one risk is reduced, because a stabilising agricultural policy is introduced, a farmer may be willing to run larger risks in other matters, for example by increased specialisation or increased investment.

International consequences

Agricultural price support in the EC meant that common trade barriers for all the Member States were raised against non-member countries. The CAP worked similarly to the EC customs union. It stimulated trade creation between the Member States and trade diversion vis-à-vis non-member countries. If the common trade barriers had merely been the average of the national trade barriers prior to the introduction of the CAP, it could be argued that the CAP was a step in the right direction. However, the common barrier was higher than the average protection levels of the individual Member States, because the EC chose the highest price levels in Germany and in Italy for its intervention prices. The CAP made it more difficult for third countries to gain access to the EC markets.

The high internal price level led to production increases which were significantly higher than the increases in demand. The EC countries were originally net importers of nearly all agricultural products, but due to the EC pricing policy and productivity increase, domestic production first squeezed out imports and then made the EC a net exporter. Because of the size of the EC's economy, its agricultural price support policy caused a decline in world market prices compared to the situation which would have prevailed under free trade.

The EC's agricultural protection was not based on fixed tariff rates, but on variable levies which were calculated as the difference between the threshold prices, which were fixed, and the world market prices which fluctuated. This system also caused wider price fluctuations on the world market than there would have been with a system with fixed tariff rates.

The production subsidies in the US agricultural policy, in the form of deficiency payments, also caused a decline in world market prices and wider price fluctuations than there would have been with free trade. However, the US agricultural policy was more flexible than the EC agricultural policy, so the world market was less "harmed" by the US agricultural policies than by the CAP.

An agricultural price support policy has been conducted by most industrialised countries, whereas the developing countries did not support the agricultural sector but taxed it, see Section 13.6. The agricultural policies of the industrialised countries did not disfavour the developing countries as a group, but lower world market prices did hurt exporting countries and favour importing countries.

The EC's cereal price policy has lowered world market prices, and this has hurt all exporters including the USA, Canada and Australia, which are industrialised, as well as Argentina which is a developing country.

The developing countries that export tropical products which do not compete with the domestic production of the industrialised countries are not hurt because these exports can normally freely enter the industrialised markets. Developing countries which export products which compete with the domestic production of the industrialised countries suffer from lack of access to the industrialised markets, lower world market prices and wider price fluctuations. The developing countries which import products which are supported by the agricultural policies of the industrialised countries benefit because the import prices are lower. It is true that the lower price level may hurt the development of domestic production in the developing country, but this effect can be neutralised if trade protection is applied.

Structural consequences

Price support policy influences the price levels of agricultural products as well as the relative prices of products, because not all products are supported to the same extent or in the same way.

From the start of the CAP in 1967-68 to the implementation of the MacSharry reform in 1992-95, the domestic price level for cereals in the EC was far above the world market price. This meant that farmers with larger acreage could thrive by specialising in cereal growing. This was also the case in a country like Denmark where the comparative advantage in agriculture had been the livestock sector.

When substitutes are not supported to the same extent or in the same way, there will be distortions in supply and demand. In the EC there were price distortions between cereals and cereal substitutes, such as oilseed products, tapioca and maize and citrus residues. Cereals were supported by high farm prices, whereas cereal substitutes were either not supported or were supported by a deficiency payment system. High cereal prices stimulated supply and reduced demand, so there was a surplus. The supply of cereal substitutes in the EC was low and the demand was high, which contributed to large import volumes. There was also price distortion between animal fat products, such as butter, and products based on vegetable oil, such as margarine and olive oil. Again the support for butter was price support, whereas the support to plant oil was deficiency payment support.

High prices caused by agricultural policy hamper the dynamic development of agriculture. Some agricultural products, such as cereals, can be used either for food or for non-food production. Ethanol, which is an additive to combustibles, can be produced from cereals, but if cereal prices are too high, ethanol will be unable to compete with the oil-based products it might replace.

Land can be used for food production or non-food production, such as the production of fibres for the textile or the cellulose industries. Again, a high price policy is a barrier to the use of land for alternative crops which do not receive support.

An agricultural policy which guarantees a minimum price for an unlimited volume reduces farmers' interest in product development and marketing activities.

The farm ownership structure may also be influenced by the agricultural policy. Price support means that the support level is higher when the production volume is higher, and this may stimulate interest in increased farm sizes and higher investment because of higher income. The risk reductions which follow from a high guaranteed minimum price for an unlimited supply may induce farmers to invest more than under a more market-oriented policy. The fact that the support policy has lasted for so long will influence long-term expectations. Farmers will expect the present support level to be maintained, so they will be less reluctant to buy more land at a high price and to enlarge their capital stock.

The agricultural policy may stimulate a higher degree of farm specialisation which can also contribute to a higher degree of disharmony between the land area and the size of animal production on individual farms. Increased specialisation may lead to less crop rotation which can depress yields in the longer term, without increased use of fertilisers and pesticides.

The neglect of social goals

The pursuit of agricultural policy can conflict with a number of other social goals.

Environmental concerns indicate that higher priority should be given to the conservation of nature. Soil fertility should be maintained, characteristic landscapes should be protected, wild life habitats should be preserved, pollution should be avoided, and there are ethical concerns about the treatment of domestic animals.

There are concerns about the survival of rural communities. With migration to the towns, there is a fear that the population base will be so depleted that the necessary services cannot be maintained in the rural areas. Migration on too large a scale creates problems of congested urban areas and thinly populated rural areas.

There is increasing public concern about the quality of food products. Food safety requires that food products should not contain bacteria to an extent that is harmful to human health. Foods must not contain residues which could cause resistance in humans to antibiotics. If there are problems, they should be easily traceable to their source.

Food quality is not only a question of food safety, it is also one of nutritional value and tastes. Obesity is a growing problem which should focus interest on foods with high nutritional value but which do not cause health problems in the long term.

The problem with the agricultural policies in the industrialised countries is that they have been very one-sided. They have only focused on solving the farm income problem. They have not taken account of the international and structural consequences discussed in the previous sections, nor of the social goals referred to in this section.

In the past, there has been a conflict between agricultural policies and environmental concerns. A high price policy induces farmers to practise more intensive farming which will often harm environmental and animal welfare goals.

Until recently, agricultural policy has focused only on farmers as producers of agricultural products. However, farmers are also stewards of large parts of the landscape and, in principle, they should be paid for producing public goods. Past agricultural policies have not encouraged farmers to avoid pollution or to maintain valuable landscapes and habitats.

Furthermore, agricultural policies have been unable to solve the problem of the steep decline in the rural population. Agricultural policy has favoured large-scale capital-intensive production, which has reduced the size of the agricultural labour force. The migration problem cannot be solved by agricultural policy; a regional policy or, even better, a land district policy should be implemented instead. Since discussions began on EU enlargement by the accession of the Central and Eastern European countries, there has been more focus on land district policy.

It has also been argued that past agricultural policies neglected the question of food quality. Farmers have been induced to focus on production volumes and to disregard product development aspects. It is only by introducing higher product standards which producers have to comply with, and by introducing a more market-oriented agricultural policy, that interest in the quality aspects can be stimulated.

It seemed as if there was a conflict between the farmers who produced and the rest of the population, who consumed. The farmers wanted an agricultural policy which could solve the farm income problem, so they focused on intensive production, which was mostly in conflict with the social goals which the rest of the population wanted farmers to deliver.

12.4 Macroeconomic policy and agriculture

Macroeconomic policy in the Western World 1750-1914

The most important economic policy during this long period was monetary policy. In feudal society, barter trade was the most common kind of trade. With more product specialisation, the money economy started to develop. Price levels were determined by the money supply which changed from period to period. In Chapter 1 there is a review of the way in which the price trends varied during different sub-periods from 1815 to 1914. In periods when the money supply increased more than the volume of transactions, prices went up, and the opposite happened when money supply declined. On the other hand, relative prices depended on the conditions of supply and demand for the different products.

The real purchasing power of farmers depended on the relative prices between agricultural products, on the one hand, and the prices of inputs and bought consumer goods, on the other hand.

Even when agricultural terms of trade were constant, it was of great importance to farmers whether the general price level was rising or falling. As agriculture became more and more commercialised, farm debt increased. When debt service payments, namely repayment instalments and interest payments, are fixed in nominal terms, farmers will gain if price levels rise and lose if price levels fall.

Monetary policy was important for the peasants because it determined the availability of credit, the interest rate and the inflation rate.

The amount of money issued in peacetime was normally associated with the stock of precious metals, such as gold and silver. The period 1870-1914 was the heyday of the gold standard. Money supply depended on the stock of gold in the central bank, and the foreign exchange rates were fixed. It was not possible to conduct an exchange rate policy at this period.

The fiscal budget was small at the time. There was some public expenditure relating to education, research, infrastructure, etc. The public budget was balanced in the sense that current expenditures should be covered by current taxes. Public capital expenditure, such as investments in railway construction, could be financed by public loans. When the peasants started to pay taxes in money, this stimulated the commercialisation process. As money was needed more than previously, the incentive to commercialise increased.

Public attitudes towards structural improvements which involved public expenditure were of great importance. Income transfers from the rich to the poor people were few. Fiscal policy, as a counter-cyclical instrument with surpluses in prosperous years and deficits in years of recession, was unknown.

Macroeconomic policy 1914-1945

When the First World War broke out, many countries left the gold standard, and foreign exchange rates were no longer fixed.

During the 1920s, there were monetary problems in nearly all countries. In Germany, Russia, Austria, Hungary and Poland, inflation was so rife that currencies became valueless and new units had to be introduced. In countries such as Britain, France and the USA, there were also high inflation rates, but of a different magnitude.

During the 1920s, exchange rates were misaligned for two reasons. Firstly, they did not reflect the cost differences which had arisen because of the varying inflation rates in the different countries since 1914. Secondly, different countries pursued different exchange rate policies. Britain, for example, wanted to return to the gold standard at the pre-war parity, whereas France returned to the gold standard at a strongly devalued parity. The misaligned exchange rates caused balance of payments disequilibria and negatively influenced the activities of industry and agriculture in countries, such as Britain, which overvalued their currencies.

When prices started to fall after the Wall Street crash in October 1929, the crisis in the USA was aggravated by a strict monetary policy. The restrictive monetary policy caused a further decline in the general price level, and this exacerbated the bank crisis. Many banks had to close down, leaving their clients unable to recover their deposits. Fiscal policy was unknown at the time. The US crisis spread to Europe through the protective trade policies of the USA, and each of the European countries soon followed suit by increased trade protection. The problem was the lack of international policy co-ordination which could have hindered the spreading of protectionism.

Up to 1933, economic philosophy was characterised by a laissez faire attitude. The market economy was considered to be a self-regulating mechanism, where a fall in prices would soon establish a new equilibrium without the need for public intervention.

Modern macroeconomic policy was introduced for the first time when Roosevelt became President of the USA in 1933. Expansionary fiscal policy was a main instrument for alleviating social distress and fighting unemployment. The key words of the New Deal in the USA were relief, recovery and reform. The theoretical basis for this intervention policy was provided by J.M. Keynes, who published his *General Theory of Employment, Interest and Money* in 1936.

According to Keynes, there is no invisible hand in the labour market which ensures full employment. The employment level depends on aggregate demand, and if aggregate demand is not sufficient, the government must stimulate aggregate demanded by running a budget deficit. In times of depression, activity should be stimulated by tax reductions and/or increased public expenditure.

Macroeconomic policy 1945-2000

Keynesian economics, focusing on the demand side, dominated the economic agenda during the period 1945-1970. During this period there was a consensus among economists about the validity of the Keynesian theory, and governments "fine-tuned" economic policy to ensure a high employment, even in the short term.

This consensus broke down when the monetarist theory and the new classical theory entered the scene in around 1970. The monetarists believed that economic policy should be targeted more towards the medium term. The fiscal budget should be balanced in the medium term and a prudent monetary policy should ensure price stability. The monetarists focused on the supply side and emphasized the importance of expectations in relation to the inflation level. Expectations about future inflation are based on past inflation and these expectations have a significant influence on wage settlements on the labour market. The new classical theory considered that the real economy and the money economy are totally disconnected, so that monetary policy should only focus on price stability, and fiscal policy was regarded as a futile instrument.

Since 1970, economic thinking has been dominated by a kind of synthesis between Keynesian theory and monetarist theory, emphasizing that both fiscal and monetary policy matter.

In the 1970s there were two sets of institutional changes in the world economy which changed the way fiscal and monetary policy interventions worked. Firstly, there was the collapse of the pegged exchange rate system, which had been instituted in 1944 at the Bretton Woods conference when the International Monetary Fund (IMF) was founded. The pegged exchange rate system was replaced by a floating exchange rate system. Secondly, since the 1970s, there was a gradual liberalisation of international capital movements. With different interest rates in different countries, an unrestricted international capital market gave rise to large capital movements which had a significant impact on foreign exchange rates. The exchange rates fluctuated much more than could be explained by changes in the relative competitiveness of countries.

Agricultural markets and macroeconomic policy

The world market for cereals is more important than the world market for animal products. The trends in the world market for cereals changed significantly during the period 1960-1990.

In the 1960s the prices fell and traded volumes only expanded moderately. In the 1970s, prices were higher and the traded volumes more than doubled. There was a dramatic shift in the world market in the first half of the 1980s. Prices fell and the trade volumes decreased. In the second half of the 1980s prices recovered and by around 1990, the traded volume nearly reached the same level as ten years previously, see Section 8.9.

The trends on the world market for agricultural products are not always closely related to general economic conditions because there are some specific factors which influence agricultural markets. The extraordinary high crop prices in the the years 1972 - 1974 were the result of harvest failures in some parts of the world, and connected with a large import demand from the Soviet Union. Apart from these erratic events, the agricultural markets were very sensitive to macroeconomic policy.

Firstly, the total demand for agricultural products is influenced by the macroeconomic policy. The US macroeconomic policy at the beginning of the 1980s, when Reagan came into power, reduced the world imports of agricultural products. Reagan, inspired by monetarist economists, wanted to fight inflation by conducting a restrictive monetary policy. At the same time, the US administration conducted an expansionary fiscal policy due to large defence expenditures and tax reductions. This policy mix led to a significant increase in interest rates around the world. Developing countries with large foreign debts were trapped by the need to finance higher interest payments. Balance of payments problems made it necessary to cut imports, including imports of agricultural products, and this reduced the world demand for agricultural products.

Secondly, the macroeconomic policies influence the exchange rates, which again have a major impact on the competitiveness of agriculture. Agricultural exports of homogenous products, such as cereals, are very sensitive to foreign exchange rate fluctuations.

During the 1960s, the USA ran into balance of payments problems, especially at the end of the decade. Given the US policy at the time, the dollar was overvalued, but because of the Bretton Woods system, the USA could not devalue. It was only when the Bretton Woods system was abandoned by the USA at the beginning of the 1970s that the dollar was devalued. The impact on the competitiveness of US cereals was clear.

While the US share of the world cereals market declined during the 1960s, it increased significantly during the 1970s.

The situation changed again in the first half of the 1980s when Reagan introduced the new macroeconomic policy in the USA, which resulted in higher interest rates. Because of the higher US interest rates, international capital flowed to the USA and created a large increase in the demand for dollars and an over-supply of other currencies. As a result, there was a sharp appreciation of the dollar, which caused a large drop in the US share of the world market for cereals. When the dollar depreciated in the second half of the 1980s, the US market share increased again.

Thirdly, the agricultural costs are influenced by the macroeconomic policy. The interest rate is important for agriculture, because it is a capital-intensive activity, which is highly indebted.

During the first half of 1980s, US farm incomes were squeezed because of the US macroeconomic policy. The turnover was low because of low world market prices and low export volumes due to the high value of the dollar. The farm costs were also high due to high interest payments.

Macroeconomic policy has a large impact on agriculture. The level of interest rates influences the world demand for agricultural products. Foreign exchange rates have a large impact on the market share of each exporter. Finally, high interest rates increase costs for farmers.

The importance of macroeconomic policy for agriculture depends on the level of integration of agriculture. Today, agriculture is much more integrated in the general economy than previously, which increases the impact of macroeconomic policy on agriculture. When the agricultural sector of a country is more internationally integrated, it will be more influenced by the agricultural policies and macroeconomic policies of other countries.

The attitudes of agriculture towards macroeconomic policy

The purpose of macroeconomic policy is to fulfil some of the economic goals of society, namely high economic growth, full employment, price stability and balance of payments equilibrium. The aim is to achieve these goals by using a mix of policy instruments, such as fiscal policy, monetary policy, exchange rate policy, wages and incomes policy, etc.

If the goal of the farmers is to obtain as high an income as possible, the optimal choice of instruments from the point of view of society at large will not be the same as the optimal choice for farmers.

Economic policy intervention

Table 12.3 illustrates how different mixes of fiscal and monetary policies influence the level of activity and the interest rate. Agriculture will be interested in higher activity, causing the income level to rise if the income elasticity for agricultural products is relatively large. On the other hand, agriculture is also interested in low real interest rates, especially if agricultural production is capital intensive.

Table 12.3: The impact of fiscal and monetary policy on activity and interest rate

Fiscal policy \ Monetary policy	Expansionary	Neutral	Restrictive
Expansionary	Activity ++ Interest rate 0	Activity + Interest rate +	Activity 0 Interest rate ++
Neutral	Activity + Interest rate −	Activity 0 Interest rate 0	Activity − Interest rate +
Restrictive	Activity 0 Interest rate − −	Activity − Interest rate −	Activity − − Interest rate 0

++ Strong increase, + moderate increase, 0 no change, − moderate decline, − − strong decline

In Western Europe and the USA today, income elasticity is around zero and farming is very capital-intensive. Therefore, farmers are interested in an expansionary monetary policy, reducing the interest rate, and they are opposed to an expansionary fiscal policy if economic activity has to be stimulated. If activity has to be reduced, farmers prefer the use of a strict fiscal policy.

As discussed in the previous section, foreign exchange rates are important for agriculture. Farmers are against overvalued currencies and favour undervalued currencies. If the real value of a currency appreciates because domestic inflation is higher than international inflation, farmers should be interested in a depreciation of the currency combined with some kind of wages and incomes policy to avoid further inflation.

Attitudes towards inflation vary between different groups of farmers. Young farmers with a high nominal debt with a fixed interest rate will gain from higher general inflation as the real value of the debt and the interest payments will fall. Older, well-established farmers without debt will not be interested in higher inflation. The same is the case for young people who want to become farmers but who have not yet acquired a farm. A higher inflation rate will be capitalized, in the sense prices for farms will go up when general inflation increases.

12.5 Summary

It is reasonable to distinguish between development policy and economic policy. Development policy includes measures aimed at promoting long-term development through structural changes. Economic policy relates to measures aimed at stabilising economic performance in the short and medium term.

In Europe and the USA, the period 1750-1914 was one in which governments intervened through development policy. Economic policy was unknown, apart from price stabilisation through trade policy.

A more comprehensive economic policy was only introduced in the 1930s, when the goal was to alleviate social distress. The true era of economic policy has been the period since 1945. The ambition has been to avoid problems before they occur through policy interventions. The goals have been to ensure economic growth, full employment, stable prices and balance of payments equilibrium.

This chapter analyses the long-term trends of three different kinds of economic policy, namely trade policy, agricultural policy and macroeconomic policy such as fiscal, monetary and exchange rate policy.

From the end of the eighteenth century up to 1875 Britain was the leading free trade nation, but there was a general trend elsewhere to move from protectionism to free trade which reached its peak in the period 1860-1875. During the period 1875-1914, there were different trends in different countries. Most countries, such as France and Germany, returned to higher tariff protection, whereas others, like Britain and Denmark, continued the free trade policy. World market prices fell due to cheaper transport, so the different trade policies effectively concerned the extent to which a country accepted the general price decline. The economic conditions differed in the different countries, so it was reasonable for different countries to choose different trade policies.

During the period 1875-1914, each country followed the same trade policy for both agriculture and industry, so there was no deliberate discrimination between the two sectors. This is in sharp contrast to the period 1945-2000, when trade in industrial products was liberalised whereas agriculture in the industrialised countries was heavily supported.

Agricultural policy, as it is known today, consists of a series of market organisations for different commodities, to which several instruments are applied. Agricultural policy was first introduced during the 1930s in Western Europe and the USA, in order to relieve the economic problems of farmers in the Great Depression. The agricultural policies of the 1930s were continued in the post-war period even though the general economic situation had changed very much to the better. It was realised that there was a farm income problem because farm incomes did not increase as much as incomes in general.

The Common Agricultural Policy, which was set up during the period 1958-1967, was considered an important element in the EC integration process. The EC conducted a high price support policy during the years 1967-1984, and the EC moved from being an agricultural net importer to an important net exporter.

The agricultural policies of the EC and the USA had some negative consequences. There was an income loss for consumers and taxpayers, which was higher than the income gain for the farmers. Price support is less efficient than income support when the transaction costs, e.g. administration costs, are disregarded.

Agricultural policy stabilised domestic market prices so that farmers were less exposed to price risks in the short run. This is not necessarily an advantage, because farmers will often specialise and invest more than they would without the support, so they will be exposed to new risks.

Agricultural policy makes the agricultural sector less dynamic. There will be less interest in new uses for traditional products, and less interest in introducing new products. When a high price for traditional products is assured, there will be less interest in product development and marketing.

Agricultural policy was one-sided from the very beginning because it focused on only one goal, namely the improvement of farm incomes. Subsequently, new social goals have arisen, namely the protection of the environment, animal welfare, the survival of rural communities and food quality and food safety.

The EC and the USA were the two big players on the world market. Their agricultural support policies meant that world market prices were lower and fluctuated more than they would have done if there had been no support.

Since the Uruguay Round of the GATT (1986-1993), the USA has focused on closer international cooperation to liberalise international trade in agricultural products. There have been some reforms since the beginning of the 1990s.

Macroeconomic policy was used during the Great Depression, but it was only in the post-war period that it became widely used. The theoretical foundation for macroeconomic stabilisation policy was provided by Keynes in 1936.

Macroeconomic policy is very important for agriculture when the sector is integrated in the general economy. The agricultural sector is especially interested in low real interest rates which reduce interest payments in a sector that has become very capital intensive. The agricultural sector is also interested in exchange rates which allow domestic farmers to compete on equal terms with foreign producers. If the macroeconomic policy is not appropriate for farmers, they will have economic difficulties which they may try to solve by demanding increased agricultural support.

The international integration of agricultural markets has increased, which means that the economic situation of farmers in one country has become more dependent on the macroeconomic and agricultural policies pursued in other countries.

13. Agriculture in the developing countries after 1950

13.1 The long-term trends in the Third World

Little development before 1950

After the Second World War, there was widespread decolonisation, and most countries in Asia and Africa became independent during the period 1945-1965.

The position of the countries that gained independence was bleak. This can be illustrated by looking at Maddison's estimates of GDP per capita in the different regions in Table 13.1.

Table 13.1: The GDP per capita in different regions in dollars[1]

	1700	1820	1870	1913	1950	2001
Western Europe	998	1204	1960	3458	4579	19256
Latin America	527	692	681	1481	2506	5811
China	600	600	530	552	439	3583
India	550	533	533	673	619	1957
Other Asia[2]	565	584	643	882	926	3998
Africa	421	420	500	637	894	1489

[1] 1990 international Geary-Khamis dollars
[2] Excluding Japan
Source: Maddison (2003)

The GDP figures, which are based on purchasing power, show that there was either no growth or very little growth in per capita incomes in Asia and Africa during the period 1700-1950. The average GDP per capita in Asia and Africa in 1950 was below the level which there had been in Western Europe in around 1700.

During the period 1700-1870, GDP per capita increased by 100 per cent in Western Europe. In the same period GDP per capita increased by

Agriculture in the developing countries after 1950

around 30 per cent in Latin America and 15-20 per cent in Other Asia and Africa, whereas there was a decline in GDP in China and India.

The period 1870-1913 was a relatively prosperous one for the developing countries, with China as an important exception. GDP per capita more than doubled in Latin America, it increased by 25 per cent in India and Africa, and by 40 per cent in Other Asia.

The increase in economic activity in Western Europe and the USA gave rise to increased demand for primary products from the developing countries. The expanding industry needed raw materials, such as textile fibres and minerals, and with increasing incomes consumers demanded tropical products, such as coffee, tea, cocoa, spices, etc. The large increase in international trade contributed to economic development in the developing countries.

During the period 1913-1950, economic development continued in Latin America, where the GDP per capita increased by two thirds. In Africa, the GDP per capita increased by one third, whereas per capita GDP fell in China and India, and stagnated in the rest of Asia.

It can be concluded that economic performance was relatively positive in the developing countries during the period 1870-1913, especially in Latin America. This economic development was based on exports of primary goods, but these exports did not give rise to industrialisation.

Bairoch has made some estimates about the history of industrialisation in the developing countries. Table 13.2 shows these figures for the Third World, including Latin America, Africa and Asia, except Japan.

Table 13.2: Manufacturing production in the Third World

	Manufacturing production index[1]	Percentage of the world total
1750	93	73.0
1830	112	60.5
1880	67	20.9
1900	60	11.0
1938	122	7.2
1953	200	6.5
1980	1323	12.0

[1] The manufacturing production in UK in 1900 = 100
Source: Bairoch (1982)

The first column shows a manufacturing production index, where 100 is equal to the manufacturing production in UK in 1900. There was a slight increase in manufacturing production from 1750 to 1830, but from 1830 to 1900, the production level halved. From 1900 to 1953 there was an increase so that by 1953 Third World manufacturing production was twice the manufacturing production in Britain in 1900. It is thus not surprising that the Third World share of world total manufacturing production has declined significantly, as shown in the second column.

Large exports of primary products, such as agricultural products, contributed significantly to industrialisation in the USA, Canada and Australia. In many developing countries in Latin America, Asia and Africa there were increasing export earnings during the period 1870-1913, but these earnings did not lead to industrialisation. Why was it so?

According to Lewis, the main reason was the high profitability of agricultural exports (Lewis, 1978). There was no economic incentive for the ruling class to industrialise. Latin America was independent, but the class of foreign traders and the class of large estate owners were neither economically nor politically interested in industrialisation. There were no entrepreneurs and it takes time to generate a class of domestic industrial entrepreneurs in countries with no industrial tradition.

In Africa and Asia, the colonial authorities opposed industrialisation, and imports of industrial products had a negative impact on the local craft industries on which industrialisation should have been based. Increased export earnings from primary exports were of limited benefit to the local population. If governments had protected domestic industries and if the increased export revenues had been invested in infrastructure and education, domestic industrialisation and internal development would have been stimulated, and the countries would have been less dependent on markets in the industrialised countries.

During the period 1913-1950, there was significant industrialisation in Latin America, which contributed to an average annual growth rate of 3.4 per cent per capita. Due to two world wars, industrial supplies from overseas were cut off, and the lack of competition from the industrialised countries gave shelter to domestic industrialisation. Interest in industrialisation also increased, because agricultural exports from Latin America fell during the Great Depression. So, it was natural for the Latin American countries to pursue a more inward looking development strategy. In the developing countries in Asia and Africa, there was no industrialisation from 1913 to 1950.

Agriculture in the developing countries after 1950

The goals adjusted during the period 1950-2000

The main idea behind economic development changed during the period 1950-2000. From 1950 to 1970, it was considered that industrialisation by means of an import substitution strategy was the best way to increase GDP per capita and modernise society. As a result, agricultural development was neglected.

The expected results were not achieved and widespread poverty continued to exist, so the focus of interest changed. The period 1970-1980 was one in which the idea of growth-with-equity entered the frame. There was increased concern about the skewed income distribution, high unemployment and the deplorable nutritional standards. Interest in agriculture increased, because most of the poverty and the attendant malnutrition were concentrated in rural areas, but the import substitution policy was continued in most developing countries.

The last period, 1980-2000, has been characterised by the idea of creating growth through policy reforms. Due to the import substitution strategy, price structures had been widely distorted in most developing countries. Macroeconomic reforms through structural adjustments were proposed and initiated. These reforms should also assist agricultural development because agriculture had been heavily taxed in the past. Other topics being discussed were food security, income generation and sustainable agriculture.

13.2 Why did the developing countries choose industrialisation?

Primary exports versus import substitutions

When the countries of Asia and Africa became independent, they had to choose a development strategy. On average, Latin America was much better off, but there were great differences between the richer countries such as Argentina, Chile, Uruguay and Venezuela on the one hand, and Paraguay, Central America and the Caribbean area on the other hand. The question was whether economic development should be based on a primary export strategy or an import substitution strategy, which had already been realised by the richer Latin American countries in the period 1913-1950. In both cases the goal would be industrialisation, but the strategy chosen differed.

The aim of the primary export strategy is to increase foreign exchange earnings which can then be invested in industrialisation. This strategy can be combined with some protection of industry. The import substitution strategy focuses on promoting domestic industrial production to substitute for imports. The import substitution strategy is associated with the infant industry argument. It is assumed that new industrial firms in the developing countries have to be protected from established competitors in the industrialised countries for an interim period. Once the new producers have survived the initial stage and built up strength, the protection should be removed. The primary export strategy focuses on the primary sector, but it can be combined with industrialisation. The import substitution strategy focuses on industry, but theoretically it can be associated with agricultural development.

After the Second World War, nearly all the developing countries focused on industrialisation as the road to development. The import substitution strategy was chosen, and it was practised in such a way that agriculture was neglected.

The choice of the import substitution strategy, combined with neglect of the agricultural sector, reflected the prevailing economic and political thinking. According to leading economists in the new discipline of development economics, development was to be achieved by industrialisation based on protection. This was the case especially in the 1950s, but also in the 1960s. There were three works of economic analysis which laid the foundations for this philosophy.

Labour supply

Lewis published an article about the unlimited supply of labour in agriculture (Lewis, 1954). His idea was that the surplus labour should be taken out of agriculture by industrialisation, which should be the driving force of economic development. Most interpretations of the Lewis model assumed that it would not be necessary to modernise the traditional agricultural sector. It was not necessary to allocate resources for the development of the agricultural sector, so agriculture could be left to itself.

This interpretation does not take into consideration two important points. Firstly, it is not possible to transfer labour from agriculture if labour productivity in agriculture is stagnant. Technological and institutional changes, combined with investments, are necessary to improve agricultural productivity and avoid a fall in agricultural output. Agricultural exports will fall or agricultural imports will increase, if resources are not allocated to agricultural development. Secondly, the success of industrialisation depends on selling the industrial output. The problem is that the large agricultural sector will not be able to buy industrial products as long as the peasants' incomes do not increase.

Linkages

Hirshman wrote about the strategy of development (Hirshman 1958), focusing on the forward and backward linkages between different economic activities. His idea was that activities which have stronger linkages should be stimulated. By increasing activity in sectors where forward and backward linkages to other sectors are strong, there would be a larger derived increase in activity than where the linkages are weak. Hirshman concluded that it was not a good idea to choose a strategy based on agricultural development because, according to him, the linkages between agriculture and the other sectors are weak.

Hirshman's analysis suffered from some weaknesses. Firstly, it was based on the economic conditions of the time. Agriculture was based on the one hand on subsistence farming, and on the other hand on export crops produced on large plantations which did not have strong linkages to the urban sector. The countries had dual economies with weak relationships between a traditional agricultural sector and a more modern urban sector, which often had closer links to the western world than to the rural hinterland. At the time, the linkages between the rural and urban sectors were weak, but this did not necessarily reflect the future possibilities. The experiences of the western world have shown that there were important backward and forward linkages between the rural and urban sectors as development proceeded. Agricultural development also stimulated non-agricultural development in rural areas.

Secondly, Hirshman focused on backward and forward linkages, and more or less ignored income linkages. When a very large sector such as agriculture develops, incomes will increase and the demand for industrial products will be stimulated.

The terms of trade

Finally, the writings of Prebisch and Singer gave rise to the Prebisch-Singer hypothesis about the long-term deterioration of the terms of trade for primary products vis-à-vis industrial products (Prebisch, 1950; Singer, 1950). Prebisch and Singer found that the terms of trade for primary products had deteriorated in the past, and they expected them to continue to deteriorate.

Why did the developing countries choose industrialisation?

According to Prebisch and Singer, there was an important structural difference between industrial countries and developing countries. In industrial countries there were trade unions that were able to increase wage levels when productivity increased, and this kept up industrial prices. In developing countries there were no trade unions, so the workers were unable to increase wage levels when productivity increased. In the monopolistic sectors, such as the mining sector which had few producers, the producers were able to set prices at a level where they could earn higher profits from the productivity gains. In the agricultural sector, with more producers and more competition, productivity gains caused a decline in commodity prices, which was beneficial to the consumers. Because of the deterioration in the terms of trade for agricultural products, the argument was that developing countries should substitute domestic industrial production for industrial imports.

There has been much debate about whether the terms of trade for primary products have deteriorated in the long term. When the prices for primary products imported to industrialised countries include costs, insurance and freight (price c.i.f.) and the export products only include costs (price f.o.b.), it is to be expected that the terms of trade will deteriorate because transport costs have fallen significantly. If the quality of industrial products improves over time, while primary products keep the same quality because they are homogenous products, one would expect a fall in the terms of trade. Over the last 100 years, the quality of a car has improved far more than the quality of wheat, so the price increase for a car has been much greater than for wheat. The figures used for the calculation of terms of trade should eliminate the effects of falling transport costs and the different trends in quality.

Terms of trade analyses show different trends, depending on the period chosen, and they also show different trends for different primary products, such as food products, textile fibres and metals. Price trends have differed, even for different food products, such as cereals, meat products, fruit and vegetables.

Even if there has been a slight deterioration in the terms of trade, this is not an argument for not continuing to export primary products. Productivity may have increased so much that it more than compensates for the fall in real prices. If so, producers would earn an increasing real income. Deteriorating terms of trade for some agricultural products is not an argument for focusing solely on industrialisation and neglecting agriculture. It is an argument for developing new productions, including new agricultural products and industrial products.

The problem with the above mentioned three economic studies is that, firstly, they contributed to the idea that agriculture was a reservoir of labour, capital, and food supplies, which could be tapped for industrialisation. Secondly, they contributed to the idea that modernisation of agriculture was not necessary, and, thirdly to the acceptance of the neglect of agriculture because the sector was declining naturally as in the case of industrialised countries.

The Soviet Union as a model

Political attitudes were also inimical to agriculture. The new political leaders in the developing countries had been marked by the colonial period and the struggle for independence. They were against capitalism and in most cases in favour of socialism. They turned to the Soviet Union as a model for development. During the 1950s, industrialisation in the Soviet Union seemed to be a great success, seen from the outside. As shown in Section 7.6, Soviet industrialisation was based on squeezing resources out of agriculture through fixing terms of trade between the agricultural and industrial sectors which were unfavourable to agriculture.

13.3 Was it wise to focus on industrialisation?

After the Second World War, the developing countries were open economies

During the period 1870-1914 there were increasing exports of agricultural products from the developing countries. Many of the tropical products exported had high income elasticity at the time. Latin America, which was independent, benefited from exports, whereas the countries under colonial rule in Africa and Asia did not benefit or did so only modestly. The colonial powers allowed free imports of manufactured goods, so there was de-industrialisation in the Third World in the period 1830-1900 (Bairoch, 1982).

In many developing countries in the period 1870-1914, the development of large plantations and large farms selling cash crops contributed to the neglect of the food producing sector, consisting of a great number of subsistence farmers.

The period 1914-1950 was difficult for the developing countries that exported primary products to the industrialised countries, due to the two world wars and the Great Depression.

Was it wise to focus on industrialisation?

After the Second World War, exports of primary products from the developing countries started again. The prospects for many tropical products such as coffee, tea, cocoa etc., were not as good as previously because the income elasticities for these products had declined in the industrial countries. Natural fibres were replaced by synthetic materials. There was no food-producing sector to fill the gap because the subsistence farming sector had been neglected. It would have been possible to stimulate subsistence farming and generate economic development, based on a surplus of food products, which could have financed industrial development, as had been the case in Western Europe 200 years before. This strategy was not followed because the agricultural sector was not considered capable of providing economic development quickly enough. Instead it was decided to develop industry through an import substitution strategy.

The experience of industrialisation in Europe and the USA did not contra-indicate protection. Industrialisation in Britain started in a closed economy and when it spread to other countries, such as Belgium and France, the high transport costs constituted a high level of protection. When Germany and the USA industrialised, they were potentially exposed to competition from Britain, but this was avoided by the transport costs and industrial trade protection, which was especially high in the case of the USA.

When the developing countries started their economic development after the Second World War, natural barriers in form of transport costs were much lower and the industrial sector was highly developed in the industrial countries. So it was natural for the developing countries to want to support their developing industries. The problem was not the support for industry, but the lack of support for the agricultural sector. In the developing countries there was disconnection between the urban and rural sectors, so that a dual economy was formed. The developing countries did not achieve the interrelationship between the two sectors which had been the experience in Europe and the USA, and which mutually stimulated economic development.

The lack of relations between the rural and urban sectors is also problematic in the longer term, when industry has to survive without support. Experience shows that an industry has difficulty in competing if it does not have a strong position in its home market. A move from import substitution to exporting is only possible when the industry expands on its home market, and such an expansion is difficult if a large part of the population engaged in agriculture does not have sufficient income to buy industrial products.

Agriculture in the developing countries after 1950

Are historical experiences relevant?

Economic development in agriculture in Western Europe started in societies with virtually no international trade. When the developing countries became independent, they chose an industrialisation strategy based on import substitution. Was it wrong not to follow the experience of Western Europe? This raises the question of the relevance of historical precedents.

Past experiences take place at given times and under given conditions. When these conditions change, it is clear that historical precedents should not be followed without considering how they should be modified to take account of the new conditions. The conditions for the developing countries after the Second World War differed from the conditions in Western Europe when economic development started in around 1750. On the other hand, when deciding on a development strategy, it would be unwise to neglect the lessons of the past which remain valid.

The demographic situations were very different. In around 1750, Western European countries were thinly populated when the population started to increase at a higher rate. In 1950, the developing countries were densely populated and the population continued to grow at a high rate. According to estimates of labour productivity in agriculture, productivity in Britain in 1810 was three times the level in Asia and Africa in the 1960s. In France, the level in 1810 was 40 per cent above the level in Asia and Africa in 1960s (Bairoch, 1975).

The need for productivity increases in the developing countries was immense. Because of the high population level, labour resources were available. The scope for putting new land under cultivation in Western Europe in 1750 was greater than in most developing countries in 1950. However, in the developing countries investments in irrigation could facilitate the move from annual cropping to multi-cropping, with a second or even third harvest per year instead of just one.

Both the high population density and the low productivity were arguments in favour of focusing on agriculture if poverty was to be alleviated.

It has been argued that in 1950 the developing countries were in a better position than Western Europe had been in 1750. The technological possibilities in 1950 were far above those in 1750, and the developing countries could start development at a much higher technological level. However, the high technological level could be considered a blessing in disguise.

Was it wise to focus on industrialisation?

Industrialisation had become more complicated in the developing countries than in early industrialised Western Europe. The new domestic industry had to compete with the efficient production of the industrialised countries, and natural protection in the form of high transport costs no longer existed.

Industrialisation had also become more difficult because the necessary capital per worker in most industries was high. In Britain the capital required per worker in 1750 was much lower than the capital required per worker in 1950 when industrialisation started in the developing countries. Due to technological developments and large economies of size, the investment required for competitive industries in the developing countries was higher and the employment effect was lower than previously.

Because of the more advanced technology, the greater need of capital and the stronger external competition, it was more difficult to emerge as an entrepreneur or industrialist from the class of the working people.

It can be concluded that there was a great need for agricultural development to create employment and increase productivity. It can also be concluded that there were a number of things that handicapped industrialisation, such as the lack of skilled labour, lack of capital and lack of entrepreneurs. The problem was not so much the attempt to industrialise through import substitution, as the neglect of the agricultural sector. The problem was that there was not simultaneous development of agriculture and industry. The experience of the western world showed the importance of the interrelationships between the two sectors. Such a strategy needs investment in infrastructure and education, and the establishment of distribution channels. During the colonial era there had been a dual economy with a small and relatively advanced urban sector and a large traditional rural sector. This dual economy structure was continued because of the industrialisation in the main cities, the neglect of agriculture and the failure to bind the two sectors together.

One important consequence of the dual economy was the large migration of people from rural areas to urban areas, which created problems in both areas.

Migration from rural to urban areas

When agriculture shifted from the short fallow cultivation system to the annual cropping system, as in Northwest Europe, a bigger workforce was needed for this investment, the more intensive production demanded a bigger workforce, and the bigger workforce had to work more. The workforce would work more regularly, as the livestock production increased in importance, and more efficiently, and labour productivity would increase. The increased agricultural supply reduced the risk of famine and it increased interest in a division of labour. When the workload increased, when the risk of famine was reduced and when the population increased, there would, for example, be an incentive for households to give up cloth making and let others specialise in textile production. There could also be people responsible for education and communication, which raised the level of knowledge in agriculture.

The shift from short fallow to annual cropping demanded more labour. This transition could be a period of considerable political and social tension because people in rural areas did not want to work harder unless they had a long-term interest in the improvements. To implement the new farming technique, it was important to combine it with institutional reforms which gave the peasants an interest in working harder. Even if the institutional changes were unsatisfactory for the peasants, they could not avoid accepting the new farming techniques when these were wanted by the landlords. Prior to industrialisation, there would be no incentive to move to the cities.

In the developing countries after the Second World War the situation was very different. There were no agricultural reforms to induce agricultural workers to stay in the countryside. Industrialisation tempted people to migrate to the urban areas to find jobs. However, the urban areas were not able to absorb all the migrants into the employed labour force, so a double problem arose, one in the urban areas and the other in the rural areas. Urbanisation created a need for major infrastructural investments, but the migrants from the rural areas, who were unemployed, did not contribute to urban development. In the rural areas, the necessary agricultural changes could not be undertaken because the workforce necessary to do the work had left for the cities.

Because of insufficient supplies, food prices rose, causing problems in the urban areas. The solution to the lack of domestic food supplies and higher prices was to open up for imports. Increased imports and lower prices were a further disincentive to undertake agricultural improvements and the flight from the countryside continued.

The only way to stop this vicious circle was to stop migration from rural to urban areas. The labour force should be kept in the rural areas to participate in agricultural development.

13.4 Production structures and patterns

No comprehensive agricultural reforms

When the developing countries in Africa and Asia became independent after the Second World War, there were agricultural reforms in the countries that turned to socialism, such as China, but these experiences were not successful. There were agricultural reforms of a kind in a few non-socialist countries, but in most countries the old production methods, the legal rights of the peasants, and the ownership of the land remained unchanged. In India, for example, there were no reforms, so the large estate owners continued to own a large part of the arable land and the caste system continued. Latin America was known as a continent with skewed land distribution, and this continued after the Second World War. There is no doubt that the right agricultural reforms would have contributed to agricultural development.

The production pattern

In developing countries there is often competition between the production of tropical crops for export and food production for local consumption. The tropical crops for export are produced in plantations owned by rich people. The labour force is hired, and the jobs on the plantations will often be more popular than work on farms producing food for domestic consumption. The work will not always be as hard, and the payment is considered reasonable compared to what can be obtained from domestic food production. So subsistence peasants produce only for household consumption and they work as wage earners on the plantations.

When the plantation sector plays a major role, there will not be agricultural development in the subsistence sector. In the longer term, earnings in the plantation sector often deteriorate because of falling real prices for the export crops.

The development of the subsistence sector is necessary in the long term, even though it its resource-demanding. There are several obstacles which make it easier to rely on plantation production.

To move from subsistence farming to commercial farming requires a change of mind-set by farmers. This change of mind-set is difficult in itself, and the obstacles are greater when markets are inefficient or non-existent.

Increased use of high yielding seed varieties combined with commercial fertilisers and investment in irrigation systems will increase productivity, but this strategy will only be possible if the necessary investments are made to establish markets and the necessary economic environment.

Finally, pricing and taxation policies matter. Output prices should be sufficiently high and input prices should be sufficiently low so that there are economic incentives for the peasants to use more modern production techniques.

Although it may be easier to promote the development of the plantation sector in the short term, a broader development strategy based on the food sector will be advisable. It will alleviate poverty and create more development in the longer term.

When the developing countries become wealthier there is a general shift in diet from plant products to livestock products. If the food sector is not already reasonably well developed, there will be pressure to establish larger livestock production units near the big cities to satisfy this demand. This will hamper the future development of the food sector which is already lagging behind.

Resource endowment, size structure and technology

Since the days of Ricardo, economists have distinguished between two ways of increasing agricultural production. Increased demand can be satisfied either by extending the area under cultivation or by intensifying production on a given land area.

The resource endowment is assumed to have an influence on the size structure of farms and the technology used. If a country has a large land area and a small population, agricultural production can be increased by extending the area under cultivation. Machinery will be used on large farms. If a country has a small land area and a large population, the farm size will be small and the land will be cultivated intensively. Higher yields are obtained by improving variable inputs (better seed, regular water supply) and by using new variable inputs (chemical fertilisers, pesticides).

If the sharp distinction between bringing new land under cultivation and improving crop yields per hectare is abandoned, the distinction between land-saving and labour-saving technology becomes less clear. The land area is considered as fixed and it can be cultivated more or less intensively depending on the needs, according to the thinking of Boserup (1965).

In the industrialised countries, the food demand has increased slowly because the population has increased slowly and the income elasticity is close to zero. Adjustments, including a reduction in the labour force, can be made in several ways. Firstly, labour can be replaced by machinery. Secondly, chemical fertilizers can be substituted for labour-intensive methods of fertilisation. Weeding by the use of chemicals can be substituted for labour-intensive methods. Thirdly, the use of chemical fertilizers on better quality land can be increased while the cultivation of poorer quality land is abandoned. Adjustments can take place either through the increased use of machinery or the increased use of chemicals.

In the developing countries there has been a large increase in the demand for food. Production can be increased by a more intensive use of resources. Agriculture can move from annual cropping to multi-cropping. Two or even three crops can be harvested per year.

Increased production can also be obtained by the increased use of industrial inputs, either by increased mechanisation or by increased use of chemical inputs. Most likely mechanisation and the use of chemical inputs will both increase. When an additional crop is grown, the use of chemical fertilizers has to be increased to avoid depleting the nutrients in the soil. Natural precipitation may not allow the cultivation of an extra crop so water has to be provided, for example through mechanised water pumps. An extra crop demands extra treatment of the land before sowing and after harvesting. This cannot be done by the available labour force, so small-scale tractors, adjusted to the small farm scale, have to be bought.

Even in densely populated areas, the full productive potential of the agricultural sector can only be exploited by the use of tractors. Land improvements may be difficult without tractors. Tractors make pasturage for draught animals superfluous, so the old pastures can be used as arable land. The use of tractors makes it possible to sow in time and to harvest quickly, when the time is right. By timely sowing and harvesting, the harvest can be increased. Finally, the use of tractors facilitates multiple cropping.

So in densely populated areas, multiple cropping is made possible by the increased use of both mechanisation and chemical inputs.

13.5 The importance of prices

The supply response and the farming system

How farmers respond to price changes depends on the kind of farming they do. If the farming sector consists of large plantations or large-scale commercialised farms, higher prices induce the owners to increase production. A production increase will only be possible if more land is bought and new investments are made, so the owners may want to enlarge their enterprises.

In Latin America and in many African countries, the agricultural structure is bimodal because there are two different kinds of farming. On the one hand there is a commercial sector consisting of plantations and large-scale farms, and on the other side there is a subsistence sector, made up of numerous smallholders. If there is a price increase, there is a risk that subsistence farmers will be squeezed out because the large farmers will want to acquire more land. In this case, the land distribution will become more skewed.

In the subsistence sector a price increase does not ensure increased supply. Subsistence farmers consume most of their production in their own households and a surplus is only sold to acquire income for buying other necessities. When agricultural prices increase, farmers can acquire the income required for buying their necessities by selling a smaller volume of agricultural products, so farmers may respond by working less. The lower production level does not reduce the farmer's consumption, because only a smaller volume needs to be sold, due to the higher prices. Another response might be to maintain the farm production level and increase the household consumption of own products, which will be possible because a smaller volume needs to be sold.

A price increase, as such, is not sufficient to induce subsistence farmers to become commercialised if it is too risky to depend on the market. General productivity has to be increased so the risk of famine is more or less eliminated in the event of a bad harvest. Only then will farmers be more interested in commercialisation.

The supply response depends on price and non-price factors

The extent to which agricultural productivity can be increased and interest in commercialisation can be realised depends on the existence of markets and the economic environment. The availability of infrastructure, inputs, innovations, information and institutions determines the structural conditions for the farming sector. These non-price factors have an important impact on agricultural supply.

When the population in the developing countries increases, it is important to support agricultural development to increase supply. What is the best strategy for increasing the agricultural supply? Should the price level be increased or should the structural conditions be improved?

Figure 13.1 shows different cases. When markets and the necessary economic environment are inadequate, there is no scope for commercialisation. In this case, a price increase will have no impact on supply. This is illustrated in Figure 13.1a, where the supply curve S_1 is assumed to be vertical, which means that the supply does not respond to price changes. When structural changes are made, the supply curve will move to S_2, so that supply will only increase if investments are made to improve the markets and the economic environment.

Figure 13.1 Supply response from price and from non-price factors

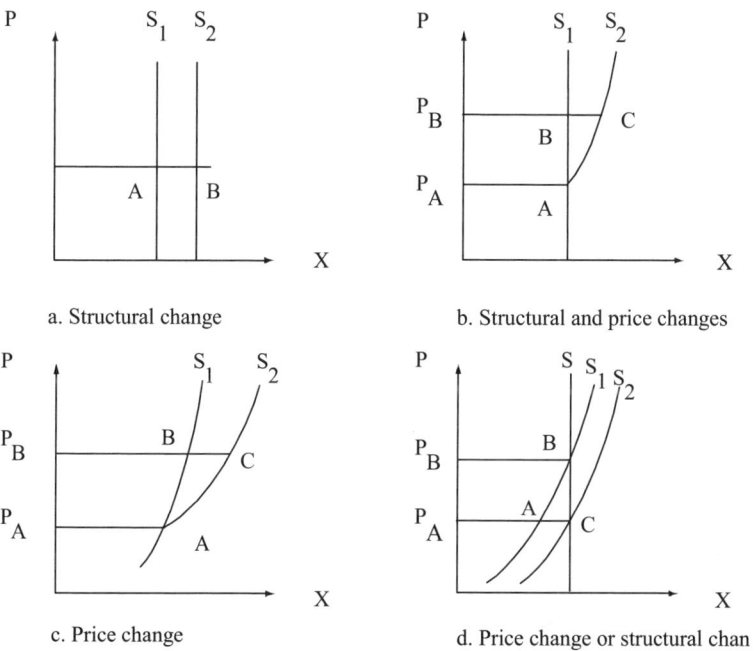

a. Structural change

b. Structural and price changes

c. Price change

d. Price change or structural chan

In Figure 13.1b, it is assumed that a supply increase from A to C can only be obtained by a combination of structural change and a price increase. Market improvements are necessary, but at the same time there must be some private investment on the farms. To stimulate this investment, it is necessary to increase the price level.

Figure 13.1c shows the situation where a price increase from P_A to P_B is sufficient to increase supply from A to C in the long term. In the short term, the supply will follow curve S_1 and the price increase will induce a supply increase from A to B. Farmers will get higher incomes, which are needed to finance the investments to increase long-term supply, as shown by curve S_2.

In Figure 13.1d, the initial price is P_A and the supply is A. The government wants to increase supply, so the new supply is equal to the level indicated by the vertical line S. The supply S_1 is the supply curve under some given structural conditions, whereas S_2 is the supply curve when these conditions are improved by public investments creating better markets and a better economic environment. Now it is clear that the supply increase to level S can be obtained either by a price increase but without public investment to improve the structural conditions, or by investment to improve the structural conditions but without a price increase.

In the country there are initially free imports and the world market price is P_A. If an import duty is imposed, the price level will be P_B, which is the price necessary to induce the farmers to increase supply. If the government wants the consumer price to stay at the initial level P_A, it has to pay consumer subsidies equal to $S \cdot (P_B - P_A)$.

The alternative solution is to invest in market improvements. It is possible to calculate which of the two solutions is the better. If the higher producer price P_B does not stimulate agricultural development to move S_1 to the right, the government will have annual expenses associated with consumer subsidies. The cost of investment in market improvements may be more than the annual consumer subsidies, but it is a one-off payment which may also create the conditions for further agricultural development.

Price matters

There is no doubt that the price level for agricultural products plays an important role in the development process. When economic development began in around 1750 with agricultural improvements, price increases due to the population increase were a major factor. The population increase and the higher prices made it more profitable to introduce new farming techniques to increase productivity, and interest was stimulated in institutional changes which could also increase productivity.

The agricultural development took place in closed economies, where increased demand induced an increase in the domestic supply of agricultural products. The structure of agricultural holdings determined who benefited from the price and production increases. Land ownership had a crucial impact on the economic and social development of a country.

The economic conditions in the developing countries in 1950 were totally different from the economic conditions in Europe in 1750. The population increase in the developing countries did not induce agricultural development because agriculture was exposed to competition from the industrialised countries. Agricultural products could be transported over long distances at low cost, so domestic agricultural development was not protected by high natural barriers.

There were important differences in agricultural productivity in different parts of Europe in around 1750, but they were very small compared to the huge differences in productivity between the industrialised and the developing countries in the period after the Second World War (Bairoch, 1975).

The large productivity increases in the industrialised countries since 1950 have caused a decline in the real world market prices for agricultural products from the temperate zone. This decline has been reinforced by the agricultural support policy which was intended to solve the farm income problem. When there is strong economic development without a high population increase, it seems to be a general problem for farmers to increase their earnings in line with average incomes. This is not only the experience of the older industrialised countries, but also of the newly industrialised countries such as South Korea and Taiwan.

Agriculture in the developing countries has been exposed to some negative external factors. Agricultural products from the temperate zone have been supplied on the world market at low and declining real prices. In addition, agriculture has been exposed to the negative internal factor of government interest in low food prices for urban populations. Governments are interested in political stability, which is why they have listened more to the urban interests than to farmers who argue for higher food prices.

It is clear that the low-price policy for agricultural products has not stimulated increased supply in the short term, nor interest in increasing supply in the long term through investments to increase productivity.

13.6 Macroeconomic policies in the developing countries

Agricultural development in Europe and the USA in 1750-1914 was very much left to market forces. Public interventions were connected with the establishment of markets and the institutional environment. When there were price interventions, it was in the form of trade policy. Macroeconomic policy, as it is known today, did not exist.

Agriculture in the developing countries after 1950

The situation in the developing countries after 1950 was very different. From 1950 to the beginning of the 1980s, most of the countries followed an inward-looking strategy based on import substitution. Some poor countries had to rely on exports of primary products, and some countries, such as South Korea, Taiwan, Hong Kong and Singapore shifted at an early stage, around 1960, to a strategy based on the export of manufactured goods.

The import substitution strategy involved severe discrimination against agriculture, because the relative prices between agriculture and industry were highly distorted against agriculture. Table 13.3 shows the nominal rate of protection in 18 developing countries in the period 1960-1984 (Schiff and Valdes, 1992). The nominal rate of protection shows the extent to which domestic prices deviated from world market prices.

Exported agricultural products (food products and agricultural raw materials for industrial processing) were directly taxed, in the sense that farmers got a price for their exports which was 16.5 per cent below the world market price level. On the other hand, imports, which were often food products, were protected by an average of 18.6 per cent of the price. This meant that there was a distortion of 35.1 per cent between the price levels of exported and imported agricultural products. If the exported and imported products are taken together, there was a net taxation of 7.9 per cent. In using the world market price level as a benchmark, it should not be forgotten that world market prices were already depressed by the dumping of surpluses from the industrialised countries, as a result of their agricultural policies.

The direct taxation of agricultural products, however, was less than the indirect taxation of the agricultural sector. 'Indirect taxation' refers to the fall in the prices of agricultural products compared with the prices for non-agricultural products, due to trade protection for industrial products and overvalued exchange rates.

When the industrial sector is protected, inputs such as fertilisers, and capital goods such as implements, installations and machinery, are more expensive than they would otherwise be. It is the same with consumer goods. Protection of the industrial sector, which has been the preferred policy of the developing countries, has amounted to taxation of the agricultural sector.

In addition, an overvalued exchange rate has hurt the sectors trading with the outside world. The home market sector, which does not compete with goods and services from abroad, is comparatively favoured by the overvalued exchange rate. Many developing countries have had overvalued exchange rates.

Table 13.3: *Direct, indirect and total nominal rate of protection for 18 developing countries, 1960-1984*[1]

Direct price intervention in agriculture	
Protection of export products	- 16.5 pct
Protection of import products	+ 18.6 pct
Protection for all agricultural products	- 7.9 pct
Indirect price intervention in agriculture	
Indirect protection due to overvalued foreign exchange rate and protection of the industrial sector	- 22.5 pct
Total direct and indirect protection in agriculture	- 30.3 pct

[1] Sample average where plus indicates protection and minus indicates taxation
Source: Schiff and Valdes, 1992

There are several reasons why foreign exchange rates were overvalued. Firstly, industrial protection reduces imports. Lower imports cause lower demand for foreign currencies, so the domestic currency is stronger when industry is protected. Industrial protection causes a real appreciation of the foreign exchange rate. Secondly, many developing countries had import surpluses, which meant that their currencies were overvalued, unless the import surpluses could be financed by foreign aid of one kind or another. Thirdly, the inflation rate has been much higher in developing countries than in industrialised countries, and the nominal exchange rate has not generally been adjusted to the higher inflation rate, which has caused the real exchange rate to revalue.

Table 13.3 shows that, in relation to non-agricultural prices, agricultural prices would have been around one third higher if the policy had been neutral vis-à-vis agriculture.

A distorted system has developed disfavouring the agricultural sector. Sometimes governments have deliberately discriminated against the agricultural sector to obtain low food prices to favour the urban poor and avoid social unrest. At other times it has been the unintended result of the import substitution strategy.

Because of the development of this highly distorted price system, a counter movement for structural adjustment began in the early 1980s. The structural adjustment theory emphasises the importance of correct pricing. Market forces should be allowed to work more freely. Prices are important signals, showing up scarcities and surpluses. Prices are important incentives for consumers and producers. As a result, import protection has been reduced and in most cases this has been combined with currency devaluation.

13.7 Summary

There was significant economic development in Europe and the USA during the period 1700-1870. In the rest of the world there was stagnation or only a slight rise in the living standard, apart from China where the GDP per capita declined.

During the period 1870-1950, economic development continued at a higher rate in Europe and the USA than in the period 1700-1870. There was also important economic development in Latin America and Japan, but these regions were exceptions in the Third World. The GDP per capita continued to decline in China, it increased only marginally in India, and in spite of some economic development in the rest of Asia and Africa, these regions lagged behind Latin America and Japan.

In around 1950, when the decolonisation started, the GDP per capita in Africa and Asia, apart from Japan, was either lower or similar to the GDP per capita in Western Europe in 1700.

It has been demonstrated in this book that the agricultural sector played a major role in economic development in Europe and the USA during the period 1700-1914. It might have been expected that the developing countries would have copied this development pattern, but this has not been the case.

Nearly all the developing countries have followed the import substitution strategy, which means that industrialisation was promoted by protection. Agriculture was considered as a reservoir from which resources could be drawn, so agricultural development was neglected. Why was it so, and was the chosen strategy successful?

Development economics was a new discipline which only became important after the Second World War when the former colonies became independent and had to choose a development strategy. To begin with, mainstream development economics was dominated by three pieces of work written by Lewis, Hirshman, and Prebisch and Singer.

Lewis wrote about the unlimited supply in the agricultural sector. This led to the view that, if industrialisation were promoted, it would create employment opportunities for the labour force which was abundant in the agricultural sector. Marginal labour productivity in agriculture was zero, so agriculture would not decline, even if its development were neglected.

Summary

Hirshman focused on linkages as a criterion for development strategy. The sectors which had strong forward and backward linkages should be supported. Hirshman believed that the forward and backward linkages in some industries were much stronger than in agriculture.

Prebisch and Singer argued that, in the long term, the terms of trade for primary products, including agricultural products, would decline compared with industrial products. Therefore it would be better for developing countries to produce industrial products which they had hitherto imported, rather than expand the production of primary products.

There were also some important ideological reasons for choosing an import substitution model and neglecting the agricultural sector in the development process. The countries which had newly gained independence were often opposed to the capitalist system, and preferred a socialist system in one form or another. Many of them looked to the Soviet Union as a model, because the Soviet economic performance had seemingly been successful during the 1930s, during the war and in the 1950s. The Soviet model was based on industrialisation in a closed economy, where resources were squeezed out of agriculture through unfavourable terms of trade.

Was the development strategy in the developing countries successful? The answer is clearly "No", and that led to new strategies. In the 1970s more attention was paid to the question about growth with equity, and in the 1980s structural adjustment reforms began to be introduced.

The problem was not that industry was supported through protection, but that the macroeconomic policy disfavoured agriculture. After all, the experience of the western world was of economic development starting in closed economies. The problem was that agricultural development was neglected. There were no productivity increases in agriculture which could have increased income levels in the rural areas. Higher incomes in the rural sector would have created a market for industrial products, and would have encouraged people not to move to the big cities looking for employment. Agricultural development would have stimulated integration between the urban and the rural sectors. Instead, the countries became dual economies with a relatively highly developed urban sector, with weak linkages to the stagnant rural sector.

What should have been done? It would have been important to introduce some agricultural reforms. This should have been done gradually, in a way which opened up for co-operation and self-organisation. The size distribution of land holdings is very important for the development path which each country takes. In countries with a bimodal structure, where one sector consists of large commercialised farms or plantations, and the other sector consists of small subsistence farms, there is a clear risk that food production in the subsistence sector will be neglected.

Increased productivity in the subsistence farming sector should be an important goal. This can only be achieved by technological and institutional changes. Total annual production can be increased by higher yields per harvest and by more harvests per year. New inputs, such as high-yielding seed varieties, fertilisers and pesticides, together with well-functioning irrigation systems, will increase productivity. The workload will increase, so it will also be necessary to mechanise to some extent. Small tractors may be very useful for overcoming seasonal bottlenecks.

There will only be technological improvements if the institutional environment is satisfactory. Inputs have to be available at reasonable prices, it should be possible to finance investments at reasonable interest rates, and there should be access to markets where the peasants can sell their products at profitable prices.

Agricultural development will only make progress if there are improvements in the infrastructure, commercial distribution channels, education, extension services, research, and credit facilities. The pricing policy and macroeconomic policy of the government are also important parts of the institutional set-up.

Export taxes, which lower domestic farm-gate prices, will not induce peasants to increase production levels through investment. The macroeconomic policy of a society influences activity, inflation and foreign exchange rates. All these elements have an important impact on the farm economy because they influence farm-gate prices, agricultural input prices, industrial consumer prices, and the interest rate borrowers have to pay. Macroeconomic policy matters not only for commercialised farmers, but also for subsistence farmers, who may be induced to shift to more commercialised farming if the policy leads to profitable opportunities.

14. The lessons of history

14.1 Different methods of analysis

The purpose of economic research is to acquire an understanding of economic relationships and processes. Such understanding can be acquired either by using the deductive method or the inductive method. When the deductive method is used, the analysis ends up with a general conclusion which is then applied to specific cases. The inductive method is based on one or a few specific cases, and the conclusions of the analysis are then applied generally.

In general economics, the deductive method is widely used. A set of assumptions is postulated, and by the use of logic and mathematics, a conclusion is drawn. Mathematical economics is a branch which only uses the deductive method. In econometrics, the task is to estimate the relationships between different economic variables, where empirical data is available, so the inductive method is used in econometrics. The same is the case when economic history is used as a way of reaching an understanding of social and economic relationships. By analysing specific cases, one tries to reach more general conclusions about causes and effects.

An example can illustrate how a given economic question can be analysed by these different methods. The question whether free trade or protectionism is to be preferred, has always interested economists. Ricardo first formulated the theory of comparative advantage based on differences in productivity in 1817. This theory is a good example of the use of the deductive method. A series of assumptions is introduced, and by the use of simple logic or simple mathematics, it can be proved that free trade is better than protectionism.

An econometric study could consist of a comparative study of different countries, where an indicator of the level of protection is correlated with the growth rate per capita. If low protection is associated with high growth, one would tend to conclude that free trade is better than protectionism.

List was a leading German economist, associated with the historical school, who did not believe in the deductive method. The historical school focused on the different conditions in different countries at a given time, and they feared that the use of the deductive method could lead to wrong conclusions being drawn. List developed the 'infant industry' argument in favour of the protection of an industry for an initial period. When his book was published in 1840, Britain was far more industrialised than the German area, and List believed it would be necessary to protect German industry against British industry, until it was sufficiently developed for competition to be on equal terms. What was good for Britain was not necessarily good for other countries, because the conditions differed between countries.

The three types of analysis, deductive analysis, econometric analysis and historical analysis, have their individual strengths and weaknesses. Deductive analysis is a rigorous analysis, where the assumptions are precise. The problem is that in the real world most of the assumptions are not fulfilled. Econometrics deals with the real world in the sense that it uses empirical data in the analysis. When conclusions are drawn, it is assumed that everything else stays the same, apart from the variables involved in the analysis. This is very seldom the case. Economic history involves a variety of elements in the analysis of economic performance. It is difficult to draw clear conclusions, because of the complexity of the analysis and the difficulty of measuring some of the important factors. However, the philosophy behind the historical school is very useful, because it appeals to cautiousness when drawing conclusions. Economic history teaches us that the economic conditions at any given moment are different in different countries, and that the economic environment changes fundamentally through time. Therefore, it is possible to learn from history, but one should be very careful not to ignore the conditions which make it difficult to postulate simple general economic laws.

The different approaches to obtaining a better understanding of economics each have their advantages and disadvantages. That is why it is important to apply all the different methods. One should not be excluded in favour of another. The different kinds of analysis should be considered as supplementary ways of acquiring knowledge.

The analysis of the past is relevant for three reasons. Firstly, economic history is important because it tells us how our present society has developed. It is enriching to know how the present conditions are rooted in the past. Secondly, economic history contributes to increased insight into the development process. When looking at the past, it is possible to learn more about the forces determining economic events. Thirdly, the lessons of the past can be useful today when developing countries have to choose development strategies. The conditions of today's developing

Agricultural development

countries differ, so one should be careful to take these differences into consideration.

14.2 General economic trends

This book is divided into three parts. The first part, *Chapters 1 and 2*, deals with the economic trends of the past. The analysis shows that some interesting changes started to occur in around 1750. The first change was the growth in population. From around 1750 there was a significant increase in the population growth rate. This trend affected not only the western world, but nearly everywhere. The second trend was an increase in the growth rate per capita. However, this trend only occurred in the western world, and not in the rest of the world. From around 1750 there was divergent development in the western world and the other parts of the world.

Economic development is associated with economic integration, which leads to increased trade. Trade between different regions within countries and international trade between countries increased significantly. However, on the basis of estimates, it can be concluded that only one per cent of the gross domestic product in the world was traded internationally in 1820. Development started in closed economies with very little international trade.

Economic development did not start suddenly. During the period 1500 - 1750, there was economic development, but it was very slow compared with the development which started in around 1750 and accelerated through the following 250 years. Economic development was not a smooth and steady process. In spite of the gradual increase in the long-term growth rate, periods of prosperity were followed by periods of lower growth and even economic crisis.

14.3 Agricultural development

The second part of the book, which comprises *Chapters 3 to 8*, analyses agricultural development in Europe and the USA from 1750 to 2000.

Long-term trends 1750 - 2000

Chapter 3 deals with the long-term trends in agricultural employment, productivity and prices from 1750 to 2000. In around 1750, up to 80 per cent of the population worked in agriculture, including a number of activities which were later separated from agriculture. Textile production is a typical example of an activity which originally took place on farms. Because of specialisation, which started in around 1750, a number of activities were separated from agriculture, and this caused a continuous decline in the agricultural share of total employment. Two other elements contributed to the migration of labour from agriculture. The agricultural share of employment will decline when the income elasticity is below one, and when there are significant increases in agricultural labour productivity. In the nineteenth century, the absolute number of people working in agriculture increased nearly everywhere, whereas there has been a dramatic decline in the absolute number in the twentieth century, especially since the Second World War.

The history of agricultural development is the history of the accelerating increase in labour productivity in agriculture. This increase has had many different causes. The change in the farming system (methods of cultivation, land ownership etc.) was very important in the period 1750 - 1914, since when the substitution of capital for labour has been its main cause, especially since the Second World War.

The terms of trade between agricultural products and non-agricultural products is as important for the agricultural sector as it is for activities in urban areas. In a market economy, agricultural prices are determined by supply and demand. Different forces shape agricultural prices in the short term, medium term, and long term. In the short term, agricultural prices are more volatile than other prices. In the long term, since the Second World War, there has been a decline in real agricultural prices.

Agricultural development in general 1750 - 1914

Chapter 4 gives a general description of the many different technological and institutional changes which started in north-western Europe (Britain, France, Germany, and Denmark) in the period 1750 - 1914. Technological innovations and institutional changes affected both agriculture and industry.

The first part of this period was characterised by a decisive increase in agricultural productivity due to changes in the farming system. The farming system depends on the methods of cultivation, the ownership of the land, and the social relations between the rural classes. The technological change was mainly connected with the introduction of new crops, such as turnips and clover, which made it possible to break out of the vicious circle of a stagnant traditional agricultural sector, mainly based on cereals, and to develop a productivity increasing system based

Agricultural development

on crops and livestock. The institutional changes were connected with the abandonment of the open-field system with common decision-making and scattered strips of land. These changes were associated with new farm-size distribution, new kinds of ownership and new relations between landowners and peasants.

Once agricultural development got started, it continued during the second part of the period, because the technological improvements continued, and the institutional changes which created economic integration between agriculture and the other economic sectors were undertaken. Economic integration was facilitated from around 1850 by the construction of a dense network of railways, and the technological advances which reduced the costs of sea transport. Communication systems improved and messages could be transmitted much more quickly.

Improved distribution channels ensured the quicker passage of commodities from producers to end-users. Agricultural universities and research stations were set up, and the dissemination of know-how was considered equally important. New markets, such as credit markets, were established. These increased savings and investments, and ensured a more efficient allocation of resources.

Agricultural reforms in different parts of Europe 1750 - 1914

Chapter 5 reviews the different developments of agricultural reforms in the different parts of Europe from 1750 to 1914. The agricultural reforms involved a series of changes in farming systems, including cultivation methods, land ownership, and the relations between landowners and peasants. The reforms were of varying comprehensiveness in different parts of Europe, and they did not all occur at the same time.

The more comprehensive the agricultural reforms were and the more rapidly they were implemented, the more positive were the effects that could be expected from them. The agricultural reforms differed from country to country, also in relation to the farm-size structure which resulted from the reforms. These differences in size structure had a great impact, not only on the future of agricultural development but on the development of society as a whole.

The reforms started in Britain, where the landlord revolution meant that the farming system became capitalist in the sense that the landlords got ownership of nearly all the land, and this was farmed by tenants on large farm units. It has been argued that capitalist farming was necessary for agriculture to develop. It has also been argued that large-scale farming made a positive contribution to industrialisation. Both arguments are problematic.

In France, the agricultural reforms were slow and France became a country with a great number of very small farms, due to the inheritance customs which demanded that all the heirs got a share of the farm.

In Germany, the agricultural reforms differed between the western and eastern parts. In the western part of Germany, the peasants acquired legal rights, and a structure based on small-scale farms was established. In the eastern part, historically the peasants had been more oppressed by the large estate owners. In eastern Germany, much of the land belonging to the smallholders was acquired by the larger farmers and estate owners, so the size distribution became much more skewed than in the west.

In Denmark, from 1784 and over the following two decades, there were comprehensive reforms of cultivation methods, land ownership and the legal rights of the peasants. This was the basis of the later successful agricultural development in Denmark.

The agricultural reforms which started in Britain were succeeded by reforms in other countries in the northern and western parts of Europe. In the Mediterranean countries and the eastern European countries, including Russia, there were few reforms, and when they came, they came late.

Agricultural performance in different countries 1815 - 1914

Chapter 6 analyses agricultural performance in north-western Europe, where the agricultural reforms took place, and in the USA in the period 1815 - 1914. The analysis of agricultural performance includes the question of trade policy, which was a major topic during this period.

Up to the last quarter of the eighteenth century, Britain was normally a net exporter of grain. Agricultural productivity was already high, and in spite of an increase in productivity, Britain became a net importer of grain. The repeal of the Corn Laws in 1846 did not hurt British agriculture, which benefited from the general prosperity of the period 1850 - 1875. When American grain exports flooded the European markets after 1875, Britain stuck to its free trade policy. From 1875 - 1914 total agricultural production in Britain stagnated. Grain production fell significantly, and livestock production increased.

In France, agriculture was protected in the period 1815 - 1850, and was then exposed to a more liberal trade regime for a period before the return of protectionism in 1875 - 1914. French agriculture only progressed slowly. The reasons for this were the lack of land reforms and the fact that the

Agricultural development

improvements in infrastructure and the necessary enabling environment came late. It was also relevant that the French economy as a whole grew slowly, because the population was virtually stagnant during the period 1870 - 1945.

The demand for agricultural products grew relatively slowly and domestic supply also grew slowly, so France was still a net importer of important agricultural products when the First World War broke out.

In France after 1875 there was an alliance between farmers and industrialists in favour of protection for both agricultural and industrial products. In Germany there was a similar alliance up to around 1890, but after that date, German industrialists shifted to favouring free trade, because German industry had become competitive.

After 1870 there was a strong increase in the productivity of German agriculture. Important agricultural reforms had taken place, to which the economic environment contributed significantly. Agricultural sciences flourished, especially chemistry, and agricultural universities and colleges were established.

In spite of the positive agricultural development following 1870, Germany turned into a large net importer of agricultural products. Due to the large population increase and the rising living standards, the demand increased more than the supply. Because of German industrialisation, there was a much more rapid decline in the relative agricultural employment in Germany than in France.

The agricultural reforms in Denmark were comprehensive, and they were implemented relatively quickly. This was a great advantage for Danish agricultural performance. A general educational system was introduced in 1814, and this contributed to the rise of an educated class of peasants who started to organise themselves culturally, politically and economically. One important result was the development of the co-operative movement which quickly spread during the last two decades of the nineteenth century.

Danish agricultural development was based on exports, especially to Britain, but also to Germany. Already from 1850, exports of livestock products increased more than grain exports, due to the changes in their relative prices. When the price of livestock products relative to cereals increased further from 1875, Danish farmers continued the move towards livestock production. The large estate owners wanted protection for cereals, but this was rejected by the peasants.

Danish agriculture was able to adjust, and agricultural development during the period 1875 - 1914 was so successful that the Danish GDP per capita increased slightly more than the German GDP per capita.

The US agricultural development is interesting because it is so closely linked to European developments. There was no need for agricultural reforms in the USA, because US agriculture had been established by large-scale European immigration during the nineteenth century. During the period 1860 - 1910, 2 million square kilometres of new land were brought under cultivation, corresponding to an area as large as Western Europe. US agriculture was based on large-scale farming, where there was a need for machinery.

The period 1860 - 1895, when agricultural prices fell, was a difficult period. The farmers were opposed to the strict monetary policy, which caused the general price level to fall. They were also against big business and the monopolies which developed during this period. The US trade policy was very protective for industrial goods, but as an exporting sector, agriculture wanted free trade. The farmers complained about the inadequate credit facilities for the settlers in the West.

When the agricultural frontier was closed, the farm situation improved. Real agricultural prices rose, and the period 1895 - 1920 was the heyday of US agriculture.

The period of two world wars and the Great Depression 1914 - 1945

Chapter 7 deals with the agricultural markets and the public interventions during the turbulent period 1914 - 1945, with two world wars and the deep depression in between.

It was during the Great Depression 1929 - 1933 that agricultural policy, understood as a series of different market interventions for each specific commodity, was introduced in Europe and the USA for the first time.

Britain wanted to give first priority to domestic agricultural products, second priority to goods from countries belonging to the British Empire, and third priority to imports from other countries. This meant it was difficult for Britain to establish high domestic market prices through tariff protection, because that would hamper imports from the Empire. Agricultural support was given through a deficiency payment system for wheat, a marketing board system for milk, an import quota system for beef and a production quota system for pork.

As a first step, France introduced higher import tariffs, and this was followed up, as a second step, by import restrictions which were more effective when prices continued to fall. The third step was a more far-reaching market intervention to create a better balance between supply and demand, in order to support prices. The demand for domestic products was stimulated and the supply reduced.

Agricultural development

Germany also introduced protective measures to deal with the crisis, but state intervention became much more comprehensive when the national socialists came to power in 1933. State import boards were widely used to increase the domestic price levels through import regulations. The French and the German agricultural policies of the 1930s had an important influence on the way the EC's Common Agricultural Policy was constructed.

The USA introduced its agricultural support policy in 1933, which was too late, because by then a deep agricultural crisis was already a reality. The agricultural crisis also aggravated the general economic crisis, because agriculture was still employing 25 per cent of the people.

The US agricultural policy had three main elements, namely a high farm-gate price, a minimum price level through the loan rate system, and a supply reduction program. This legacy of the past can be found in the US agricultural policy after the Second World War.

A major problem in the interwar period was the lack of international co-operation. There was no co-operation in trade policy or in exchange rate policy and the attempts to improve the agricultural situation by international commodity agreements failed. The absolute number of people working in agriculture fell during the period 1920 – 1945, but the production level continued to go up because labour productivity increased more than the decline in employment.

The Bolshevik Revolution in Russia in 1917 was the foundation of the Soviet Union, where dramatic changes took place in agriculture. The period of War Communism was replaced by the New Economic Policy, where private ownership was allowed and private markets existed. In the years 1924 - 1926, there was a lively debate about the role of agriculture in the development of a socialist society between Bukharin, who believed in the market mechanism, on the one hand, and Preobrazhensky, who favoured a planned economy, on the other hand. Finally, Stalin decided to follow a collectivisation strategy, which started in 1929.

Agricultural difficulties 1945 - 2000

Chapter 8 analyses the period 1945 - 2000, which is characterised by the continuation of agricultural support policies in the industrialised countries. After the Second World War it became clear that the long-term real price of agricultural products would decline. Demand has increased less than supply, in spite of the large migration of labour from agriculture.

In Western Europe, the EEC Treaty signed in Rome in 1957 led to the establishment of the Common Agricultural Policy (CAP). The principles on which the CAP was to be based were fixed during the period 1958 - 1962. In the following years, 1962 - 1967, the different market organisations for agricultural products were established in detail, and the policy of a high market price level was chosen from the very beginning.

The EC decision-makers allowed nominal prices to rise so much that the real prices of agricultural products remained constant during the period 1973 - 1984. This policy was in contradiction to market forces, which would have led to falling real prices if they had been allowed to operate. The high price policy caused problems of surpluses in the EC, and in response, nominal prices were only allowed to increase marginally from 1984 until the MacSharry reform in 1992. Supply management, in the form of a milk quota system, was also introduced in 1984.

In the USA it was expected that agriculture would suffer from problems of surpluses after the Second World War. These were postponed until after the end of the Korean War in 1953, and during the period 1954 - 1960 there was excess supply, boosting public stocks. There were some adjustments in the 1960s through the introduction of a comprehensive supply-management programme.

The 1970s was a prosperous period for US agriculture. World market prices, although fluctuating, were relatively high and US farmers became more competitive because of the depreciation of the dollar after the pegged exchange rate system was abandoned.

US agriculture became increasingly dependent on the world market, so it suffered from the reduction in world demand, followed by falling prices during the first half of the 1980s. At the same time, the dollar was greatly appreciated, so the US share of the world cereal market fell. The result was the most severe crisis in US agriculture since the Great Depression.

Because of this crisis, the USA demanded that an international agreement on agriculture should be negotiated when the GATT Uruguay Round started in 1986. It had been possible for the EC, the USA and other industrialised countries to conduct protectionist agricultural policies because agricultural products were exempted from the main GATT rules.

The EC MacSharry reform opened the way for a compromise so that an international agreement on agriculture was implemented during the period 1995 - 2000, with the aim of creating more discipline, and less trade-distorting support.

There were two important trends during the post-war period. Firstly, agricultural exports became more important for the USA and the EC/EU, so that agricultural policy for each of the two areas became more important for the other part and for the rest of the world, and international interdependency increased.

Secondly, macroeconomic policy became more important to the agricultural sector. Agriculture became more specialised, which meant that larger amounts of inputs had to be bought and indebtedness in agriculture increased, making the sector more sensitive to changes in interest and inflation rates. Agriculture has also been sensitive to foreign exchange rate changes, which are heavily dependant on the macroeconomic policy.

14.4 A development model

In *Chapter 9*, a development model has been put forward. A framework for a development model consists of two sectors, a rural sector and an urban sector, where development is interlinked in the commodity, service and factor markets. Economic development in both sectors depends on resources, technology, institutions and attitudes. Each of these four elements is important. The importance of changing attitudes should not be underestimated. The liberal ideas of the second half of the eighteenth century influenced attitudes towards agricultural reforms. Economic integration, both nationally and internationally, was facilitated by liberal ideas about removing political obstacles to trade such as tolls, tariffs and restrictions. At the end of the nineteenth century, socialist ideas gained a foothold in Europe. In the Soviet Union, a socialist regime was established, based on a planned economy. In Western Europe and the USA, the Great Depression stimulated ideas on economic stabilisation policies through increased public interventions.

The model is dynamic in the sense that it shows the sequential development stages. Some exogenous changes in resources, technology, institutions, and attitudes can be considered as shocks, which start a development process. When economic changes take place, they feed back into resources, technology, institutions and attitudes.

Resources, technology, institutions, and attitudes are interlinked through the economic system, but there are also some direct links between them, as can be illustrated by a couple of examples.

Technology determines the relative scarcity of production factors. When agricultural development started in Europe, land was a scarce resource because the available technology only gave low yields. Today, land in the industrialised countries is abundant, due to the advanced agricultural technology which gives extremely high yields.

The lessons of history

When there are different classes with different interests, the power structure and the way in which political decisions are made is extremely important. Those who own the resources may belong to the politically powerful class, which has a major influence on the prevailing attitudes and laws, which again determine the institutions.

In around 1750, nearly all the European states could be characterised as feudal societies, with a class of landlords, a class of clergy, a burgher class of artisans, traders and merchants, and a class of peasants. The feudal society was a stationary society with little development. It was a conservative society, which more or less reproduced itself, without dynamic changes.

The agricultural development can be divided into different stages. The different characteristics of the different stages are presented in Figure 14.1.

Figure 14.1: The different characteristics of the different stages in agricultural development

	1750	1850	1914	1950	2000
Stage	1	2	3	4	5
Main characteristics:	Productivity increase	Economic integration	Relief and recovery	Farm income problem	Externalities
Technology:	Crop-livestock husbandry. Development based on internal resources	Technological progress connected with increased labour force	Technological progress connected with decreasing labour force	Specialisation, mechanisation, bigger units with less labour	Fulfil environmental, ethical, safety and nutritional goals
Institutions:	Agricultural reforms	Markets and economic environment	Agricultural policy	Agricultural policy and macroeconomic policy	Rural policy and consumer policy
Attitudes:	Specialisation and liberal ideas	Liberal ideas and public initiatives	Lack of international co-operation	Lack of international co-operation in agriculture	International co-operation in agriculture.

It was suggested by W.W. Rostow that economic development in different countries follows a given pattern (Rostow, 1960). Rostow put forward a 'stage theory', showing how development progresses. This idea is used in the theory of agricultural development in Chapter 9. On the basis of historical developments, it is assumed that agricultural developments can be grouped into four stages. There is no clear demarcation line between the different stages, because the specific features of each stage overlap with the other stages. It is also clear that each country goes through the different stages at different times, because some countries are pioneers and others are laggards in relation to agricultural and economic development. Nevertheless, it is suggested that for the countries in north-western Europe, agricultural development can be split into four stages, each with a dominant feature. These stages are: 1. Productivity increases 1750 – 1850; 2. Economic integration 1850 – 1914; 3. Relief and recovery 1914 – 1950; and 4. Farm income problems 1950 - 2000. It is reasonable to assume that we have already entered a fifth stage where the main issues are connected with the relationship between agricultural production and the environment, ethics and human health.

14.5 Productivity increases and agricultural reforms

Chapter 10 analyses the first stage, when the agriculture moves from a stagnant feudal system to a system where productivity is increased. In around 1750, agriculture was most advanced around the urban centres in the Low Countries, around London and Paris, and around the cities in the Rhine valley in Germany and the Po valley in northern Italy. The agricultural revolution which started the development process began in Britain.

Agricultural reforms

The start of economic development in around 1750 is most often associated with the start of industrialisation. However, studies show that the agricultural revolution preceded the industrial revolution. It is impossible to believe that economic development could have started without being preceded by dynamic changes in the agricultural sector where up to 80 per cent of the population was employed.

The productivity increases which started in the eighteenth century reduced the threat of famine in years with bad harvests. That opened up for new attitudes. The risk of not getting sufficient food was reduced, so it was no longer necessary to be a subsistence farmer, more or less self-sufficient in agricultural products, textile products and other products. Now, it became much less risky to specialise.

The higher agricultural productivity increased the supply of food, and the improved level of nutrition contributed to increased labour productivity. The higher agricultural productivity also made it possible to release labour for the major agricultural investments which were connected with the agricultural reforms.

There are reasons for believing that countries that were successful in implementing agricultural reforms obtained a higher growth rate. This is difficult to prove, because it is not possible to find a reasonable measure which takes all the different elements of the agricultural reforms into account. In addition, it should be remembered that agricultural reforms set in motion a series of changes which came to create new possibilities.

There is no doubt that the increase in the population growth rate from around 1750 contributed to the agricultural revolution. Through rising prices, the greater demand increased interest in agricultural reforms, and the increased labour supply made it possible to initiate the labour-intensive investments connected with the agricultural reforms.

Malthus argued that agricultural production determined the size of the population (Malthus, 1798). Esther Boserup argued that population density influences the farming system, so that a population increase will induce agricultural reforms (Boserup, 1965). The agricultural development in the eighteenth century can be considered as a combination of both theories. The population increase contributed to the reforms which increased production, which again made it possible to sustain a greater population.

Size structure and path dependency

The kind and the extent of agricultural reforms had an important impact on how societies developed. The farm-size structure depended on how the agricultural reforms were implemented.

It is not possible to conclude that large-scale farming was in general better than small-scale farming. The performance of a farm of a given size depends on the economic environment. When the economic environment is adequate, small-scale farmers will be able to take advantage of the possibilities. When the economic environment is inadequate, it will be easier for the large estate owners to overcome the obstacles. Even if, at the time, the large estate owners were more productive than the small-scale farmers, because of the inadequate economic environment, it could be a good strategy to focus on the peasant class. An active peasant class could contribute to the removal of the bottlenecks which were a hindrance to development. The question of

Productivity increases and agricultural reforms

the optimal size structure of farming should be considered in a dynamic perspective.

By focusing on large-scale farming, Britain may have obtained a short-term advantage over France which had a large number of small farms. But in the longer term it might have been better to focus on a class of middle-sized freeholders, as in the case of Denmark, because it set in motion a development which soon created new opportunities.

The farm-size structure, resulting from the agrarian reforms, was shaped by the political struggle between different groups with different interests. The size structure had far-reaching consequences because of 'path dependence'. The first step along the path determines the direction, which creates new opportunities which influence the next step, which further determines the course of development. Path dependence, showing how the first step leads to the second step which leads to the third step, is often the only way in which development can be explained. For example, the success of Danish agricultural development can only be explained by the succession of different steps which can be traced back to the agricultural reforms in the second half of the eighteenth century.

Interrelationships between agriculture and industry

When agricultural development started, and when the agricultural reforms took place, it was based on the use of the internal resources of agriculture. However, agricultural development was important for the industrial revolution.

Agricultural demand stimulated industrialisation. Improved productivity increased agricultural incomes, which augmented the demand for non-food products, such as textiles and other consumer and investment goods. The development of the British textile and iron and coal industries was greatly dependant on agriculture. Industrialisation began in closed economies, so industrial production could only be sold in an economy where agriculture was the overwhelmingly dominant sector.

Agriculture supplied the resources for industrialisation. The wealthy class of merchants in the cities in Britain were not the entrepreneurs who started the industrialisation. Most of the entrepreneurs came from agriculture, which also delivered the labour force, the capital and the necessary food surplus.

When the industrialisation process got going an important and dynamic interrelationship between agriculture and industry was established. Industrial development stimulated the demand for agricultural products,

The lessons of history

especially livestock products, and industry supplied consumer goods and important inputs to agriculture.

14.6 Economic integration, markets and economic environment

In the first stage, agricultural development is based on the crop-livestock model and the implementation of agricultural reforms. In the second stage agricultural development accelerates because of new technological progress and new institutional changes. The second stage is characterised by economic integration, which is made possible by improved and extended markets, and by the establishment of the necessary economic environment.

Chapter 11 focuses on the markets and institutions which are so important for economic development in the second stage.

The importance of markets and the economic environment

It is important to realise that the market mechanism is a very important signalling system, which contributes to the dynamics of economic development. Firstly, with a given amount of resources, the market mechanism allocates the resources more efficiently in a static society. In a dynamic society, with population growth and capital accumulation, but without technological progress, the market mechanism will have a dynamic effect because competition induces producers to invest and to produce more efficiently in order to increase profits and stay in business. When there are technological innovations, there are further benefits because information about the new possibilities is diffused through the economic system and will induce producers to take advantage of the new possibilities.

Secondly, the market mechanism reveals bottlenecks either through high prices or lack of availability. These bottlenecks are made apparent to private entrepreneurs and to governments, who have the opportunity to remove them. Development can be seen as a process in which there is an interaction between opportunities and bottlenecks. At any given moment there are some bottlenecks, and there are some private and public incentives to remove them. When they are removed, new opportunities arise and then new bottlenecks occur. There is never equilibrium, because the economy moves from one disequilibrium to another due to the ever emerging bottlenecks. The bottlenecks can be of different kinds such as resource constraints, lack of technology, inadequate institutions or inappropriate attitudes.

Agricultural development depends on markets and how they function, which again depends on a series of factors, namely:

> Transport and communication
> Distribution channels
> Human resources
> Innovation based on research
> Diffusion of innovations and information.

Agricultural development needs investment, so the existence of credit institutions, where the peasants can deposit their savings and borrow the necessary funds, is important. When most peasants' children can leave agriculture due to increased labour productivity, migration from agriculture to industry will be facilitated if there is a labour market.

The establishment of markets and the economic environment demands many resources. A large part of the agricultural savings has to be spent on major investments. Not all the resources at any given time should be spent on one activity, but they should be allocated between different activities, because the utilities of the different activities are interlinked. The benefits of research and innovations depend on the existence of extension services and an information system and these in turn depend on the ability of the peasants to recognise the new possibilities and to undertake the necessary investments. Theoretically, it is easy to conclude that resources should be allocated to those activities where the marginal rate of utility is highest. In the real world it is difficult to get a clear picture of these utilities, because of different class interests, because the utility is not the same in the short and the long term, and because the marginal utility of a single activity will often be less than the sum of the marginal utilities of a combination of activities.

To establish markets and the institutions around markets is a major task which takes time. At this stage of development, the public sector only has few resources, so the initiatives and financing cannot be undertaken by the public sector alone. The private sector also has to contribute, but it is of course a great advantage when the public sector plays an active role in the development process. This can only be done if the government intervenes in a supportive manner. The government has to understand the role of agriculture in the development process. To support agricultural development is not only important because it is a large sector, it is also important because of the significance of agricultural development for the establishment of markets and institutions. If agricultural development does not have a high priority, it is easy to neglect resource-demanding investments where the benefits will only be apparent in the longer term.

Markets and institutions of special importance to agriculture

Markets are of special importance to agriculture because the producers are geographically dispersed in contrast to industry, where fewer producers are often concentrated in urban centres. In agriculture, the infrastructure is vital and the co-ordination of decisions taken by many dispersed producers to satisfy the needs of many dispersed consumers can only be achieved through the market.

Institutions are also very important in agriculture because agriculture is a biological production where the "external framework" for production is not fixed. Agricultural production is seasonal, which makes it more difficult for agricultural labour to specialise and to obtain constant employment throughout the year.

The tasks of agriculture at any given moment are determined by external factors. The weather and the incidence of disease tell the farm operator what to do at a given time. The farm operator must make daily decisions about what to do and how to do it. Therefore, it is important to have an institutional set-up which induces the peasants to take the right decisions. If the owner of a farm, the operator of the farm, and the worker on the farm, are one and the same person, there are reasons for believing that the decisions taken and the work done will be in the interests of the owner of the farm. Attitudes towards risk determine, for example, whether private ownership or share-cropping are to be preferred. From a profit-maximisation point of view, private ownership is preferable to a share-cropping system, when risks are not taken into consideration. In share-cropping, the risks are smaller than with private ownership. When production risks are high, share-cropping may be a preferable system, although it is less productive under normal circumstances.

Agriculture is exposed to climatic risks as well as market risks. These risks can be reduced when appropriate institutions are established. Risk reductions will often create a more positive environment for new productions, new production methods and investments.

The importance of the market mechanism in promoting economic development can be illustrated by comparing the performances of the planned economy in the Soviet Union with the market economies of the West after the Second World War.

During the Great Depression, 1929 - 1932, industrial production in the Soviet Union increased 83 per cent, while industrial production in

Germany and the USA fell by 47 per cent in the same period. In the first decades after the Second World War, the production increase in the industrial sector was high in the Soviet Union.

In contrast to the industrial sector, agriculture always had problems in the Soviet Union. In 1950, productivity in Soviet agriculture was a little more than one third of productivity in Danish agriculture. In spite of the low level, the productivity ratio fell even further during the post-war period. In 1990, the Soviet productivity had fallen to a little under 20 per cent of productivity in Danish agriculture.

The problems of Soviet agriculture underline the special importance of markets and institutions to agriculture. The Soviet model was based on the assumptions that the planning system was efficient, that there are large economies of size, and that collective or state ownership promotes productivity. Experience shows that none of these assumptions was correct.

14.7 Economic and agricultural policy intervention

There are good reasons for distinguishing between the periods 1750 - 1914 and 1914 - 2000. During the first period, agriculture played a dominant role in the economic development process. Agriculture was originally the engine of growth, and was a prerequisite for successful industrialisation. During the second period, agriculture was no longer as important as previously. Agriculture started to experience problems so that extensive policy interventions were needed. In short, during the first period society depended on agriculture, and during the second period agriculture depended on society.

Chapter 12 analyses the different economic policies that influenced the agricultural sector, namely trade policy, agricultural policy, and macroeconomic policy. Before 1914, different countries had trade policies and monetary policies, but these policy interventions were far less extensive than the interventions made during the period 1914 - 2000.

Trade policy

From the second half of the eighteenth century, when the ideas about the benefits of free trade emerged and up to 1875, there was a general trend towards reduced protection. This resulted in a situation which was very close to free trade in the years 1860 - 1875. International trade grew not only because the political barriers were lowered, but also because of improved transport and communication systems

From 1875 - 1914, France, Germany, and many other European countries as well as the USA followed a protectionist trade policy. Other countries, such as Britain, Denmark and the Netherlands continued a free trade policy. In spite of the protectionist policy of some European countries, economic integration continued because the reduction of transport costs was greater than the typical increase in tariff protection.

There was no correlation between trade policy and agricultural performance. Britain chose to follow a free trade policy, and British agriculture suffered, whereas the free trade policy in Denmark was combined with a prosperous period when agricultural production shifted from arable crops to animal husbandry. Agriculture in France was protected, but did not perform well. In Germany, agricultural protection was accompanied by high productivity increases. Thus, trade policy did have an impact, but agricultural performance also depended on a series of other factors.

The trade policy vis-à-vis agricultural and industrial products was more or less the same in each country. Either a country supported both agriculture and industry by protection, like France, or it supported neither industry nor agriculture, as was the case in Britain and Denmark.

The pattern after the Second World War was very different. The industrialised countries removed industrial protection, but agricultural protection was increased before some more liberal reforms were introduced in the 1990s.

Agricultural policy

Agricultural policy, as a series of more or less complex market interventions, was first introduced during the Great Depression in the 1930s. Agricultural policy was meant to be a relief measure during the 1930s, but it continued after the Second World War, in spite of the totally different economic conditions. The general economy was prosperous and the agricultural sector was not in crisis. However, from the mid-1950s, farmers were not able to get income increases at the same rate as the rest of society. Now the aim of agricultural policy was to solve the relative-income problem of farmers.

There was little change in agricultural policy from the 1930s to the post-war period. The US agricultural policy was based on deficiency payments, minimum market prices and a set-aside programme. The Common Agricultural Policy of the EC was based on high market prices implemented through a high protection level and export subsidies. There were also internal support mechanisms, such as intervention prices and direct payments to farmers. There are series of problems connected with agricultural support policy, and these are all discussed in Chapter 12.

Macroeconomic policy

Macroeconomic policy, such as fiscal policy, monetary policy and exchange rate policy, only started to be consciously pursued in earnest during the 1930s, and it played a major role in the last half of the twentieth century.

Monetary policy was known before the 1930s. When the barter economy is gradually replaced by a money economy and when a monetary system with a central bank is established, there will automatically be a monetary policy. The monetary policy determines the money supply, which has a great impact on the general price levels in the economy. In some periods, the general price level goes up, and in other periods it goes down, and these changes in the general price level affect farmers. When farmers are net debtors, they suffer from a general price decline.

The agricultural price decline in the USA in 1929 and the following years caused a decline in farm incomes, and this reduced the demand for industrial products. An early price support policy combined with an increase in the money supply could have avoided the cycle of recessionary forces in the economy. At the time it was not understood how important it was to stabilise the economy through intervention. The laissez-faire policy was dominant, and it was believed by economists that self-regulating market forces would soon create a new equilibrium, with acceptable employment and incomes.

The theory of counter-cyclical demand policy was introduced by Keynes, and his theory was the basis of economy policy in the post-war period up to 1970. It was a period with pegged exchange rates and restrictions on capital movements. The way the policy instruments worked was changed when floating exchange rates were introduced in 1973, and when capital movements were gradually liberated.

The macroeconomic policies had impacts on agricultural markets in several ways. Firstly, indebted countries in the Third World had balance-of-payments problems when interest rates rose and this caused a reduction in their agricultural imports. Secondly, the macroeconomic policies influenced exchange rates, which in turn had a major impact on the competitiveness of the agricultural sector in many countries. Thirdly, agricultural costs were influenced by the macroeconomic policies, especially through interest rates.

The lessons of history

Agricultural incomes are insensitive to changes in employment in society, because the income elasticity of farm products is nearly zero in industrialised countries. On the other hand, agricultural incomes are highly sensitive to the level of interest rates, because agriculture is a capital-intensive activity, and often highly indebted. To keep down interest rates, farmers are interested in a policy mix consisting of a strict fiscal policy and a lax monetary policy.

14.8 Post-war experiences of the developing countries

Chapter 13 focuses on the developing countries after the Second World War. They did not follow the lessons of economic development in the western world. Was this because the lessons of the past were no longer relevant because of the changed conditions, or were there other reasons? The GDP per capita in China, India, other Asian countries and Africa in around 1950 was either at the same level or below the level of the GDP per capita in Western Europe 250 years before. Due to colonisation and other factors there was little economic development in the developing countries, except in Latin America.

Agricultural development played an essential role in economic development in the western world during the first and second stages. This has been overlooked by the developing countries which have focused on industrialisation and neglected the agricultural sector.

The developing countries could choose

It is clear that conditions for the developing countries in 1950 were very different from the conditions in around 1750, when the western world started the development process. The western world did not have an option between focusing on agriculture or industry. It had to focus on agriculture because nearly all the resources were connected with agriculture and there was little or no possibility of importing know-how and capital. The developing countries did have the possibility of focussing either on industry or agriculture.

In around 1750, there was no option for the western world between pursuing strategies focusing on international trade or trade protection, because development had to be based on the internal resources of a closed economy. Due to the high natural barriers and the political barriers to trade, agricultural development could only be based on domestic purchasing power. After the Second World War the developing countries were not protected by high transport costs eliminating competition from

Post-war experiences of the developing countries

the industrialised world. The developing countries had to choose between a free trade policy and a more or less protectionist policy.

In a sense, it can be argued that in 1950 the developing countries were in a more favourable position than the western world in 1750. The developing countries could get resources from the western world in the form of loans or development assistance. The developing countries could draw on the technology and experience of the institutions which had been developed in the western world.

However, the technology, institutions and attitudes of the developed countries were alien to the economies of the developing countries, so it was a mistake to assume that they could be successfully introduced in a short time in the developing world.

The lessons from the development model in Chapter 9 show the importance of the interrelationship between resources, technology, institutions and attitudes on the one hand, and the economic and social development on the other hand. These interrelationships are developed through time. Therefore, it is wrong to regard the technology and institutions of the western world in 1950 as exogenous elements which could be introduced into the economies in the developing countries. The principal lesson from the development model in Chapter 9 is that technological, institutional and behavioural changes are an integral part of the development process.

Agriculture was neglected

The developing countries forgot the importance of agriculture in the development process. Instead, they focused on industry and did not realise that successful development hinges on the mutual relationships between the urban and the rural sectors. It was difficult for the developing countries to industrialise because of competition from the western world, because of the need for capital and because of the lack of domestic demand. When the western world industrialised, natural trade barriers in the form of high transport and communication costs constituted protection. At that time, the capital costs associated with industrialisation were much smaller because the economies of scale were much smaller. Industrialisation in the western world was very much demand driven, because the increased incomes of agriculture created a market for industry.

After the Second World War the developing countries restricted competition from the western world by protectionist trade policies. The capital needs of industry were high, and this meant that the available capital was only able to create relatively few jobs. The industrialisation was to a large extent supply driven and there was insufficient demand for the industrial products because of the neglect of the large agricultural sector.

It has been argued that agricultural development was easier in the western world because of the large land area which could be integrated into the production. This argument is not valid, because agricultural production in the developing countries should have focused on more intensive use of the land resources by shifting from annual cropping to multi-cropping, getting more than one harvest a year.

The fact that the agricultural land area was relatively limited, combined with a large population, should have provoked greater interest in agricultural development, employing the large labour force in rural development in general, as was the case in the western world during the period 1750 - 1914. The lack of agricultural development has caused large migration to the urban sector where mega-cities have grown up without the capacity to employ all the new arrivals.

The agricultural sector was neglected from the very beginning, and this attitude was self-reinforcing. Due to the backwardness of agriculture there was migration to the urban centres which strengthened the urban interests. There were no fundamental agricultural reforms and institutional changes corresponding to those which had initiated and sustained agricultural development in Europe in the past. The neglect of the agricultural sector was also apparent when it came to agricultural price policy and macroeconomic policy. The urban sector wanted low food prices, and the peasants wanted high food prices. Governments have generally chosen to keep agricultural prices below the world market prices, which were already artificially low in many cases, because of the agricultural support policies of the industrialised countries. The macroeconomic policies which protected the industrial sector created high inflation and caused real exchange rates to be overvalued, contributing to lower the real incomes of the peasants. Agricultural supply depends on the existence of markets and how well they perform, and these in turn depend on the enabling environment. In most cases insufficient public resources have been allocated to these tasks.

The neglect of agriculture caused problems

The neglect of the agricultural sector has been detrimental to the development of society for several reasons. Firstly, it has made it difficult for industry to develop because of the lack of demand. Secondly, too many people have moved from the rural sector the urban sector. Cities have become overcrowded, and large public investments have been spent in the cities in the attempt to cope with the problem of congestion. In the rural areas there have been too few people to undertake the necessary agricultural changes. Thirdly, a dual economy has emerged, with the urban sector disconnected from the rural sector. The establishment of markets and the necessary economic environment, which could have facilitated economic integration, have been neglected. Fourthly, poverty alleviation has been indirectly neglected. Most poor people live in the rural areas. When resources are spent in the urban centres, any possible trickle-down effect to poorer segments in the cities will leave the rural poor unaffected. Fifthly, the lack of agricultural development has made it difficult for agriculture in developing countries to compete with agriculture in the industrialised countries.

A simple calculation shows why the poorer developing countries have had increasing difficulty in competing with the more advanced agricultural production of the western countries. According to the estimates of Bairoch (1999), productivity in the most developed countries was around 15 times the productivity of the poorer developing countries in 1950. When the wage rates in the rich countries were around 60 times the level in the poorer countries, this meant that, un 1950, the costs of agricultural products in the rich countries were four times the level in the poorer countries.

This picture was totally changed by 1980. At that time, productivity in the most developed countries was around 60 times higher than in the poorer developing countries. The wage disparity had decreased, so that the wage rate in the rich countries was around 30 times the level in the poorer countries. This meant that the costs in the rich countries were only around 50 per cent of the level in the poorer developing countries.

This simple calculation shows a dramatic shift. However, these calculations should be treated with caution as they depend on the reliability of the data and upon the choice of wage rates and foreign exchange rates.

Why was agriculture neglected?

Why did the developing countries choose industrialisation and neglect agriculture? Mainstream economic thinking at the time contributed to the belief that industrialisation was the right choice. Many of the new leaders in the newly independent former colonies were marked by socialist thinking, and many of them looked to the Soviet Union as a model for economic development.

Literature

Allen, Robert C. (1992), *Enclosure and the Yeoman*, Oxford, 1992.

Bairoch, Paul (1969), "Agriculture and the Industrial Revolution" in Cipollo C.M. (ed.), *The Fontana Economic History of Europe*, volume 3, London, 1969.

Bairoch, Paul (1975), *The Economic Development of the Third World since 1900*, Berkley, 1975.

Bairoch, Paul (1976), *Commerce extérieur et development économique de l'Europe au XIX siècle*, Paris, 1976.

Bairoch, Paul (1982), "International Industrialization Levels from 1750-1980", *Journal of European Economic History*, 11, 1982.

Bairoch, Paul (1999), *L'Agriculture des Pays Développés,* Economica, Paris, 1999.

Barro, Robert J. and Xavier Sala-i-Martin (2003), *Economic Growth*, MIT Press, 2003.

Basch, A. (1943), *The Danube Bassin and the German Economic Space*, New York, 1943.

Baykov, A. (1946), *The Development of the Soviet Econoic System,* Cambridge, 1946.

Benedict, M.R. (1953), *Farm Policies of the US 1750-1950*, New York, 1953.

Benedict, M.R. (1955), *Can We Solve the Farm Problem*, New York, 1955.

Binswanger, Hans P. and Vernon W. Ruttan (1978), *Induced Innovations: Technology, Institutions and Development*, Baltimore and London, 1978.

Bloch, M. (1931), *Les caractères originaux de l'histoire rural francaise*, Paris, 1931.

Boserup, Ester (1965), *The Conditions of Agricultural Growth*, London, 1965Boserup, Ester (1981), *Population and Technology*, Chicago, 1981.

Braun, R. (1967), "The rise of a rural class of industrial entrepreneurs". *Journal of World History*, volume 10, 1967.

Brenner, Robert (1976), "Agrarian class structure and economic development in pre-industrial Europe, *Past and Present*, 70. Reprinted in Aston, T.H. and C.H.E. Philin (eds.), *The Brenner Debate*, Cambridge, 1985.

Brenner, Robert (1997), "Property relations and the growth of agricultural productivity in late medieval and early modern Europe" in Bhaduri, Amit and Rune Sharstein (eds.), *Economic Development and Agricultural Productivity*, Edward Elgar, 1997.

Bukharin, Nikolai I. (first edited 1920), *Economics of the Transition Period*, New York, 1971.

Campbell, Bruce M.S. and Mark Overton (1991), *Land, Labour and Livestock: Historical Studies in European Agricultural Productivity*, Manchester University Press, 1991.

Chambers, J.D. and G.E. Mingay (1966), *The Agricultural Revolution 1750-1880*, London, 1966.

Christensen, Jens (1983), *Rural Denmark 1750 – 1980*, Copenhagen, 1983.

Chapham, J.H. (1938), *Economic History of Modern Britain* Cambridge 1938.

Clapham, J.H. (1966), *The Economic Development of France and Germany 1815 – 1914*, Cambridge, 1966.

Clark, Colin (1940), *The Conditions of Economic of Economic Progress*, London, 1940.

Clark, G. (1993), "Agriculture and the industrial revolution, 1700 – 1850" in Mokyr, J. (ed.), *The British industrial revolution; an economic perspective*, Oxford, 1993.

Literature

Cochrane, W.W. (1958), *Farm Prices: Myths and Reality*, Minneapolis, 1958.Cohen, Stephen F. (1974), *Bukharin and the Bolshevik Revolution: A Political Biography 1888 – 1938*, London, 1974.

de Vries, J. (1984), *European Urbanization 1500 – 1800*, Cambridge, 1984.

de Vries, J. and Ad van der Woude (1997), *The First Modern Economy: Success, failure and perseverance of the Dutch economy, 1550 -1815*, Cambridge, 1997.

Domar, E.D. (1957), *Essays in the Theory of Economic Growth*, New York, 1957.

Duby, G. and A. Wallon (1975 – 76), *Histoire de la France rural*, volume 1-4, Paris, 1975 – 76.

Ellman, M. (1981), "Agricultural Productivity under Socialism", *World Development*, volume 9, 1981.

Feldman, G.A. (first edited 1928), "On the Theory of Growth Rates of National Income" in Spulber, N (ed.) *Foundations of Soviet Strategy for Economic Growth: Selected Soviet Essays, 1924 – 1930*, Indiana University Press, 1964.

Friedman, M. (1973), *A Monetary History of the United States 1967 – 1960*, National Bureau of Economic Research, 1973.

Fussell, G.E. (1952), *The Farmer's Tools, 1500 – 1900*, London, 1952.

Gardner, B.L. (1992), "Changing Economic Perspectives on the Farm Problem", *Journal of Economic Literature*, March 1992.

GATT (1958), *Trends in International Trade: A Report by a Panel of Experts*, Genova, 1958 (The Habeler Report).

Hansen, Svend Aage (1984), *Økonomisk væksti i Danmark*, Akademisk forlag, 1984.

Harrison, Mark (1996), "Soviet Agriculture and Industrialization" in Mathias, Peter and Johan A. Davis (eds.), *The Nature of Industrialisation*, volume 4, Blackwell, 1996.

Hayami, Y. and W.W. Ruttan (1985), *Agricultural Development*, John Hopkins University Press, 1985.

Heaton, H. (1968), *Economic History of Europe*, New York, 1968.

Heywood, Colin (1986), "Agriculture and Industrialization, 1870 – 1914" in Mathias, Peter and John A. Davis (eds.), *The Nature of Industrialization*, volume 4, Blackwell, 1996.

Hirschmann, A.O. (1958), *The Strategy of Economic Development*, New Haven, 1958.

Historical Statistics of the United States 1789 – 1945 (1949), United States Department of Commerce, Washington DC, 1949.

Hoffman, W.G. (1955), *British Industry 1700 – 1950*, Oxford 1955.

Ingersent, Ken A. and A.J. Rayner (1999), *Agricultural Policy in Western Europe and the United States*, Edward Elgar, 1999.

Jensen, Einar (1937), *Danish Agriculture*, Copenhagen, 1937.

Johnson, D. Gale (1963), "Efficiency and welfare implications of US agricultural policy", *Journal of Farm Economics,* volume 45, 1963.

Johnson, D. Gale (1973), *Farm Commodity Programs: An Opportunity for Change*, American Enterprise Institute, Washington DC, 1973.

Jones, E.L. (ed.) (1967), *Agriculture and Economic Growth in England, 1650 – 1815*, London, 1967.

Josling, T.E, S. Tangermann and T.K. Warley (1996), *Agriculture and GATT*, Macmillan, 1996.

Kerridge, E. (1967), *The agricultural revolution*, London, 1967.

Keynes, John Maynard (1936), *The General Theory of Employment, Interest and Money*, 1936.

Kjaergaard, T. (1994), *The Danish evolution 1500 – 1800. An ecohistorical interpretation*, Cambridge, 1994.

Koning, N. (1994), *The Failure of Agrarian Capitalism*, London, 1994.

Literature

Kuznets, S. (1966), *Modern Economic Growth*, Yale University Press, 1966.

Lewis, W. Arthur (1953), *Economic Survey 1919 – 1939*, London, 1953.

Lewis, W. Arthur (1954), "Economic development with unlimited supplies of labour", *Manchester School of Economics and Social Studies*, volume 22, 1954.

Lewis, W. Arthur (1978), *Growth and Fluctuations 1870 – 1913*, London, 1978.

List, Friedrich (1840), *Das nationale System der politischen Ökonomie*, 1840.

Lorimer, F. (1946), *The Population of the Soviet Union*, Geneva, 1946.

Maddison, Angus (1995), *Monitoring the World Economy 1820 – 1992*, OECD, Paris, 1995.

Maddison, Angus (2001), *The World Economy: A Millennial Perspective*, OECD, Paris, 2001.

Maddison, Angus (2003), *The World Economy; Historical Statistics*, OECD, Paris, 2003.

Mahalanobis, P.C. (1955), "The approach of operational research to planning in India", *Samkhya: The Indian Journal of Statistics,* volume 16, 1955.

Malthus, T (1798), *An Essay on the Principles of Population*, 1798.

Martin, Michael V. and Ray F. Brokken (1983), "The Scarcity Syndrom: Comment", *American Journal of Agricultural Economics*, 1983.

Marx, Karl (1867), *Das Kapital*, 1867.

Mathias, Peter and John A. Davis (eds.) (1996), *The Nature of Industrialisation*, volume 4, Blackwell, 1996.

Messerlin, P.A. and S. Becuwe, "Intra-Industry Trade in the Long Run: The French case 1850 – 1913 in D. Greenaway and P.K.M. Tharakan (eds.) *Imperfect Competition and International Trade*, Sussex, 1986.

Mingay, G.E. (1975), *Arthur Young and his times*, London, 1975.

Mingay, G.E. (ed.) (1989), *The agrarian history of England and Wales, 1750 – 1850*, Cambridge, 1989.

Mitchell, B.R. (ed.) (1981), *European Historical Statistics, 1750 – 1975*, Maximillan, London, 1981.

Molle, Willem (1990), *The Economics of European Integration*, Dartmonth, 1990.

Mundlak, Yair (2000), *Agriculture and Economic Growth, Theory and Measurement*, Cambridge, 2000.

Newell, William H. (1973), "The Agricultural Revolution in Nineteenth Centry France", *The Journal of Economic History*, 33, 1973.

North, D.C. and R.P. Thomas (1973), *The Rise of the Western World*, Cambride, 1973.

North, D.C. (1990), *Institutions, Institutional Change and Economic Performance*, Cambridge, 1990.

North, D.C. (1993), "The ultimate cause of growth" in A. Szirmai, B. van Ark and D. Pilat (eds.), *Explaining Economic Growth: Essays in honour of Angus Maddison*, Amsterdam 1993.

O'Brien, Patrick and Caglar Keyder (1978), *Economic Growth in Britain and France 1780 – 1914*, London, 1978.

Olsen, E. (1962), *Danmarks økonomiske historie siden 1750*, København, 1962.

Overton, Mark (1996), *Agricultural Revolution in England, The Transformation of the agrarian economy 1500 – 1850*, Cambridge, 1996.

Paarlberg, Don (1984), "Tarnished gold, US farm commodity programs after 50 years", *Food Policy*, February 1984.

Pokrovsky, M.N. (1933), *Brief History of Russia*, London, 1933.

Prebish, R. (1950), *The Economic Development of Latin America and its Principal Problems*, United Nations, New York, 1950.

Preobrazhensky, E. (first edited 1925), *The New Economics*, Oxford, 1965.

Literature

Quesnay, F. (1758), *Tableau Economique*, 1758.

Rasmussen, Wayne D. (1962), "The Impact of Technological Change on American Agriculture: 1862 – 1962", *The Journal of Economic History*, 22, 1962.

Ricardo, David (1817), *The Principles of Political Economy and Taxation*, 1817.

Rostow, W.W. (1960), *The Stages of Economic Growth: A Non-Communist Manifest*, Cambridge, 1960.

Sah, R.K. and Joseph E. Stiglitz (1984), "The Economics of Price Scissors", *The American Economic Review*, March 1984.

Saloutos, T. (1982), *American Farmer and the New Deal*, Iowa State University Press, 1982.

Scheiber, H., H.G. Vatter and H.U. Faulkner, *American Economic History*, New York, 1976.

Schiff, M.V. and A. Valdes (1992), *The Political Economy of Agricultural Pricing Policy*, volume 4, Washington DC, 1992.

Schultz, G.E. (1945), *Agriculture in an Unstable Economy*, New York, 1945.

Schumpeter, J.A. (1943), *Capitalism, Socialism and Democracy*, London, 1943.

Singer, H.W. (1950), "The distribution of gains between investing and borrowing countries", *American Economic Review*, volume 41, 1950.

Skrubbeltrang, F. (1953), *Agricultural Development and Rural Reform in Denmark*, FAO, Rome, 1953.

Smith, Adam (1776), *An Inquiry into the Nature and Causes of the Wealth of Nations*, 1776.

Timmer, C.P. (1988), "The Agricultural Transformation" in Chenery, H. and T.N. Srinivason (eds.), *Handbook of Development Economics*, volume 1, Amsterdam, 1988.

Tracy, Michael (1982), *Agriculture in Western Europe, Challenge and Response 1880 – 1980*, Granada, 1982.

Literature

Tracy, Michael (1996), *Agricultural Policy in the European Union*, Brussels, 1996.

Usher, A.P. (1970), *History of Mechanical Inventions*, Cambridge, 1970.

USDA (1942), *Agricultural Statistics*, 1942.

van Bath, B.H. Slicher (1963), *The Agrarian History of Western Europe A.D. 500 – 1850*, London, 1963.

van Bavel, Bas J.P. and Erik Thoen (eds.) (1999), *Land Productivity and Agro-systems in the North Sea Area,* Brepols Publishers, 1999.

van Zanden, J.L. (1999), "The development of agricultural productivity in Europe 1500 – 1800" in van Bavel, Bas J.P. and Erik Thoen (eds.). *Land Productivity and Agro-systems in the North Sea Area*, Brepols Publishers, 1999.

Wade, W.W. (1981), *Institutional Determinants of Technical Change and Agricultural Productivity Growth, Denmark, France and Great Britain, 1870 – 1965*, New York, 1981.

Weber, E. (1977), *Peasants into Frenchmen – the Modernisation of Rural France*, London, 1977.

Weber, Max (1905), *Die Protestantische Ethik*, München, 1905.

Wisner, R.N. (1990), *World Food Trade and US Agriculture*, Des Moines, Iowa 1990.

Writht, Gordin (1964), *Rural Revolution in France*, Stanford, 1964.

Yatsunsky, V.K. (1965), "Formation en Russie de la grande industrie textile sur la base de la production rurale" in *Second International Congress of Economic History, 1962*, volume 2, Paris 1965.

Index

A
Agricultural development
- agriculture 1815-1914
  - performance 151-179
  - trade policy 151-179
- agriculture 1914-1945
  - adjustment 181-183
  - performance 197-199
  - Soviet Union 200-208
  - support 183-196
- agriculture 1945-2000
  - adjustment 213-214
  - agricultural policy 216-230, 232-236, 238-239
  - economic policy 236-238
  - GATT 214-216, 231-232
- and markets 115-118, 300
- institutional changes
  - first stage 104-108, 119-120
  - second stage 112-115, 120-122
- population growth 286-288
- technological changes
  - first stage 103-104, 119-120
  - second stage 108-112, 120-121
Agricultural policy
- inter-war period
  - Europe 183-191, 325-327
  - USA 191-195, 325-326
- post-war period
  - Europe 216-217, 218-230, 328-330
  - USA 217-218, 232-236, 328-330
Agricultural policy consequences
- fluctuations and risks 331-332
- internationally 332-333
- neglect of social goals 335-336
- short term 330-331
- structural 334-335
Agricultural prices
- livestock and feed 90-91
- long term 88-92
- medium term 87-88
- real prices 93-95
- short term 85-87
Agricultural production
- heterogeneity 303
- seasons 302-303
- variability 303
Agricultural reforms
- attitudes and incentives 107-108
- different elements 105-106
- different parts of Europe 123-150
- farm size 288-290
- path dependence 290-291
Agricultural revolution
- Britain 127-130
- gradual change 17-18
- start 277-278
Agricultural sector
- and economic policy 336-342
- and industry 280-286
- and institutions 304-308
- and markets 301-302
- and population 286-288
- and trade policy 321-325

Index

- engine of growth 277-280
- management 302-304
- two sector models 245-252

Agricultural surplus
- and development 280
- importance 383-384

Agriculture
- demand 84-85
- labour force 73-76
- labour productivity 79-84, 197-200
- land productivity 82-84, 197-200
- yield 79-80, 126-127

Allocation
- and growth 41
- and markets 295-296

Attitudes
- definition 248
- different policies 319-342
- farming system 306
- importance 107-108
- stage theory 381-382

Austria –Hungary
- agricultural reforms 144-145

B

Balkan countries
- agricultural reforms 144-145
- inter-war period 190

Baltic area
- feudal system 125

Bottlenecks
- and development 248-249, 296
- and markets 296

Britain
- agricultural performance 152-155, 197-199
- agricultural policy 184-185
- agricultural reforms 127-133
- feudal system 126

- imperial preferences 155, 184-185

Business cycles 33-34

C

Capital
- accumulation 36-42
- deepening 38-39
- vintage 39-40
- widening 38-39

Capital markets
- and development 114, 264

Capital movements 60

Capitalist farming
- consequences 130-132

Cobden treaty 53-54, 156-157

Common Agricultural Policy
- and the GATT 231-232
- green currencies 224-225
- implementation 222-223
- price policy 222-223, 228-230
- principles 221-222
- reforms 238-240, 329-330
- structural policy 224

Common market 219-220

Comparative advantage
- and transport 320-321
- theory 53

Competition
- foreign exchange rate 235-236
- importance 295

Co-operative movement
- Denmark 168-169

Corn Laws
- Britain 52-53, 152-153

Customs union
- EEC 219-220
- Zollverein 53-54, 161-162

D

Data estimates 18-19

Index

Decision making
- agriculture 301
- and institutions 304-308

Delimitation of periods
- agricultural revolution 277-278
- different stages 255-256
- industrial revolution 278
- modern era 17-18

Demand
- Determinants 84-85

Denmark
- agricultural performance 166-169, 195-199
- agricultural policy 190-191
- agricultural reforms 140-143
- self-organisation 165-166

Developing countries
- choice of technology 360-361
- development choices 354-355
- industrialization
  - economic arguments 350-354
  - political arguments 354
- lack of reforms 359-360
- long-term, trends 347-349
- macroeconomic policies 365-367
- manufacturing 348-349
- migration 357-358
- production pattern 359-361

Development economics
- special discipline 251-252

Development model
- determining factors 247-248
- dynamic relations 248-249
- general model 245-252
- interaction between
  - development factors 250-251
  - framework and economy 249-250
- linkages 246
- stage characteristics 381-383

- stage theory 255-276

Development policy
- definition 319

Development strategy
- developing countries 350-354
- inward looking, see import substitution strategy
- manufacturing exports 366
- market economy 299-300
- master plan 117-118
- primary exports 350-351
- Soviet Union 204-208

Distribution channels
- and integration 113, 260-261

E

Economic development
- factor behind 34-43
- in the world 21-24
- long-term changes 28-33

Economic integration
- and institutions 112-115
- and markets 259-260
- definition 47
- natural barriers 47, 54-58
- political barriers, see trade policy
- through the ages 47-69

Economic policy
- definition 319
- see, macroeconomic policy

Education
- and development 261-262

Employment
- different sectors 73-76

Enabling environment 115-116, 295

Extension service
- and development 262-263

407

Index

F
Farm income problem 225-228
Farm size structure
 - and reforms 105-109
 - best structure 288-290
 - importance 290-291
 - Soviet Union 312-313
 - unimodal and bimodal 107-108
Fair trade 155
Farming system
 - alternatives 306-307
 - and population growth 286-288
 - crop-livestock 103-104, 257-259
 - definition 102, 123
 - developing countries 359-361
 - effect of urban centers 254, 287
 - feudal system 124-127, 252-254
 - focus on
  - human resources 261-262
  - innovation and diffusion 262-263
  - inputs 260-265
  - transport and distribution 260-261
 - open-field system 102-103
 - scientific farming 173-175
 - see, agricultural reforms
Feudal system
 - common characteristics 252-254
 - in different regions 124-125
First World War
 - adjustment problems 61-66, 181-183
Five "ins" 115
France
 - agricultural performance 133-137
 - agricultural policy 185-188
 - agricultural reforms 133-137
 - feudal system 125

French revolution
 - and agricultural reforms 132-133
 - and trade 49-50

G
GATT
 - agricultural agreement 238-240, 329-330
 - agriculture excluded 214-216, 324-325
 - and the CAP 231-232
 - different rounds 231-232
General economic trends
 - GDP, population, prices 17-45
 - integration and trade 47-69
Germany
 - agricultural performance 161-166
 - agricultural policy 188-200
 - agricultural reforms 137-140
 - feudal system 125
Great Depression
 - agricultural policy
  - Europe 183-191
  - USA 194-196
 - agriculture in the USA 191-192
 - exchange rates 65
 - industrial production 64
 - international co-operation 196-197
 - New Deal 193-194
 - trade 65-66
Gold standard 60
Gross domestic product
 - different trends 28-33
 - in the world 21-24
Growth with equity 350

H
Historical experiences

Index

   - relevance 356-357
Historical lessons
   - developing countries 347-370, 392-395
   - development theory 245-276, 381-383
   - economic integration 295-317, 386-389
   - policy intervention 317-345, 389-392
   - productivity 277-293, 383-385
Historical school 371-372

I
Imperial preferences
   - Britain 155, 184-185
Import substitution strategy
   - arguments behind
      - labour supply 351-352
      - linkages 352
      - Soviet Union 354
      - terms of trade 352-353
   - content 350-351
Industrial revolution
   - first revolution 100
   - gradual change 17-18
   - second revolution 101
   - start in different countries 278
Industrialisation
   - and agriculture 280-284
   - in Europe 24-28
Infant industry argument
   - content 350-351
   - Germany 56, 162
   - USA 56-57, 172
Information
   - and institutions 111-112
Infrastructure
   - importance 112-113
   - improvements 55, 57-58
Innovations

   - and development 262-263
   - and institutions 110-111
Inputs
   - and institutions 110-111
   - new inputs 109-110
Institutions
   - alternatives 306-308
   - and agriculture
      - first stage 104-108
      - second stage 112-115
   - and climate risks 303-304
   - and decision-making 304-305
   - and market risks 306
   - deficiencies 36-37
   - definition 99-100, 247-248
   - stage theory 381-383
Integration, see economic integration
International co-operation
   - before First World War 60-61, 196
   - inter-war period 61-66, 196-197
   - post-war period 66, 218-223, 231-232
International trade
   - and GDP 50-51
   - and growth 42
Interrelationships
   - agricultural policy in the EU and the USA 237
   - agriculture and industry 283-286
   - Europe and the USA 174-175
   - technology and institutions 108-112
   - technology, institutions and growth 36-43

L
Labour emigration 60
Labour force

- different sectors 73-76
Labour markets
  - and development 264
Labour productivity
  -and growth 34-35
  -in agriculture 79-83
Land productivity
  - in agriculture 79-83
Liberalism
  - Adam Smith 49
  - see, trade policy
Linkages
  - and development 352
  - two-sector model 246
Low Countries 123, 277

M
Macroeconomic policy
  - and agriculture 237-238, 336-342
  - developing countries 363-368
Manufacturing
  - labour force 73-76
Markets
  - and development 295-296
  - and enabling environment 115-116, 297
  - and integration 259-260
  - and risks 252-253
  - definition 113
  - implementation 116-117, 298-300
  - importance in agriculture 301, 386-389
  - main description 248
  - static and dynamic effects 295-296
Mediterranean countries
  - agricultural reforms 143-144
Mercantilism 48
Methodology

  - different analyses 371-372
  - free trade as case 371-372
Modern era
  - start 17-18

N
Natural resources
  - and growth 41
Netherlands
  - advanced agriculture 127
  - inter-war period 191
  - see, Low Countries

P
Path dependence 290-291
Physiocrats 49
Population growth
  - and agriculture 286-288
  - Black Death 124-126
  - in Western Europe 21-22
  - in the world 19-20
Prices
  - see, agricultural prices
  - different trends 28-33
  - non-price factors 362-364
  - supply response 361-365
Primary export strategy 350-351
Protection
  - see, trade policy
  - direct 365-367
  - indirect 365-367

R
Real prices
  - long-term trends 93-95
  - post-war trend 225-228
Risks
  - climate 305-306
  - farming system 306-307
  - market 306
Russia

Index

- agricultural reforms 145-147
- agricultural performance 309-310
- see, Soviet Union

S

Second World War
- immediate post-war period 213-214
- adjustment in the 1950s 216-218

Serfdom
- definition 146
- in Russia 145-146

Services
- labour force 73-76

Share-cropping 306-307

Soviet Union
- agricultural performance 309-310
- collectivisation 201-204
- development strategy
  - Bukharin 204-208
  - Preobrazhensky 204-208
- Great Depression 64
- inter-war performance 200-201
- inter-war economic policy 201-204
- new economic policy 202-203
- problems with
  - economies of size 312-313
  - labour incentives 313-314
  - planning system 310-311

Specialisation
- and risks 252-253

Stage theory 255-276
- characteristics of different stages 381-383
- delimitation of stages 254-256
- first stage 119-120, 257-259
- second stage 120-122, 259-265
- third stage 265-267

- fourth stage 267-270
- fifth stage 270-273

Structural adjustment 350

Structural policy 224

Supply response
- farming system 361-362
- non-price factors 362-364
- price matters 364-365

T

Technology
- agriculture
  - first stage 103-104
  - second stage 108-112
- and integration 54-55
- deficiencies 36-37
- definition 99
- stage theory 381-383

Terms of trade
- and economic growth 35
- for agricultural products 93-95
- two-sector model 246

Trade barriers
- see, economic integration
- see, trade policy

Trade policy
- and agricultural performance 321-323
- fair trade 155
- infant industry 320
- price stabilization 320
- through the ages 47-69, 320-325

Transport
- and integration 260-261
- declining costs 57-58, 353
- railway constructions 55

U

USA
- adjustment
  - after First World War 181, 191

411

Index

- after Second World War 213-214, 217-218
- agricultural performance 171-175, 197-200
- agricultural policy
  - inter-war period 194-195
  - post-war period 232-236
- frontier movement 169-170
- Great depression 191-192
- New Deal 193-195

W
World market
  - dependency 236-237
  - post-war period 234-236

Y
Yield
  - different parts of Europe 126-127
  - historically 79-80